Democracy Prevention
The Politics of the U.S.-Egyptian Alliance

When a popular revolt forced long-ruling Egyptian president Hosni Mubarak to resign on February 11, 2011, U.S. president Barack Obama hailed the victory of peaceful demonstrators in the heart of the Arab World. But Washington was late to endorse democracy – for decades, the United States favored Egypt's rulers over its people. Since 1979, the United States had provided the Egyptian regime more than $60 billion in aid and immeasurable political support to secure its main interests in the region: Israeli security and strong relations with Persian Gulf oil producers. During the Egyptian uprising, the White House did not promote popular sovereignty but instead backed an "orderly transition" to one of Mubarak's cronies. Even after protesters derailed that plan, the antidemocratic U.S.-Egyptian alliance continued. Using untapped primary materials, this book helps explain why authoritarianism has persisted in Egypt with American support, even as policymakers claim to encourage democratic change.

Jason Brownlee is Associate Professor of Government at the University of Texas at Austin. He has been traveling to Egypt and conducting research there for seventeen years. In addition to his previous book, *Authoritarianism in an Age of Democratization* (Cambridge 2007), Professor Brownlee's writings have appeared in *Current History*, the *Journal of Democracy*, and numerous scholarly journals. In 2010 and 2011, he was a Visiting Fellow at the Woodrow Wilson International Center for Scholars.

Democracy Prevention

The Politics of the U.S.-Egyptian Alliance

JASON BROWNLEE
University of Texas, Austin

CAMBRIDGE
UNIVERSITY PRESS

CAMBRIDGE UNIVERSITY PRESS
Cambridge, New York, Melbourne, Madrid, Cape Town,
Singapore, São Paulo, Delhi, Mexico City

Cambridge University Press
32 Avenue of the Americas, New York, NY 10013-2473, USA

www.cambridge.org
Information on this title: www.cambridge.org/9781107677869

First published 2012

Printed in the United States of America

A catalog record for this publication is available from the British Library.

Library of Congress Cataloging in Publication Data

Brownlee, Jason, 1974–
Democracy prevention : the politics of the U.S.-Egyptian alliance / Jason Brownlee.
    p.   cm.
Includes bibliographical references and index.
ISBN 978-1-107-02571-4 (hardback) – ISBN 978-1-107-67786-9 (paperback)
    1. United States – Foreign relations – Egypt.   2. Egypt – Foreign relations – United
States.   3. Egypt – Foreign relations – 1952–   I. Title.
✓E183.8.E35B76 2012
327.73062–dc23   2012004673

ISBN 978-1-107-02571-4 Hardback
ISBN 978-1-107-67786-9 Paperback

To Joan and Eleanor

Even if one supposes that the visible misgovernment of Egypt, in its bearing on the life of the inhabitants, did impart some unselfish element to our conduct, no one would suggest that as an operative force in the direction of our imperial policy such motive has ever determined our actions.

– John Atkinson Hobson, *Imperialism: A Study*

America allies itself with dictatorships because it is easy to deal with despots, while it is difficult to work with democratic states.... America spends years negotiating with democracies, while it can reach agreement with an autocrat in just a few minutes. But what America gains quickly, it loses just as fast!

– Moustafa Amin, *Mirthful America . . . Long Ago*

Contents

Preface and Acknowledgments

On June 16 and 17, 25 million Egyptians – half the electorate – selected the country's first president since a popular uprising deposed Hosni Mubarak. On the top of the ballot was Ahmed Shafiq, a retired air force general who had served as Mubarak's last prime minister and had edged out two major revolutionary candidates in initial voting on May 23 and 24. Next came Mohamed Morsi, of the Muslim Brotherhood and head of its Freedom and Justice Party (FJP). Morsi had topped the field in May, and his candidacy in the runoff offered Egyptians an unprecedented chance to choose a civilian leader from the opposition. With 51.7 percent of the vote, Morsi prevailed – only to be encircled by Egypt's military oligarchy, the Supreme Council of the Armed Forces (SCAF).

The narrative of this book concludes with the parliamentary elections of 2011–2012. During the first half of 2012, Morsi's FJP and other parties began establishing popular sovereignty for the first time in the history of the Egyptian republic. The SCAF and its clients, however, manipulated Egypt's pliable institutions and, in a dizzying set of decrees, obstructed the electorate's will. On June 13, two weeks after the decades old State of Emergency had expired, the Ministry of Justice gave soldiers and security personnel the right to arrest civilians. On June 16, after Egypt's highest court declared the country's chief electoral law unconstitutional, the SCAF dissolved the main chamber of parliament. The generals then usurped legislative authority and claimed sweeping influence over the country's constitutional assembly.

Opposition leaders called it a coup. Finally, as polling stations closed on June 17, the SCAF amended its own Constitutional Declaration from March 30, 2011, effectively stripping the president of authority over national security and foreign affairs. Although Egyptians had voted, the leaders they chose could not steer the ship of state.

Many colleagues, friends, and family members selflessly responded to this project as it developed. I am deeply indebted to them.

My father, Mac, who died suddenly in April 2010, lovingly encouraged my writing and research. While creating this book, I fondly recalled our discussions of politics. I have also cherished the guidance I received from the late, brilliant Mohamed El-Sayed Said. Mohamed introduced me to the problems this study covers and the courage Egyptians have shown addressing them.

Robert Vitalis has been my most patient and generous colleague, reading countless manuscripts from the inception of this book to its completion. My friend and periodic partner in the field, Joshua Stacher, provided invaluable suggestions over months of phone calls and e-mails. Robert Jensen advised me as I sought to write a book for political scientists and general readers. Gary Freeman and my home department at the University of Texas at Austin kindly sponsored a manuscript workshop in the spring of 2011. Laurie Brand, Clement Henry, and Robert Springborg took part in the workshop and made this project far more fruitful than it otherwise would have been.

While bearing sole responsibility for any errors that remain, I express my sincere gratitude to the numerous individuals who lent a hand or an attentive ear, invariably improving this book in the process: Jon Alterman, Jonathan Argaman, Matthew Axelrod, Mahmoud Al-Batal, Kirk Beattie, Joel Beinin, Eva Bellin, Catherine Boone, Nathan Brown, Abhishek Chatterjee, Noam Chomsky, Yoav Di-Capua, Mohamed Elmenshawy, Tulia Falleti, F. Gregory Gause III, Ellis Goldberg, Gretchen Helmke, Steven Heydemann, Donald Horowitz, Susan Hyde, Saad Ibrahim, Marcia Inhorn, Amaney Jamal, Melvyn Leffler, Ellen Lust, Tarek Masoud, Patrick McDonald, Pete Moore, Nagla Mostafa, Ami Pedahzur, Anne Peters, Jim Rigby, Hesham Sallam, Matthew Schroeder, Jeremy Sharp, Julia Simon, Hillel Soifer, Joel Suarez, Chantal Thomas, Eric Trager, David Waldner, Lucan Way, Lisa Wedeen, Sean Yom, Marilyn Young, and audiences at Case Western Reserve University, Cornell Law School, the

Middle East Studies Association, Princeton University, the University of Pennsylvania, and Yale University.

For invaluable institutional and intellectual support, I thank Pauline Strong, director of the Humanities Institute at the University of Texas at Austin, who graciously included political scientists in the institute's fall 2009 faculty workshop on intellectuals during moments of crisis. During the 2010–2011 academic year, Haleh Esfandiari and Michael Van Dusen warmly hosted me at the Woodrow Wilson International Center for Scholars (WWICS) in Washington, DC. WWICS Fellow Aaron David Miller helped me arrange many of the interviews used in this book. My sincere thanks go to him, to those who agreed to be interviewed, and to those who wanted to meet but were unavailable because of time constraints.

While researching and producing this book, I undertook no consulting work with U.S. or foreign intelligence agencies.

This study of the U.S.-Egyptian alliance was immeasurably helped by Albert Nason and the staff of the Jimmy Carter Library, Paul Rascoe of the Perry-Castañeda Library at the University of Texas, and Dagne Gizaw, Michelle Kamalich, and Janet Spikes at the WWICS Library. Matthew Buehler, Allyson Hawkins, Rachel Sternfeld, and Philip Wiseman provided timely and careful research assistance. Steven Brooke was indispensable during the last stages of production. At Cambridge University Press, Lewis Bateman shepherded the manuscript from précis to finished work. I cannot thank him enough. Two outside readers provided thoughtful and incredibly constructive comments.

Permissions to use material that appeared, in earlier form, in journal articles were granted by *Political Science Quarterly* and *Current History*.

To my mother, Becky, who has supported me studying Egypt and politics since college, I give heartfelt thanks. Finally, my wife, Joan Asseff, and our daughter, Eleanor, shared their boundless love and energy with me while I pursued this project, sometimes away from home for weeks. I dedicate this book to the two of them with all my love.

Jason Brownlee
Austin, Texas

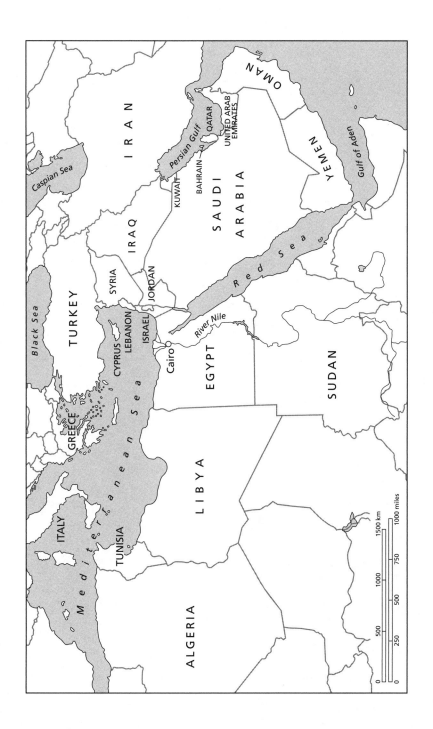

xv

Introduction

In July 1980, a dozen F-4 fighter jets traveled from Moody Air Force Base, Georgia, to Cairo West, where they would fly in joint U.S.-Egyptian maneuvers. Operation Proud Phantom was the U.S. Air Force's first tactical deployment to Egypt, and it symbolized the two governments' nascent partnership. An aerial photo of Egyptian- and U.S.-piloted F-4s passing the pyramids conveyed, in the words of one National Security Council (NSC) staffer, "the sense of cooperation and benefits to regional states that we have emphasized throughout the security framework."[1]

The framework, designed to counter Soviet influence in the Persian Gulf and absorb the aftershocks of Iran's revolution, almost collapsed the following year during Egypt's "Autumn of Fury." Egyptians faulted President Anwar Sadat for mismanaging the economy, hoarding power, and accepting a bilateral treaty with Israel that enabled Israeli aggression instead of bringing regional peace. Rather than answering these objections, the embittered ruler jailed fifteen hundred of his critics. But a small band of militants struck back. During an October 6, 1981, ceremony – which commemorated Sadat's military success eight years prior – they shot and killed the president. The assassins took Sadat's life, but they did not upset Egypt's role in U.S. geostrategy. Vice President Hosni Mubarak succeeded to the presidency, and his counterpart in Washington, Ronald Reagan, fortified the U.S.-Egyptian alliance by increasing military aid.

Thirty years and $60 billion of U.S. aid later, President Mubarak and his U.S. partners watched tens of thousands of Egyptians assemble in a "Day of Rage." The January 25, 2011, protests began a national uprising that eclipsed the Autumn of Fury in scope and impact. As anti-Mubarak demonstrators occupied Cairo's central square for more than two weeks, Egyptian and U.S. officials struggled to quell the crisis. Realizing that the crowds, which eventually encompassed millions, would not disperse as long as Mubarak headed the regime, they hoped to install ex-intelligence chief and newly appointed vice president Omar Suleiman in power. A smooth transition to Suleiman could placate Mubarak's critics without disrupting U.S.-Egyptian cooperation.

But representatives of the uprising rejected any dialogue with the regime and would not accept a government headed by Suleiman. The opposition refused to leave the square, even as police and thugs killed hundreds of demonstrators and injured thousands more. On February 8, 2011, tens of thousands went on strike or joined in protests to oust Mubarak. The groundswell forced the Egyptian Supreme Council of the Armed Forces (SCAF) and U.S. policymakers to rescind support for Mubarak and Suleiman. On February 11, Suleiman announced that Mubarak was stepping down, the SCAF took responsibility for governing the country, and U.S. president Barack Obama praised the outcome. This transition was more open than elites in either country had envisioned, exposing Egyptian domestic and foreign policy to the will of the Egyptian public. Without firing a shot, the opposition had cracked the edifice of Egyptian autocracy, rattled the U.S.-Egyptian alliance, and launched the Middle East's largest democratic experiment.

Mubarak's overthrow is one of the most consequential developments of the early twenty-first century. Not since the Iranian shah fled into exile in 1979 has a popular movement swept away a key U.S. client in the Middle East so abruptly. Nevertheless, democracy in Egypt is no more certain after Mubarak than it was after Sadat. When it intervened, the SCAF circumscribed the uprising and safeguarded its ties to Washington. Similarly, U.S. officials accepted a change in leadership that would protect their interests. The bulwarks of authoritarianism had not vanished. Egyptians debated constitutional reforms and new election laws under the supervision of the military, which had been the arbiter of Egyptian politics since 1952. Six months after Mubarak's resignation, the SCAF sought to reassure the public that it had no desire to rule after Egyptians had elected a new parliament and president, and ratified a new constitution. Observers doubted, however, that the military would submit to civilian control.

This book seeks to explain why Egyptians who joined the Day of Rage in winter 2011 managed a political triumph that had eluded them in the Autumn of Fury of 1981. It also seeks to show why protesters replaced a ruler but not a regime. Answering these questions depends on showing not only what changed but also what remained the same across these periods. Scholars have identified two major political components to the durability of authoritarianism: domestic coercion and international support.[2] One of the remarkable aspects of the January 25 Revolution is that both factors were at least as strong in 2011 as they had been in 1981. The pillars of Mubarak's rule had not crumbled before the initial Day of Rage. Yet, in the absence of preexisting rifts within the Egyptian state and its international support network, protesters overcame security forces and prompted elites to recalibrate their support for Mubarak. Grassroots mobilizing, rather than intraregime cleavages, propelled the January 25 Revolution. While the result fell short of regime change, because the Egyptian army remained in control, the uprising showed how mass movements in Egypt contested the foundations of durable authoritarianism.[3]

Arguably the best guide to Egypt's dynamic and evolving present is a clear understanding of U.S. support, internal repression, and domestic opposition in Egypt's recent past. This book investigates the historical and contemporary obstacles to Egyptian democracy, analyzing the Egyptian security state that Sadat erected, Mubarak expanded, and the united States enhanced. It also chronicles the opposition's uphill battle for an accountable government. Official U.S.-Egyptian relations have been at odds with domestic public opinion in Egypt. Rather than fostering democracy in an incremental fashion, U.S. and Egyptian officials have promoted an autocratic security state that supports a U.S.-led regional order built around Israeli security and the projection of U.S. influence over the Persian Gulf.[4] By contrast, public opinion in Egypt favors a regional security order less dominated by the United States and Israel, and a government that respects political competition and civil liberties.

I consider authoritarianism an international phenomenon, and this book treats Egyptian authoritarianism as co-constituted by local and foreign actors.[5] Beginning with the 1979 Egyptian-Israeli peace treaty and extending past the January 25 Revolution, the United States has been a coalitional partner of Sadat, Mubarak, and the SCAF. This participation in Egyptian authoritarianism has not been all-determining or immutable. Rather, the United States has shaped the regime's longevity and posture in specific and contestable ways.[6] The United States has protected Egyptian rulers from foreign threats, heavily subsidized the Egyptian armed forces, and bolstered the Egyptian security services.[7] At the same time, the U.S. alliance with the Egyptian regime has been influenced by events inside Egypt. During the January 25 Revolution, Egyptian demonstrators induced the Obama administration to curb U.S. support for Mubarak. They showed that while "strategic interests" may be quite rigid, the calculus by which the United States pursues those interests can shift. By February 10, 2011, a transition without Mubarak or Suleiman had become the best bet for preserving the U.S.-Egyptian alliance.

Authoritarianism under Liberal Hegemony

Prolonged autocracy in one of the United States' closest allies challenges ideas about U.S. democracy promotion and the triumph of liberal values after the Cold War.[8] Scholars and practitioners have documented U.S. efforts to spread democracy.[9] Carter is credited with helping the opposition win an election in the Dominican Republic; Reagan purportedly pushed for democratic outcomes in El Salvador, the Philippines, South Korea, and Chile; and after George H. W. Bush overthrew Manuel Noriega in Panama, the country's multiparty democracy resumed.[10] Yet, Washington's support for autocratic regimes is also well known.[11] During the Cold War, the pattern was clear: When the incumbent was pro-United States, the United States was pro-incumbent. John F. Kennedy's administration would only experiment with democracy in the Dominican Republic, for example, when a communist takeover had been definitively precluded. "There are three possibilities in descending order of preference," Kennedy explained. "A decent democratic regime, a continuation of the [Rafael] Trujillo regime or a [Fidel] Castro regime. We ought to aim at the first, but we really can't renounce the second until we are sure that we can avoid the third."[12] The implications for popular sovereignty in the Dominican Republic became clear when Kennedy's successor oversaw a military intervention in 1965 that enabled Joaquín Balaguer, a former aide to Trujillo, to claim the presidency over anti-Trujillista Juan Bosch. Balaguer ruled continually until 1978.[13] Reagan's ambassador to the United Nations, Jeane Kirkpatrick, defended the "double standards" by which U.S. leaders denounced human rights abuses committed by communist regimes and ignored them in its anticommunist allies.[14] Only when circumstances impelled the White House to accept the opposition – as in the Philippines – would the United States realign.

Given the historical pattern in U.S. foreign policy, U.S. support for autocracy in Egypt and other Middle Eastern allies becomes easier to understand. Many states in the Middle East have had greater geopolitical significance for the United States than the Dominican Republic or the Philippines. Further, the strategic significance of the Middle East predated and outlasted the period known as the "third wave of democratization," roughly 1974–1991.[15] On October 6, 1973, Egypt and Syria launched a surprise attack against Israeli forces occupying the Sinai Peninsula and Golan Heights. The war (discussed more fully in Chapter 1) turned quickly in Israel's favor, thanks to a U.S. resupply effort and Sadat's limited strategic ambitions. When news leaked that the United States was airlifting military supplies to Israel, however, the Kingdom of Saudi Arabia led Arab oil producers to gradually cut production and, later, to completely freeze Arab oil exports to the United States, the Netherlands, and a small number of other states. Active hostilities ceased later that month, and the Arab supply cuts ended the following spring. The crisis brought two U.S. strategic imperatives into focus: preventing another major Arab-Israeli war and maintaining reliable ties with Gulf oil exporters.[16] This vision of regional security belongs in any explanation of why democratic currents have barely touched the Middle East. Post-1973 U.S. foreign policy promoted the continuity of friendly Middle Eastern autocracies during the Cold War and afterward.

U.S. support for Middle Eastern regimes since 1989 represents an anomaly for the leading prognoses of post–Cold War world politics. Under the pressures of "liberal hegemony," autocrats were expected to democratize or be ostracized.[17] In some regions, such as Central

Europe, the U.S. government and U.S.-based nongovernmental organizations (NGOs) helped opposition movements bring down authoritarian regimes.[18] But international liberal norms lacked transformative
power in the Middle East. Updating Kennedy and Kirkpatrick's preferences for a postcommunist world, U.S. politicians who celebrated
the defeat of tyranny in Eastern Europe or sub-Saharan Africa showed
little zeal for advancing democracy among the United States' Arab
partners.[19] Instead, they promoted current regional allies over their
domestic opponents. It was not that interests trumped norms. Rather,
U.S. policymakers normatively preferred the U.S. framework for
Middle East security over local democracy.[20]

America and the Egyptian Regime

Scholars have explained the persistence of autocracy in the Middle East
with a number of variables, including oil income and domestic political
institutions.[21] This book joins a growing body of work looking at the
contribution of the United States to robust authoritarianism.[22] Steven
Levitsky and Lucan Way have cited the "linkage" and "leverage"
between Western states and developing countries to explain variations
in authoritarianism and democratization after the Cold War.[23] In the
conventional sense of those terms, there has been no autocracy more
linked to and more leveraged by the United States than that of Egypt.[24]
Rather than siding with the opposition, however, America backed the
ruling coalition of an authoritarian regime.[25]

   The contemporary U.S.-Egyptian relationship began after the 1973
War. It was sealed after the Iranian Revolution. After Great Britain
withdrew from the Persian Gulf in 1971, Iran became the centerpiece of
U.S. strategy in the area.[26] U.S. president Richard Nixon and National
Security Advisor Henry Kissinger even discussed with the shah of Iran,
Mohammed Reza Pahlavi, "contingency plans" for an Iranian intervention in Saudi Arabia should the kingdom fall.[27] Playing the role
of regional gendarme, the shah ordered $20 billion of U.S. materiel
from 1970 through 1978, a quarter of all U.S. foreign military sales
during that period.[28] A Senate report called the U.S.-Iranian military
sales program "the largest in the world in terms of dollar value and
the number of Americans involved in implementation."[29] Such lavish
expenditures were expected to secure the Persian Gulf while supporting

U.S. arms merchants. At the end of 1977, Carter toasted the shah as leading "an island of stability in one of the more troubled areas of the world."[30] Yet, heavy equipment was no panacea for the shah's political woes. Advanced submarines could patrol the Indian Ocean but could not stop the protests against his profligate and brutal regime. One year after Carter had raised his glass, protests were sweeping the country.

Meanwhile, Carter was working to translate the Camp David Accords into a permanent treaty. After thirteen days of grueling negotiations at Camp David in September 1978, he achieved a framework that would prevent another Egyptian-Israeli war. But this diplomatic feat coincided with political calamity. The shah fled in January 1979. His downfall upset U.S. strategy for the Persian Gulf. The next month Secretary of Defense Harold Brown toured the Middle East, in search of allies – and arms buyers for the wares previously destined for Tehran. Peace between Egypt and Israel served both aims. When the two countries signed a peace treaty in March, Washington offered unprecedented military assistance to help them acquire U.S. weapons and vehicles.

The aid symbolized how important Egyptian-Israeli peace and U.S.-Egyptian cooperation had become for the White House's interests in the Middle East. The NSC staffer commenting on the photo from Operation Proud Phantom noted the irony that "only a decade ago, Israeli F-4s were conducting deep-penetration raids in this same general area."[31] The peace treaty had virtually eliminated the threat of a major Arab-Israeli land war while freeing Egypt to assist U.S. operations from Afghanistan to the African Horn. In January 1980, Carter issued his self-titled doctrine, vowing the United States would forcibly defend the "free movement of Middle East oil." But U.S. intervention in the Persian Gulf depended on logistical cooperation with Egypt and speedy passage through the Suez Canal. Otherwise, the United States would have trouble projecting its power to what Secretary Brown called "areas far from but vital to us."[32] Carter left office ignominiously, but presidents from both parties would uphold his strategy and guard against revolution toppling another U.S. ally. The U.S. military, positioned discretely "over the horizon," would provide a check against hostile revolts while arming its clients to the hilt. Defending a controversial sale of high-tech radar to Saudi

Arabia, Reagan intoned, "We will not permit [Saudi Arabia] to be an Iran."[33]

As the United States ensured Israel's security and supported friendly Arab oil exporters, Egypt remained a key partner. With the exception of the Desert Shield and Desert Storm operations, Egyptian troops would not join U.S. forces in combat, but the Egyptian government shared intelligence and enabled the movement of U.S. forces from the Mediterranean to the Persian Gulf. When the U.S. military was fighting in Afghanistan and Iraq in 2005, Egypt provided an average of twenty overflight permissions a day to U.S. aircraft crisscrossing its territory. Even at times of diplomatic strain, as in the mid-1980s and 2000s, bilateral tensions did not interfere with strategic cooperation. When democracy promotion became a prominent feature of U.S. foreign policy during the George W. Bush administration, for example, officials sought to safeguard security cooperation with Cairo. Similarly, when lawmakers attempted to condition military aid to Egypt in 2007, they sought to elicit greater Egyptian cooperation on Israeli security, not change the Egyptian regime's domestic behavior. Genuine leverage served U.S. interests (in that case, weakening Hamas) rather than democracy in Egypt.

Analytic Framework

Examining the United States' role in Egyptian authoritarianism is difficult, because Egypt is often understood as a case of failed or incomplete democracy promotion, rather than an exemplar of U.S. geostrategy. Those who have recently written on U.S.-Egyptian relations have generally provided two kinds of accounts. Public analysts, such as Michele Dunne and Steven Cook, have discussed the United States' vexed efforts to nurture democracy in Egypt through conditional aid and stern diplomacy.[34] Investigative journalists like Jane Mayer and Stephen Grey have highlighted the two governments' joint work fighting al-Qaeda.[35] These works illuminate different aspects of the relationship. While the democracy discourse has occupied the foreground, security cooperation has been the alliance's operational core. Officials may allude to the repressive side of the U.S.-Egyptian alliance, but they seldom acknowledge that antidemocratic norms pervade the relationship.[36]

The United States and Egypt's mutually advantageous relationship comprises massive economic support, joint military exercises, intelligence sharing, and high stakes diplomacy. Officials from the two countries form a network of common interests, values, and practices.[37] This network has served U.S. security interests in the Middle East and the interest of Egyptian incumbents in retaining power. While collaborating bilaterally, leaders have prevented the rise of a more representative Egyptian government and have reinforced Egypt's strategic alignment.

Just as officials within each government have their differences, participants in the U.S.-Egyptian network periodically disagree. More importantly, however, they share certain assumptions, taken-for-granted ideas that establish the conceptual frameworks within which they identify and solve problems. For example, the primary functions of post-1973 U.S.-Egyptian relations – Israeli security and U.S. force projection to the Gulf – are not on the table for discussion; they are the frame of reference for everyone at the table. Two other core assumptions undergird the bilateral alliance: distrust of popular sovereignty and an acceptance of U.S. primacy.

Although some U.S. officials advocate liberalizing reforms in Egypt, they accept that a sudden opening of public participation could bring unknown figures to power and jeopardize strategic cooperation. No U.S. president, much less his Egyptian interlocutors, wants Egypt to follow the way of Iran, whether through elections or revolution. Indeed, even a subtler mix of populism and nationalism could jeopardize Egyptian support for U.S. strategy. It follows that elections and political reform are welcome only insofar as they impede extremists and enhance stability.

The second area of consensus is a binational hierarchy. Despite the two countries' codependency, Egypt has been a vital subordinate in U.S. foreign policy, not an equal partner. This arrangement stems from political and economic asymmetries that thirty years of linkage have not ameliorated.

U.S. antagonism toward overt Islamist movements shows the power of the unspoken assumptions of the U.S.-Egyptian alliance.[38] After the USSR collapsed, U.S. policymakers began regarding religious conservatism in the Muslim World as a strategic challenge to U.S. power. Washington opposed any traditional Islamic group taking power, even through elections, at the expense of a pro-U.S. government. Assistant Secretary of State for Near Eastern and South Asian Affairs Edward Djerejian vowed the United States would not accept "one man, one vote, one time."[39] He implied that Islamist movements would use democracy to take power then shut it down after they had won elections. Given U.S. reticence about democracy, however, his stance had more to do with preventing assertive nationalism than preempting authoritarianism. When Djerejian spoke, the only serious electoral challenge to Mubarak's National Democratic Party (NDP) in Egypt was the Muslim Brotherhood, a leading critic of U.S. and Israeli policies. The problem for Washington was not that pro-U.S. authoritarianism would be followed by more authoritarianism, but that the successor government, democratic or not, could turn Egyptian policies away from U.S. preferences. Hence, U.S. officials worked to check Islamic political activity, either by cultivating a liberal option between the NDP and the Muslim Brotherhood or by squarely backing Mubarak.

Foreign Aid and Regime Survival

Political scientists have already theorized that U.S. aid, especially military aid, can make authoritarianism more robust. Beyond observing a general aggregate relationship, however, they seldom specify the causal role of aid in regime survival.[40] Thus, it is worth asking: Through what mechanisms does Washington's support sustain nondemocratic rule in Cairo? To answer this question we must situate the material aspect of aid in the political relationship between the U.S. government and Egyptian regime.

The United States' influence on Egyptian decision makers extends beyond a normal bilateral relationship. Given the stakes for both sides, the United States is less like an external force and more like a local participant in the ruling coalition.[41] The U.S. government plays a role analogous to those of domestic coalition members (the director of intelligence, the minister of the interior, the minister of defense), shaping the calculations, priorities, and resources of the regime. Continued U.S. support for the authoritarian apparatus impedes the opposition. Conversely, a U.S. defection from the ruling coalition would increase the likelihood of regime change and the development of democracy.[42] At the time of this writing, such realignment has not occurred. Although the White House rescinded support from Mubarak, it did not stop supporting the Egyptian security state he had commanded.

Turning to aid, it is worth recognizing that billions of dollars of military hardware (financed through oil revenues) did not guarantee the survival of the Iranian monarchy. Therefore the political implications of aid flows to Egypt merit scrutiny. During the thirty-two years from the signing of the Egyptian-Israeli treaty to the January 25 Revolution, the United States strengthened local incumbents in four respects: national defense, coup proofing, macroeconomic stability, and domestic repression. First, U.S. support tends to check the aggression of neighboring states.[43] This effect has been especially strong in the wealthy but militarily vulnerable Gulf states, including Saudi Arabia, which have enjoyed a U.S. "security umbrella."[44] In Egypt's case, the main modern military adversary was Israel. Even after the end of hostilities with that neighbor, however, Egyptian presidents contended with Muammar Qadhafi in Libya. Washington reinforced Egypt's power vis-à-vis the heavily equipped Libyan military and deterred infringements on Egyptian territory. This contribution to Egyptian national security, although difficult to measure, all but eliminated the threat of military defeat.

The United States has also diminished the incentives for a hostile coup. More leaders in developing countries have lost power through military coups d'état than through foreign invasion or opposition victory.[45] Postcolonial leaders, including Sadat and Mubarak, worried about rivals in the military and tried to "coup proof" their regimes.[46] While coup proofing typically entails creating internal security forces to counterbalance the traditional military, another way of reaching the same goal is to reduce the incentives for a takeover.[47] $1.3 billion in annual military financing helped keep the armed forces from seizing power outside of a major domestic crisis. Even after Mubarak resigned, the Egyptian military continued collaborating with Washington.

The next greatest challenge to the regime comes from the populace. Ever since the Egyptian price riots of January 1977 and the Iranian Revolution, leaders in the Middle East and United States have striven to quiet mass unrest. The initial aid package was an attempt to rescue Sadat after he lost Soviet economic aid and mounting debt to Western creditors prompted him to make unpopular subsidy cuts.[48] Subsequently, the U.S. Agency for International Development (USAID) in Egypt has overseen several hundreds of millions of dollars annually in economic aid, which largely went to consulting and infrastructure projects, as well as food subsidies. Probably more consequential than the ongoing USAID presence has been the periodic interventions by which the United States, and sometimes Western Europe, have helped to revive a sagging Egyptian economy. Debt forgiveness from the United States and the Paris Club in 1991 saved Egypt from a fiscal crisis. Washington's readiness to ease economic hardship in Egypt – if and when it appears to threaten political stability – limits the risk that the coercive apparatus will collapse, a standard precondition for revolution.[49]

Finally, U.S. aid has helped the Egyptian regime expand its repressive forces over time. This link, however, is smaller than the substantial military aid package implies. The bulk of Egypt's nearly unparalleled military financing program goes toward heavy armaments, including fighter jets, tanks, and even naval vessels that have little to no role in domestic policing. For the Egyptian leadership, this use of aid makes sense; low-tech police gear and torture paraphernalia are ubiquitous and inexpensive.

Structure of the Book

The contemporary U.S.-Egyptian alliance, initiated under Nixon and consolidated by Carter, flourished during a stretch of history that tossed dozens of dictatorships on the ash heap and left political scientists asking why Middle Eastern autocracies had dodged the trend. Tracing the evolution of bilateral relations over more than three decades, I show that the Egyptian regime has benefited from consistent and substantial U.S. support.[50] When the United States and Egypt restored diplomatic ties in 1974, security ranked ahead of democracy. These priorities endured, even as geopolitics changed. What originated in the 1970s as a military-strategic alliance focused on peace with Israel and the projection of U.S. forces to the Persian Gulf shrank after the Cold War into a narrow security portfolio: the defeat of radical Islamist movements like the Islamic Group in Egypt, al-Qaeda internationally, and Hamas in the Gaza Strip. As the relationship evolved, Washington's need for interlocutors in Cairo continued. This reliance circumscribed democracy promotion, whether it was a footnote to foreign policy, as in most administrations, or a dominant theme, as during the tenure of George W. Bush. To the extent that the edifice of Egyptian authoritarianism cracked in winter 2011, credit goes to the masses who defied Mubarak's armed agents.

The book's five empirical chapters draw on a variety of primary sources, including government publications, memoirs, news reports, the Jimmy Carter Library archives, interviews with participants in the bilateral relationship, and State Department cables published by the whistleblower Web site Wikileaks. Chapter 1 shows that U.S. post-1973 strategy in the Middle East was advanced by repression in Egypt. Through authoritarianism at home, Sadat guaranteed bilateral peace with Israel and reliable logistical support for the Pentagon.[51] This combination of international diplomacy and internal security climaxed in the Autumn of Fury and the Egyptian president's assassination. Chapter 2 turns to U.S.-Egyptian relations under Mubarak during the late Cold War and early post–Cold War periods. While assisting the Central Intelligence Agency (CIA) to capture Islamic militants abroad, Mubarak smothered internal dissent.

Chapter 3 charts how the Bush White House expanded intelligence cooperation, even as U.S. and Egyptian leaders questioned who, after Mubarak retired or passed away, would preserve the bilateral security relationship. Mubarak and his son Gamal were plotting a dynastic succession, a prospect that galvanized the regime's critics. Chapter 4 examines a rare moment of U.S. congressional pressure on the Egyptian regime. After the Palestinian elections of 2006, as Bush's "Freedom Agenda" receded, Congress threatened to withhold part of the annual $1.3-billion assistance package provided to the Egyptian military. Using the aid for leverage, representatives succeeded in getting the Egyptian Ministry of Defense to more vigilantly interdict smugglers whose activities (funneling weapons into the Gaza Strip) threatened communities in southern Israel.

Chapter 5 follows the groundswell of opposition to Mubarak that began during Bush's final years in office and continued into the Obama administration. Like Sadat before him, Mubarak reaped the fruits of his misdeeds and caprice. Rampant poverty, bogus elections, and unchecked police brutality – capped by the inspiring example of nearby Tunisia – generated a popular uprising that forced Mubarak's resignation and induced the SCAF to pledge a democratic transition. The revolt also augured a potentially dramatic drop in Washington's influence over Egypt. The implications of Mubarak's ouster for Egyptian democracy will hinge on how a new cohort of Egyptian leaders reckons with their country's security relationship with the United States and its domestic imprint.

The conclusion distills the book's main lessons. In diplomatic lore the Sadat-Carter-Begin collaboration is remembered as a template for resolving other conflicts and a progressive step toward Egyptian democracy. Peacemaking and democratization, however, were in tension during Sadat's presidency and have been ever since, because the regional strategy shared by U.S. and Egyptian officials runs counter to the aspirations of many Egyptians.

This pattern carries clear implications for contemporary debates. Whereas democracy promotion advocates have spoken of using the U.S.-Egyptian security relationship to influence the Egyptian government's domestic policies, the pattern has been the opposite: U.S. officials have selectively invoked the need for political reform inside Egypt as leverage over the foreign policy and security efforts of their Egyptian peers. Rather than being taken as given, the tenets of U.S. strategy and Washington's approach to Egypt can and should be problematized. One alternative to expecting an authoritarian regime to mold or ignore Egyptian public opinion around existing U.S. preferences would be to take Egyptian attitudes more seriously when formulating U.S. foreign policy.

What follows is a study of why and how the United States has partnered with the Egyptian regime as it suppressed and then retreated before the people of Egypt.

I

Peace before Freedom

From 1952 until 1967, the Egyptian regime cooperated with the United States. After Israel devastated the Egyptian military in the 1967 War, however, Cairo severed diplomatic ties with Washington. Seven years later, the two governments reconciled. While Anwar Sadat sought territory and foreign investment, the White House wanted a strategic advantage over the Soviet Union. The mutual benefits of a U.S.-Egyptian alliance only became clear to both sides, though, after Sadat took Egypt to war. What followed was one of the most tectonic shifts of the Cold War: the complete return of the Sinai Peninsula to Egypt; a lasting peace between Israel and Egypt; and a strategic pact between the United States and Egypt, previously a key client of the Soviet Union. By the end of the decade, Egypt was integral to U.S. preparedness to intervene in the Persian Gulf.

Bold diplomacy required fierce autocracy. Sadat's foreign peers understood that the Egyptian regime could handle terms that would be untenable in a truly democratic polity. If needed, Sadat could impose consensus from above rather than sway the public through open debate. The Egyptian president confirmed these expectations. After signing the Egyptian-Israeli Peace Treaty he aggressively policed the Egyptian public. But neither internal violence nor foreign assistance could rescue his presidency. Sadat slipped into a vicious spiral of fiscal desperation, diplomatic overextension, and mass detentions. This maelstrom claimed Sadat's life. His successor, Hosni Mubarak, would continue the heavy-handed tactics that protected Egypt's alignment while repressing its people.[1]

Sadat's presidency and the negotiations at Camp David have been incisively treated elsewhere.[2] Instead of reprising that history, this chapter links Sadat's diplomacy to his reincarnation of the Nasserist security state – the bulwark of Egyptian authoritarianism – and shows how internal violence meshed with international peacemaking. Three main accomplishments punctuate Sadat's tenure and organize the analysis. Between taking office in 1970 and signing the first disengagement agreement with Israel in 1974, he succeeded, through war, in gaining U.S. attention and reclaiming a sliver of Egyptian territory on the east bank of the Suez Canal. From 1974 until 1977, he oversaw economic and political liberalization, pledging to open Egypt's markets and its single-party system. That period closed abruptly after price riots rocked the country in January 1977. From then until the signing of the Egyptian-Israeli peace treaty in March 1979, Sadat poured his energy and political capital into cementing a strategic alliance with the United States and regaining the remainder of the Sinai Peninsula. After accomplishing most of what he wanted, the Egyptian president struggled to convince his people a peace dividend was imminent. When Egypt's alliance with the United States and peace with Israel proved neither as lucrative nor as comprehensive as Sadat had intimated, dissidents confronted a revived security state. The regime jailed hundreds during the 1981 Autumn of Fury before Sadat fell to a small band of militants.

Limited War

Sadat's early career gave little hint of the heights to which he would rise. As a junior military officer, Sadat participated in the July 23–26, 1952, overthrow of King Farouk and the establishment of the Egyptian republic in 1953. But in the new regime he was an innocuous underling of coup-leader-cum-Prime Minister (and, from 1956, President) Gamal Abdel Nasser.[3]

Nasser practiced tough diplomacy and tougher domestic politics. He was a pioneer of non-alignment, refusing to side with the United States or the USSR. In 1956 he nationalized the Suez Canal Company and withstood the subsequent "Tripartite Aggression" of Great Britain,

France, and Israel. Before the 1967 War, Nasser's most spectacular *failures* were a bid at joining Egypt and Syria (the short-lived United Arab Republic of 1958–1961) and military intervention in Yemen. During the 1952 to 1967 period, Nasser and his advisors communicated closely with the U.S. government, and Cairo received intermittent aid from Washington. Their relationship, while modest in comparison to the later U.S.-Egyptian alliance, presaged the strains and strengths of bilateral cooperation between the White House and later Egyptian presidents.

Through aid, U.S. policymakers sought "to moderate the behavior of the Egyptian government" so that Egypt would not interfere with U.S. interests.[4] Congress and the White House assisted Nasser only insofar as he would distance himself from the Soviet Union and pursue peace talks with Israel.[5] When the Egyptian president, rather than coming to heel, showed ambitions of regional leadership, the United States scrapped plans for sending military aid and long-term economic aid, although food aid was still offered. For their part, Egyptian officials hoped that U.S. support would provide breathing room economically without imperiling Egypt's interests or independence. The Public Law 480 (PL 480 or "Food for Peace") program, while limited, became the most successful component of U.S. aid. It granted surplus U.S. grain to Egypt and enabled Nasser to spend his country's foreign reserves in other areas of development.[6] By 1963 Egypt was the "world's largest per capita consumer of American food aid."[7] Nasser emphasized, however, that the Egyptian people would oppose any relationship that bound them to an outside power in a colonial-style relationship.[8] He rebuffed President Lyndon Johnson's emissary when the White House tried to link food aid to changes in Egyptian foreign policy. "We don't mind troubles," Nasser told an audience in Port Said in December 1964. "But we are not going to accept pressure. We are not going to accept gangsterism by cowboys."[9]

In contrast to the White House and Congress's approach, the Kremlin offered military aid, as well as grain, to Nasser without attaching political strings. Thus, Egypt enjoyed Soviet assistance, including advanced weaponry, without making concessions on the Arab-Israeli conflict or appearing to compromise national sovereignty.[10] Meanwhile, the gaps between Egyptian policies and U.S. priorities grew. In summer 1967, USAID officials recognized that the United States should not have expected "President Nasser would abandon or significantly modify political action which he determined to be in his own and Egypt's best interests in consideration of continued American wheat imports."[11]

When it came to domestic control, Nasser mused, "We could rule this country the way Papa Duvalier rules Haiti," implying that he had the power to terrorize Egyptians into submission.[12] The threat was far from hypothetical; a vast intelligence network foiled foreign spies and preempted putsches.[13] In the words of one British official, Nasser ran the Egyptian republic as a "complete police state."[14] While hunting enemies inside Egypt, Nasser exposed his country to foes from without. Having sent tens of thousands of Egyptian soldiers to Yemen, Nasser was stunned by a surprise Israeli attack on June 5, 1967. In less than a week, Israel had trounced not only the Egyptian military – including laying waste to much of the Egyptian air force while it was still on the ground – but also Jordan's and Syria's forces.

Nasser euphemistically called his country's defeat the "Setback," but Israel controlled the Sinai Peninsula, the Gaza Strip, the West Bank (including East Jerusalem), and the Golan Heights. His prestige in tatters, the Egyptian president could no longer play the superpowers off each other. He severed diplomatic ties with Washington, Israel's chief patron during the war, and accepted Moscow's help rebuilding his decimated army. His final military venture was a war of attrition to gain ground near the Suez Canal and deter Israeli air raids, which flew as far west as Cairo. Ever the Arab ombudsman, Nasser mediated between the Palestinian Liberation Organization (PLO) and Jordan. At home, he created a paramilitary police organization – the Central Security Forces (CSF) – to help maintain internal order.[15]

In the twilight of Nasser's rule, a new movement for democracy in Egypt was dawning. The president had pinned defeat on his military and intelligence leaders. In a November "heart-to-heart" before Parliament, he faulted "centers of power" who had corrupted the intelligence services and vowed that those responsible would be tried before a revolutionary court.[16] Some Egyptians may have been mollified, but others hungered for more tangible change. On February 20, 1968, the regime seemed to renege on its vows of accountability; air force leaders charged with negligence received sentences no longer than fifteen years. The next day, workers in the industrial town of

Helwan began demonstrating. Soon thousands of students in Cairo and Alexandria were in the streets. Protests lasted six days, the biggest student uprising of Nasser's presidency.[17] Yelling "Down with the Security State!" protesters called for resentencing the derelict officers and retiring Nasser's secret police.[18] The democracy movement revealed the courage of Egyptians living under Nasser, but the president conceded little. On March 30, he promised to reform the ruling party (the Arab Socialist Union [ASU]), strengthen the legislature, ensure the right of Egyptians to litigate in court, and limit the tenure of top officeholders.[19] Although a popular referendum ratified the March 30 declaration, one year later, U.S. reports still depicted an "extensive and efficient intelligence apparatus which reaches into almost every corner of Egyptian society."[20]

Nasser died of a heart attack in September 1970. Nine months earlier he had appointed Sadat vice president. After an interim period as acting president, Sadat succeeded to the office through a national plebiscite. To many top officials, including ASU chief Ali Sabri, Sadat was an accidental president, an undistinguished subordinate elevated by circumstance. Sabri and fellow Nasserists supported Sadat's nomination because they considered him weak and pliable. They expected him to be their marionette.

But Sadat took his own cues. Rather than adopt pro-Soviet policies and escalate the confrontation with Israel – in other words, continue Nasser's policies – he reversed land reforms and floated an Arab-Israeli peace proposal. Incensed, Sabri's clique tried to derail Sadat's presidency by resigning en masse in May 1971. Sadat had beaten the conspirators to the punch. He had recruited second-echelon intelligence and military officials; they arrested Sabri and his collaborators.[21] In addition to countering the coup, Sadat worked to regain the public's trust. He publicly incinerated the Ministry of the Interior's surveillance tapes, torching an emblem of the "security state."[22] He also closed detention centers and declared an end to arbitrary arrests.[23] These liberal steps, however, did not reduce the president's powers. A new constitution, adopted in September 1971, took steps – albeit small ones – toward safeguarding individual liberties, expanding judicial institutions and property rights.[24] Yet it also allotted tremendous powers to the chief executive and retained language allowing for a martial law-like "State of Emergency." The Emergency Law (No. 162 of 1958) allowed the president to close newspapers, censor media, and

subject his opponents to indefinite detention without trial or sentenc-
ing through extrajudicial security courts.[25] For the time being, these
repressive tools were held in reserve.

Seeing a Soviet hand in Sabri's plot, Sadat wanted to swap Moscow's
patronage for Washington's.[26] As early as April 1971, he privately
signaled to the Nixon administration that he was keen on achieving
peace with Israel.[27] In July 1972, after having signed a long-term
Egyptian-Soviet Friendship and Cooperation Treaty the prior year,
Sadat expelled some ten thousand Soviet military advisors.[28] Egyptians
found themselves in a state of "no peace, no war."[29] In light of Egypt's
military weakness, however, neither the United States nor Israel wanted
to alter the status quo. In fact, from the perspective of Nixon's national
security advisor, Henry Kissinger, this limbo was ideal: "a prolonged
stalemate that would move the Arabs toward moderation and the
Soviets to the fringes of Middle East diplomacy." Kissinger appreciated
the expulsion of the Soviet advisors, but did not reward Sadat's move.[30]
He and his Egyptian counterpart, Hafez Ismail, met once in 1972,
but the back-channel discussions were mainly a stopgap while Nixon
campaigned for a second term.[31] Sadat had declared 1972 the "Year
of Decision," but it passed, as the Nixon administration preferred,
without any major advance in Arab-Israeli politics.

Much like Sadat's domestic rivals, U.S. officials dismissed the
Egyptian president as a lightweight. The Suez Canal had been closed
since the 1967 War and U.S. strategy focused not on Egypt, but on Iran
and Saudi Arabia, the "two pillars" of Persian Gulf security.[32] Over
the short term, Washington did not seek to change this arrangement.
With Saudi help, the White House planned to wean Sadat off the Soviet
dole without contesting Israel's post-1967 occupations. Reestablishing
ties with Egypt, however, was a minor goal. "Where possible," a 1973
NSC memo suggested, "the US will also try to find ways of developing
its own bilateral relationship with Egypt, within the constraints set
by the Arab-Israeli conflict."[33] The Egyptian president chafed at those
constraints, which perpetuated deadlock. Defying Kissinger's predic-
tion of "moderation," Sadat turned from diplomacy to battle.

On October 6, 1973, Egyptian forces penetrated the Bar Lev Line, a
massive defensive fortification on the eastern bank of the Suez Canal,
and challenged Israel's control of the Sinai. Simultaneously, the Syrian
military attacked the Golan Heights. U.S. officials were astonished

by the actions, which Sadat and Syrian President Hafez al-Assad had secretly been planning for months. The two leaders' goals differed dramatically, however. Assad envisaged a reconquest of lost territory. By contrast, Sadat was not seeking to retake land by force or challenge Israel's pre-1967 borders (a scenario he foreswore to the White House early in the fighting). Rather, he aimed to compel the superpowers to start peace talks that would return to Egypt the whole Sinai Peninsula, reopen the Suez Canal, and let the country move from costly military spending to economic recovery.[34] It was a "limited war ... to change the agenda."[35]

Neither the war itself nor the diplomacy that followed matched Sadat's expectations. Initially Egyptian and Syrian forces made dramatic headway, but Sadat then held the Egyptian army on the east bank of the canal, rather than advancing and capturing the crucial Gidi and Mitla passes that cut through Sinai's mountainous northern terrain.[36] While Egyptian soldiers stood still, Israel hammered the Syrians. The Pentagon also began ferreting millions of tons of military supplies to Israel. When news spread that Nixon's administration was intervening on Israel's behalf, the Arab states of the Organization of Petroleum Exporting Countries (OPEC), led by Saudi Arabia, reduced their overall oil exports and stopped selling oil to the United States and a limited set of Western countries. Before the war, OPEC had opted to raise the price of oil. The supply reduction, coupled with poor domestic energy policies in the United States and other Western states, spiked fuel costs and brought shortages.

Meanwhile, Sadat's military was losing ground. When Egyptian forces belatedly advanced into the Sinai, they were pummeled by Israeli aircraft. Israeli soldiers also crossed to the west bank of the Suez. Only the Arab oil embargo compelled U.S. attention and saved Egyptian troops from an utter rout.[37] OPEC's actions forced Kissinger to accelerate work on ending the conflict.[38] On October 22, the UN Security Council (UNSC) adopted Resolution 338, which called for an immediate ceasefire, the implementation of UNSCR 242 (1967) affirming the principle of "land for peace" (Israel would relinquish the land captured in 1967 in exchange for a commitment to peace from the Arab states), and negotiations "toward a just and durable peace in the Middle East." The ceasefire did not take hold at first, and Israel encircled Egypt's Third Army. Hostilities were suspended, however, after the Security Council passed a second resolution (340, on October 25) and Sadat said he was ready to engage in talks before an Israeli withdrawal.[39]

The end of the war revitalized U.S.-Egyptian relations. In November, Kissinger visited Cairo, where he discussed reestablishing U.S.-Egyptian diplomatic ties and arranging an Arab-Israeli peace conference in Geneva, Switzerland.[40] The U.S. and Egyptian governments posted "persons of ambassadorial rank" in their respective outposts. Career foreign service officer Hermann Eilts was the U.S. emissary to Cairo.[41] Just before Christmas, the Americans, the Soviets, and the main belligerents of the October War gathered in Geneva. The multilateral talks, however, did not disentangle Israeli and Egyptian forces. Kissinger took up that task, "shuttling" between Jerusalem and Cairo for ten days in January. His diplomacy yielded the Sinai I disengagement agreement, under which Israel withdrew its forces twelve to thirteen miles east of the Suez Canal. On February 28, 1974, the U.S. embassy in Cairo reopened. For the next five years Eilts would lead it, meeting Sadat almost daily.[42]

In June, Nixon left behind the Watergate hearings and took refuge in his foreign policy success, visiting Egypt, Saudi Arabia, Syria, and Israel.[43] It was, in Eilts's words, "a kind of triumphal tour, to cap a very triumphal period of U.S. diplomacy." The pleasant visuals, which included a presidential handshake by the Pyramids, belied Nixon's anguish and detachment from the political reality of Washington.[44] Weeks later Sadat received a fantastic list of weapons and equipment that Nixon proposed to sell him: $180 million worth of sensors, radar equipment, TOW missiles with launchers, torpedoes, bombs, helicopters, and fighter jets – none of which would get through Congress without a fight.[45] It was a pipe dream, but one that Sadat would keep chasing. When Nixon resigned in October, the offer vanished. Still, to mitigate the chance the Egyptians would reach out to Moscow, Gerald Ford implored Sadat "to turn the Soviets down" and give the United States' "unilateral effort" toward peacemaking more time. He also pledged $250 million in economic support for Egypt, an unprecedented disbursement from the United States to Egypt but not a military aid package. Even in terms of economic assistance, the aid paled in comparison to the Egyptian government's fiscal needs.[46] Still, Sadat acceded to Ford's request.

Egypt achieved some economic relief from a second disengagement agreement. After another round of shuttle diplomacy, on September 4, 1975, Egypt and Israel signed "Sinai II." The accord provided $2 billion in aid for Israel, moved the Israeli military twelve to twenty-six miles farther eastward, and established a UN-managed buffer system between Egyptian and Israeli forces.[47] The pullout allowed Egypt to reclaim its eastern oil fields, which generated an estimated $1 billion annually.[48] Egypt also reopened the Suez Canal, which would provide half a billion dollars worth of tolls in 1976.[49]

Liberalization

Before the October War, Sadat had struggled to finance Egypt's wheat imports.[50] Afterward, he hungered for capital to rebuild the Egyptian military and the country's infrastructure. In April 1974, Sadat enjoined Egyptians to lead the reconstruction but admitted, "We still have a great need for foreign resources."[51] Through the Open Door policy (codified in Law 43/1974), he lifted Nasserist restrictions on foreign investment.[52] Generous tax exemptions induced Arab investors in the Persian Gulf to bring their surplus wealth to Egypt. But Gulf Arabs put their money in enclaves that were relatively safe, highly profitable, and capital, rather than labor intensive. In 1976, petroleum projects comprised 48 percent of foreign investment, while housing, tourism, and construction absorbed 23 percent. The Open Door thus failed to kick start industries that would create local jobs and high-value products.[53]

While Egypt struggled to produce internationally competitive goods, luxury items and junk food flooded the Egyptian market. By 1975, imports exceeded 30 percent of gross domestic product (GDP). As inflation hit an estimated 20 to 35 percent, most Egyptians could not afford the new goods or handle the corresponding rise in basic prices.[54] Rather than bringing the country's population (approximately 34 million in 1974 and growing by more than a million per year) new opportunities, the Open Door caused working class Egyptians to resent the elite bankers and businessmen who benefited from the influx of foreign capital.[55] In January 1975, labor protests erupted in Cairo. Two months later, forty thousand workers in the factory town of Mahalla al-Kubra went on strike.[56] Sadat responded with force. Police with clubs and machine guns dispersed Cairo bus drivers when they went on strike in September 1976.[57]

Although U.S. politicians welcomed the Open Door – a showcase of western capitalism on the Nile – they did not help Sadat reduce the trauma it was inflicting on Egyptian society. Strategically Egypt still played second fiddle to Iran and Saudi Arabia, countries the White House relied on to safeguard "the rapidly increasing importance of Gulf oil" (set to "account for two-thirds of all oil moving in international trade in the next decade"). "[S]upporting Sadat's regime" was an afterthought.[58] Military aid proved a particularly tough row to hoe. In 1975 Egypt's military expenditures totaled $6.1 billion, more than half the gross national product.[59] In March 1976, in a fresh bid for U.S. military assistance, Sadat told Parliament to cancel Egypt's friendship treaty with the USSR.[60] In April, he denied Soviet ships access to Egyptian ports (although the Soviet Union remained, for the time being, Egypt's largest trading partner). After Sadat snubbed Egypt's former patron, Washington began selling C-130 military transport aircraft to Egypt.[61] Six C-130s were delivered in 1976, but only after Kissinger promised Congress that the sales would not constitute a precedent and that there would be no further Egyptian requests for materiel that calendar year.[62] For the next fiscal year, bilateral economic aid and food subsidies to Egypt would top $1 billion – a hefty appropriation from Congress, but not enough for an economic recovery.[63]

While workers slammed the Open Door, Sadat ended single-party rule and allowed voters to choose between rightist, centrist, and leftist "platforms" in the fall 1976 parliamentary elections. It was another nod to western liberalism, but Egypt's return to multiparty politics was immediately eclipsed by social turmoil.[64]

At the close of 1976 Sadat faced a $2 billion budget deficit. Foreign debt exceeded GDP, and the size of debt repayments equaled approximately 70 percent of exports.[65] To balance the books, the government slashed state subsidies on cooking gas, rice, and sugar, which totaled $1.7 billion that year.[66] The reductions would trim the deficit by 20 percent, but raise the cost of living for an average Egyptian by 15 percent.[67] The risky step to retrench subsidies rather than curb military spending, debt servicing, or investment reflected the government's deference to its core domestic and foreign constituencies.[68] Yet price hikes could not have come at a worse time. Washington had resumed PL 480 grain shipments to Cairo and "one of every three loaves of bread consumed by urban Egyptians was a product of PL 480 wheat."[69] By keeping bread prices below the market rate, food aid backstopped the regime. That protection would vanish if Egyptian families were forced to spend more money on other essentials. Without consulting the recently elected parliament, Sadat's cabinet publicized its decision on January 17.[70]

The subsidy cuts sparked the greatest social unrest Egypt had seen in twenty-five years. On January 18 and 19, tens of thousands rioted in cities up and down the Nile. At one point, 30,000 demonstrators clashed with police in Cairo.[71] The situation prompted Sadat, vacationing in southern Egypt, to revoke the austerity measures and send in the military to regain control of the streets. An estimated eighty people were killed, hundreds were wounded, and 1,200 to 2,000 were arrested.[72] The price revolt traumatized Sadat, some say permanently.[73] He "was 100 percent changed by the experience" and "became aggressive," recalled then minister of defense Abd al-Ghani Gamassy, who had led the military's intervention.[74] Sadat, who fancied himself to be liberalizing Egypt, warned that democracy had "fangs one hundred times sharper than the extraordinary measures" of dictatorship.[75] During a two-hour television broadcast on February 3, he pinned the riots on Soviet agents and communist remnants from Nasser's administration. Egypt's enemies had exploited the November 1976 elections to sow doubt and propaganda. In order to preserve national unity and prevent another "uprising of thieves," Sadat would rollback his earlier reforms, criminalize strikes and demonstrations (on penalty of life imprisonment with hard labor), and confine electoral competition to government-sanctioned parties. "We hereby end one period," Sadat proclaimed, "and we begin a new one."[76] A February 10 plebiscite approved the measures with a suspicious 99.4 percent.[77]

As violence roiled Egypt, the young administration of Jimmy Carter hoped to help Sadat survive a dicey period. The United States, Carter's team believed, could shore up the government in Cairo by providing arms and pushing for peace. Secretary of State Cyrus Vance toured the Middle East in February and explained that

> The importance of American arms sales to Sadat is primarily political. He does not expect arms sales of an amount which would affect

the arms balance in the area. He sees modest American arms sales as a means of strengthening support of the all-important Egyptian military establishment for him and the peace effort in which he is engaged. Sadat believes the U.S.-Egypt relationship has come a long way in the last three years but that the principal missing ingredient is the lack of an arms relationship.... Sadat knows he must retain the loyalty of his military if he is to stay in power and thereby must continue his peace policy. He also knows Egypt must maintain some degree of military credibility if his diplomatic initiative is to succeed. On the other hand, elements of the armed forces have expressed opposition to Sadat's turning to the West precisely because it has resulted in curtailment of the Soviet arms supply. Should there be no progress in negotiations within a reasonable time frame and, at the same time, there is further erosion of the combat capabilities of the armed forces, the pressure on Sadat to change his policies or leave office will become inexorable. The ousting of Sadat from power in Egypt under these circumstances would start a destabilizing process in Egypt, the ramifications of which are difficult to forecast but which could be extensive and very damaging to United States interests in Egypt and throughout the Middle East. For starters, it would probably begin the unraveling of all that has been accomplished since the end of the October 1973 war.[78]

After years of indifference, the United States was giving Sadat the attention he craved.

Popular unrest and military dissatisfaction in Egypt provided the White House a powerful incentive. In April, the two presidents met in Washington, discussed the threats of pro-Soviet governments in eastern Africa, and shared their hopes for Middle East peace. Carter toasted Sadat as a "good friend" and described him as a "shining light" in the Middle East.[79] Carter's friendship would prove to be a double-edged sword for the Egyptian president. It gave Sadat unprecedented access to the White House, but it also exposed him to intense pressure. Rather than alleviating Sadat's domestic difficulties, Carter exacerbated them by expecting his Egyptian counterpart to ignore public opinion.

Given Carter's commitments to promoting human rights, his attitude toward Egyptian domestic politics was ironic. In his inaugural address, Carter imagined a distinctly ethical foreign policy: "Because we are free, we can never be indifferent to the fate of freedom elsewhere. Our moral sense dictates a clear-cut preference for those societies which share with us an abiding respect for individual human rights." Later, he elaborated on this theme and stressed the primacy of "human freedom" for the United States' role in the world. Renouncing the practice of tacitly supporting dictators, he asserted that the U.S. government "can have a foreign policy that is democratic" while "reject[ing] the arguments of those rulers who deny human rights to their people."[80] Nevertheless, when it came to Egypt the White House tacitly accepted Sadat's arguments about "fanged democracy."

White House staff struggled to reconcile U.S. interests with Carter's rights advocacy:

> Day by day, country by country, human rights considerations are being weighed against other foreign policy objectives, such as... strategic arms limitation, peacekeeping in the Middle East.... While there is no necessary inconsistency among these objectives, they will, on occasion, compete for primacy.... There will clearly be instances in which efforts to achieve our human rights goals will have to be modified, delayed or curtailed in deference to other important objectives. But by the same token, making human rights a principal goal of our foreign policy means that promotion of human rights will not be viewed as a lesser objective.[81]

Human rights would be defended when not superseded by other foreign policy goals – like preserving the Egyptian regime.

Strategically, Egypt was helping the United States keep Soviet clients in check, and would be integral for Arab-Israeli peace. On May 25, 1977, Sadat provided pilots to support Zairean strongman and U.S. ally Mobutu Sese Seko in his fight against communists.[82] Economic assistance to Egypt reached $900 million, exceeding the sum of all other such programs for Latin America and Africa. A fifth of the funds went toward supplementing the country's food supply and preempting further price riots.[83] Meanwhile, Egypt was buying light weapons commercially from U.S. suppliers during 1976–1979, including 350 gas grenade launchers, more than 150,000 gas grenades, and more than 2,400 handguns with 328,000 rounds of ammo.[84]

Diplomacy and Dissent

Egyptian-Israeli negotiations had been stalled since Sinai II. Carter and Sadat wanted to resume talks, but in May 1977, Israeli voters gave the right-wing Likud Party the opportunity to form a government.

Whereas Carter saw the West Bank becoming part of a "Palestinian homeland," the new prime minister, Menachem Begin, considered it Israeli territory.[85] Undeterred, the White House worked with the Kremlin to convene a second Geneva summit. When that plan bogged down, Carter, in his words, "decided to play my only hole card – a direct appeal to President Sadat."[86] In a handwritten letter, Carter reminded Sadat that he had offered to assist "at a crucial moment" in the search for Middle East peace: "We have reached such a moment, and I need your help.... The time has now come to move forward, and your early public endorsement of our approach is extremely important – perhaps vital – in advancing all parties to Geneva."[87]

The message tapped Sadat's fondness for grand gestures, and the Egyptian leader replied that he would call for an international summit in East Jerusalem. Carter nixed the idea; he still wanted the parties to meet at Geneva.[88] Sadat spoke before the Egyptian parliament on November 9 and said a Geneva conference would enable Arab leaders to promote a Palestinian state and regain the land lost in 1967.[89] But, with characteristic flair, he also dropped a bombshell:

> I am ready to go to Geneva.... More so, I am ready to travel to the ends of the earth if it saves a single soldier or officer from harm, much less death.... And Israelis will be surprised when they hear me say, before you now, that I am ready to go to their house, to the Knesset itself, and address them.[90]

It was a provocative move; no Arab ruler had visited Jerusalem since 1967. Sadat's foreign minister, Ismail Fahmy, resigned in protest. The Carter administration gave tentative support, wary of blowback for Sadat.[91] Ambassador Eilts wondered if the Egyptian cabinet was about to collapse and asked Defense Minister Gamassy if he would follow in Fahmy's footsteps. "I think the President's totally wrong in what he's doing," replied Gamassy, "but I'm a soldier and I will stand by him."[92] For the moment, other Egyptian officials followed suit.

On November 19, at Begin's invitation, Sadat flew to Jerusalem. The next day he addressed the Knesset and called for comprehensive peace: "total Israeli withdrawal from Arab lands and the recovery of the Palestinians' rights, including their right to set up an independent state."[93] Arab leaders condemned Sadat's trip to Israel and "froze" diplomatic relations with Egypt. In response, Sadat broke ties with

Syria and four other rejectionist states (Algeria, Libya, Iraq, and South Yemen).[94] The Egyptian public, however, was tired of war and supported Sadat's terms.[95] An estimated 77 percent of Egyptians approved of Sadat's approach, versus 18 percent for the "PLO [Palestinian Liberation Organization] strategy" (of rejecting talks).[96] Among student respondents at American University in Cairo, a proxy of the "Westernized bourgeoisie," the bulk (60 percent) agreed that "Egypt should make peace with Israel only on condition that she returns *all* the occupied Arab territories, including the Golan Heights of Syria, and permits creation of an independent Palestinian state on the West Bank of the Jordan."[97] But the U.S. Embassy in Cairo reported that even if a separate (Egyptian-Israeli) peace resulted, many educated Egyptians were "ready for it."[98] Gamassy and other cabinet members hoped the Jerusalem trip would benefit Egypt but doubted talks would progress without U.S. pressure on Israel.[99]

Months later there was no breakthrough. Sadat had imagined, perhaps naively, that Israel would respond to his trip by accepting peace with Egypt and the other Arab states and returning the land conquered in 1967. Instead, Begin simply agreed to start talking.[100] In late December Israelis and Egyptians met in the Egyptian city of Ismailiyya. Begin insisted on keeping settlers in the Sinai and retaining control over the other occupied territories. His stance frustrated the Egyptian delegates, including Sadat's new foreign minister, Muhammad Ibrahim Kamel.[101] Sadat was livid; the deadlock on Palestinian issues made it look like he was pursuing a separate peace.[102] That winter he vented his frustrations to Carter during meetings in Egypt and the United States.[103] Carter dissuaded Sadat from publicly criticizing Begin, but he had yet to bridge the gap between the two men.[104]

While Egyptian-Israeli talks stalled, the U.S.-Egyptian relationship progressed. To date, the United States had helped Egypt maintain the country's Soviet MiGs, provided another fourteen C-130s, and begun an officer training program in the United States (paid for with $200,000 of International Military Education and Training [IMET] for fiscal year [FY] 1978).[105] Sadat requested forty F-5E fighter jets to help him build an "Africa Corps" patrolling the northeast corner of the continent.[106] The notion was fantastical, but the White House worked on selling fighters to Egypt, as well as to Saudi Arabia.[107] Lawmakers worried that such major arms sales to Arab states would upset the

regional balance and threaten Israel.[108] Anticipating congressional
resistance, Carter bundled weapons packages to Israel, Egypt, and
Saudi Arabia for a single vote, refusing to let senators peel off the Arab
acquisitions. The $2.5-billion deal passed, providing "seventy-five
F-16s and fifteen F-15s to Israel, sixty F-15s to Saudi Arabia, and fifty
F-5Es to Egypt."[109] The package opened a long-term process of "mode-
rnizing" – meaning de-Sovietizing – the Egyptian armed forces. Elated,
Carter and Sadat exchanged congratulatory letters.[110] The sales to
Egypt, however, did not come with U.S. aid to finance them. Saudi
Arabia agreed to cover the cost of Egypt's purchases.[111]

The sales delighted Sadat, but his popularity at home was waning. Early in the year, Israel had responded to a lethal attack by
Palestinian militants by invading southern Lebanon. Israeli forces
killed more than a thousand civilians, angering many Egyptians and
undercutting Sadat's peace efforts.[112] When the left-wing Tagammu
Party decried the Israeli action, Sadat shut down its newspaper. He
then held a referendum on expelling dissident members of parliament
for inciting "a bloodbath and class warfare."[113] Officially, 98.29 percent of voters approved the six-point measure on May 21, 1978.[114]
Protesting the new restrictions, the Tagammu shuttered its publication completely. The center-right New Wafd Party also suspended
operations.[115]

U.S. State Department officials regretted Sadat's "de-liberalization,"
writing that Egyptians had historically lived under "benevolent autocracy" and that "Sadat had done quite well in countering this authoritarian tradition." Suppressing the opposition, however, carried a "pre-
ventive" upside in peace talks: "The further flexibility that will be
required provides additional ammunition for his opponents at home
and within the Arab world. Sadat, therefore, would want to assure
maximum domestic tranquility before moving into the most difficult phase of the peace process."[116] If "flexibility" in foreign policy
demanded strong-arm tactics, then Sadat would need to make difficult
concessions to the Americans and Israelis, while imposing compliance
on his fellow Egyptians.[117] But as the U.S. government observed Sadat
using "extraordinary powers to quell his detractors" and suppressing "chronic dissent," more and more Egyptians wondered if he had
simply been duped.[118]

The time had come, Carter decided, for another bold venture. In early August, he invited Begin and Sadat to join him at the presidential retreat at Camp David, where the three leaders could address all outstanding issues. In such a high-profile venture, failure would be catastrophic for Carter's political future and for the chance of real peace. At the same time, he hoped the isolated and bucolic setting could elicit compromises that had so far eluded the parties.[119]

Bilateral Peace

On September 5, U.S., Egyptian, and Israeli negotiators began crafting "a framework for peace in the Middle East."[120] Rather than advancing a comprehensive Arab-Israeli peace, however, the agenda at Camp David focused on an Egyptian-Israeli accord. Sadat was willing to accept solutions that were anathema to many Egyptians, including some members of his own negotiating team. Carter played on Sadat's purported ability to make decisions unilaterally in the face of public opposition. Because Sadat could override the objections of his fellow citizens and delegates, he could be counted on to seal the deal.[121] The surfeit of power vested in Egypt's president put his side at a disadvantage, whereas Begin could buttress his positions by invoking the Israeli electorate.[122]

Sadat entered the talks mistakenly thinking he and Carter were conspiring against Begin. "[The Israelis] are not really being responsive to anything, as you know," he remarked to Eilts.[123] At Camp David, Sadat treated Carter as his confidante and his own ministers as gadflies.[124] He initially laid out maximalist positions to knock Begin onto his heels, but the Israeli premier pushed back just as fiercely. Carter soon decided that rather than having the two leaders talk to each other directly, he would deal with each one individually.[125] He later recalled that Sadat "seemed to trust me too much, and Begin not enough."[126] In fact, while Carter thought Sadat enjoyed "freedom of action," the Egyptian leader depended heavily on his friend in the White House.[127] Compounding this handicap was Sadat's tendency to sequester himself in his cabin, leaving the legwork to his staff.[128]

For days Carter tried to reconcile the differences between the Egyptian and Israeli leaders. When the gaps appeared unbridgeable,

Carter counted on Sadat to make unpopular decisions on his own. "It is generally held that Sadat is flexible," he told the Egyptian team, "while his close associates are hard-liners; and that Prime Minister Begin is a hard-liner while his close associates are flexible.... [I]f it is true, then it constitutes a useful and desirable balance."[129] But Sadat did not counterbalance Begin. Even if the two sides could be equally obstinate, when Sadat became the fulcrum of debate, the scales tipped against the Egyptians. Carter explicitly encouraged this lopsidedness and preferred to circumvent the Egyptian president's advisors: "On any controversial issue, I never consulted Sadat's aides, but always went directly to their leader."[130]

U.S. and Israeli officials commented on the expediency of dealing with Egypt's autocratic ruler, who could impose major national policy changes without building a popular consensus. In one of the summit's more relaxed discussions, Carter records Begin making a "good debating point" as the Israeli premier described how Sadat had realigned Egypt from Soviet to U.S. support and taken his country from war to peace: "It was obvious that under strong leadership, the opinion of the Egyptians could be changed."[131] By contrast, Begin answered to a broad governing coalition. The point echoed a previous remark by Israeli defense minister Ezer Weizman: "Sadat continually spoke of agreement or disagreement on the part of the Egyptian people even though he was clearly able to ensure the adoption of almost any decision he wanted, whereas Begin had to consider many others, in his party and out."[132] Consistent with this understanding of Sadat's domestic leverage, Carter presumed the Egyptian leader could disregard his constituents, while the Israeli premier needed to convince his.

As the possibility of regional peace slipped away, the prospects of a U.S.-Egyptian alliance against the USSR came into view. On September 12 (day 8), Carter explained to Egyptian foreign minister Mohammed Ibrahim Kamel that negotiations over the West Bank, the Gaza Strip, and Jerusalem would need to occur later, for the negotiators could not "solve all problems at once." Egypt, he argued, should seize the chance to end its conflict with Israel, which would serve all three sides' interests in checking Soviet influence. As Carter put it,

> The Soviet Union is roaming freely in the Horn of Africa and the
> Middle East because it knows that Egypt has five whole regiments

pinned down along the Suez Canal which cannot be moved. Were we
to reach a peace agreement between Egypt and Israel, there would be
no need for the five regiments to be held up on the Canal. President
Sadat would be free to deploy them in whichever manner he chose.
This would force the Soviet Union to rethink its strategy and make it
more likely to observe more caution.

That argument played into Sadat's hope "to become not only America's ally, but also America's policeman in the area," yet Kamel was
not persuaded.[133] "Pardon me, Mr. President," he replied, "but we
are meeting here to find a solution to the Arab-Israeli conflict, not to
deal with the policies of the Soviet Union!"[134] The foreign minister
feared that by putting a U.S.-Egyptian partnership ahead of the return
of Arab territory, Sadat would squander the achievements of 1973 and
consign the West Bank to "be chewed up by Israeli settlements."[135]

For a moment, Sadat was ready to heed Kamel's counsel and break
off talks. On September 15, he began to storm out of the conference because the Israeli delegation had not made sufficient compromises. Carter caught up to Sadat and warned that their friendship, as
well as any chance for a stronger U.S.-Egyptian alliance, would end
if he walked away.[136] There would be no second chance for Carter.
Midterm elections loomed in November, and Camp David was fraught
with implications for his reelection bid in 1980.[137] His team understood: "The President has got to come out of this meeting with something."[138] The ultimatum stopped Sadat in his tracks. U.S. national
security advisor Zbigniev Brzezinski recorded: "President Sadat, who
saw Camp David as an opportunity to collude with the United States
against Israel, ended with much of the pressure directed against him.
His choices were either to walk out or to agree to whatever we could
get the Israelis to accept. Sadat chose the latter."[139] From that point,
the Egyptian leader was resigned to whatever Carter could deliver.[140]
Sadat stunned his delegation by saying he "would sign anything proposed by President Carter without [even] reading it."[141]

The first part of the Camp David Accords, the Framework for the
Conclusion of a Peace Treaty between Egypt and Israel, showed how
much Sadat had retreated during the summit. Carter had identified "six
no's" in Begin's stance (no withdrawal from the West Bank, no end
to settlement activity, no withdrawal from the Sinai, no acknowledg-
ment that UN Resolution 242 applied to the West Bank and Gaza, no

Palestinian self-rule, no consideration of refugees); Sadat came away with a single "yes" (Sinai withdrawal).[142] Begin had demanded that 2,000 to 2,500 Israeli settlers be allowed to remain in the eastern Sinai Peninsula after Israel withdrew.[143] But Sadat insisted that all settlements be vacated.[144] After twelve days at Camp David (four times the planned duration), Begin agreed, but made the pullout contingent on Knesset approval.[145] Hence, Begin anchored an unpalatable concession in domestic electoral institutions, a tactic unavailable to Sadat. Moreover, even the return of the Sinai entailed flexibility from the Egyptians. Because of Carter's intercessions, the Israeli pullout would stretch over a three-year period – not the two years Sadat preferred.[146]

The second portion of the accords, the Framework for Peace in the Middle East, offered vague recommendations for talks among Israel, the Arab states, and the Palestinians.[147] It did not specify that Israel would need to vacate other occupied territories, nor did it link Egyptian-Israeli peace to comprehensive peace. Regarding the deal as an abandonment of Arab solidarity and Sadat's own earlier pledges, Foreign Minister Kamel resigned in protest.[148] The parties signed the Camp David Accords on September 17, 1978. The next day Begin reasserted that the occupied West Bank was part of Israel. He also envisioned only a ninety-day freeze in settlement construction, not an indefinite halt until the broader Arab-Israeli peace was finalized, as Carter had understood.[149] Carter acknowledged what had troubled Kamel: "It seemed that suspicions at Camp David were proving well founded. Begin wanted to keep two things: the peace with Egypt – and the West Bank."[150] Of course, the U.S. administration was well aware of the Israeli premier's hard-line views.[151] Yet the summit's wake was an inconvenient time for Israel to reassert its claims on the West Bank, particularly when the Camp David Accords mentioned Palestinian autonomy.

In spring 1978, Sadat had stressed to Carter the need for "[a]ttracting the other Arab parties to join us in the process of the negotiations."[152] His evolution toward a bilateral peace deal reflected desperation more than duplicity. Losing ground before a steadfast Israeli leader and a U.S. president determined to close a deal, Sadat took what he could and left the rest for later. His paramount goal was regaining the entire Sinai Peninsula. The second imperative was forging a partnership with the United States that would rescue the Egyptian economy and rehabilitate the Egyptian military. Theoretically, these accomplishments were compatible with a long-term strategy of helping the Palestinian and Syrians regain their lands. The Sinai I disengagement treaty had been followed by a similar pact between Israel and Syria; an Egyptian-Israeli accord could be the springboard for deals among the other parties.[153]

The Camp David Accords drew mixed reactions in Egypt and the Arab world. The Egyptian army approved, even though the deal limited Egyptian force deployments to a sole division in the Sinai.[154] Likewise, the Egyptian public largely backed an agreement that would liberate the Sinai. Sadat's fellow Arab rulers, by contrast, thought Sadat had sold out the Palestinians and Syrians. In November 1978, the Arab League agreed to expel Egypt if it signed a formal treaty with Israel. In response, Sadat severed ties with the governments denouncing him and boasted, "Egypt isn't isolated in the Arab world, the Arabs are isolated from Egypt."[155]

The opening of 1979 strengthened the desire in Washington and Cairo to conclude an Egyptian-Israeli treaty. In the middle of January, the shah of Iran fled into exile and the United States lost its main "pillar" of Persian Gulf security. Of the White House's allies in the Middle East, "Egypt came the closest" to being a possible replacement for Iran, mused Secretary of Defense Harold Brown. But Egypt lacked significant oil wealth and would need outside resources to expand its military. The United States could finance arms sales to Egypt, but only after Sadat signed a peace deal with Israel. Director of National Intelligence Stansfield Turner worried that enlarging Sadat's role in U.S. strategy could threaten his presidency:

> [I]t will be difficult to turn Sadat away from his concept of being a Middle East policeman, but there are real dangers in our encouraging that role. There is a danger that he will ignore his domestic problems, ignore the military dissatisfaction with such a policy, and that he could end up generating the same kind of problem that we have just seen in Iran.[156]

True to form, Sadat proposed to Brown in February that Egypt step in for Iran "on an even grander scale than had been assumed by that country under the shah."[157] Brown communicated that the United States could provide more aid after Egypt and Israel signed a peace treaty.[158] Sadat did not object to this conditional offer. U.S.-financed arms sales stood to strengthen relations between the president and the army, mitigating some of the instability that concerned Turner.[159]

Sadat was not going to replace the shah, but the Egyptian-Israeli treaty could stabilize one corner of the region.[160] On March 7, Carter flew to Cairo to seal the deal with more compromises from Sadat: "Once more, I wanted Begin to have his way with particular phrases and depended on Sadat to be flexible on language and to take the long view concerning the effect of the agreement."[161] The Egyptian leader gave Carter, in Brzezinski's words, "carte blanche for his subsequent negotiations with the Israelis."[162] In exchange, Sadat was promised a "massive" U.S.-Egyptian military and economic relationship after the treaty.[163] Reprising the pattern of Camp David, Carter relished Sadat's autocratic efficiency: "Over the opposition of some of his closest advisers, Sadat accepted the troublesome texts, and *within an hour* he and I resolved all the questions which still had not been decided after all these months."[164] Carter's work in Israel, by contrast, stretched over three days, during which he lobbied Begin, the cabinet, and the entire Knesset.[165] With a modified text in hand, Carter hopped back to Egypt for final approval: "There was some equivocation among his advisers, but after a few minutes Sadat interrupted to say, 'This is satisfactory with me.'"[166]

On March 17 and 19, Secretary Brown concluded the details of U.S. military assistance, the linchpin of peace.[167] Israel would receive approximately $2.2 billion in military financing, plus support for building new air bases to compensate for abandoned airfields in the Sinai. Egypt would get $1.5 billion "in loans to finance procurement through fiscal year 1982 of defense articles and defense services," as well as $300,000 in economic assistance.[168] The arrangement created an informal norm that aid to Israel and Egypt would follow a 3:2 ratio. On March 26 in Washington, Sadat and Begin signed the Egyptian-Israeli Peace Treaty, along with texts covering West Bank autonomy talks, normalization of Egyptian-Israeli relations, and Egyptian oil sales to Israel.[169] The treaty also capped Sadat's long quest for U.S. weaponry. That summer, the United States sold Egypt "several hundred air-to-air and air-to-surface missiles," 550 armored personnel carriers, "twelve batteries of Improved Hawk air-defense missiles," and 35 F-4E Phantom fighter-bombers.[170] Saudi Arabia had pulled its prior financing for the F-5Es and effectively killed the deal as part of the post-treaty Arab boycott, but the faster and longer-range Phantoms made up for that loss.[171] These were tools of war, to satisfy the Egyptian military and engrain its security alignment.[172]

Autumn of Fury

The Egyptian-Israeli treaty marked the culmination of Carter and Sadat's collaboration and the apex of Sadat's presidency. The Arab League expelled Egypt, relocated its headquarters from Cairo to Tunis, and boycotted Egyptian companies that worked with Israel.[173] Inside Egypt, thirteen MPs wrote a letter faulting Sadat for accepting a separate peace with Israel, for allowing Israel to infringe on Egyptian sovereignty in the Sinai, and for wasting precious resources on military adventures in Africa.[174]

Overruling the dissenters, 329 MPs approved the treaty on April 11, 1979.[175] Sadat then put the peace agreement up for public referendum and promised steps for "consolidating democracy."[176] His democracy was beginning to look a lot like Nasser's security state. A 99.95 percent result ratified the treaty and called for new elections.[177] It was another implausible display of unanimity; foreign journalists videotaped men stuffing ballot boxes.[178] Ensuing parliamentary elections were just as distorted. During a brief six-week campaign period, candidates were barred from criticizing the treaty and the opposition struggled to be heard in the state-dominated media.[179] When voting took place in June, none of the Tagammu's thirty-one candidates even made it to a runoff.[180] Sadat's newly formed National Democratic Party took 86.4 percent, while a loyal pack of oppositionists got 8.4 percent of contested seats.[181] From the field of peace treaty critics, only two were reelected, one thanks to supporters who brandished submachine guns to ensure a fair vote tally.[182] The other candidate managed an upset, even though, he said, government agents "kicked out my representatives, put in fake ballots, and did everything imaginable to make me lose."[183]

After silencing critics of the bilateral peace, Sadat offered to help Carter with Iran and Afghanistan.[184] The U.S. president had let the ailing shah enter the United States for medical treatment. On November 4, 1979, Khomeini supporters stormed the U.S. embassy in Tehran and captured dozens of Americans. In response, Sadat proposed a far-fetched joint U.S.-Egyptian strike upon Iran.[185] While the White House formulated more feasible approaches to the hostage situation, on Christmas Eve the Soviets invaded Afghanistan. Suddenly Saudi Arabia and other Arab states in the Gulf looked vulnerable. Again leaping to help, Sadat said his country stood ready to assist U.S. forces "to defend all these Arab countries."[186] Top administration officials envisioned a smaller supportive role than Sadat did.[187] Rather than operating through regional "pillars," they considered direct U.S. intervention with local logistical assistance. Sending forces eight time zones away would require access, basing, and overflight (ABO) rights Egypt could help to grant.

In his next State of the Union address, Carter slammed the USSR for endangering "the free movement of Middle East oil" and vowed that "An attempt by any outside force to gain control of the Persian Gulf region will be regarded as an assault on the vital interests of the United States of America, and such an assault will be repelled by any means necessary, including military force."[188] Egypt helped Carter implement his doctrine. In early 1980, the CIA funneled Egyptian stockpiles of old Soviet weapons to Afghan anti-Soviet fighters.[189] In April 1980, under the guise of conventional operations, Carter used Egyptian airbases to launch a mission to rescue the hostages in Iran.[190]

The hostage rescue operation failed, and eight service members perished during the attempt, but it ushered in a new era of U.S. military operations in the Persian Gulf. To execute these missions, the White House sought launching pads around the region, including in Egypt. Visiting Washington, Egyptian vice president Hosni Mubarak explained to two congressmen that Egypt would only be comfortable with letting the Pentagon use Egyptian "facilities."[191] Sadat offered to orally commit to allow U.S. use of the southern town of Ras Banas.[192] The offer was shelved, however, because Congress needed a written agreement and the Egyptians viewed any such deal as an infringement on national sovereignty.[193] The U.S. military would henceforth use Egyptian facilities, without establishing sovereign bases as it had in West Germany and South Korea. The Pentagon would also conduct joint maneuvers with Egyptian forces, practicing in an environment much like that of the Persian Gulf. In mid-July the U.S. Air Force flew a squadron of F-4Es to Egypt, where U.S. and Egyptian pilots conducted Operation Proud Phantom.[194] That fall, soldiers from the 101st Airborne joined with Egyptian paratroopers in Operation Bright Star, an elaborate ten-day war game that later became a biennial event.[195] It was the debut abroad of Carter's new Rapid Deployment Force, the contingency mechanism for intervening in the Middle East and a forerunner to Central Command (CENTCOM).[196]

As Sadat bolstered U.S. strategy, he lost the battle for public opinion. Israel had begun gradually pulling back from the Sinai in two-month intervals, starting with the northern coastal city of El Arish on May 25, 1979. But Begin had not budged when it came to talks on Palestinian autonomy.[197] Further, he corroborated the fears of Fahmy and Kamel by increasing the number of West Bank settlements.[198] Anticipating no major breakthroughs, the Carter administration tried to shield Sadat from the political fallout.[199] During a meeting among Carter, Sadat, Brzezinski, and Saudi Arabian emissary Prince Bandar bin Sultan, the U.S. president asked for Saudi Arabia to help advance the peace process.[200] Tagging on to Carter's request, Sadat defended his incremental approach:

> I have recovered 80% of the Sinai, all the oil, etc. We have started on a road, but we cannot insist that Begin promise everything at once. To ask for everything is to give him the golden opportunity to do nothing. . . . I made this breakthrough not to recover the Sinai alone but because it is the only way. We now have U.S. and world public opinion on our side. Let us exploit it.[201]

Although Bandar and Sadat exchanged pledges of reciprocal assistance, an Egyptian-Saudi rapprochement did not create regional momentum. Egypt and Israel had opened embassies in Tel Aviv and Cairo, but the first anniversary of the Egyptian-Israeli treaty brought little cause for celebration.[202] When the original May 26, 1980, deadline for Palestinian autonomy talks came and went, William Quandt wrote that most observers saw "the Camp David approach to Middle East peace" as being "at a dead end."[203]

After the price riots, Sadat had asked Egyptians to "Wait Until 1980" for relief. The wait was over and the economy was in shambles; inflation hovered at 30 percent.[204] The Egyptian president tried to compensate for economic and diplomatic failure through tight political control. On May 22, 1980, he held another plebiscite. The measure, which passed with 98.96 percent of the vote, changed article 2 of the Egyptian constitution and established the tenets of Islamic law as the principle source of legislation. It also eliminated the term limits that would have ended Sadat's presidency in 1982.[205] Further, the referendum criminalized transgressive speech through Law 33/1980 "protecting values from shameful conduct," otherwise known as the "Law of Shame."[206]

Afterward, Tagammu leader Khaled Mohieddin remarked: "[A] lot of intellectuals who did not believe in Camp David did feel that democracy might prevail in this country after the peace treaty. But all those hopes have gone."[207] Politicians and intellectuals mobilized as a National Front. In a pair of missives, they demanded a more assertive foreign policy and more accountable government. Sadat had not created an "outright dictatorship," they allowed, but he had also not established "a democracy, nor even a pseudo-democracy."[208] White House officials acknowledged they had weakened Sadat. Two staffers told the national security advisor, "We are increasingly asking Egypt to do things that move the balance from 'what is good for Egypt' to 'what is good for the U.S.'"[209] There was little, however, they could do to help after Carter lost reelection.

In January 1981, Sadat watched for the third time as his U.S. interlocutor left office in defeat. Unfortunately for Sadat, incoming president Ronald Reagan and Secretary of State Alexander Haig were more interested in reasserting U.S. might than in mediating between Israel and the Arab states. Israel was conducting airstrikes in Beirut and, in June 1981, bombed the Osirak nuclear reactor in Iraq. The region bore little resemblance to Sadat's 1977 call for "total Israeli withdrawal from Arab lands."[210] Even the president's handpicked "opposition," the Socialist Labor Party, rescinded its approval of the peace treaty in protest of Israeli settlements in the West Bank.[211] In early August, Sadat visited the White House and communed with Reagan over the threat Libya posed in the Mediterranean Sea and northeastern Africa.[212] He also pushed for the U.S. government to send Egypt more military aid and restrain Begin. A gracious host, Reagan extolled the Egyptian president's "majestic sense of decency and dedication to universal human principles." Privately, he brushed off Sadat's pleas for help.[213]

Whereas Sadat's foreign policy first seemed brave, it now looked irresponsible. Rather than ushering in regional peace, Egypt's bilateral treaty appeared to have enabled Israeli aggression.[214] Sadat still wagered that the completion of Israel's pullout from the Sinai on April 25, 1982, would vindicate his decisions. All that stood between him and the recovery of the Sinai was a handful of months and a legion of critics. Fearing his opponents would sabotage the withdrawal to discredit him, the Egyptian president reverted to Nasserist levels of surveillance.[215] In May 1980, he had formally lifted the state of emergency, but this alleged step toward democracy did not stop Sadat from acting with impunity.[216] According to a sympathetic biographer, tapes of salons and private discussions confirmed his presidency was politically bankrupt: "Reports were presented to Sadat, video reports and audio recordings on the discussions that were circulating in these meetings. They were all against the peace treaty. The question was... 'Where was the prosperity that Sadat had promised the masses?'"[217] Instead of delivering an economic boon, Sadat expanded the old Egyptian security state, tripling the number of riot police in the CSF to 300,000.[218]

In September 1981, the Ministry of the Interior arrested or detained more than 1,500 party activists and leading cultural figures, including the Coptic pope and the General Guide of the Muslim Brotherhood.[219] The dragnet swept up secularists, leftists, liberals, and Islamists. One victim was a young man in southern Egypt named Mohamed Islambouli. On October 6, Mohamed's brother Khaled and three fellow Islamic militants assassinated Sadat during a military parade commemorating the war in 1973.[220] Vice President Hosni Mubarak survived the shooting and assumed the presidency.[221]

Conclusion

The core interests of the U.S.-Egyptian alliance – securing Israel and sustaining friendly relations with Arab oil exporters – indelibly shaped the two governments' collaboration. After the 1973 War, Egypt and the United States reestablished diplomatic ties, conceived a massive aid relationship for modernizing Egypt's armed forces and reviving its economy, and began integrating their militaries to enable U.S. force projection to the Persian Gulf. Price riots in 1977 and the Iranian Revolution in 1979 underscored Washington's need for steady leadership in Cairo. Although Carter prided himself on being a human rights advocate, he refrained from criticizing Sadat about his plebiscites, censorship, and police repression. In fact, he depended on Sadat's autocratic prerogatives to conclude the Egyptian-Israeli peace treaty. The domestic repercussions of this approach proved more than Sadat's presidency could withstand. The U.S. aid program for Egypt aimed to keep the military loyal and the people quiet: Advanced jets and tanks would deter the Egyptian army from turning against Sadat and back to the Soviets, while economic support funds would prevent a popular revolt. But while U.S. officials helped Sadat avoid the fate of the shah, the violence they enabled and encouraged brought other risks for their Egyptian partner.

2

Mubarak's War on Terrorism

Sadat's death launched Mubarak's rule. Egyptians welcomed a change of leadership – no matter its provenance – and U.S. policymakers realized they could no longer take the Egyptian president for granted. With renewed domestic and foreign support, Mubarak pursued a cautious foreign policy. He cooperated with the United States, communicated with Israel, and reached out to Arab states without ignoring Egyptian public opinion. The longer Mubarak stayed in power, however, the more he resorted to the repressive tactics of his forerunners. After a period of détente between the regime and Islamic militants associated with Sadat's assassination, the two sides plunged into an internal war. Mubarak eventually won, but only after cracking down on moderate, as well as radical, opposition. Under the aegis of antiterrorism, Mubarak consolidated his rule and blocked alternative movements from gaining control of government.

In the 1980s, U.S.-Egyptian relations fell and rose as the countries coped with hijackings at sea and in the air. In matters of war and peace, Egypt supplemented U.S. policy, such as in Lebanon and with the Iran-Iraq War. But the Egyptian-Israeli Peace Treaty had vitiated the heft of the Egyptian army in the Middle East and, after the Cold War ended in 1989, the Egyptian military role in Africa diminished. Soon trans-Atlantic intelligence sharing would matter far more than joint maneuvers on the Egyptian coast. Operation Desert Storm showcased the strategic contribution of the conventional Egyptian military, and it brought massive, and much needed, debt relief for Mubarak. The war to liberate Kuwait, however, did not change the reality of post–Cold War geopolitics: The United States was the sole superpower and its most audacious challengers were small cells of militants, not rival states. In the fight against those organizations, Egypt offered both partner and role model.

When an Egyptian cleric who had approved Sadat's killing was tied to the 1993 World Trade Center bombing, Washington joined Mubarak's war on terrorism. Under the supervision of Egyptian spymaster Omar Suleiman, U.S. and Egyptian forces began capturing suspected terrorists abroad and bringing them to Egypt, where they were detained, tortured, and, in some cases, executed. Extraordinary renditions signaled the core of the U.S.-Egyptian relationship was evolving from strategy to intelligence. Meanwhile, authoritarianism in Egypt thrived. As Mubarak became the longest-ruling president in his country's history, his political security remained integral to U.S. planning.

State of Emergency

The October 6, 1981, attack stunned the U.S. intelligence community. CIA agents had trained Sadat's security detail, which had failed utterly, and their surveillance network in Egypt focused on the government and external foes, ignoring domestic opposition. CIA director William Casey groused to his subordinates, "[G]et some people out in the fucking street to see if someone's going to shoot Mubarak."[1] Reagan and Secretary of State Haig worried that Sadat's death could shake Egypt's international commitments. They feared, as then-ambassador to Egypt Alfred Leroy Atherton explained, that the Egyptians would renege on commitments and, after reclaiming the Sinai, "reassert their old belligerency toward Israel."[2] Reassuring Washington, Mubarak called the treaty a "legal obligation to be observed and respected."[3] Given the circumstances, however, such promises still depended on calming the political climate inside Egypt.

The same day as the attack on Sadat, the Egyptian cabinet reinstituted the state of emergency, which enabled "the president to . . . detain opponents without trial and break up unauthorized public gatherings."[4] It was the first time the Egyptian government had imposed the state of emergency since the end of hostilities with Israel.[5] A week later 98.6 percent of Egyptian voters ratified Mubarak's succession in a single-candidate plebiscite.[6] Meanwhile, the regime stamped out an insurrection that began after the assassination. Mubarak's forces quelled an uprising in the southern city of Asyut that left nearly fifty dead and his police arrested some 2,500 suspected militants and conspirators.[7] The Ministry of the Interior tortured many of the men it captured, including Ayman al-Zawahiri. Zawahiri was a young leader in the Jihad organization, which sought to seize power in Egypt through a coup d'etat. He and his fellow radicals, however, had not plotted Sadat's assassination.[8] In addition to the police response, the military expelled more than 130 suspected sympathizers with Islambouli for "extremist religious leanings." Nonetheless, Mubarak and Defense Minister Abdel Halim Abu Ghazala insisted the army was uncorrupted.[9]

As vice president, Mubarak had been Sadat's military liaison with Washington and had argued, unsuccessfully, for Egypt to receive advanced fighter aircraft from the United States.[10] After succeeding Sadat, he found a more receptive audience. On October 15, the United States deployed two aerial radar and command stations known as AWACS (Airborne Warning and Control System) to prevent a Libyan surprise attack. After the AWACS left, on October 28, 4,000 U.S. troops began arriving for Operation Bright Star. Besides improving interoperability between U.S. and Egyptian forces, the war games displayed a common front against Qadhafi's adventurism.[11] Shrewdly, Mubarak invited Soviet technicians back to Egypt to fix aging equipment while pressing the White House for larger and faster arms supplies.[12] U.S. military financing to Egypt rose by $400 million.[13] Henceforth, U.S. military aid to Egypt would hover at $1.3 billion annually (and after 1984, it would be in the form of grants, not loans).[14] The F-16 fighters and air-to-air missiles Egypt purchased sustained the prestige of the Egyptian armed forces without contesting Israel's military dominance in the subregion.[15] Introducing Egyptian officers to U.S. ideas and methods was as valuable as updating their equipment. U.S. assistance also included millions of dollars in IMET funds. In 1982, 343 Egyptian officers traveled to the United States to take advanced courses and interact with their U.S. counterparts: more than all the cohorts who had visited during Sadat's presidency combined.[16]

Whereas the U.S. and Egyptian militaries grew closer during Mubarak's first year in office, Egyptian-Israeli relations remained

tense.[17] During his first presidential visit to Washington, Mubarak
and Reagan underscored their shared commitment to pursuing comprehensive peace as structured by the Camp David framework.[18] While
honoring Egypt's obligations, though, Mubarak would not extend
himself much further, for the Palestinians or the Israelis. He decou-
pled Sinai withdrawal from the need for progress on the West Bank
and Gaza.[19] When Begin's government annexed the Golan Heights of
Syria in December 1981, Mubarak denounced the move but took no
punitive measures against Israel in response.[20] There was talk of the
Egyptian president visiting Israel. The plan collapsed, however, when
Begin insisted the itinerary include Jerusalem. Mubarak preferred a
low-profile tour of other cities.[21]

Israel's withdrawal from the Sinai proved the most contentious
issue between the two governments.[22] Defense Minister Ariel Sharon
objected to Egypt exceeding its permitted four-thousand-troop presence in the middle north-south strip of Sinai known as "Zone B"
and demanded Mubarak prevent weapons smuggling to PLO forces in
Gaza.[23] The two sides also failed to agree on the status of Taba, a strip
of beach at the Sinai Peninsula's easternmost corner, and set it aside
for subsequent mediation.[24] No issue created more tumult, though,
than Israeli settlements in the Sinai. Sharon oversaw the relocation of
settlers, many of them unwillingly, from the town of Yamit in north-
east Sinai.[25] "Resistance to the withdrawal lasted several days," writes
historian Avi Shlaim, "and was accompanied by heartbreaking scenes
on television."[26] Nonetheless, Sharon razed the physical structures left
behind and ended Israel's presence in Sinai by the agreed-upon date of
April 25, 1982.

Agreeing to Disagree

Six weeks after the Israeli army withdrew from the Sinai it moved into
Lebanon.[27] In Egypt the move caused "active hatred and total distrust
of the Jewish state," according to Egyptian sociologist Saad Eddin
Ibrahim.[28] The invasion, said Atherton, crippled Egyptian-Israeli ties
after a promising start: "I have a feeling that at least there were some
people in Egypt who were committed to trying to make it work better,
this relationship with Israel. They may have been a minority, but there
were some. After that, they didn't speak up."[29] One member of this

minority was Anis Mansour, a writer known for working with his Israeli peers. "We had reconciled with Israel, looking forward to a comprehensive peace," he rued, "It turned out to be a mistake. . . . The most optimistic among us knows now that it will take another 34 years to correct that mistake."[30] Mubarak criticized Israel's offensive but initially took no diplomatic action in protest. In September 1982 Sharon allowed Lebanese Christian militia members to enter refugee camps in Beirut, where they murdered up to eight hundred Palestinian refugees: the Sabra and Shatila massacre.[31] Mubarak then recalled his ambassador from Tel Aviv. He did not, however, end commercial air traffic with Israel or close the Egyptian embassy there.[32] Reagan's new secretary of state, George Shultz, tried unsuccessfully to convince belligerent foreign forces, Israeli and Syrian, to withdraw, and to persuade Mubarak to restore the Egyptian ambassador.[33]

In Beirut, the Reagan administration hoped to demonstrate U.S. strength in the Middle East and erase Americans' post-Vietnam fears about intervening abroad.[34] Rather than easing concerns about military entanglements in foreign countries, Lebanon reinforced them. The Marines had arrived in Beirut in the summer of 1982 to supervise and ensure the departure of Yasser Arafat and the PLO. After achieving that goal – and posting a "Mission Accomplished" sign on Navy carriers offshore – the U.S. military remained in the area, ostensibly to end fighting among Israel, Lebanon, and Syria.[35] As negotiations failed to bring peace within reach, U.S. personnel fell under attack from Lebanese militias. In April, a suicide bomber struck at the U.S. embassy, killing more than sixty people, among them seventeen Americans.[36] On October 23, another suicide attacker rammed into the Marine barracks, leaving 241 service members dead. Reagan vowed that the United States would not back down before terrorism, but in a matter of months he "redeployed" U.S. peacekeeping forces from Beirut.[37]

Reagan saw the Middle East through the lens of Cold War politics. He had wanted to establish a pro-U.S. government in Lebanon to block Soviet influence. Mubarak saw the conflicts in the Middle East through a regional prism and sought to ensure Egypt did not become further isolated. Thus when Iraq and Iran fought one of the most destructive wars in the history of the region, Egypt supported Baghdad. Mubarak's efforts yielded success and, by the end of 1988, he had restored diplomatic relations with nearly all Arab governments.[38] In 1990 the Arab League returned to Cairo, and the following year member states tapped Egyptian foreign minister Ahmed Abdel Maguid to lead the body as secretary-general.[39] Even while steering his country back into the Arab fold, Mubarak gave attention to the White House's anti-Soviet causes. Egypt continued helping the United States' secret campaign in Afghanistan. When Nicolas Veliotes, Atherton's successor, reached the embassy in 1983, U.S.-Egyptian cooperation on Afghanistan ranked second, after consolidating the Egyptian-Israeli treaty, on his list of priorities.[40] At an estimated cost of $30 to $50 million a year, the CIA and Saudi Arabia purchased Soviet arms from Egypt's old stockpiles and smuggled them, via Pakistan, to Afghan fighters.[41]

When it came to Libya, a local issue for Mubarak, the two presidents again differed. The Egyptian leader considered Qadhafi a serious nuisance.[42] From Reagan's perspective, he was a strategic threat who took Soviet weapons and sponsored terrorists.[43] In the summer of 1985, the National Security Council proposed an Egyptian land assault, with U.S. air cover, to correct Qadhafi's behavior, if not remove him from power. One State Department official snapped to Veliotes, "You won't believe what these madmen in the White House have come up with now." The ambassador and Shultz tried in vain to deter their president from pursuing the idea with Mubarak, but Reagan insisted on sending his deputy national security advisor, Vice Admiral John Poindexter, to Cairo.[44] Mubarak did not even let Poindexter finish his proposition: "Admiral, thank you," he interrupted, "I think I know where you're going with this, and let me tell you, some day, Egypt might decide to invade Libya, but if we do, it will be for our reasons, not yours. So the answer here is absolutely not."[45]

A concern about international terrorism linked the U.S. government's losses in Beirut with its antagonism toward Qadhafi. Attacks on U.S. civilians and officials abroad, often conducted by secularist militants seeking attention for a particular cause, became more frequent during the 1980s. Outside of Lebanon, the number of deaths was low, particularly in comparison with the millions of Americans traveling abroad every year.[46] But even when most victims were physically unharmed, hijackings stirred traumatic memories of the U.S. embassy hostage crisis.

The loosely organized Shia partisans behind the 1983 bombings in Beirut had coalesced into Hezbollah (the Party of God). In June 1985, members of the group took over Trans World Airlines Flight 847, killed one U.S. passenger (a navy Seabee), and held the remainder, including thirty-nine Americans. The hijackers landed the plane, which had originated in Cairo, in Beirut, where they removed the hostages from the aircraft – negating the possibility of a rapid rescue mission. Reagan's cabinet proceeded gingerly to make sure the incident did not grow a national crisis. After seventeen days, Hezbollah released the hostages, while Israel freed some seven hundred Shia prisoners. U.S. and Israeli officials disavowed any linkage, maintaining they did not strike deals with terrorists.[47]

That fall it was Mubarak's government who negotiated with hijackers, in an imbroglio that brought U.S.-Egyptian relations to their lowest point since the restoration of diplomatic ties in 1974. Attacks between Israel and the PLO were on the rise. When Palestinians killed three Israelis in Cyprus in September 1985, Israel bombed the PLO headquarters in Tunis.[48] In a separate incident, an Egyptian policeman in the Sinai tourist town of Ras Burqa turned his weapon on Israeli tourists, murdering four children and three adults.[49] According to Veliotes, the string of international and local attacks set the "Egyptian establishment on edge."[50] Then, on October 7, four members of a fringe Palestinian militia took control of an Italian cruise ship named the *Achille Lauro*. The *Achille Lauro* carried tourists to Egypt, dropped them off in Alexandria for inland sightseeing, and then picked them up from Port Said. The hijacking occurred after the ship had disembarked from Alexandria. Nineteen Americans were still aboard, including an elderly couple, Marilyn and Leon Klinghoffer. Mrs. Klinghoffer was terminally ill with cancer. Members of the Klinghoffers' synagogue had accompanied them on a farewell tour for her.

When they learned of the hijacking, Shultz and Veliotes scrambled to locate the vessel, which had left Egyptian waters and was heading toward Syria. Egyptian officials got the ship back into their national waters and, over a period of days, struck a deal for the hostages' release. In exchange for recovering the hostages, the U.S., British, French, German, and Italian governments (all of which had citizens aboard) would guarantee that the hijackers would be turned over to fellow Palestinians, not extradited or prosecuted. This arrangement shielded

Mubarak from any domestic outcry that would have come from trying the hijackers in Egypt. The Western governments assented with the understanding that no passengers had been or would be harmed.[51]

Veliotes reached the ship, moored off the Egyptian coast, around midnight. He found a grief-stricken and apologetic captain, who explained that Mr. Klinghoffer, who was wheelchair bound, had been shot and killed, then thrown overboard. Klinghoffer's death scotched the deal for leniency from the United States, and Veliotes swore into an unsecure sea-to-land line that Egypt would have to "prosecute those sons of bitches." He then returned to Cairo, but Mubarak refused to receive him or any other foreign dignitaries. The Egyptian president had reportedly turned the hijackers over to the PLO the prior day and they had left Egypt.[52] But the White House had eavesdropped on Mubarak's calls and learned the Egyptian leader had just then packed the four hijackers – along with their leader, Abu Abbas, and one other co-partisan – onto an Egyptian jet bound for Tunis.[53] Determined that Klinghoffer's killers would not evade justice or enjoy a hero's welcome at the PLO's headquarters, Reagan sent navy fighter jets to intercept the plane. The airmen forced Abu Abbas's plane to land at a nearby NATO base in Sigonella, on the island of Sicily. The drama was not over, however, for as soon as Delta Force troops had encircled the hijackers, the Americans found themselves surrounded by Carabinieri. Asserting Italian sovereignty, the police arrested the Palestinians. Although the Italian government would put the hijackers on trial for murder, they released Abu Abbas and the sixth man.[54]

The end of the *Achille Lauro* crisis satisfied none of the three main governments involved. Mubarak called the interception of the hijackers an "act of piracy," and, by grounding an Egyptian plane in Sigonella, the United States had violated Italy's airspace and sovereignty.[55] For the United States, the daring high-altitude intervention had failed to bring the terrorists into U.S. custody. It fell to Veliotes to try to repair his and Reagan's relationship with Mubarak. Little could be done to roll back the "sons of bitches comment" – "Certain elements of the [Egyptian] press were calling for my assassination," the ambassador remembers – but he worked to bridge the distance between Cairo and Washington. Days after the crisis, he conveyed a letter from Reagan to Mubarak that reached out to the Egyptian leader but stopped short of an apology. Veliotes then publicly expressed "regret" over the incident.

An upbeat visit to Egypt by Shultz warmed bilateral relations a bit more.[56]

Ironically, it was another hijacking that restored comity between Reagan and Mubarak. In late November 1985, Libyan-backed Palestinians seized Egypt Air Flight 648, bound from Athens to Cairo, then landed and held it in Malta. Mubarak planned a rescue operation, but Egypt's fighters did not have the range to fly CAP (combat air patrol) and stop Libya from attacking the plane of Egyptian commandos en route. Mubarak asked the White House for two navy fighters from the Sixth Fleet to accompany the Egyptian antiterrorism squad. Reagan agreed and sent the same kind of planes whose derring-do had recently soured Mubarak.

Bilateral rapprochement preceded an operational catastrophe for the Egyptians.[57] The commando team botched the demolitions job to board the plane and unintentionally ignited parts of the fuselage. Fifty-eight of ninety-eight passengers died, most from smoke inhalation or the initial explosions.[58] Dark humor circulated in the cafes of Cairo: "What's worse than being hijacked by Palestinian terrorists? Being rescued by Egyptian commandos." Any lingering ill will over the *Achille Lauro* dissipated while Egyptians coped with the Malta tragedy, and the White House sent a fresh ambassador, Frank G. Wisner, to Cairo.

Even in the immediate wake of the *Achille Lauro* hijacking, U.S. military aid to Egypt and bilateral cooperation continued. In fact, the Pentagon and the Egyptian army were growing closer. In 1987, Egypt became a seminal member of U.S. "major non-NATO allies" (MNNAs). The U.S. government sold – or occasionally donated – weapons, vehicles, and materiel to MNNAs that other countries could not receive. Egypt thus gained preferential treatment in acquiring U.S. military technology and bidding on U.S. contractors.[59] In Egypt, Mubarak called off negotiations on Ras Banas, prompting the U.S. Department of Defense to expand its arrangements in the Persian Gulf.[60] The Pentagon kept using Egyptian facilities, however, including Cairo West Air Base, for refueling, maintenance, and predeployment. Additionally – and crucially for movement between the Mediterranean and Gulf – the U.S. Navy gained special permission to pass nuclear-powered vessels through the Suez Canal.[61] In emergency cases when ships needed to move rapidly though the canal, the Egyptians would waive the regulations meant to safeguard the waterway from a nuclear accident.[62] There were still areas of debate, largely about military doctrine. While the U.S. government hoped to modernize the Egyptian army into a leaner and faster institution, Egyptian officers preferred acquiring tanks and aircraft.[63]

Domestic Challengers

Mubarak had inherited a severe debt burden, but the specter of 1977 haunted him and his ministers. Fearing revolt, they refused to retrench spending – food subsidies were nearly inviolable.[64] Rioting in October 1984 prompted Mubarak to reverse plans for raising the price of inexpensive bread from one piaster (an Egyptian penny) to two.[65]

The Egyptian military and international financiers concerned Mubarak as much as the masses. Four-fifths of the state budget went to interest payments, the military, subsidies, and public sector salaries. In 1985, defense spending consumed more than a quarter of the budget, placing Egypt eleventh in the world in that area.[66] The country suffered from a multibillion-dollar trade deficit, which eventually reached $5.8 billion. The national debt would hit $50 billion by the end of the decade. Interest payments on the debt eventually absorbed more than a fourth of the revenues coming from exports.[67] Seeking to appease the army and foreign creditors, Mubarak and his government gingerly redirected revenues. They froze the hiring and wages of public servants. The real value of public-sector salaries fell by 45 percent between 1973 and 1989.[68] College graduates hoping for government employment found the doors closed.

Nonproductive rents helped the Egyptian economy hobble forward. Economic support funds poured in, including $4.5 billion during 1982 through 1986. But the U.S. Agency for International Development, which administered programs in Egypt, often "couldn't spend the money as fast as Congress appropriated it."[69] Funding that entered Egypt typically flowed back to U.S. consulting firms, which conducted surveys and studies that could have been performed by Egyptians. Some aid dollars went to infrastructure, including a revamp of the Cairo sewer system that went largely unappreciated.[70] Larger and more significant were remittances from Egyptians working in the Persian Gulf, revenue from tourists, and local oil income. These funds rose and fell, though, on the vagaries of the regional political economy. In Mubarak's first year as president, remittances provided the base for nearly 20 percent of government revenue, and during 1982–1989, they delivered $3.4 billion per year.[71] Money from tourism reached $2 billion by the end of the decade. These rent sources helped to offset the precipitous decline in Egypt's oil export revenue. Whereas the country had brought in $2.9 billion from petroleum sales in 1983, after the oil bust of 1985–1986 this figure shrank to $1.36 billion.[72]

Eventually the government's modest cost-cutting efforts provoked a large-scale backlash. Mubarak had expanded the paramilitary Central Security Forces, which numbered nearly half a million soldiers by 1986. Of these men, 60 percent were uneducated and of modest origin, conscripted into the CSF because they did not qualify for conventional military service. The conditions of service compounded any class-based resentment these young Egyptians already felt. As indentured cops, they received only two meals a day, were barely paid (four dollars a month), and often stood guard before glitzy foreign embassies and tourist sites that underscored their deprivation. When the government proposed to lengthen the CSF's required term of service from three to four years, 17,000 of the draftees rampaged through Cairo. On February 25, 1986, they set fire to hotels, shops, and countless public and private vehicles. The insurrection stunned Mubarak and he took a full day before responding. On February 26, he declared a curfew that mitigated the chance the riots would spread. In actuality, that threat had already passed. Although millions of Cairenes (some estimated a third of the city's population) turned out into the streets, they did not join with the mutineers.[73]

At Mubarak's behest, Defense Minister Abu Ghazala moved to restore order. The Egyptian army ushered Cairenes back to their homes and suppressed the rioters with tanks, helicopter gunships, and heavy firepower. The crackdown left an estimated 107 people dead; thousands more were detained. After a week and a half Mubarak rescinded the curfew, but his presidency had suffered. The riots, coming on top of the *Achille Lauro* mess and the Malta fiasco, had diminished his stature, leaving him in the shadow of the intrepid Abu Ghazala.[74] Sadat had appointed Abu Ghazala defense minister in 1980. Mubarak kept him in place, benefiting from the field marshal's gift for working with Washington. Even before the riots, however, Abu Ghazala had begun to outshine the president domestically.[75] For days on end during the crisis it looked like Mubarak's defense minister was running the country. Like many a presidential rival before him, Abu Ghazala soon found celebrity was his doom.

Egyptians re-elected Mubarak for a second six-year term in 1987. In the spring of 1989, he executed a "bloodless, bureaucratic coup" that enabled him to rule for decades. Promoting Abu Ghazala to the previously nonexistent post of presidential assistant, Mubarak condemned the field marshal with superficial praise. The move severed Abu Ghazala from the armed forces he had so capably commanded and it reestablished Mubarak's dominance. During subsequent months, Abu Ghazala would shuffle through ceremonial and managerial roles while fading from political life.[76]

Opposition parties were hardly a source of concern for Mubarak, especially in comparison to the CSF conscripts and Abu Ghazala. The Egyptian president allowed parties like the Tagammu and the Wafd, and even the Muslim Brotherhood, to publish their views and expand their role in parliament. He pledged to bring "democracy in doses," and during his first-term elections became gradually freer and more competitive.[77] In 1984, voters selected members of parliament (MPs) for the People's Assembly through voter lists, a system that brought a Wafd-Muslim Brotherhood partnership fifty-seven seats (12.7 percent), while the ruling NDP absorbed the remainder. These electoral rules were eventually overturned and a court order created a blend of party lists and individual candidacies. In elections during the spring of 1987, the Wafd garnered thirty-six seats (8.8 percent), and a Muslim Brotherhood-Socialist Labor Party alliance saw fifty-six of its members elected (12.5 percent).[78] All the same, it was the People's Assembly, firmly controlled by the NDP, that nominated Mubarak for his second six-year term in 1987 and dutifully renewed the state of emergency in 1984, 1986, and 1988. Moreover, opposition parties had no real leverage over the Ministry of the Interior, the main instrument of domestic repression. In the winter of 1987–1988, students and political activists demonstrated against the Israeli crackdown upon the Palestinian intifada (uprising) in the Gaza Strip and West Bank.[79] The CSF aggressively policed their rallies.[80]

Strategic Rents

Western creditors put more pressure on Mubarak than Egyptian dissidents had. After oil rents took a nosedive, Egypt struggled to pay the half-billion dollars in military debt financing owed annually to the United States (military debt itself had reached $4.5 billion). In 1987, Egypt and the United States turned to the IMF to renegotiate Egypt's debt financing and free up funds that could cover the interest on military debt. The Paris Club and Egypt struck a deal in April 1987 for lower interest rates in exchange for serious spending cuts. By fall, Mubarak, wary of controversial austerity measures, had reneged on his pledge.

The White House and Congress then took the unusual step of making $230 million of economic aid to Egypt conditional on significant economic reforms. Mubarak insisted that any radical adjustments would destabilize Egypt, but he was up against a wall. If he failed to trim the country's constant budget deficit and secure debt financing, Egypt risked losing not just economic assistance, but all of the aid coming from Washington. A statute known as the "Brooke Amendment" stipulated if a country fell more than a year behind in making repayments on military debt owed the United States, all aid would be suspended. In summer 1989, the deadline for the Brooke Amendment was imminent. Mubarak entered a second round of talks with the IMF. He also drew on an obscure escrow fund, filled by prior debt repayments, that allowed him to resume servicing the military debt. The State Department then bolstered his position by releasing half of the frozen $230 million in August – without substantial budget cuts by the Egyptian government.[81] To a great extent, Egypt's geostrategic importance and the constant threat of domestic upheaval help explain why Mubarak was able to manage an extraordinary series of multibillion-dollar deals, broken pledges, and renegotiations.[82]

While Mubarak had dodged the Brooke Amendment, the Egyptian public began to feel the pinch of foreign-mandated cutbacks. Per capita gross national product (GNP) declined during the second half of the decade, while inflation rose, reaching 25 percent in 1990.[83] Staples became more expensive as U.S.-subsidized wheat imports boosted meat and poultry consumption among upper-class Egyptians while undermining traditional domestic produce.[84] Egyptian workers who organized faced repression. When steel workers went on strike in summer 1989, the Ministry of the Interior detained more than a thousand of them and their supporters.[85] Meanwhile, as the government selectively retrenched subsidies and held public wages constant, well-connected businessmen, often partnered with military officers, converted access into lucrative transactions.[86]

More relief was on the way, for Mubarak, if not for the Egyptian masses. As Reagan's vice president, George H. W. Bush had followed Mubarak and learned to appreciate the Egyptian leader's priorities. During Bush's presidency, the two men became closer than any U.S.-Egyptian pair of leaders since Carter and Sadat. No subsequent occupant of the Oval Office replicated Bush's rapport with "Hosni" (as he called his Egyptian peer in his memoirs). In November 1989, the Berlin Wall fell and both superpowers soon declared the end of the Cold War. The Soviet Union was in eclipse. The United States had a unique opportunity to reshape world affairs. Bush and his confidante, national security advisor Brent Scowcroft, wrote that, in this new era, Mubarak provided a "reliable and valued sounding board" whom the president would phone regularly for brief chats or extended discussions.[87] Thanks in large part to Iraq's ill-conceived invasion of Kuwait, Bush and Mubarak's personal friendship delivered a windfall for the Egyptian treasury.

In the summer of 1990, Iraqi president Saddam Hussein accused Kuwait and the United Arab Emirates (UAE) of costing Iraq $14 billion as a result of oil overproduction.[88] On July 19, he moved two divisions of his Republican Guard up to the Kuwaiti border. Mubarak and U.S. ambassador to Iraq April Glaspie recommended Bush give Hussein room to back down.[89] After meeting with the Iraqi president, Glaspie cabled back to Washington that Hussein wondered, "How can we make them [Kuwait and the UAE] understand how deeply we are suffering?" He did not see the Bush administration as an enemy, however, and he implored the United States to "not force Iraq to the point of humiliation at which logic must be discarded."[90] Briefly the United States, with Egyptian and Saudi help, pursued a diplomatic initiative to get Hussein to de-escalate while saving face. But in the early hours of August 2, Iraqi tanks rolled into Kuwait. The invasion had begun.

Bush checked in with Mubarak, who offered to help find an intra-Arab solution to the crisis.[91]

As Iraqi soldiers swarmed over Kuwait, Bush and Scowcroft hoped to put U.S. troops in Saudi Arabia and deter an Iraqi push into that country's territory as well. King Fahd would only accept a U.S. presence if other Arab states, such as Egypt and Morocco, also participated. Therefore Bush and Scowcroft realized it would be impossible for the United States to act against Iraq without an "Arab coalition" on their side.[92] Under Bush's instruction, Secretary of Defense Dick Cheney relayed this message to Mubarak. The Egyptian leader would not yet commit troops, but he allowed a U.S. Navy battle group to pass through the Suez Canal, U.S. Air Force fighters to fly over Egyptian airspace, and U.S. forces to use "Egyptian bases for refueling and transport."[93] Mubarak's most consequential role, though, came in the diplomatic arena. At an emergency meeting of the Arab League on August 10, Egypt gathered a majority of member states that sought to protect Saudi Arabia. "Mubarak had prevailed," Bush later wrote. "It was a very favorable result and put an umbrella over our troop movements." The next day, Bush thanked Mubarak, and "Egyptian and Moroccan troops began to arrive in Saudi Arabia...and with them stark evidence for Saddam that the Arab world too would stand up to him."[94]

Egypt won enormous economic benefits for enabling Operation Desert Shield. Bush asked Capitol Hill to forgive all of Egypt's military debt to the United States and in early November, with congressional approval, he wrote off $6.7 billion Cairo owed Washington. Saudi Arabia, Kuwait, Qatar, the UAE, and the Gulf Cooperation Council also forgave $7 billion in Egyptian debt. These packages relieved Mubarak of $1 billion in annual debt service payments.[95]

As the United States and Iraq edged toward military conflict, Bush found Mubarak willing to do whatever was needed, including using Egyptian troops, to help evict Hussein's army from Kuwait. "I saw eye-to-eye with him [Mubarak] on almost all of the issues," the U.S. president writes.[96] On January 9, 1991, Secretary of State Jim Baker presented Iraqi foreign minister Tariq Aziz with a letter from Bush stipulating that Hussein comply with UN Security Council Resolution 678 and withdraw completely from Kuwait by the fifteenth of the

month or face military action by the U.S.-led coalition.[97] Coalition air
strikes against Iraq began on January 17, opening the offensive military phase of Operation Desert Storm. The ground war in Kuwait soon
followed, and Iraqi units fled over the border.[98] Egyptian and Saudi
forces did not engage in combat against Iraqi soldiers, but the Arab
militaries were the first to enter, and then hold, Kuwait City after its
liberation, thus avoiding the appearance of a Western occupation.[99]
The coalition's success spurred a second phase of debt reduction
for Egypt. In May, the Paris Club met and initiated a write-off of
$10.1 billion – half the funds owed by Egypt – and rescheduled the
other half. The program promised an additional $1 billion reduction in
Egypt's yearly interest payments.[100] Not since 1979 had an Egyptian
president so effectively cashed in on security cooperation with the
United States.[101]

Diplomatic cooperation was also strong. In fall 1991, the United
States, the Soviet Union (on the brink of dissolution), Egypt, Israel,
Jordan, Syria, Lebanon, and Saudi Arabia sent leaders or top emissaries to Madrid, Spain, for three days of multilateral discussions.
Palestinians took part in a joint delegation with the Jordanians. Substantively, the meeting delivered no surprises. Procedurally it was a
breakthrough, bringing the parties into direct dialogue.[102] Mubarak
was instrumental in making the gathering a success.[103]

The New Enemy

Ironically, the Gulf War marked the swan song of the conventional
Egyptian military for U.S. geostrategy. Contingency planning for
deploying U.S. forces to a desert environment had paid off in Kuwait,
but the end of the Cold War diminished the value of the Egyptian
army for regional security.[104] While cooperation against *states* was
becoming less essential, security cooperation against *nonstate actors*,
such as Islamist cells, grew in value. This element of U.S.-Egyptian
relations soon dominated the two countries' alliance in the post–Cold
War period.

On December 26, 1991, in a coincidence that marked a strategic
watershed, the Soviet Union dissolved and Algerians voted in national
multiparty elections. After decades of military rule, the North African
state had begun a limited shift to multipartyism. In the first round

of voting for the country's legislature, candidates from a conservative religious movement, the Islamic Salvation Front (Fronte Islamique du Salut; FIS) won 188 of 231 seats (81.4 percent). In runoffs, the FIS was poised to command a large legislative majority. Rather than let the elections proceed normally, however, the Algerian military froze voting the next month. The Bush administration accepted this antidemocratic coup. As Secretary of State Jim Baker later explained, "Generally speaking, when you support democracy, you take what democracy gives you.... If it gives you a radical Islamic fundamentalist, you're supposed to live with it. We didn't live with it in Algeria because we felt that the radical fundamentalists' views were so adverse to what we believe in and what we support, and to what we understood the national interests of the United States to be."[105] At the time, the White House and Pentagon were interested in perpetuating U.S. global supremacy. Opposition movements to U.S. allies in Algiers and Cairo were anathema to this vision.[106] Baker's point man for Middle Eastern affairs insisted the United States would not support elections in which Islamist movements could take an electoral mandate and then shut down future elections, a scenario he dubbed "one man, one vote, one time."[107] In practice, the White House would continue endorsing pro-U.S. autocrats, whether generals, monarchs, or presidents-for-life.[108]

Algeria provided one way of preventing Islamist-led governments in the Arab world, and the implications for Egypt were clear. In fact, Mubarak had never allowed elections as competitive as those the FIS nearly won. The opposition boycotted Egypt's legislative polls in 1990 in protest over unfavorable electoral rules (the country had abandoned proportional voting) and a lack of judicial supervision. Although Mubarak kept the lid on elections, his rule was threatened from another corner: the militant organization known as the Islamic Group (al-Jama'a al-Islamiyya).

In the late 1980s, the Islamic Group had resurfaced after years underground. Its members propagated a highly traditional brand of Islam. They spread their message in rural communities and the shantytowns of Cairo, tapping into feelings of economic deprivation. By 1989, the Islamic Group had leaders who had returned from the anti-Soviet war in Afghanistan. The movement formed an armed wing and, that December, tried unsuccessfully to assassinate

Interior Minister Zaki Badr. After the conscript riots, Badr had become
Mubarak's iron-fisted enforcer. He once defended his brutality toward
religious activists by saying, "I only want to kill one percent of the
population." In fall 1990, another attempt on Badr's life went awry.
Gunmen targeted the wrong limousine, slaying Speaker of the Parliament Rifaat Mahjub instead.[109] The killing triggered a massive
crackdown by the Egyptian state and began the bloodiest decade of
Mubarak's presidency.[110]

The Islamic Group made its most infamous hit in June 1992, when
two militants on a motorcycle gunned down social critic Farag Foda,
whom the movement dubbed an "apostate" for his secularist views.[111]
Six months later, the regime fought a battle royal over the western Cairo slum of Imbaba – or "the Islamic Republic of Imbaba,"
as its righteous defenders called it. Activists harking to the Islamic
Group typically hailed from depressed rural areas. In Imbaba, though,
a twenty-seven-year-old preacher known as Sheikh Gaber proved that
the group could "Islamicize" communities at the country's heart. For
three years, Gaber's followers had been enforcing strict Islamic moral-
ity in Imbaba, establishing an Islamic microstate on the fringe of Cairo.
To shatter Gaber's urban emirate, Mubarak deployed 14,000 police
with armored personnel carriers. Despite this manpower, it took the
state three weeks to prevail. Each side suffered more than a hundred
casualties.[112]

In early 1993, the ripples of Islamic extremism in Egypt seemed to
reach the United States. Barely a month after Bill Clinton took office,
a Kuwaiti-born man named Ramzi Yousef and a handful of fellow
militants detonated a large truck bomb under the North Tower of the
World Trade Center. Yousef was one of the "Arab Afghans," those
who had fought the Soviet occupation, with U.S. support, and then
planned attacks upon the United States and its allies. The explosion
killed six people. In the investigation that followed, federal inves-
tigators identified an Egyptian cleric named Omar Abdel Rahman
(the "Blind Sheikh") as the attackers' spiritual mentor. Years earlier,
Abdel Rahman had fled Mubarak's interior ministry for the relative
safety of New York City. For his role in the plot, he was sentenced
to life imprisonment.[113] Abdel Rahman's background suggested that
Mubarak's fight, if successful, could make Americans safer.

After the 1993 World Trade Center bombing, the Clinton administration gave Mubarak's intelligence forces a central role in the U.S.

campaign against Islamic radicalism. The man handling this portfolio was a former military intelligence officer named Omar Suleiman,
whom Mubarak appointed in 1993 to head the Egyptian General Intelligence Services (GIS).[114] Previously, the GIS had been Egypt's equivalent of the CIA, an instrument for spying abroad.[115] Under Suleiman,
GIS collected intelligence overseas *and* supervised domestic security.
By the end of 1993, Mubarak had exceeded Sadat in numbers of arrests
and detentions (25,000 to 19,000) and of casualties from political violence (2,386 to 250) that had taken place on his watch. His war on
the Islamic Group brought 1,106 casualties that year alone (including
more than one hundred civilian deaths), accounting for 41 percent of
all Egyptians killed and wounded in internal political violence since
1952.[116] Against this grim backdrop, Mubarak won a third six-year
presidential term with an official 96.3 percent of the vote.[117]

The Clinton administration endorsed Mubarak's repression,
although it flew in the face of the White House's rhetorical commitment to spreading democracy. The U.S. president cited academic literature on the "liberal democratic peace" and asserted that "Democracies don't attack each other. They make better trading partners
and partners in diplomacy. That is why we have supported...the
democratic reformers in Russia and in the other states of the former Soviet bloc."[118] Egyptian dissidents received no such support.[119]
Martin Indyk, senior director of Near East and South Asian affairs
on the National Security Council, said that the administration would
focus on "the free-flow of Middle Eastern oil," Israeli security,
and settling "the Arab-Israeli conflict," while also fighting Islamic
militants:

> Decades of neglect and dashed hopes for political participation and
> social justice have nurtured some violent movements cloaked in reli-
> gious garb that have begun to challenge governments across the Arab
> world with the potential of destabilizing the region. Our...challenge
> is to help the people and governments of the Middle East confront
> this emerging threat, in part by pursuing peace with vigor, in part by
> containing extremism throughout the region, and in part by holding
> out an alternative vision of democratic political development and free
> market economic development.[120]

Because pro-U.S. autocracies were "containing extremism" effectively,
the White House supported the Egyptian regime taking whatever steps

were necessary to retain power. Only after abuses were committed would U.S. officials chide their Egyptian peers. The "bargain," as Indyk characterized security cooperation, meant that the United States would "stand by Mubarak while he brutally suppressed his extremist opponents." The U.S. public would hear their government criticize the Egyptian regime, but official admonitions were not meant to deter Mubarak or Suleiman. "There were occasional expressions of concern at human rights abuses cautiously documented by the State Department," explained Indyk, "but the Egyptians were far more sensitive to this mild criticism than the administration expected them to be."[121]

Retaliation

In 1995, the White House joined Mubarak's war on the Islamic Group. The militants had failed to galvanize popular support inside Egypt. They had been attacking tourists since 1993, a campaign that devastated the economy and alienated Egyptians.[122] Even in decline, the movement went down shooting. On June 26, 1995, Islamic Group members brazenly attempted to assassinate Mubarak during a high-profile diplomatic visit to Addis Ababa, Ethiopia. Urged by GIS director Suleiman to cancel the trip due to security concerns, Mubarak insisted on traveling but accepted Suleiman's suggestion that he at least move in an armored car. Although the shooters mistimed their attack, and Mubarak's car escaped without taking any fire, the spymaster looked prescient.[123]

Henceforth, Mubarak would exhibit an obsession with security, secluding himself in Sharm El-Sheikh, strangling the press and civil society, and giving no quarter to Islamists.[124] In the fall of 1995 the opposition rejoined elections for the People's Assembly, but the NDP took 94 percent of seats amid heavy violence that left at least three dozen dead.[125] In elections for the lawyers' and doctors' syndicates (analogous to unions), the Muslim Brotherhood won controlling majorities – until the People's Assembly passed legislation that brought the unions under government control. Mubarak refused to discriminate between the Islamic Group, which was shooting tourists, and the Muslim Brotherhood, which tried to negotiate a ceasefire.[126] In 1995, military courts sent fifty-four members of the Muslim Brotherhood to prison. The Ministry of the Interior held thousands more in "administrative detention."[127] Secular dissidents were not much safer. The People's Assembly passed a tyrannical law on the press (Law 93/1995) that drew such sustained outrage from journalists that the parliament actually repealed it. A second law (Law 96/1996) boosted reporters' liberties but still criminalized some forms of speech under the pretext of "libel."[128] Civil society organizers also faced prosecution under legislation passed by the 1995–2000 People's Assembly. Law 153/1999 prohibited associations from engaging in "political" activities, which, it later became clear, meant challenging the president and any of his allies.[129]

As Mubarak swept aside nonviolent opposition, Suleiman brought the Islamic Group to heel.[130] Egyptian forces captured or killed the organization's seasoned fighters, and the movement exhausted its resources just tending to the families left behind.[131] In July 1997, the historic leaders of the Islamic Group declared a unilateral ceasefire, which Sheikh Abdel Rahman endorsed from a U.S. prison cell. In November, a rogue faction spurned the move and carried out a shooting spree in Luxor that killed fifty-eight foreign tourists and four Egyptians. The massacre isolated any remaining rejectionists within the group, and a second ceasefire, proposed in March 1999, held.[132]

While Egypt's insurrection cooled, the U.S. war on Islamic militants heated up. Days before the Addis Ababa attack, Clinton issued a presidential decision directive that identified terrorism as a threat to U.S. national security to be combated by "all appropriate means."[133] The directive authorized a program of extraordinary renditions: apprehending and transferring alleged terrorists to third countries without formal arraignment and extradition proceedings.[134] It began with the United States providing Egypt with charter jets and intelligence agents to help catch Islamic militants abroad.[135] Michael Scheuer, a CIA officer who helped craft the program, later explained the goal was to get belligerents "off the street" by turning them over to the "Arab tyrannies" who wanted them.[136] The circumstances of Sadat's assassination and the 1993 World Trade Center bombing made Egypt the "obvious choice" for the United States to deliver suspects.[137] Under Suleiman's supervision, Cairo became a hub for renditions, receiving eleven alleged militants from 1995 through 2000.[138] With respect to the high likelihood that Mubarak's agents would mistreat detainees, the U.S. ambassador to Egypt at the time, Edward Walker, professed,

"We had to have an assurance from the Egyptian security authorities that people would be retried, and they'd have a fair trial, and they wouldn't be tortured."[139] Scheuer later scoffed at such promises, testifying, "If you accepted an assurance from any of the Arab tyrannies who are our allies that they weren't going to torture someone, I have got a bridge for you to buy."[140] Indeed, the program's first subject, Talaat Fouad Qassem, had been sentenced to death in absentia for involvement in Sadat's shooting. After U.S. agents whisked Qassem from Croatia to Egypt in September 1995, he was covertly executed.[141] Two Egyptians rendered from Albania in the summer of 1998 were also executed, whereas three others from the same cell were tortured but not killed.[142]

Extraordinary renditions tied the United States to the repressive policies of Sadat and Mubarak that had spawned a new generation of militants. On August 4, Zawahiri responded in the Arabic press to the renditions of the Albanian cell. After leaving Egypt in the 1980s, he had become Osama bin Laden's deputy in Afghanistan.[143] Regarding the latest round of renditions, Zawahiri wrote: "We are interested in telling the Americans, in brief, that their message has been received, and a reply is currently being written. We hope they read it well as, God willing, we will write it in the language they understand."[144] Three days later, truck bombers struck nearly simultaneously at the U.S. embassies in Nairobi, Kenya, and Dar es Salaam, Tanzania. The first attack killed 12 Americans and 240 others, most of them Kenyans, and injured more than 5,000. The second bomber found his way blocked by a water tanker but detonated his device anyway and managed to kill eleven people in the area.[145] Clinton retaliated by firing missiles at suspected al-Qaeda bases in Afghanistan and an alleged chemical weapons factory in Sudan.[146] The following year, CIA agents delivered to Egypt two of Zawahiri's brothers, one of whom was completely unconnected to Jihad and its kindred movements. Clinton's struggle with al-Qaeda reached its lethal climax on October 12, 2000. Two suicide bombers struck the USS *Cole*, harbored at Yemen, killing seventeen sailors and tearing a forty-foot hole in the destroyer's hull.[147]

The Clinton administration was no more successful at finding Arab-Israeli peace than it was at stamping out al-Qaeda. A July 2000 summit at Camp David ("Camp David II") between Arafat and Israeli premier Ehud Barak ended in bitter recriminations from all three sides.

During the meeting, Egypt had been confined to the margins. Clinton approached Arab-Israeli peace as a series of bilateral talks (Israeli-Palestinian, Israeli-Jordanian, Israeli-Syrian), calling on Mubarak only when a logjam occurred.[148] Daniel Kurtzer, U.S. ambassador in Cairo at the time, recalls that the administration essentially shut Mubarak out for the duration of the summit:

> We never really activated Arab diplomacy. It was a sense that we had a monopoly on what was happening.... Even in critical periods like Camp David... Arab states weren't involved, weren't briefed.... During Camp David... I was trying to get briefings out of the team in Washington, and I couldn't. They just wouldn't return phone calls, so I couldn't brief Mubarak.[149]

Although Egypt still had a passive role to play in maintaining the treaty with Israel, the active agenda with Washington was antiterrorism, Suleiman's bailiwick.

In November 2000, after Sharon visited the Temple Mount in Jerusalem, Palestinians began a second intifada. Mubarak withdrew Egypt's ambassador from Israel, and he assigned Suleiman to handle Israeli-Palestinian issues.[150] The intelligence chief's evolution into domestic enforcer and foreign diplomat showed how the U.S.-Egyptian relationship was changing.

Compared to the agile and indispensable GIS, Egypt's traditional armed forces were an outdated behemoth. During Desert Storm, Egyptian units in the field had worked with a mishmash of Soviet and U.S. equipment.[151] Egypt received $9.98 billion in vehicles and hardware during 1990 through 2000, and 1,407 trainees returned from U.S. programs.[152] Yet, interoperability with U.S. forces remained a distant goal. After a hiatus owing to Desert Storm, the Bright Star war games resumed in 1993. They expanded in 1996 to include a number of Middle Eastern and European militaries.[153] In 1999, with tension again escalating between Washington and Baghdad, eleven countries and nearly 70,000 troops took part.[154] At the exercises, Secretary of Defense William Cohen declared that "Saddam Hussein remains an outlaw in his own neighborhood. Over his horizon, he should see that Bright Star demonstrates that the countries of this region, backed by the United States, Britain and other European allies... are building a long-term partnership that will provide the security that our people want and the stability that they deserve."[155] In spite of Cohen's veiled threat, the relevance of Bright Star, and of conventional U.S.-Egyptian military cooperation, was fading as asymmetric warfare overshadowed traditional conflict. While receding strategically, the military entrenched economically. Army officers controlled substantial manufacturing industries, producing household appliances, agricultural goods, and bottled water, as well as military hardware. This industrial niche drew on conscript labor, operated outside of the tax-collecting authority, and was not subject to parliamentary oversight. The Egyptian armed forces thus enjoyed an "off budget" revenue stream that kept them invested in the regime.[156]

Corruption permeated the Egyptian economy, even as it seemed to recover. Gulf War debt relief, along with a quick return of tourism and remittance revenue, gave Mubarak leeway to pursue structural adjustment.[157] He signed on to a neoliberal Economic Reform and Structural Adjustment Program with the World Bank and IMF in 1991.[158] The government deficit dropped to 4.7 percent in 1993, then 2 percent in 1994, and it remained low for years. GDP growth rose from 2 percent in 1992 to 6.3 percent in 1998–1999.[159] But strong growth figures cloaked a pernicious weakness in exports. Government infrastructure projects, including an irrigation boondoggle at Toshka (New Valley), inflated GDP numbers, while exports as a share of GDP fell from 31.2 percent in 1990 to 24.6 percent in 2000. Meanwhile the ranks of the jobless swelled, mostly from a growing youth bulge but also from hundreds of thousands of Egyptians who had been forcibly repatriated from Iraq to rural areas in Egypt, where labor was already abundant.[160] In 1995, unemployment reached 20 percent.[161] Privatization proceeded apace for the first half of the decade. Without a politically accountable government, however, well-connected investors and officers captured the process.[162] Much like rulers in postcommunist Russia and Central Asia, Mubarak used economic "reform" to recruit wealthy clients.[163] After the highest-quality government factories had been purchased, structural adjustment slowed.[164] In 1999, Mubarak's younger son Gamal arrived on the political stage, toting an entourage of cronies eager to leech off the treasury.

Superficially, Egypt had shed its dilatory habits and, therefore, earned top marks from the White House. Vice President Al Gore and

Mubarak engaged in a high-level dialogue about shepherding structural adjustment, although in Indyk's recollection, "the Egyptians dictate[d] the pace."[165] From Kurtzer's vantage in Cairo, the changing Egyptian economy provided a ray of light in an often bleak scene:

> [I]f you look at Egypt's economic development in the '90s, it was almost a model of success. The IMF said that the Egyptian program, the IMF program for structural reform, was one of the best they had ever done. The Egyptians established serious benchmarks. They met those benchmarks – in some cases exceeded them. There was a dynamic aspect to the program. In combination with that, you had the Gore-Mubarak [Initiative], which was designed to move Egypt from a heavy state-oriented economy to a private sector economy. By the late '90s, that was happening.[166]

Simultaneously, U.S. economic aid to Egypt was shrinking. In 1998 Israeli prime minister Netanyahu negotiated to phase out U.S. economic aid to Israel while increasing military aid by a smaller amount. The move promised a net gain for the United States. To maintain the traditional 3-to-2 ratio between post-treaty assistance to Israel and Egypt, the United States planned to reduce economic aid to Egypt as well. This process, known as the "glide path," halved the Egyptian government's receipt of economic support funds over the next decade (from $821.5 to $411 million).[167] Annual foreign military financing for Egypt remained $1.3 billion.

The White House did not pressure Mubarak to lift the state of emergency or relax political restrictions, leaving it to the Egyptian president to make some of the most explicit remarks about democratization in Egypt. In the summer of 1999, Mubarak received an honorary degree from George Washington University, where he addressed Egypt's trajectory:

> The road to democracy is a long one, and we travel it with confidence. We have not turned back under the most difficult conditions, economic hardships, social pressures, malicious terrorism and narrow-minded intolerance. And we will not turn back, nor will our belief in the rule of law be shaken. We will work towards consolidating our democracy gradually, steadily, and in the spirit of tolerance and cooperation that is known about the Egyptian people.[168]

Gradualism was the watchword. That September the seventy-one-year-old Egyptian president won a fourth term. By the end of the year, he had led Egypt longer than Nasser.

Conclusion

As dozens of autocracies around the world fell in the wake of the Cold War, Mubarak thwarted domestic challenges to his presidency and capitalized on U.S. support. During tight economic times, he prevented a repeat of the 1977 price riots and survived the much smaller mutiny by CSF conscripts. He then marginalized the officer who had quelled that insurrection and who represented his most serious elite rival. Like Sadat, the longer Mubarak stayed in power, the more he aggressed on the citizens he professed to be leading. In the 1990s the Egyptian president and Suleiman targeted peaceful and violent opposition movements, turning their regime into an exemplar of authoritarianism in an ostensibly liberal era.

From Mubarak's tumultuous succession through his second decade in power, domestic stability inside Egypt was integral to U.S. operations in the Middle East. Although Washington did not gain sovereign bases in Egyptian territory, the Pentagon enjoyed de facto ABO rights, which proved integral in pushing Iraqi forces from Kuwait. When the primary threat shifted from nation-states to terrorist cells, the Egyptian GIS became the United States' premier partner in the global campaign against Islamic militants. Republican and Democratic administrations were clear about what they wanted from the Egyptian regime: reliable security cooperation and the defense of key U.S. interests in the region, guaranteed by Mubarak and his lieutenants.

3

The Succession Problem

Paradoxically, September 11, 2001, brought new urgency to security cooperation between Washington and Cairo *and* brought democracy to the fore of official discourse. George W. Bush believed that the attacks, which killed nearly three thousand people on U.S. soil, necessitated Washington revisit its relations with Arab autocrats. This rethink, however, did not alter the United States' basic approach to the Egyptian regime. Although it sometimes appeared Bush was at loggerheads with Mubarak, their biggest disagreements concerned U.S. regional policies, not internal Egyptian politics: Mubarak had misgivings about the U.S.-led invasions of Afghanistan and Iraq, while Bush balked at Mubarak's call for direct Arab-Israeli peace talks. Nonetheless, joint covert operations expanded – even as Bush publicly enjoined Mubarak to liberalize and Mubarak slammed Bush's approach to the Palestinians and Iraq. Compared to the presidents' substantial arguments about the United States' role in the Middle East, their disagreements about democracy promotion in Egypt were tactical, concerning different ways of reaching the shared goal of regime continuity. Whereas Mubarak wanted to groom his son for the presidency, Bush's advisors favored a more seasoned and reliable successor, such as Omar Suleiman.

This chapter revises the dominant narrative about the Bush administration's Freedom Agenda. Observers have widely billed and accepted Bush's democracy promotion policies as a strategic watershed. Whereas past White Houses palled around with dictators, the 9/11 attacks made "political liberalization, even democratization ... a central feature of U.S. national security policy."[1] The Bush White House "intensified its focus on democratization in the Arab world" and effected "a major shift in the traditional U.S. foreign policy approach to the Middle East."[2] Egypt provided the crucible of "Bush's firm commitment to promoting democracy in the Arab world."[3] Yet, despite an aura of altruism, U.S. support for democracy during Bush's tenure, as under his predecessors, remained yoked to long-standing security interests. Even as Bush called on Mubarak to lead the Middle East toward democracy, the United States depended on the Egyptian president to interrogate al-Qaeda suspects, ease U.S. craft through Egyptian waters and airspace, and keep tabs on Gaza after Israel withdrew. Political reform was pushed only so far as it helped ensure the post-Mubarak regime would be pro-American. Hence, the Freedom Agenda was not a turning point for U.S. foreign policy, but a variant of the existing approach.

The political context inside Egypt was what differentiated the Freedom Agenda from earlier White House approaches to the Egyptian regime. When Bush took office, Mubarak was seventy-two years old, had not appointed a vice president, and had already escaped one assassination attempt. Were Mubarak to perish without an orderly succession plan in place, his departure could jeopardize Egypt's alliance with the United States. When Bush and his national security team urged Mubarak to reform, they sought to broaden the spectrum of Egyptian politics to allow sustainable pro-U.S. alternatives, other than Mubarak's heir apparent and the religiously conservative Muslim Brotherhood.

The War on Terrorism

When Arab hijackers crashed passenger planes into the World Trade Center and the Pentagon they strengthened the arguments made by unilateralists – such as Paul Wolfowitz, the deputy secretary of defense; Douglas Feith, undersecretary of defense for policy; and Elliott Abrams on the National Security Council – that the United States had to fight not only al-Qaeda but the circumstances that fostered it. Egypt, birthplace of lead hijacker Mohammed Atta, was a particular source of concern. Michele Dunne, who served at the Cairo embassy and on the National Security Council during Bush's first term, explained:

There was a general feeling that the Middle East was beset by some very large problems . . . that [were] at the root of why the terrorist attacks happened, and that one of these large problems was lack of democracy, repression, human rights abuses, etc. And that the United States had found itself on the wrong side of that question. . . . Egypt was seen as a leading case of this.[4]

C. David Welch, U.S. ambassador to Egypt at the time, elaborated: "It's not unusual for the United States to be concerned about human rights and political liberties globally, but the focus throughout the Middle East had gotten really more intense after 9/11."[5]

While giving repressive regimes a second look, the White House still called on Mubarak to help with the United States' War on Terror and the conventional war in Afghanistan known as Operation Enduring Freedom.[6] Unlike his father, Bush sought no grand alliance with Arab governments, and he abjured new Arab-Israeli peace talks.[7] Instead, Secretary of Defense Donald Rumsfeld and Secretary of State Colin Powell conducted bilateral discussions about how different states could assist.[8] Egypt again helped gather intelligence on al-Qaeda and facilitate the passage of U.S. forces to the Persian Gulf.[9] "Intelligence was one of the most difficult challenges," Feith described. "It was understood right from the beginning that we had enormous military capabilities and extremely limited intelligence."[10] And, he recalled, the Pentagon "had access, basing, and overflight [ABO] considerations all along the various routes from Europe and the United States to Afghanistan."[11] Overflight requests granted to U.S. military aircraft through Egyptian airspace for 2001 through 2005 averaged more than twenty per day.[12] A report from the Departments of State and Defense issued in 2002 remarked that the "importance of Egypt's cooperation for Suez Canal access and security, as well as overflight clearances, cannot be overstated."[13] Mubarak's Egypt was also cited as an antiterrorism exemplar. "Egypt . . . is really ahead of us on this issue," commented Powell. "They have had to deal with acts of terrorism in recent years in the course of their history. And we have much to learn from them, and there is much we can do together."[14]

Confirming Powell's forecast, the CIA and the Egyptian General Intelligence Services turned extraordinary renditions into a massive intelligence sweep.[15] One of the first post-9/11 rendition flights occurred in mid-November 2001, when a privately registered Gulf-stream jet flew from Johnston County, North Carolina, to Egypt, and then on to Sweden, where a binational U.S.-Egyptian team absconded with two Egyptian men, both alleged terrorists who were seeking asylum in Sweden.[16] In another rendition case, a man named Ibn al-Sheikh al-Libi (also known as Ali Abdul Aziz al-Fakhiri) was captured by Pakistani forces while fleeing Afghanistan in the fall of 2001. He passed from the custody of the Federal Bureau of Investigation (FBI) to the CIA, when, as an ex-FBI official described, "They duct-taped his mouth, cinched him up and sent him to Cairo."[17] Al-Libi's Egyptian captors reportedly threatened him with a "long list of methods" which "would [make him] confess because three thousand individuals... before him... had [all] confessed." Prompted "that the next topic was al-Qa'ida's connections with Iraq," al-Libi assembled a story built around names of actual al-Qaeda operatives he had encountered that placated the interrogators and warded off harsher interrogation methods.[18] Two al-Qaeda agents, he fibbed, had gone to Iraq for training in chemical and biological weapons. This claim, which some intelligence agents immediately doubted and al-Libi later retracted, would resurface in the Bush administration's rationale for invading Iraq.[19]

Even as they depended on the Egyptian regime for security assistance, some U.S. officials favored spreading democracy. If the United States hoped to defeat al-Qaeda, it would have to win the "war of ideas" and draw future Attas away from the radical ideologies that seemed to thrive under authoritarianism. Democracy could help inure would-be terrorists against the retrograde notions of Osama Bin Laden. It followed that political change in Egypt and other al-Qaeda points of origin was a vital U.S. interest.[20] "This idea that lack of freedom and repression was... one of the things that caused... al-Qaeda... resonated very much with President Bush personally," said Dunne. "This was something he embraced."[21] The ideational approach stood in contrast to the notion that economic conditions and U.S. backing of the Israeli occupation of the West Bank and Gaza were the wellspring of anti-U.S. sentiments. Proponents of advancing Arab-Israeli diplomacy, including professionals in the State Department and the intelligence community, were inclined to address "root causes" and doubted the security dividends of pushing for democracy in places like Egypt or Saudi Arabia.[22] For the most part, however, the

War on Terror would be understood as a war against antidemocratic ideology, not a war to remedy Palestinian or Egyptian deprivation and its radicalizing effects.[23]

Bush portrayed Mubarak as a key partner in the War of Ideas. "There are some in the world who don't like President Mubarak because of what he stands for, a more open society," said the U.S. president when his counterpart visited Washington in March 2002. "He's been a great leader of Egypt, and there are extremists who don't like him. And to the extent that we can help round up those extremists that would do harm to the President or his government or the people of Egypt, we will do so."[24] At that time, Bush also initiated a new program at the State Department, the U.S.–Middle East Partnership Initiative (MEPI), and began to articulate a general argument for reform in the Middle East.[25]

Behind the scenes the two governments disagreed sharply about how to approach Israeli-Palestinian peace. Nabil Fahmy, then the Egyptian ambassador to Washington, observed, "Before [9/11], we and you always gave each other the benefit of the doubt, even if we differed, even if you were angry one day, you know . . . that guy is not the problem. There's something wrong here, but he's not the problem. . . . The debate [afterward] was, well, you actually may be the problem."[26] Dunne also recalls a distance in relations from the start of Bush's term: "There had been, I think, a kind of a slow . . . change in perceptions of Egypt. . . . [T]here were more negative perceptions of Mubarak for reasons having to do with the Arab-Israeli peace process . . . and I don't think the Bush Administration came into office with quite as rosy a view of Mubarak as had existed before that."[27]

With these distinct perspectives, Bush and Mubarak watched conflict grow among the right-wing government of Israeli prime minister Sharon, the Palestinian Authority led by Yasser Arafat, and Palestinian militants carrying out suicide bombings inside Israel. In June 2002, the two presidents met at Camp David. Questions from the press corps revealed significant differences in how they regarded Arafat. Bush thought Arafat should be replaced for not doing enough to stop attacks on Israelis. But Mubarak wanted to give Arafat the benefit of the doubt. Asked whether the chairman could accomplish the "Palestinian reforms that President Bush says have to happen," Mubarak answered. "Look, we should give this man a chance. . . . Such a chance will prove that he is going to deliver or not.... If he's not going to deliver, his people will tell him that."²⁸ Noting Mubarak's "interesting point of view," Bush remarked, "There is plenty of talent in – amongst the Palestinians.... if we develop the institutions necessary for the development of a state, that talent will emerge."²⁹ In fact, Bush had already decided to stop dealing with Arafat. Earlier in the year, amid a wave of suicide bombings, the Israeli government had intercepted a shipment of arms bound for the Gaza Strip, allegedly sent by Iran and approved by Arafat.³⁰ Although Arafat denied foreknowledge, Bush records in his memoirs: "We and the Israelis had evidence that disproved the Palestinian leader's claim. Arafat had lied to me. I never trusted him again. In fact, I never spoke to him again. By the spring of 2002, I had concluded that peace would not be possible with Arafat in power."³¹ No significant Arab-Israeli talks occurred in this period, although Saudi crown prince Abdullah announced, and the Arab League endorsed, a major peace plan in March.

Despite Egyptian intercessions, the White House swept Arafat aside. On June 24, Bush announced from the Rose Garden that his administration supported the creation of a Palestinian state under new leadership. Sidelining Arafat without uttering his name, Bush's speech reflected input from throughout the administration. It also fit broad themes pushed recently by Natan Sharansky, a member of the right-wing Israeli government.³² The White House had worked through multiple drafts, and several journalists credited Sharansky, an ex-Soviet dissident, for prodding Bush to isolate Arafat.³³ The president called for "new leaders, new institutions, and new security arrangements."³⁴ (This coupling of the two-state solution with Palestinian leadership changes [plus an Israeli settlement freeze and partial redeployment in the West Bank] provided the basis for the "Road Map to Peace," which the "Quartet" [the United States, the European Union, Russia, and the UN] proposed in 2003.³⁵)

The speech anticipated how Arab allies would fit into the White House's promotion of democracy.³⁶ Bush reasoned that "free societies are peaceful societies," but his plans for an "externally supervised effort to rebuild and reform the Palestinian security services" gave key roles to the governments of Egypt and Jordan.³⁷ Thus, while the White House rejected one Arab leader, it relied on others who were just as susceptible as Arafat to criticism of their democratic practices.³⁸ The difference hinged on whether Arab rulers were fueling terrorism or fighting it. Bush saw Arafat and Mubarak on opposite sides of that question: While Arafat abetted lethal assaults on Israelis, Mubarak could help the Palestinian Authority combat anti-Israeli bombings.[39]

Pushing Mubarak

When it came to Egyptian domestic politics, the Bush administration sought small openings of the regime, which Mubarak either rejected out of hand or tailored to bolster his power.

In the spring of 2001, one of Egypt's notorious state security courts had sentenced sixty-three-year-old sociologist Saad Eddin Ibrahim to seven years in prison. A naturalized U.S. citizen, Ibrahim taught sociology at the American University in Cairo and had founded the Ibn Khaldun Center for Development Studies. The organization produced academic reports, managed microcredit programs, and, when the occasion arose, conducted election monitoring. Early into a 2000 election monitoring effort, Ibrahim was arrested for accepting foreign funding without government authorization, detained for over a month, and released on bail, at which time his group persevered in watching that fall's elections.[40] Then, for six months he stood trial, accused of embezzlement, illegally receiving foreign funds, and "spreading false reports overseas of electoral fraud and religious persecution to undermine state interests."[41] In addition to convicting Ibrahim, the court gave twenty-seven codefendants sentences of one to seven years.[42] An upper court called for a retrial in early February 2002, releasing Ibrahim temporarily.[43] Claiming "we have all kinds of democracy," Mubarak rejected the suggestion he was using the criminal justice system to punish political activists.[44] Coincidentally or by design, Mubarak's one-on-one meetings with U.S. presidents (Clinton on August 29, 2000, and Bush on April 2, 2001, and June 8, 2002) took place during Ibrahim's stints outside of prison.[45]

On July 29, Ibrahim's three-month-long retrial concluded – with a second conviction and another seven-year sentence.[46] The *Washington Post* and *New York Times* faulted the White House for supporting Mubarak with billions in aid while pledging to advance democracy in the Arab World.[47] Foreign affairs doyen Thomas Friedman slammed the administration for feckless diplomacy that made the United States less secure: "The State Department, in a real profile in courage, said it was 'deeply disappointed' by the conviction of Mr. Ibrahim.... 'Disappointed'?... I'm 'outraged' and expect America to do something about it. I'm also frightened, because... if there is no room in Egypt for Saad Ibrahims, then we will only get more Mohamed Attas."[48] *Post* writer Jackson Diehl likened Ibrahim to one of the most famous Soviet dissidents, chiding Bush for his silence over "the jailing of an Arab Andrei Sakharov."[49]

In an unusual move, the White House responded by suspending a potential $130 million in supplemental funds over Ibrahim's ordeal. The annual package of foreign military financing and economic support funds, however, would be unaffected.[50] Although the Bush administration earned plaudits for its stance, Congress was unlikely to have approved the supplemental funds even if Ibrahim had remained free.[51] In this respect, the White House reaped symbolic benefit from sequestering money that was going to disappear anyway. To the delight of Ibrahim's defenders, the professor won his appeal and left prison on December 3.[52]

Beyond withholding the supplemental funding, it was unclear how Bush would further operationalize his ideas.[53] In December, the Department of State launched the Middle East Partnership Initiative. Directed by Elizabeth Cheney (daughter of Dick Cheney, the vice president), MEPI was crafted by Secretary of State Colin Powell and his deputy, Richard Armitage, as a way to encourage socioeconomic development. The program would later become the flagship of the Freedom Agenda, but it originated to advance development generally, not democracy and human rights in particular. Egypt was the core case for MEPI's work, recalled Armitage, but the project did not seek to challenge Mubarak or push for domestic political reforms: "[W]hen MEPI started... It was [about] empowerment of women, it was education, it was transparency, and... anticorruption," not democracy promotion.[54]

While Powell and Armitage did not consider MEPI a democracy program, other members of the Bush administration expected it would spotlight domestic politics under the Egyptian regime and other autocratic U.S. allies. Previewing the initiative, Richard Haass, the State Department director of policy planning, gestured toward the goal of expanding democracy abroad but refrained from spelling out what that would mean for U.S. relations with rulers like Mubarak. When asked about the consequences if Mubarak "[gave] power to his son without benefit of very much consultation with the people," Haass demurred:

> What I'm basically saying is we're going to have a foreign policy in which the dimension of democracy is going to get greater emphasis than it's had in the past. But how in particular circumstances we are going to weigh our promotion of democracy against our other interests, I don't know any other way to answer it except it depends.... an effective democratization policy has to be tailored and it's got to reflect the specifics of individual situations.[55]

Haass's prepared remarks represented a "meeting of the minds" among Bush's foreign policy team, but his answers signaled the difficulty of going from a thematic consensus to meaningful implementation.[56] Although the White House argued that the promotion of freedom would advance shared U.S.-Arab interests, the logistics of democracy promotion were trickier, particularly when the effort flowed through a department charged with strengthening international relationships. When Powell officially introduced MEPI the next week, he anchored the program to three "pillars:" the economy, political participation, and education. (Women's empowerment later became a fourth.)[57] "[H]ope begins with a paycheck," the secretary contended, as he linked MEPI to the United States' "deep and abiding national interest" in resolving the Israeli-Palestinian conflict.[58]

U.S. personnel in Cairo also appreciated the underlying causes of Arab discontent. Welch favored an approach that would not antagonize Mubarak or gratuitously stir controversy:

> My own view of this, sitting there as ambassador, was there are some responsible things that could be done here that might even work, and those are run on a spectrum from economic reform measures, which are a feature of the assistance program, all the way through education reform to working with civil society to having a dialogue about political reform to the far end of that envelope, 'promoting democracy.'... my own view of that was the ones that were directly and publicly associated with pushing democracy were the most difficult, because the Egyptians... are very nationalistic. Everybody is nationalistic in the world, but they tend to have this view that they don't

like foreigners preaching to them about this, and it reaches beyond
the regime.[59]

None in the administration wanted to alienate Mubarak. Bush
accepted the tenets of U.S. strategy that predated his presidency, including the importance of having a strategic alliance with Egypt for Israeli
security and U.S. interests in the Persian Gulf. The White House harbored concerns about what would happen in Egypt after Mubarak was
gone, but cherished his cooperation in the present, never more so than
in the lead-up to Operation Iraqi Freedom.

Iraq had concerned many members of Bush's national security team
before 9/11, but al-Qaeda's attacks gave an old cause new urgency.[60]
Arguments about security and democracy mixed during the run-up
to war.[61] Saddam Hussein presented a "very powerful moral case for
regime change," said National Security Advisor Condoleezza Rice.
"This is an evil man who, left to his own devices, will wreak havoc
again on his own population, his neighbors, and, if he gets weapons
of mass destruction and the means to deliver them, on all of us."[62]
In late August 2002, Cheney informed the Veterans of Foreign Wars
that "Saddam Hussein now has weapons of mass destruction" and
was "amassing them to use against our friends, against our allies, and
us." Citing early successes in Afghanistan, he anticipated "a future
of stability, self-determination, and peace" after Iraq's regime change.
At the UN the following month, Bush declared, "Liberty for the Iraqi
people is a great moral cause, and a great strategic goal." He envisaged a renaissance as the "people of Iraq . . . join[ed] a democratic
Afghanistan and a democratic Palestine, inspiring reforms throughout
the Muslim world."[63] Others argued that victory in Iraq was a prerequisite for bolstering the prospects of Arab-Israeli peace.[64] Inside
the administration some hoped to establish a new U.S. and Israeli ally
in the Arab world, something promised by longtime Iraqi exile and
U.S. client Ahmad Chalabi. "[T]he siren song of Iraq at the time that
Ahmed Chalabi was singing was multidirectional; first of all, we will
be the Middle East pillar of democracy . . . We will allow you to use
our bases to pressurize Iran . . . We will recognize Israel . . . That was
the song."[65]

Although public opinion in Egypt opposed the war and Mubarak
also argued against it, Egyptian intelligence had provided key

"evidence" for the case against Saddam.[66] A National Intelligence Estimate published in January 2003 called the confession from al-Libi "credible reporting."[67] In the six months before the war, Bush and his colleagues warned over twenty times of links between Saddam and al-Qaeda.[68] In an evening address to the nation on March 17, Bush said the Iraqi regime had "aided, trained and harbored terrorists, including operatives of alQaeda." He then issued an ultimatum for Saddam Hussein and his sons to "leave Iraq within forty-eight hours" or else invite "military conflict, commenced at a time of our choosing."[69] U.S. airstrikes on Iraq began March 19; the ground invasion started the next day.

In a further reminder of how useful authoritarianism could be, the Egyptian regime helped U.S. planners circumvent objections from democratic Turkey. A North Atlantic Treaty Organization (NATO) member and participant in the ad hoc "Coalition of the Willing," Turkey had balked at letting the United States use Turkish territory and bases for the attack.[70] As the Pentagon adjusted its plans to compensate, U.S. warships from two battle groups moved from the Mediterranean Sea through the Suez Canal and on to the Persian Gulf. The Defense Department also redirected the Fourth Infantry Division, some thirty thousand soldiers, to fly from the United States to the Persian Gulf, while the division's high-tech equipment, waiting off the Turkish coast, was shipped via Suez.[71]

Had Mubarak weighed public opinion more carefully, Egypt would have been less accommodating. Survey data show that the share of Egyptian respondents expressing "favorable/unfavorable" views of the United States was 15/76 in 2002 and 13/79 before the invasion.[72] Polled in February and early March 2003 about the likely consequences of a U.S.-led war on Iraq, large majorities thought the conflict would reduce democracy (63 percent) and peace (79 percent) in the Middle East.[73]

Once the war began, these attitudes manifested in the largest show of popular dissatisfaction since January 1977. On March 20, an estimated twenty thousand people converged upon Tahrir Square. Egyptians of many ideological leanings came together a show of national pride, Arab solidarity, and opposition to U.S. hegemony. Some participants marched on the U.S. embassy, only to be turned back by the CSF.[74] The vibrant demonstration carried pointed messages for Mubarak and

Bush: "Down with the USA, we won't be ruled by the CIA! We won't be ruled by imperialism!" and "Down Bush, down Blair, down Aznar!" (a reference to the British and Spanish premiers allied with Bush). Poking fun at MEPI, one banner read, "Down with Powellian democracy." A leftist parliamentarian declared that "The Egyptian people hereby announce the closure of the Suez Canal." Calls for Mubarak to step down also percolated. Demonstrators held the square from the afternoon through late evening, at which time security forces began using dogs to disperse the crowd. Afterward, opponents of the Iraq invasion tried to resume demonstrations, but the Ministry of Interior began rounding up and assailing leaders of the main rally, including two elected MPs.[75]

Later that year, when the search for weapons of mass destruction in Iraq came up empty, Bush began invoking democracy promotion more frequently. On October 2, David Kay reported on the progress of the Iraq Survey Group that sought Saddam Hussein's alleged stockpiles of biological and chemical weapons. His group had located a "clandestine network of ... safehouses," a "prison laboratory," and other signs of weaponry programs in the recesses of the fallen state but had "not yet found stocks of weapons." That admission dominated the news.[76] Bush argued Kay's findings underscored the problem Iraq had posed for years: "He's saying Saddam Hussein was a threat, a serious danger."[77] It was a debatable position, though, and it did not match the sense of urgency that had driven the prewar debate. After Kay's report, freedom became a fixture of Bush's rhetoric on Iraq and the Middle East. As tallied by Feith, who favored sticking to the security argument, Bush spent less than a paragraph discussing the threat Saddam Hussein had posed in his next twelve major addresses about Iraq. The same speeches averaged eleven paragraphs, maintaining that Iraqi regime change would deliver Arabs a freer future.[78]

On November 6, 2003, with the U.S. presidential election only a year away, Bush delivered the seminal address of the Freedom Agenda. The occasion was the twentieth anniversary of the National Endowment for Democracy (NED), Reagan's creation for aiding anti-Soviet dissidents and the backbone of U.S. democracy programs after the Cold War.[79] Bush declared "a new policy, a forward strategy of freedom in the Middle East." He dismissed doubts about rapid reform, calling them a form of the same "cultural condescension" that had wrongly forecast undemocratic fates for Germany, Japan, and India. His volume rising with indignation, Bush scoffed, "Time after time, observers have questioned whether this country, or that people, or this group, are 'ready' for democracy – as if freedom were a prize you win for meeting our own Western standards of progress."[80] The United States would emulate prior administrations that had nurtured democracy after World War II and after the Berlin Wall fell. Already, Bush saw "the stirrings of Middle Eastern democracy" in Bahrain, Jordan, Kuwait, Morocco, Oman, and the "multiparty political system" of Yemen. He challenged Saudi Arabia to give its people "a greater role," and he pronounced that "The great and proud nation of Egypt has shown the way toward peace in the Middle East, and now should show the way toward democracy in the Middle East." The line drew hearty applause. Democratic development would take time, but Bush implied that the clock was ticking: "Sixty years of Western nations excusing and accommodating the lack of freedom in the Middle East did nothing to make us safe – because in the long run, stability cannot be purchased at the expense of liberty."[81]

The implications for U.S. foreign policy were potentially vast. If officials genuinely saw democracy inside Egypt as a precondition for U.S. security, then the United States would need to shift from backing an iron-fisted autocrat to accepting popular sovereignty, wherever it might lead. However, the strategy behind Bush's words did not entail such a radical break. Even the most ardent democracy promoters did not want to risk, much less seek, Mubarak's downfall. The septuagenarian had no vice president, and White House officials wondered about succession.[82] Opinion polls from Egypt showed an almost total rejection of U.S. strategic priorities – attitudes that would surely shape official Egyptian policy if there were ever to be a democratically elected government. In the absence of a clear and friendly successor, opposition figures – whether religious conservatives or secular nationalists – could take power and potentially revise their country's international alignments, especially since Egypt's top-heavy political system granted the president tremendous discretion. In November, concerns grew that the Egyptian regime might face a sudden change of ruler; midway through a nationally televised address, Mubarak faltered and took an unscheduled thirty-minute break. Members of the presidential entourage called it a case of severe flu, but Egyptian and foreign observers speculated anew about how long Mubarak would last.[83]

Within the Bush administration, there were two main perspectives about the urgency of pressuring Mubarak to adopt stabilizing reforms that would safeguard the U.S.-Egyptian alliance against disruptions. One camp contended that Mubarak needed to broaden the political system to give more space to non-Islamist movements that were sympathetic to U.S. interests. A more competitive playing field would safeguard Egypt's alignments in two respects. First, it would eliminate the binary choice Egyptian voters and U.S. policymakers faced of dealing with either the NDP or the Muslim Brotherhood. Second, it would provide Mubarak's successor an institutional basis of legitimacy, mitigating the need for that figure to drum up anti-Americanism to garner public support. An alternative view, more consistent with the approach of prior administrations, was that the United States should encourage political change holistically, by continuing to support gradual socioeconomic development, and should not try to directly influence how Mubarak handled succession or other domestic policy matters. Advocates of this approach also emphasized the need for progress on Arab-Israeli peace talks. In sum, there was a group for "democracy promotion," aggressive about raising issues of political reform but still interested in stabilizing the regime, and a constituency for "diplomacy promotion," which sought to maintain a productive bilateral relationship with Mubarak on regional issues and envisioned reforms in Egypt occurring over the long term.

Elliott Abrams had worked on human rights issues under Reagan and stood at the fore of the democracy promotion camp under Bush.[84] In June 2001, Abrams had been brought into the National Security Council as senior director for democracy, human rights, and international operations.[85] The following year he was put in charge of the Middle East portfolio at the NSC. When it came to Egypt and the Middle East, Abrams's interest in democracy meshed with his defense of U.S. regional interests, including Israeli security, a subject of his writings while outside of government.[86] He explained that encouraging democratic change in Egypt was more complicated than in Chile and other cases he had worked on during his time in the Reagan administration. In the Latin American regimes, pro-U.S. opposition forces were poised to come to power "if the military would just get out of the way." For Egypt under Mubarak the challenge was twofold: build-ing up the opposition and subsequently prodding the ruler to step aside.[87] Officials floated various scenarios for post-Mubarak Egypt, but Abrams explained that "nobody was even talking about getting rid of Mubarak." Rather, "the question was just [about] pushing a little bit."[88]

From Strain to Estrangement

Mubarak was less offended by the NED speech than by how Bush handled the Israeli-Palestinian peace process. A snafu in 2004 made Mubarak look complicit in unprecedented White House assurances to Israel and brought U.S.-Egyptian relations to their lowest point since the *Achille Lauro* hijacking.

In June 2003, the Quartet had discussed the Road Map to solve the Israeli-Palestinian conflict. Following on Bush's Rose Garden speech, the Road Map laid out conditions by which both sides would end the occupation and establish a Palestinian state adjacent to Israel by 2005.[89] Mubarak hoped for tangible progress toward that goal. Instead, Israel, with U.S. support, seemed to be obviating the pos-sibility of a viable Palestinian state in the West Bank and the Gaza Strip.

In December 2003, Sharon announced that Israel would end its presence in some areas of the occupied territories if the Road Map could not be speedily implemented. The implication of this "Disen-gagement Plan" was that Israel would unilaterally withdraw from the Gaza Strip, removing twenty-one settlements and eighty-five hundred settlers.[90] At the same time, by departing from the framework of the Road Map, Sharon opened the prospect that Israel would claim lands in the West Bank and predetermine a portion of any final Israeli-Palestinian agreement. With respect to the Gaza Strip, if the Knesset approved Sharon's plan, it would be the first time, since the Sinai with-drawal of 1982, that Israel relinquished territory gained in the 1967 War. The disengagement also required major Egyptian involvement. After Israel withdrew, the Egyptian Ministry of Defense would be responsible for securing Gaza's eight-mile southern border. Mubarak accepted an expanded role in security around Gaza but publicly repudi-ated the White House's waning commitment on Palestinian statehood.

In April 2004, Bush and Mubarak met at Bush's ranch in Crawford, Texas. The setting implied atypical comity between the two presidents. "Getting invited to Crawford is supposed to be the ultimate thing," remarked Ambassador Fahmy, "and we initially took it that way, but it seemed to be your side was taking it as, 'We'll get him to Crawford to soften him up to get him to accept something.'"[91] "Something" turned out to be U.S. assurances to Sharon that Palestinian refugees would not return to live within Israel's pre-1967 borders and that existing West Bank settlements would be taken into account when drawing a final border between Israel and the prospective Palestinian state.

By Abrams's account, the visit by Mubarak also provided a chance for Bush to prod the Egyptian leader to open up politically. These discussions occurred when Mubarak – and Gamal, who accompanied him – were peeled off from their colleagues. Bush's team worked out a way of broaching issues from the Freedom Agenda with the minimum possible resistance: "In the Crawford meeting, we thought about how to do this, and our conclusion was that you should, first of all, get Mubarak away from everybody else. He had those big delegations of ministers.... All of them were [a] very bad influence, and not one of them was for a democratic opening."[92] Having separated the Egyptian president, Bush raised the issue of reform, but Mubarak "didn't bite." Abrams explains:

> He changed the subject, and he went off on tangents two or three times, and after – I don't know – half an hour of this or something, the others [from the Egyptian delegation] arrived, and we moved on to discussing with him the fact that the President was about to give Sharon what became the April 14th letter [of assurances]. So that was the closest I think they [Bush and Mubarak] ever came to having a conversation about this, and it didn't work.[93]

Mubarak cautioned Bush against promising support for the Israelis without making analogous pledges to the Palestinians. In a meeting before lunch, recalled Fahmy, "Mubarak explain[ed] why you can't give assurances to one side and not the other [when you are supposed to be an arbiter].... Second, he explain[ed] the problems with the substance of the assurances."[94] Bush proved as resistant to Mubarak's positions on Israeli-Palestinian issues as Mubarak was to Bush's democracy agenda. After initially getting no response, Mubarak raised the issues a second time, at which point Bush evaded making any commitment. "Clearly, this [was] not getting anywhere," Fahmy said.[95] The Egyptians made scant headway during the rest of their stay.[96]

At a closing press conference, both presidents expressed guarded support for Sharon's withdrawal, so long as it was part of the Road Map and negotiated peace.[97] Asked how Egypt would assist, Mubarak answered that his government "could help a lot in Gaza by training the police." Bush praised Mubarak for fighting terrorism and supporting "Iraq as it transitions to democracy and stability," and he reaffirmed that "[Egypt] will set the standard in the region for democracy by strengthening democratic institutions and political participation."[98] The conference's closing joint statement also acknowledged "the need for political and economic reform in the region" and "President Mubarak['s] . . . commitment for a continuing reform process."[99] The Egyptian regime was not about to turn over a new leaf, but it had a crucial role to play in monitoring the Egypt-Gaza border and strengthening Palestinian security forces.[100]

After the summit, Mubarak lingered in Texas, and Bush welcomed Sharon on a scheduled visit to the White House. At a joint news conference, Bush endorsed Sharon's plan for unilateral disengagement from Gaza and provided the assurances that Mubarak had advised against. Instead of affirming a two-state solution along the pre-1967 borders, Bush said that some Israeli settlements in the West Bank had to be accepted: "In light of new realities on the ground, including already existing major Israeli population centers, it is unrealistic to expect that the outcome of final status negotiations will be a full and complete return to the armistice lines of 1949." He also prejudged how the parties would honor Palestinians' right of return, saying that such a solution "would need to be found through the establishment of a Palestinian state and the settling of Palestinian refugees there, rather than Israel."[101] The new positions were enshrined in an exchange of letters.

According to a former member of Mubarak's cabinet, Ali El Dean Hillal, Bush had delivered a "public humiliation" to his Egyptian counterpart.[102] Fuming, Mubarak announced he was "shocked" by Bush's move, which abrogated the Road Map and put a U.S. imprimatur on an Israeli land grab in the West Bank. The timing gave the impression that Mubarak had abetted what some Egyptians called high perfidy.[103] Stopping in Paris on his trip back, the Egyptian president used a newspaper interview to blast the White House's policies and affiliate with the mood in the Middle East: "Today there is hatred of the Americans like never before in the region.... People have a feeling of injustice. What's more, they see Sharon acting as he pleases, without the Americans saying anything."[104] After returning to a maelstrom of controversy in Egypt, Mubarak suspended his customary annual visits to Washington.[105]

Some students of the period have attributed Bush's and Mubarak's estrangement to the Freedom Agenda.[106] But both Abrams and Fahmy trace the break to the Bush-Sharon exchange of letters: "It is entirely about Bush-Sharon," recalled Abrams. Bush and Mubarak

> left on perfectly good terms. The problem was that Mubarak stayed in the country.... That is what did it. He was very pissed off, and maybe it's bad staff work that we sort of didn't realize that this would matter to him so much, being in the country, but it did. That is what chilled the personal relationship and led to his not coming back to the United States after that.[107]

Asked whether Mubarak avoided the United States because of Bush's promotion of democracy, Fahmy was emphatic: "No, no, no, no, no. He didn't come back because of Iraq and the fact that he had just been embarrassed.... [After] crazy things like assurances and then Iraq. Why in the world should [he] come back?"[108] All the same, according to Abrams, Mubarak's wounded pride did not damage his support for U.S. policies: "If you asked how did it change Egyptian policy on anything – America, Israel, Gaza, the Canal – nothing, it didn't change anything."[109] "It just became a chilly [relationship]," described David Schenker, who worked with Feith at the Pentagon. "I think it was really atmospherics more than anything else, because the strategic relationship is really on autopilot."[110]

Even as Mubarak distanced Bush – and an estimated 98 percent of Egyptians held an "unfavorable" view of the United States – their two governments cooperated closely.[111] By the end of the year, Egypt had "trained 250 Iraqi police and 25 Iraqi diplomats" and conducted a joint infantry exercise with 134 Iraqi soldiers.[112] Egypt had also received dozens of extraordinary rendition victims.[113] In FY 2004,

Egypt took in $3 million from the State Department's Antiterrorism Assistance Program. One hundred Egyptian agents attended antiterrorism courses in Virginia and Louisiana.[114] Incongruously, "antiterrorism" trainees came from the same police forces cited in the State Department's 2004 human rights report as responsible for torture, extralegal detention, mass arrest, and unlawful killing.[115] The connection between Egyptian and U.S. security forces suggested an unused lever for influencing Mubarak's domestic policies: if U.S. officials objected to how the Egyptian leader treated his own people, they could stop training his people and sending them detainees. "We had no illusions about what we had with Mubarak, and Omar Suleiman was known very well to us," said Armitage, "but they were very helpful to us in the Palestinian question, and . . . the obvious implications for Israel were real, and that's the way we generally saw Egypt."[116]

Without reducing collaboration with the Egyptian repressive apparatus, the Bush administration continued to push political reform publicly – and invite high-profile objections from Arab rulers. Mubarak was a conspicuous no-show when the administration introduced another endeavor for promoting Middle East reform, the Greater Middle East Initiative, in June. Egypt and Saudi Arabia had already replied to a leaked draft of the program, asserting that Arab states were already embarked on "development, modernization and reform," and they would brook no foreign "imposition" of reform. Tossing blame for regional instability back at Washington, they advocated "finding a just and fair solution to the issues of Arab and Islamic countries," starting with "Palestine and Iraq."[117] Mubarak warned, "Anyone who imagines solutions or reform can be imposed from the outside on any region or society is delusional." "It is the nature of the peoples [of the region]," he continued, "to reject all who attempt to subdue them or force their ideas upon them."[118] With Iraq in flux and the peace process moribund, European leaders echoed Arab skepticism about this latest U.S. scheme for political engineering.[119] When the initiative was finally announced on June 9, it had evolved into the cumbersome Partnership for Progress and a Common Future with the Region of the Broader Middle East and North Africa, and "BMENA" states were free to accept or decline its provisions.[120] The authors conceded that "change should not and cannot be imposed from outside," and a third of the text discussed the Arab-Israeli conflict and Iraq.[121]

Authoritarianism on the March

As Bush headed into his second term, the White House could cite signs of economic and political reform in Egypt. These currents, however, stemmed from close regime affiliates on one side and diehard activists who opposed U.S. foreign policy on the other.

Mubarak had reshuffled his cabinet in the summer of 2004 to bring in more neoliberal figures. Canadian-trained information technology specialist Ahmed Nazif became prime minister, and associates of Gamal's acquired the portfolios of Finance, Investment Development, Industry, and Foreign Trade.[122] Already, Gamal's coterie had influenced the 2000 legislative elections and subsequent leadership choices within the ruling party. Now this so-called New Guard had the opportunity to sell off state-owned companies to their political clients. The promotion of a Gamal-centered clique galvanized opponents of the Mubaraks.[123] A new group called the Egyptian Movement for Change rallied on December 12 in downtown Cairo. Although demonstrations occurred periodically during Mubarak's tenure, this occasion was unusual for its blunt criticism of the president. Some covered their mouths with stickers that declared "Kefaya!" (Enough!), and hundreds showed that they opposed Mubarak and his brood.[124] The group's chief slogans were "No to [term] extension! No to hereditary succession!"[125] Members of Kefaya, as the Egyptian Movement for Change quickly came to be known, also denounced the Nazif government and criticized U.S. policies in the region. At the same time, some of the group's members credited Bush's rhetoric with giving them a chance to push the envelope. "[T]here is no denying that there was a period of . . . some kind of protection," recalled Dina Shehata. "All eyes were on Egypt, and it was hard for the regime to be too heavy-handed."[126]

Events far from Cairo also seemed auspicious for the Freedom Agenda. Hundreds of thousands of Ukrainians had taken to the streets in the Orange Revolution. Decrying electoral fraud by ex-Soviet politicians, they hoisted pro-U.S. candidate Vicktor Yushchenko into the presidency.[127] Just a year earlier, Georgia's Rose Revolution had brought another Washington favorite, Mikheil Saakashvili, into office.[128] In early January 2005, Palestinians chose Mahmoud Abbas in free and fair voting that gave Americans and Israelis a new negotiating partner.[129] Later that month, Iraqis would go to the polls to choose a constitutional assembly.[130]

These campaigns for popular emancipation provided the backdrop when Bush gave his second inaugural address. "We are led, by events and common sense, to one conclusion: The survival of liberty in our land increasingly depends on the success of liberty in other lands. The best hope for peace in our world is the expansion of freedom in all the world." The mission for U.S. foreign policy was epic: "to seek and support the growth of democratic movements and institutions in every nation and culture, with the ultimate goal of ending tyranny in our world." Addressing dissidents around the globe, Bush pledged that "The United States will not ignore your oppression, or excuse your oppressors. When you stand for your liberty, we will stand with you."[131] The next month, in the State of the Union address, he again called for Egypt to "show the way toward democracy in the Middle East."[132]

Democracy promotion still meant nudging Mubarak to broaden participation, without "ending tyranny" in Egypt.[133] But during the second term, Bush's foreign policy team was more ready to confront Egyptian officials about human rights abuses. The two NSC sections Abrams had headed in the first term (Democracy, Human Rights and International Operations and Near East and North African Affairs) were placed under Global Democracy Strategy, which he would run as "democracy czar."[134] After assisting her father's campaign, Liz Cheney returned to again head MEPI.[135] Rice replaced Powell at the State Department.[136] Her appointment promised to better connect the State Department to the White House and, when needed, challenge the foreign service bureaucracy.[137] Stephen Hadley, Rice's former deputy at the White House, rose to become national security advisor. Overall, the group promised a less ambivalent implementation of democracy promotion than in the first term. As Abrams explained, Bush's appointees understood the policy for democracy promotion from "the NED speech and the second inaugural," and they had "experience" and "a sense of what the President wanted."[138]

Their work on Egypt for the remainder of the year revolved around elections, and in particular around a qualitative shift to presidential voting introduced by Mubarak. His prior four terms had come through single-candidate plebiscites, an antiquated practice codified in article

76 of the Egyptian Constitution. This highly autocratic system had a vulnerability that oppositionists could potentially exploit: Parliament nominated the sole presidential candidate. There remained the remote possibility that a charismatic figure opposing Mubarak or, more likely, his would-be successor could sway enough MPs to get on the ballot – and seize the presidency by default. Remedying this problem, on February 26, Mubarak asked the parliament to draft a constitutional amendment allowing multicandidate presidential elections – something opposition forces had long demanded.[139] Intimating that his initiative was part of his planning for succession, Mubarak confided to visiting members of Congress that the amendment was for "the future, not for me."[140]

The change enabled contested leadership elections, something the White House had applauded in the Palestinian Authority and Afghanistan. After some initial wariness, Bush pointed to Mubarak's move as another advance in Arab democracy.[141] The "prospect of competitive, multi-party elections for President [of Egypt] in September," along with municipal elections underway in Saudi Arabia, marked "small but welcome steps" on the "path of reform."[142] For their part, the Saudis had cleared a relatively low bar: Women could not vote, and the elections filled half the seats on councils that had only advisory power.[143] Contested presidential elections in Egypt offered a bigger spectacle, but not necessarily a more substantive one. Mubarak had not introduced multicandidate elections as a concession to Washington or to the domestic opposition. "The Egyptians themselves did it," said Ambassador Welch. "I can't argue that we were a part of that decision, and we certainly weren't prescriptive about how they might implement democratic reform."[144] Similarly, Ambassador Fahmy stated, "The idea did not come from the United States, but yes, the fact that there were two forces happening – an opening up in Egypt and an interest in America – kept . . . the issue of democracy topical."[145]

Groups like Kefaya wanted not only multicandidate presidential elections but also the conditions that would enable free political organizing, starting with a repeal of the Emergency Law. Seeing none of that, one outspoken newspaper editor, Ibrahim Eissa, dismissed the announcement as "a way to improve [Mubarak's] image with the Americans and to please them with some formal changes . . . [while] keeping everything else unchanged."[146] In fact, the shift had the potential to serve U.S. interests if it bolstered pro-U.S. candidates. If not, however, it would perpetuate the binary choice between Mubarak and the Muslim Brotherhood.

In Abrams's view, contested elections would constitute meaningful reform only if they broadened the political center:

> Every time somebody tries to have a moderate centrist, even [a] moderate Islamist party, that actually could take votes from the Brotherhood, it is crushed. So the dichotomy is one of [Mubarak's] making, and we should not fall into his trap. What we should be doing is demanding that he open the political system more, so that those voices can be heard.[147]

On that score, the referendum approving the amendment boded poorly. A wide range of movements boycotted the referendum and faulted Bush for "[giving] the NDP a green light . . . to manipulate political reform in its favor."[148] The measure passed amid state-organized assaults on peaceful demonstrators.[149] Asked a week later whether Egypt was "on pace for . . . free and fair elections," Bush temporized, "I urged [Mubarak] once again to have as free and fair [an] election as possible. . . . He assured me that that's just exactly what he wants to do."[150]

A free and fair election presupposed multiple viable candidates, but a legal cloud hung over Mubarak's most serious challenger. Ayman Nour was a forty-one-year-old lawyer who had twice won election to parliament as a Wafd candidate before creating his own party, al-Ghad (Tomorrow), in 2004. In late January 2005, authorities arrested and charged Nour with forging nearly 1,200 of the signatures used in his party's registration.[151] The accusation was dubious given Nour's local popularity and the case arose despite the government's own initial approval of al-Ghad's registration papers. (Subsequently one of the main witnesses against Nour stated that his testimony had been coerced through torture.)[152] It looked as if the regime was again criminalizing dissent. Nour represented the kind of incremental liberalization sought by democracy promoters like Abrams, a change that would free the United States from relying on Mubarak as the sole alternative to Islamic rule. Nour's campaign for the presidency would be a barometer of reform. Rice raised the case with Egyptian foreign minister Ahmed Aboul Gheit and postponed a visit to Egypt in protest.[153]

From jail, Nour declared that he was running. Later released on bail and charged with forgery, he began campaigning.[154]

Rice eventually traveled to Egypt in June. Speaking at the American University in Cairo, she underlined that the administration wanted to see improved elections.[155] After praising Egypt's regional leadership, the secretary addressed her hosts in unusually pointed terms:

> President Mubarak has unlocked the door for change. Now, the Egyptian Government must put its faith in its own people.... The Egyptian Government must fulfill the promise it has made to its people – and to the entire world – by giving its citizens the freedom to choose. Egypt's elections, including the Parliamentary elections, must meet objective standards that define every free election.

Although Rice insisted that the United States was not imposing its will, she struck a confrontational pose. Faulting "undemocratic governments," the secretary gestured to "impatient patriots" across the region, including "right here in Cairo."[156] Rice later met with some of these restive oppositionists, including Nour.[157]

Events that summer highlighted the contrast between democracy promotion and security cooperation in bilateral relations. Two days after Rice's speech, Egypt became the first Arab country to restore full diplomatic relations with the new government in Baghdad. It was a daring gesture that came at a steep price.[158] Within a month Iraqi insurgents had abducted and murdered Egypt's ambassador-to-be, Ihab al-Sherif.[159] Back in Egypt, in July, a series of bomb attacks in the Sinai (the second such assault in less than a year) rocked Sharm El-Sheikh, killing seventy people, most of them Egyptians.[160] As Mubarak's forces cracked down on suspected Bedouin militants, they also prepared to patrol the border with Gaza. In August, Egypt trained "5,000 Palestinian policemen" in Gaza. Mubarak's government also signed a "$2.5 billion deal for the sale to Israel of Egyptian natural gas," an agreement that would later provoke domestic controversy.[161] By September 12, Sharon's government had removed all Israeli settlers, bases, and military personnel from the Gaza Strip.[162] Israel would no longer have a major presence on the inside of the border between Egypt and the Gaza Strip. Therefore, the disengagement vested Egypt with significant responsibility over the sole external passage for the Palestinians of Gaza, the border crossing in the town of Rafah.

While it aided Washington on regional issues, the Egyptian regime defied U.S. input about electoral reform. During the two-and-a-half-week campaign, Nour and other candidates were blocked from publicizing their candidacies, while Hosni Mubarak took to the campaign trail in a U.S.-style tour stage-managed by Gamal. The heir apparent and his adjutant, Mohammad Kamal (a Johns Hopkins–trained political scientist), used focus groups to hone their candidate's message and employed the NDP's local branches to excite party cadres.[163] Such measures probably had more to do with refurbishing the party than tipping the election. As soon as Hosni Mubarak entered the race, most observers considered the results a foregone conclusion. On September 7, some 7 million voters cast ballots, and "as free and fair ... as possible" proved hardly fair for the opposition. Mubarak racked up 88.6 percent of the vote, 5 percent less than his performance in the last single-candidate plebiscite. Nour came in a distant second, with 7 percent.[164]

Bush congratulated Mubarak by phone, and a White House statement termed the election "an important step toward holding fully free and fair competitive multi-party elections."[165] The administration's proponents of change in Egypt saw little more that could be done. Stephen Krasner, then the head of policy planning at the State Department, explained, "You had a very clear commitment to this democratization agenda, people absolutely tied to American national security in a direct way, and yet having said those things and believed them, it wasn't clear what you could do to actually implement the policy."[166]

Bush's team responded to Mubarak's self-serving reforms with a mix of praise and censure. Following the election, Liz Cheney met with Gamal. According to a U.S. embassy rapporteur, she "pressed Gamal to identify areas that he thought could be improved in future elections." Due to a provision of the amendment, in the next presidential race aspiring candidates from official parties would need to have 5 percent of parliamentary seats to qualify, a criterion no party had met since the 1980s (under more liberal election rules). Gamal was indifferent when Cheney "asked if any opposition party" would clear the bar. Parties, he responded, would have to "get their acts together" and demonstrate their seriousness, apparently by making stupendous gains against his party and the security apparatus. If opposition groups were free to nominate their own candidates without having the requisite seats in parliament, "chaos" would ensue.[167] The amendment to article 76 looked increasingly like a way of promoting Gamal into the presidency against cherry-picked opponents – dynasticism behind a democratic fig leaf.

Parliamentary elections soon confirmed the improbability of a serious presidential election under Mubarak's system. After Egyptian security forces menaced Nour's constituents in the lead-up to voting, Nour lost reelection – an improbable result had the contest been free and fair.[168] His district proved to be a bellwether. Election observation teams were excluded from watching the process and slammed Egyptian authorities for "[falling] well short of their previously stated commitments to establish a fair and transparent election."[169] In plain view, NDP candidates and the Ministry of Interior intervened with impunity. Egyptian police abandoned any pretense of protecting the public. Law enforcement officers pushed aside legally mandated judicial supervisors.[170] Sometimes they "cordoned off and blocked" polling stations or "[used] tear gas and . . . sticks" to obstruct voters turning out for opposition candidates.[171] Government-sponsored thugs roamed freely. In Alexandria, Egypt's second-largest city, journalists photographed blade-wielding hooligans threatening voters.[172]

Violence against opposition voters resulted in fifteen deaths and at least five hundred injuries.[173] By contrast, Egyptians ready to cast their ballots for the NDP were spared the hazards, given premarked ballots, and enticed with bribes of thirty-five Egyptian pounds (seven dollars).[174] These tactics guaranteed the NDP's supermajority in parliament. The party's bloc shrank nominally, from 88 percent to 73 percent, but remained comfortably above the two-thirds majority needed to renew the state of emergency and advance new constitutional amendments.[175] The biggest losers were candidates like Nour from the non-Islamist opposition parties. They held sixteen seats in the outgoing parliament but won only twelve races (2.7 percent of elected seats) in 2005.[176]

Egypt was headed for another five years of NDP hegemony. Rather than boosting a pro-U.S. alternative like Nour's al-Ghad Party, elections had reproduced the Mubarak–Muslim Brotherhood dichotomy. In fact, the Muslim Brotherhood had achieved an unprecedented eighty-eight seats, nearly a fifth of the elected seats in the People's

Assembly.[177] A State Department spokesman drew attention to "one of the biggest gains of independent seats in the history of Egyptian parliamentary elections" and averred that "These elections overall represent an important step in the democratic reform process in Egypt."[178] Likewise, the embassy in Cairo cautioned a visiting U.S. official not to be shocked by the results, saying that the "Egyptians [in the regime] have a long history of threatening us with the MB [Muslim Brotherhood] bogeyman." The embassy warned that if the official visitor's "interlocutors" tried to portray Muslim Brotherhood's gains as a reason to slow liberalization, he ought to "push back that, on the contrary, the MB's rise signals the need for greater democracy and transparency in government."[179] No matter how sound that logic, few in Washington would cheer the success of a group the U.S. government kept at arm's length, almost never referred to by name, and whose readiness for democracy was openly questioned.[180] Mubarak had used the parliamentary elections to reassert control, neutralize Nour, and clear Gamal's path to succession.

The tumult of 2005 had not quite ended, for as soon as the elections were over, the legal case against Nour resumed. On December 24, a court sentenced Nour to five years in prison on forgery charges that increasingly appeared to have been concocted by Egyptian security.[181] It was a dramatic close to Mubarak's year in the spotlight. "So much for holding Egypt up as a beacon of burgeoning democracy in the Middle East," opined the *New York Times*.[182] Subdued, the Bush administration said the conviction "call[ed] into question Egypt's commitment to democracy, freedom, and the rule of law."[183] It also raised questions about how far the White House would go in confronting the Egyptian regime. Two weeks prior to the conviction, U.S. ambassador to Egypt Francis Ricciardone had told Vice President Cheney, "We've beaten up everyone short of Mubarak on [Nour's case]."[184]

The Freedom Agenda was coming full circle. Ricciardone opined that Egypt was witnessing "the slow sunset of a quarter century of benevolent but authoritarian rule."[185] But Mubarak was no more domestically constrained than he had been before Bush entered office, and the Egyptian regime remained just as integral to U.S. strategy in the Middle East. Days after the jailing of Nour another grim episode marred Cairo's relations with Washington. On December 29, the Ministry of Interior used lethal force to disperse a tent city of Sudanese refugees in downtown Cairo. The assault killed twenty-seven Sudanese and underscored the Egyptian government's proclivity for employing excessive, arbitrary force. A U.S. embassy cable reported that the parliamentary elections, the conviction of Nour, and the repression of the Sudanese had "undermined Mubarak's credibility as a leader of democratic reforms, and . . . strained our ties with Egypt." Still, the incidents would not infringe upon security cooperation: "The bedrock of our strategic interests with Egypt . . . remains as important as ever."[186]

Conclusion

In their speeches, Bush and Rice publicly abjured the United States' "sixty years" of cozying up with Middle Eastern dictators; in practice, they reproduced that tradition. To be sure, during his first five years in office George W. Bush incorporated democracy and human rights into U.S. foreign policy as no president had since Jimmy Carter. As in the late 1970s, however, rights advocacy in the 2000s was circumscribed by considerations of U.S. security and geostrategy. The intelligence collaboration that Clinton had expanded became invaluable after the September 11 attacks. Mubarak was a vital partner in the Bush administration's war on terrorism and its war against Saddam Hussein. The White House also remained a key partner of the Egyptian regime. Military and economic aid continued steadily, although economic support funds shrank gradually based on the "glide path" established under Clinton. Egyptian security forces traveled to and received training in the United States. All of this material and logistical assistance proceeded while Mubarak and his son orchestrated an autocratic leadership succession under the cover of political reform.

When it came to Egyptian domestic politics, succession concerned the Bush administration most. Just as Carter's team saw economic development as a way of stabilizing Egypt, the Bush White House used democracy promotion as an instrument to anchor Egypt's alignment before Hosni Mubarak passed away. In a less constricted political arena, moderates like Ibrahim and Nour could excel. Such would serve as an alternative to the current authoritarian leadership (the Mubaraks) and to the likely beneficiaries of any future elections that were free (the Muslim Brotherhood). The regime gave no quarter, however, and even if it had, the cultivation of pro-U.S. Egyptian politicians was unlikely to bolster U.S. strategy. Public opinion surveys regularly showed that the Egyptian mainstream rejected U.S. policies from Baghdad to Gaza. Because any freely elected government would likely follow suit, the Egyptian regime was holding at bay not only the Islamists, but also a broader swath of nationalist forces.

4

Gaza Patrol

Sadat had envisioned replacing Iran as a Middle East gendarme, but in 2006–2008, Egypt looked more like a small town sheriff's deputy. Bush administration officials did not seriously consult with Mubarak on matters of war and peace, and they regarded Minister of Defense Mohammed Hussein Tantawi as more of a nuisance than an asset. Obsessed with state-on-state warfare, the field marshal demurred from retooling his forces to meet post–Cold War challenges. Meanwhile, intelligence chief Suleiman was tackling terrorism and the other twenty-first-century threats that troubled Washington. Politicians from the White House and Congress relied on Suleiman for managing the Israeli-Palestinian conflict and fighting al-Qaeda. Many preferred him to Gamal Mubarak as a presidential successor. Meanwhile, they relegated the Egyptian military to border duty.

After Palestinians freely elected a Hamas-led government, U.S. politicians demanded the Egyptian regime work harder to secure the Gaza Strip and prevent Palestinian attacks on Israeli towns. Even as U.S. officials wanted to bolster Mubarak and prevent the Muslim Brotherhood from replicating Hamas's achievement, some members of Congress argued Mubarak was not doing enough to weaken Hamas and pacify Gaza. The debate on Capitol Hill culminated in the first attempt to condition post-1979 U.S. *military* aid on the behavior of the Egyptian regime.

In 2007, U.S. congressional representatives stipulated that Mubarak must reform the judiciary and police to receive the full amount of aid.

They focused their conditionality proposal, however, on the Egyptian Ministry of Defense, which was responsible for Egypt's external borders. By withholding a portion of military aid, Congress sought to impel the Egyptian army to destroy underground tunnels that circumvented an international blockade on Gaza and allowed smugglers to bring in arms and supplies. Sensitive to the Pentagon's rapport with the Egyptian armed forces, the Bush administration waived the conditionality. Nonetheless, Congress had sent a message; the Egyptian military expanded its antismuggling operations. The episode was instructive. Washington had publicly exerted leverage on Egyptian officials – not to promote democracy in Egypt, but to enhance security inside Israel and advance U.S. interests. Whereas the Palestinian elections underscored the risks of popular sovereignty, Mubarak and Suleiman demonstrated the benefits of an authoritarian regime that favored U.S. strategy over the local public.

Elections and Double Standards

On January 25, 2006, more than three-quarters of voters in the Palestinian Authority turned out to choose 132 Palestinian Legislative Council members. The vote was peaceful, internationally certified, and highly competitive.[1] Hamas, which had originated as a branch of the Egyptian Muslim Brotherhood in the 1940s, beat President Abbas's Fatah party by 3 points in the national popular vote.[2] Electoral rules, which Fatah and Hamas had coauthored, magnified this narrow margin into a 56 percent majority (seventy-four seats). Hamas could choose the next prime minister and cabinet.

The elections bookended the Freedom Agenda. In 2002, the White House advocated elections in the Palestinian Authority to marginalize Arafat. Four years later, free and fair voting had carried a U.S.-designated "foreign terrorist organization" into the political mainstream.[3]

Bush dismissed the election as a protest vote, a rebuke against Fatah – not a mandate for Hamas.[4] "The people are demanding honest government. The people want services," he asserted.[5] Further, even if Palestinians genuinely favored Hamas, the United States would not accept the group. "A political party that articulates the destruction of Israel as part of its platform," Bush insisted, "is a party with which

we will not deal." Rice said, "You cannot have one foot in politics and another in terror."[6] At her direction, the Quartet stipulated
that Palestinian Authority officials "renounce violence" and "accept
Israel's right to exist" or lose international funding. On January 30, the
Quartet declared a halt to foreign payments to the Palestinian Authority until the new government accepted the Road Map. At the urging
of U.S. officials, incumbent ministers from Fatah rebuffed Hamas's
proposals for a broad-based coalition government. Hamas leaders rejected the Quartet's attempt to undermine their success and
formed a government without Fatah and with a few independents.[7]
"The U.S. and Israel have no right to prevent the Palestinian people from choosing their leadership," said a Hamas official based in
Damascus.[8]

Bush's team shared his father's administration's skepticism about
popular sovereignty in Arab countries: Hamas was the new FIS. But
rather than concede publicly that U.S. interests trumped Palestinian
democracy, the White House described the new Palestinian government as less than democratic. A new National Security Strategy was
published in March. It specified that the United States' goal was to
foster "effective" democracies. In support of that goal, elections like
those won by Hamas were necessary but insufficient:

> The Palestinian people voted in a process that was free, fair, and
> inclusive. The Palestinian people having made their choice at the
> polls, the burden now shifts to those whom they have elected to take
> the steps necessary to advance peace, prosperity, and statehood for
> the Palestinian people.... The international community has made
> clear that there is a fundamental contradiction between armed group
> and militia activities and the building of a democratic state. The
> international community has also made clear that a two-state solution
> to the conflict requires all participants in the democratic process to
> renounce violence and terror, accept Israel's right to exist, and disarm
> as outlined in the Roadmap. These requirements are clear, firm, and
> of long standing.[9]

The United States' imprimatur depended on the Palestinian government's external *and* internal behavior: "Any elected government that
refuses to honor these principles cannot be considered fully democratic,
however it may have taken office."[10] The National Security Strategy
spent nearly as much ink on the question of effective democracy in

the Palestinian Authority as the entire section on "ending tyranny" in North Korea, Iran, Syria, Cuba, Belarus, Myanmar (Burma), and Zimbabwe.

Until Hamas changed its stance on Israel and armed struggle, the group belonged with the rogues, if not a more ostracized caste. David Schenker described how the Bush administration saw the matter:

> People say that we want democracy and elections, but we don't want the results, right? . . . I think the administration certainly in Palestine, the way we viewed it was – 'Listen, people are entitled to vote for who they want to, and we are entitled to have our policy toward those people, too, right?' . . . If you vote for a terrorist state, we don't have to trade with you. We don't have to accept everybody and talk to everybody just because you vote for them, so we had no problem with that.[11]

For Abrams there was a precondition – democratic political parties – that the Palestinians lacked and that would need to be in place before democratic elections could take place: "You can't have democratic politics without democratic political parties. . . . We are great at election monitoring, but that is the end. That just measures whether you succeeded or failed. It doesn't help you succeed."[12] These criteria gave Hamas and its constituents a catch-22: avoid elections and be accused of being undemocratic, or participate successfully and be punished for policy stances endorsed at the ballot box.[13]

The Bush administration's reaction to the Palestinian elections so qualified U.S. advocacy of democracy as to render it almost meaningless, for although it had only been applied in practice to two main cases (Algeria and the Palestinian Authority), it anticipated how the United States would respond under analogous conditions elsewhere. International legitimacy stemmed from alignment with U.S. security needs, not accountability to the local populace. So long as parties who threatened U.S. interests could prevail at the ballot box, full-blown democratic elections would be deemed precipitous, whether that judgment was made beforehand, as with Egypt, or after the fact, as with the Palestinian Authority.[14] "The people" were sovereign only insofar as they chose leaders who did not contest U.S. power. Otherwise, ultimate authority remained with the ruler: the Algerian military, Mahmoud Abbas and the Israeli government, or Mubarak.

Mubarak saw Hamas as an extension of the Muslim Brotherhood and had no problems isolating the Palestinian group. Publicly,
though, Egyptian officials tried to avoid looking like they were abetting U.S.-Israeli antagonism against the new Palestinian government.
While Mubarak and Suleiman worked to reestablish Fatah's control,
Suleiman began reaching out to Hamas. A mid-February U.S. embassy
cable reported the Egyptian intelligence chief had met Hamas leaders in
Cairo and pressed them "to adopt realistic and responsible positions:"

> Unless Hamas lives up to the PA's [Palestinian Authority] inter-
> national obligations, abandons violence, and recognizes Israel,
> Suleiman had warned the Hamas leaders, they would not get Egypt's
> support. Suleiman reported that Hamas leaders appeared to under-
> stand that they needed Egypt and seemed ready to fulfill the PA's
> international obligations and adhere to a cease-fire with Israel, but
> that they were still balking at recognizing Israel's right to exist.[15]

The Bush administration wanted the Egyptians to apply more pressure, but Suleiman resisted freezing international funding for the
Palestinian Authority. Foreign Minister Ahmed Aboul Gheit also
objected to the Bush administration's approach. At a press conference alongside Rice, Aboul Gheit told journalists that Hamas would
"develop" and "evolve" and that it should be given more time. While
trying desperately to drum up support, Rice dropped the democratic
evangelism of her 2005 American University in Cairo speech. Calling
Mubarak "a president who has sought the consent of the governed,"
she forswore U.S. paternalism: "We can't judge Egypt. We can't tell
Egypt what its course can be or should be."[16]

Lawmakers from both parties also wanted the United States to be
tough on Hamas and easy on Mubarak. Hasty democracy promotion, they asserted, could produce new autocrats or, when it came to
Egypt, topple an incumbent autocrat who helped the United States.
"Hamas's victory takes this beyond theory," cautioned Representative
Christopher Smith (R-NJ). "Free and fair elections can usher into
power brutal dictatorships with a seemingly popular mandate."[17]
When it came to stalwart allies like Egypt, Congresswoman Shel-
ley Berkley (D-NV) argued the United States should stop "pushing our friends too hard to attain an ideal situation...[that] will
ultimately overthrow...regimes...that are relatively friendly to the

United States in favor of terrorist organizations like Hamas that are taking over in quite legitimate democratic elections."[18]

Annus Horribilis

The Palestinian elections posed the first challenge of a difficult year for U.S. policy in the Middle East. Violent conflicts, from the Gaza Strip to Iraq and Lebanon, demanded Washington's attention and, often, Cairo's assistance.

For more than a year, Hamas had been observing a unilateral ceasefire (*tahdi'ya*, literally "quieting") toward Israel. During this period the group abstained from joining in a campaign of shooting primitive rockets from the Gaza Strip into southern Israel.[19] On June 9, 2006, however, Israel killed two Hamas notables in missile strikes and was suspected of targeting a third. Hamas promptly renounced its ceasefire and resumed offensive operations. On June 25, fighters from Hamas's militant wing and two other paramilitary groups sprang from a 0.3-mile tunnel burrowed from the Gaza Strip, attacked an Israeli military base, killed two Israeli soldiers, and seized a nineteen-year-old Israeli Defense Force (IDF) corporal named Gilad Shalit. That same day Hamas and Fatah signed a National Conciliation Document, which signaled Hamas could accept a two-state solution along the 1967 borders and the two factions could potentially form a coalition government for the sake of improving the local situation. Shalit's abduction, however, vitiated any possible Israeli or U.S. goodwill Hamas might have earned by accepting a condition of the Quartet. Between June 28 and July 18, Israel fired a thousand artillery shells in Gaza, while Hamas continued shooting rockets. One Israeli soldier was killed in the fighting, and eighty-four Palestinian adults and sixteen Palestinian children perished.[20]

Over in Iraq, the showcase of the Freedom Agenda was becoming a cautionary tale. Sunni militants bombed the golden-domed al-Askariya Shrine in Sammara on February 22, 2006. Shia death squads then slew hundreds in Baghdad. Fighters from the Sunni minority struck back. As militias targeted Iraqis based on their sectarian identity, communities segregated themselves for protection.[21] During July, 3,184 Iraqi civilians died, the most in a single month since the U.S.-led invasion.[22] The Iraqi civil war put Bush on the defensive. While visiting Russia that summer, Bush was asked about discussing democracy with President Vladimir Putin. "I talked about my desire to promote institutional change in parts of the world like Iraq, where there's a free press and free religion," answered Bush, "and I told him that a lot of people in our country would hope that Russia would do the same thing." Putin pounced. "We certainly would not want to have the same kind of democracy as they have in Iraq, I will tell you quite honestly."[23]

Most Egyptians also disdained U.S. foreign policy in the Middle East. By June 2006, 76 percent of Egyptians polled saw Hamas's electoral victory as good for the Palestinian people, and 83 percent thought the war in Iraq increased the risk of terrorism. Substantial majorities ranked the Israeli-Palestinian conflict (68 percent) and the U.S. presence in Iraq (56 percent) ahead of Iran (14 percent) and North Korea (14 percent) as threats to world peace. Ten percent supported the U.S.-led War on Terror, and only 8 percent expressed either "a lot" or "some" confidence in the U.S. president's international leadership.[24] Egyptians already were appalled by how Bush approached the Palestinian Authority and Iraq were soon outraged by his handling of Lebanon.

On July 12 the Shia movement Hezbollah shot diversionary rockets at IDF troops in northern Israel.[25] Hezbollah fighters then captured two Israeli soldiers and killed three others. By seizing Israeli service members, Hamas and Hezbollah leaders intended to trigger prisoner swaps that would liberate their imprisoned co-partisans. Israel rejected the possibility of any such exchanges and retaliated by launching military strikes into Lebanon. Hezbollah officials charged Israel with trying "to alter the regional map" by forcibly disarming and neutralizing the group.[26] In fact, disarmament had been an aim of United Nations Security Council Resolution 1559 (2005), which called for demobilizing all Lebanese militias, removing all foreign forces (Syrian and Israeli), and holding free and fair presidential elections. Israeli leaders sought to downgrade Hezbollah's ability to strike northern Israel and drive a wedge between Hezbollah and the Lebanese public. The IDF fired on buildings and facilities connected to Hezbollah, as well as civilian infrastructure (roads, bridges, airport runways, seaports) and populated areas such as south Beirut. Within two weeks, more than 350 Lebanese civilians had been killed. During the same period, Hezbollah fired thousands of missiles into Israel, averaging 150 to

200 missiles per day.[27] These attacks killed forty-four Israeli civilians.[28]

As the war in Lebanon continued, the Bush administration resisted calls for the United States to push for a quick diplomatic solution. On July 21, Rice minimized the need for an immediate intervention that restored the status quo: "What we're seeing here, in a sense, is the growing – the birth pangs of a new Middle East. And whatever we do, we have to be certain that we are pushing forward to the new Middle East, not going back to the old one."[29] Mention of a "new Middle East" played into Hezbollah claims that Israel was attempting to turn a skirmish into a strategic game changer, redrawing the political map in the Levant through overwhelming military force. Rice also seemed inured to the deaths of hundreds of Lebanese civilians. Nine days after her remarks, an Israeli airstrike on an apartment building in Qana, Lebanon, killed twenty-eight civilians, including sixteen children, although initial media reports placed the number of deaths higher.[30]

The Qana attack provoked sorrow and anger across the region. Mubarak called for a ceasefire, but he could not quiet the Egyptian public. State and independent newspapers labeled the strike a joint U.S.-Israeli operation.[31] Kefaya and the Muslim Brotherhood led protests against Israeli aggression and U.S.-Egyptian complicity. Demonstrators likened Hezbollah leader Hassan Nasrallah to Nasser, and chants of "Oh beloved Hezbollah, strike, strike Tel Aviv" mixed with cries of "Down, down with Mubarak." In early August, with the war still going on, rallies drew more than 5,000 participants – enormous by the metrics of tightly policed Egypt. Had parliament and the universities not been in summer recess, the crowds would likely have been much larger. Participants called on Mubarak to withdraw Egypt's ambassador from Tel Aviv, expel the Israeli ambassador from Cairo, and revoke the Egyptian-Israeli peace treaty. One hundred MPs marched from the People's Assembly to the vicinity of the U.S. embassy.[32] Rights activists reported that the war was radicalizing Egypt, boosting the popularity of the Muslim Brotherhood, and further isolating the ever-embattled NGO community. One legal advocate said, "We have been set back 2–3 years. . . . reform advocates do not want U.S. pressure now for domestic reform, because if they welcome American support, they will be tainted as being traitors and accomplices of the war crimes the U.S. and Israel are committing in Lebanon." Another said, "All momentum for political reform in Egypt has been lost."[33]

On August 11, the UN Security Council unanimously adopted resolution 1701, which called for an end to hostilities, the withdrawal of Israeli forces, and the placement of UN peacekeepers to assist the Lebanese army.[34] On August 14, after eleventh-hour volleys that demonstrated neither side had been vanquished, fighting between Hezbollah and the IDF stopped.[35] The Israel-Hezbollah War had lasted thirty-four days and taken the lives of 1,187 Lebanese, combatants and civilians, and 160 Israelis, soldiers and civilians. Hundreds of thousands of Lebanese had also been forced to relocate.[36]

The war drew the Bush administration's attention back to the Arab-Israeli conflict and demonstrated that the United States still needed diplomatic help from its Arab allies. Welch, who was then Assistant Secretary of State for Near Eastern Affairs, explains that, "The Middle East kind of smacked us in the face with all its problems. 2006 was annus horribilis."[37] He continues:

> We certainly didn't want to alienate any of our friends, because we already had enough problems and the Egyptians were helpful in working some of them. . . . I think, realistically, people took a look at their priorities and gave them a bit of a rethink. Reality forced that upon us. Iraq . . . the Palestinian situation . . . a war in Lebanon . . . take your pick. Our hands were full.[38]

Whatever rhetorical weight Bush and Rice had assigned democracy promotion before 2006, the days of hectoring their Egyptian counterparts were over. William Inboden, who served on the National Security Council at the time, described the election of the Hamas government and the war in Lebanon as "the two events that were most jarring for the Freedom Agenda, or that certainly caused it to be revisited."[39] The result was a "softening line towards Mubarak and Egypt and the belief that, okay, we need to deal with this guy to keep Hamas reined in and as well as to keep Hezbollah reined in and get this Lebanon war resolved."[40] "[M]issing from '06 onward," averred Dunne, "was really the kind of fairly energetic, private diplomacy that went on in [2004 and 2005]."[41]

The Scion and the Spy

Events in 2006 erased any ambiguity about whether Mubarak's constitutional amendment served multiparty democracy or his family's
ambitions. The People's Assembly postponed for two years the elections to Egypt's municipal councils, which were a necessary step under
the amended constitution if nonlicensed opposition groups like the
Muslim Brotherhood were to field a presidential candidate.[42] Parliament also renewed the state of emergency for another two years,
abrogating a campaign pledge of Mubarak's to replace the Emergency
Law with an antiterrorism law. Decrying the extension, MPs from the
Muslim Brotherhood donned black sashes that read "No to Emergency" and forced a rare formal vote in parliament (which came up
257–91 for passing the measure). That spring, judges Mahmoud Makki
and Hisham al-Bastawisi endured disciplinary hearings for exposing outcome-changing electoral fraud the prior fall. Members of the
Muslim Brotherhood and Kefaya protested the proceedings. By the
middle of May, police had cordoned off much of downtown Cairo
and detained hundreds of protesters. The hearing board exonerated
Makki and reprimanded al-Bastawisi, a warning lest other jurists challenge Mubarak.[43] After the protests Kefaya struggled to grow in size
and the group's momentum ebbed.[44]

With Nour behind bars and independent judges under attack,
observers suspected Mubarak of tailoring Egypt's electoral system
for Gamal. In February, his son had become one of three assistant
secretaries-general in the NDP, a post that augmented his visibility
and political credentials. Meanwhile, no opposition figures qualified to
seek the presidency. "The issue of presidential succession is the hottest
single issue on Egypt's domestic political scene," stated an April cable
from the U.S. embassy. "Both Gamal and his father have repeatedly
denied that there is any plan for a 'succession scenario.' More important than such words, many Egyptians tell us, are the actions of Gamal,
his father, and others, which appear to be setting the stage for the young
Mubarak's rise to power."[45] The "others" included Bush's top advisors. On May 12, while demonstrations in Cairo raged, a journalist
outside the White House caught Gamal Mubarak entering. The sur-
reptitious visit included meetings with Cheney, Rice, National Security

Advisor Stephen Hadley, and, in an unscheduled drop-by, Bush himself.[46] The president had previously demurred from addressing the succession question publicly, but his chat with Gamal signaled his private assent.[47]

Although Gamal was the heir apparent, some members of the National Security Council questioned whether he was the best figure to guarantee Egypt's foreign policy alignment after Hosni Mubarak's tenure.[48] "It's the path of least resistance to be supportive of this particular autocratic regime," said Inboden, "but over time, that's not necessarily going to be reliable for our security interests ... especially ... [with] a real murkiness around the question of his successor. It is probably going to be Gamal, but who knows?"[49] If Gamal struggled to establish his authority, a dynastic succession could actually set back U.S. interests. "Whoever ends up as Egypt's next president likely will be politically weaker than Mubarak," reported the U.S. Embassy. Consequently, "the new president will likely adopt an anti-American tone in his initial public rhetoric, in an effort to prove his nationalist bona fides to the Egyptian street, and may possibly extend an olive branch to the Muslim Brotherhood as did previous Egyptian presidents at the beginning of their terms."[50] Abrams also reasoned that an electorally weak president, such as Gamal, might seek legitimacy through "anti-Americanism" and "a kind of populism that appeals to the street by distancing them from us and even from Israel and from the peace treaty."[51]

Suleiman was expected in Washington the same month Gamal visited, although the intelligence chief eluded the media.[52] According to the April 2006 U.S. embassy cable about succession, Suleiman was the only viable possible successor to Mubarak besides the president's son.[53] A later cable noted that "Our intelligence collaboration with Omar Suleiman is now probably the most successful element of the [U.S.-Egyptian] relationship."[54] Suleiman's military background, intelligence work, and policy experience made him a more reliable bet for U.S. policy than Gamal. If the logic held that anti-Americanism was a crutch of weak politicians, the veteran spy could rule from day one without excessive demagoguery. Moreover, Suleiman had proven himself a staunch ally of the United States and Israel, working to free Shalit and weaken Hamas.[55] During an October 2006 meeting in Cairo with foreign diplomats, Suleiman said, "The most important thing to

remember is that the Hamas government must not be allowed to succeed. It has to fall."[56]

Freedom in Reverse

Compared to the Palestinian elections, in 2006 Mubarak's authoritarianism evoked minimal concern on Capitol Hill and at the White
House. Diplomatic tensions over trade and NGO funding, while periodically heated, did not disrupt security cooperation or U.S. efforts to
squeeze the Hamas government. When the situation in the Gaza Strip
worsened in 2007, however, and U.S. policymakers began to think
Mubarak was not doing enough to weaken Hamas, Congress imposed
conditions (with an optional waiver for the executive branch) on U.S.
military aid to Egypt. The move harked back to efforts to "moderate"
Nasser's behavior by tugging on aid.[57] As in the earlier period, the
heart of conditionality aimed at changing Egyptian foreign policy, not
curbing internal repression.

Although the Bush administration sparred with the Mubarak regime
over a free trade agreement and restrictions on U.S.-backed NGOs in
Egypt, neither episode disturbed the core of the bilateral relationship.
After Nour went to prison, the Bush administration stopped pursuing
a U.S.-Egyptian free trade agreement (FTA). Although members of the
administration had been working on the deal for years, the final outcome was a tempest in a teacup. A sufficient number of congressional
representatives already opposed a U.S.-Egypt FTA for domestic economic reasons. Therefore, the agreement was improbable under the
best of circumstances.[58] Moreover, enthusiasm on the Egyptians' side
was waning. Although the neoliberals of the Nazif government sought
a free-trade agreement, Mubarak was not as interested. When the deal
flopped, he showed little disappointment.[59]

With respect to NGO funding, the Bush administration had long
objected to how Mubarak's cronies blocked U.S. aid dollars from
reaching Egyptian civil society organizations. In 2002, the Egyptian
government passed a law (Law 84/2002) that limited foreign funding for NGOs to approved groups and imposed regime supervision
on otherwise independent activity. Saad Eddin Ibrahim's Ibn Khaldun
Center and other groups circumvented the law by calling themselves
"civil companies," not NGOs. In 2005, as part of MEPI, the Bush

administration had granted the Ibn Khaldun Center and five other organizations grants of $1 million each. This money, distinct from economic support funds, was supposed to be administered without the Egyptian government being involved.[60] Egyptian officials argued, however, that the civil companies should have applied for a license, because their work fell under the purview of Law 84/2002.[61] In November 2005, members of Bush's foreign policy team tried again. Attending the second annual Forum for the Future in Manama, Bahrain, U.S. delegates attempted to generate a fund for NGOs that would not be subject to Egyptian approval. Foreign Minister Aboul Gheit insisted that recipient NGOs first be licensed by their respective governments.[62] Four other Arab delegations concurred with Egypt's position and quashed the Americans' idea.[63]

In summer 2006, the focus of the NGO controversy shifted from Egyptian organizations to U.S. groups operating in Egypt. On June 3 an independent Egyptian newspaper quoted Gina London, country director for the International Republican Institute (IRI), as saying, "There has been a democratic movement in Egypt for over twenty-five years, but it has not succeeded in speeding up change." London allegedly traced the impasse to lack of funding, claiming the Egyptian movement had not been granted the "assistance received by the democratic movements in Romania and Ukraine." IRI had operated in Egypt for nearly a year and had reported on the 2005 parliamentary elections. But the mention of Ukraine suggested to some Egyptians that the United States was fomenting an "Orange Revolution" against Mubarak. A Ministry of Foreign Affairs spokesman dubbed London's remarks "blatant interference in Egypt's internal affairs." The ministry then forced IRI to halt its activities.[64] London, who claimed her remarks had been misreported, later resigned her post and left Egypt. Although the Bush administration could continue offering small grants, as it had in 2005, the Egyptian government would oversee the much larger pot of democracy promotion money in the economic support funds. The fiscal year 2007 budget allocated $50 million of the total $455 million for "democracy, governance, and human rights programs," with at least half going to "nongovernmental organizations for the purpose of strengthening Egyptian civil society organizations."[65] As far as Mubarak and foreign minister Aboul Gheit were concerned, those NGOs would need to be formally approved and registered under Law 84/2002.

The White House and most of Congress opposed pressuring Mubarak through aid to change his domestic policies, however much they inconvenienced IRI and other pillars of the democratization industry. An *unsuccessful* attempt at conditionality exposed how much Washington appreciated its reliance on the Egyptian regime. In the spring of 2006, Congressman David Obey (D-WI) cited human rights violations in Egypt and tried in committee to tie $200 million in military aid to political reform.[66] Secretary Rice pushed back, asserting in a letter to committee members that any aid cuts would damage a "strategic partnership" that was "a cornerstone of U.S. policy in the Middle East."[67] The Wisconsin representative then took a modified version of his original proposal to the House floor.

Obey, Tom Lantos (D-CA), and Henry Hyde (R-IL) cosponsored an amendment to transfer $100 million from the economic support funds for Egypt to refugee assistance in Sudan and Bush's HIV/AIDS initiative. Calling himself no "naïve peddler of global democracy," Obey acknowledged that free elections had wrought "disastrous consequences" in the West Bank and Gaza – but the situation in Egypt presaged an even larger catastrophe. He said that Egyptian "backsliding on municipal elections, an extension of emergency laws, repression of judicial freedoms and a crackdown on demonstrations and rallies" harmed moderates and empowered the Muslim Brotherhood. Although Egypt's aging ruler had "done many constructive things . . . in the interest of peace in the region and . . . helped promote [U.S.] national interests," Obey concluded that "Congress has an obligation . . . to act before it is too late to salvage the situation."[68] For his part, Lantos was "sickened" that Nour would be imprisoned "on transparently manufactured charges when . . . his only real crime was having the temerity to wage a political campaign against Mr. Mubarak." Lantos excoriated the regime for manipulating elections, intimidating judges, and shuttering IRI. "I do not denigrate the importance of our alliance with Egypt, and I deeply appreciate the importance of the Israeli-Egyptian peace," Lantos offered. "But I do feel that we deserve more, much more for our generosity than the laundry list of problems I have only partially described."[69]

Speaking in opposition, lawmakers from both parties warned against jeopardizing an alliance that served U.S. security. "The main reason we do foreign assistance is we do it in the American national interest," argued Roger Wicker (R-MS):

We do not have a lot of friends over there. But one friend we have in that area is Egypt.... Talk about national interests: When we went in with Operation Iraqi Freedom, some of our allies, Turkey, for example, would not let us through ... By contrast, Egypt has allowed us to use the Suez for that purpose. They have allowed us continuous overflights. And just recently, they have been instrumental in helping with the unilateral Israeli withdrawal from the Gaza [Strip].... My friends, these people in Egypt have stood by us in a tough, tough neighborhood. And I do not think this amendment is the sort of thing we do to our friends. It might make us feel good, but it is terrible foreign policy.[70]

Representative Carolyn Kilpatrick (D-MI) pointed out that "Egypt supports us in the Gaza Strip and the Egyptian border.... They buy our U.S. military equipment ... hundreds of millions of dollars [in U.S. aid were] being spent for our own security."[71]

The argument about Egypt's help in the Gaza Strip resonated. Long-serving congressman David Price (D-NC) noted his advocacy for human rights in Egypt, including several years working on Ibrahim's case. He then stressed Suleiman's management of Israeli-Palestinian issues:

Egyptian leaders like General Suleiman have intervened in discussions and negotiations when the U.S. simply cannot do so.... In an effort to prevent Fatah's disorganization from enabling a Hamas victory in Palestinian elections, General Suleiman worked with Abu Mazen [Mahmoud Abbas] in December 2005 to try to mediate between splinter parties. In December 2004, during a period of heavy attacks against Israel, General Suleiman initiated a dialogue with Hamas and the Islamic Jihad and other Palestinian militant groups to seek an end to the attacks. Mr. Chairman, we are facing a critical period in the Middle East. The political crisis caused by Hamas's victory makes Egyptian mediation more, not less, critical. That is decisive for me.[72]

Suleiman's intelligence work may have sealed the amendment's fate. Two years earlier an initiative by Lantos to shift military aid to economic support had failed 287 to 131.[73] When a vote was taken in 2006, the Obey-Hyde-Lantos amendment failed by a slim margin, 198 to 225.[74] Had Price and thirteen colleagues switched sides, the aid cut would have passed.

Observers who had hailed the Freedom Agenda in 2005 chided the U.S. government for switching from democracy promotion to security promotion. "Apart from freezing negotiations for a free-trade agreement," wrote two Washington-based Egypt experts, "the administration has kept a low profile on Egypt's disturbing political developments." They continued, "Most strikingly, without any objection from the Bush administration, Congress recently approved yet again a multibillion-dollar economic and military aid package for Egypt, without asking anything in return from the Mubarak regime regarding political reform."[75] What the White House was seeking from Mubarak had little to do with democracy and human rights, and everything to do with controlling the Gaza Strip.

The Gaza Takeover

In fall 2006, the Bush administration escalated its campaign to dislodge Hamas. Armed forces loyal to Fatah, some seventy thousand strong, outnumbered the twelve thousand men in Hamas's police and militias. In October, Rice encouraged Abbas to take action against the Islamist movement; he demurred. The administration then began funneling materiel to Abbas's security chief, Mohammed Dahlan, through Arab allies. While Dahlan prepared for a confrontation, Hamas and Fatah were abducting, torturing, and in some cases murdering each other's members in a feud that killed dozens.[76] In late December, four trucks arrived from Egypt for Dahlan carrying two thousand rifles and two million rounds of ammunition. In January, the U.S. State Department announced it would provide $86 million to strengthen Fatah's security forces against Hamas and diminish the influence of Iran – the presumptive beneficiary of crises in the Palestinian Authority, Lebanon, and Iraq.[77] That winter, the Palestinian Authority verged on civil war. On February 1, 2007, Dahlan's forces set several buildings aflame at the Islamic University of Gaza, which was affiliated with Hamas. Before both sides went over the brink, however, Saudi Arabia offered to mediate between them. On February 8, Fatah and Hamas accepted the Mecca Agreement, a power-sharing deal in which Hamas held on to the prime ministership, Fatah officials retained several key posts, and Saudi Arabia bankrolled the salaries of officials from both groups.

This diplomatic breakthrough did not change the demands of the Bush administration and the Quartet. Hamas still needed to accept past agreements, renounce violence, and recognize Israel. Rice's team outlined a course for Abbas to dissolve the National Unity Government if Hamas did not accept the Quartet's conditions. This political step would be backed up by force: Fatah would receive additional resources, plus training in Egypt and Jordan, to defeat Hamas militarily.[78] In the middle of May, five hundred newly trained, well-equipped, and crisply uniformed men from Abbas's National Security Forces arrived in Gaza from Egypt. The next month Fatah requested "dozens of armored cars, hundreds of armor-piercing rocket-propelled grenades, thousands of hand grenades and millions of rounds of ammunition" to be delivered from Egypt.[79]

Reports of U.S. attempts to overthrow Hamas had already leaked to the Jordanian press. The expansion of Dahlan's apparatus signaled a putsch was imminent. On June 12, Hamas assaulted Fatah's security buildings in Gaza rather than waiting for Fatah to strike first. Despite their lucrative U.S. support and Egyptian training, Dahlan's fighters could not muster an effective counteroffensive. Hamas razed Dahlan's office and house, took over Abbas's residence in Gaza, and, by June 16, controlled all other buildings in the area associated with Fatah.[80] The battle tore the Palestinian Authority in two. Hamas held the Gaza Strip. President Abbas dissolved the unity government and tapped a new prime minister, Salam Fayyad, to administer the Fatah-controlled West Bank half of the Palestinian Authority.[81] In response, the United States announced it would resume aid to the government of Abbas, partially ending the post-election embargo. Suleiman's security forces, which had been on the losing side, pulled out of Gaza.[82]

After Hamas took control of the Gaza Strip, fingers on Capitol Hill pointed at Egypt. The House Appropriations Committee, under Democratic control, proposed striking $200 million in assistance unless the Egyptian government safeguarded judicial independence, curbed police brutality, and did more to fight tunnel smuggling into Gaza.[83] On the House floor, Lantos asserted that:

> The nightmare that is unfolding in Gaza is in no small measure the responsibility of the Government of Egypt. Egypt has a huge military, and it boggles the mind to assume that the Egyptian military would

not have been able to seal Gaza from the constant flow of drugs, weapons and persons being trafficked into Gaza had they attempted to do so.[84]

The bill imposing conditionality sailed through (241 to 178).[85] Compared to the vote a year earlier, the threatened cut to military assistance appeared driven by an acute concern about Hamas, rather than by chronic repression in Egypt.

As it happened, Egyptians were shouldering more responsibility for security in Gaza than they had originally expected. The 2005 arrangement for Israel's redeployment assigned a three-party Israeli–Palestinian Authority–European staff to control the Gaza side of the Rafah border crossing with Egypt. After Hamas expelled Dahlan's soldiers, the monitoring mission departed. Henceforth, the Gaza Strip's sole external crossing (to exit Israel and the Palestinian Authority) was Rafah at the Gaza-Egypt border, and it remained nearly completely shut. Egypt was left enforcing the international embargo on goods. Flows of workers and basic commodities ground to a halt, consigning most of the 1.5 million inhabitants of the Gaza Strip to unemployment and impoverishment. When conditions worsened for Palestinians, Egypt appeared to be a junior warden to Israel.[86]

Like U.S. and Israeli officials, Mubarak and his lieutenants wanted to undermine Hamas by restricting supplies entering Gaza. During a July 2007 meeting with members of the Knesset, Suleiman argued for letting the population barely subsist: "The people of Gaza must not be starved, but there's no need to help them too much. Keep them going on the minimum." When told by the parliamentarians that Gaza residents needed one hundred tons of fuel a day, the intelligence czar answered, "There's no need to give them one hundred tons; thirty to forty tons is enough for vital needs."[87] In November, after more rocket fire from Gaza, Israel cut food supplies into the area by half and limited the flow of fuel and foreign currency coming in.[88] Despite these measures, Hamas nearly doubled its stocks of munitions in a matter of months.[89]

A key suspected passage for materiel was the underground tunnels that stretched from houses on the Gaza side of Rafah into the Sinai Peninsula. This subterranean network had existed since 1982, when the Israelis left Sinai. Under the embargo, it had expanded prodigiously. As demand and prices for basic goods rose, the money made by smugglers and tunnel managers soared. On the Egyptian side, the security services and armed forces repeatedly attacked the Bedouin population in northern Sinai to repress communities aiding the smugglers.[90] As for destroying tunnels or manning the border more effectively, the 1979 peace treaty limited the Egyptian Ministry of Defense to 750 border police in the area and prohibited heavy military vehicles.[91] For the Ministry of Defense, it was a no-win situation: The longer the border stayed closed, the more profitable smuggling and tunnel construction became. As the Egyptian military attaché in Washington, Major General Mohamed Elkeshky, later argued, the problem was on the demand side, within Gaza, and no external power could seal the border completely: "No one can secure this border one hundred percent. Look to your borders [between the U.S. and Mexico] . . . the tunnels will never stop until we allow the people to get their human needs."[92]

Egypt's actions and constraints did not stop U.S. and Israeli officials from demanding greater vigilance. In the fall of 2007, Yuval Diskin, the director of Israel's internal security agency (Shin Bet), complained that Suleiman had not followed up on Israeli intelligence about known traffickers and was not "cleansing the Sinai" as he had promised. Even more troubling than the tunnel entrances in the Sinai were the smuggling routes farther south. Goods came overland, mostly from Sudan, and Egypt was not exploiting its considerable assets in that country to stop the problem at its source.[93] The Bush administration offered to provide Minister of Defense Tantawi with outside experts to propose technical improvements. As reported from the U.S. embassy, Egypt's military commander partially "relented and permitted a U.S. Army Corps of Engineers team to assess the border situation," but his government insisted it had to act with care because of political sensitivities surrounding Gaza: "The Egyptians continue to offer excuses for the problem they face: the need to 'squeeze' Hamas, while avoiding being seen as complicit in Israel's 'siege' of Gaza." Egyptian officials also cautioned the United States that if the border were not opened periodically and at key periods, like the season of pilgrimage to Mecca, then "Hamas would blow a hole in the wall and the Egyptians would not be able to control the influx that ensued."[94]

Unfazed by the Egyptians' arguments, Congress moved closer to conditioning aid. The argument Obey and Lantos made about sending Egypt a message dovetailed with Israeli frustration about arms entering Gaza. Traditionally, pro-Israel lobbyists had advocated sustaining assistance to Egypt. In 2007, those same figures were notably quiet about the impending linkage of military aid to Egyptian policy changes.[95] The Senate did not include the House's conditionality article in its version of the appropriations bill, and the differences were set to be reconciled in conference committee. Tipping deliberations toward the aid restrictions, senators from the U.S.-Israel Joint Parliamentary Committee on National Security encouraged one of their Israeli colleagues to write the Senate and support conditionality in the final bill. MP Yuval Steinitz of the Likud Party distributed a letter to all 100 senators, charging that "Egypt's de facto behavior in the field supports Hamas.... As long as Egypt is not required to pay a real price for this behavior, weapons and financial aid will continue to flow into the hands of Hamas and other terrorist groups in Gaza."[96]

In December, Congress passed, and President Bush signed, an appropriations act that included half of the original aid cuts.[97] For FY 2008, $100 million in economic and military aid to Egypt would depend on the secretary of state certifying that Egypt had met the conditions on policy reform and smuggling efforts *or* on her waiving those conditions for national security reasons.[98] Although Congress seemed to have outdone Bush in his signature area of democracy promotion, representatives had mainly backed the bill to fight smuggling and protect Israel – to good effect, some claimed. "Egypt is an ally," commented Representative Nita Lowey (D-NY), "but it is important to make clear that they must do more to eliminate smuggling tunnels and networks that lead from Egypt to Gaza." The message had gotten through, as Steve Israel (D-NY) observed: "From the moment Congress began circulating the language conditioning aid to Egypt, the Egyptians began to make an effort to close the tunnels."[99]

Return to Diplomacy

While Congress was finalizing the budget and aid conditionality, Bush was making a late entry into multilateral peace efforts. It was a lopsided endeavor, given that he continued to exclude Hamas, but it constituted a significant uptick in U.S. diplomatic efforts on the Arab-Israeli conflict. In mid-July, he affirmed his goal of a Palestinian state free of terrorism and pledged another $80 million to Abbas's security forces "to strengthen the forces of moderation and peace among the Palestinian people."[100] His remarks echoed the 2002 Rose Garden speech, although Hamas had replaced Arafat as Bush's bête noire. But in 2007, he proposed an international conference, with significant participation from Egypt, Jordan, and possibly even Syria. Annapolis, Maryland, was selected as the conference location, and the event became a focus of State Department efforts.

Belatedly, the Bush administration was coming back to the diplomatic approaches of its forerunners. This shift presupposed warmer relations with Mubarak. As Abrams recalled:

> I think one of the things that happened... was that [Rice], in particular, became deeply devoted to, and involved in, the Israeli-Palestinian peace negotiations in 2007–2008.... And... once you do that... You lose all your focus on Egypt the country. All you care about is Hosni Mubarak and his foreign minister and their role with respect to Israel.... I think once that happened... the president and she pulled their punches more and were not as candid in '07 and '08 as they had been in '05 and '06.... they hadn't been hostile to Egypt, but they had put some pressure on.[101]

Likewise, Ambassador Fahmy saw bilateral ties improving as the White House focused on regional diplomacy: "At the presidential level, there was a rapprochement."[102]

Diplomatic outreach coincided with massive arms sales to U.S. allies. In Sharm El-Sheikh at the end of July, Rice and Secretary of Defense Robert Gates offered a $20-billion package of advanced weaponry, equipment, and vehicles, the bulk of which would go to Saudi Arabia, along with smaller amounts of materiel for nearby Bahrain, Kuwait, Oman, Qatar, and the United Arab Emirates. Fortifying the Arab Gulf states against Iran, though, would arguably reduce Israel's relative military advantage.[103] To ensure Israeli dominance, the White House pledged $30 billion in foreign military financing for Israel during the next decade, a 25 percent increase.[104] Military assistance to Egypt would be $13 billion for the next ten years, rounding up amounts that were already near $1.3 billion annually. For U.S. policy on Iran, Egypt was a second-tier player compared to Israel and Saudi Arabia. By not substantially raising military aid to Egypt above current levels, the agreement ended the historic 3:2 ratio of U.S. assistance to Israel and Egypt.[105]

After participating in the Annapolis peace conference in late November, the Egyptian government was shocked by Congress's conditions on military aid.[106] The economic support funds, Egyptians thought, shielded the $1.3 billion going to the Egyptian armed forces. According to Ibrahim, Mubarak saw military aid as a red line: "[Once] I heard him personally say . . . that so long as he keeps the military happy, with the continuous flow of supply of arms, the U.S. can do whatever is needed to be done, to get through Congress and so on, with the civilian part."[107] According to the U.S. embassy, Egyptian officials "thought their self-interest in [wanting Hamas to fail] was so obvious to us, to Abu Mazen [Mahmoud Abbas], and to the Israelis – as it is to Mubarak's domestic opposition – as to be beyond all question." Suleiman dubbed Israel's lobbying in Washington a "hostile act."[108] The Foreign Ministry rejected Congress's move as outside interference in Egyptian affairs.[109]

By early 2008 the furor had mostly subsided. Israeli defense minister Ehud Barak visited Egypt before the New Year on a fence-mending mission.[110] At the start of January, Congressman Steve Israel conveyed to Mubarak that the debate was over and Egypt was already doing a better job of tackling the smuggling problem.[111] On January 30, an Israeli official echoed the sentiment: "There has been dramatic progress made with the Egyptians with regards to sealing the open border in Rafah."[112] By that time, though, the Egyptians had been proven right about Gaza being a pressure cooker. On January 18, responding to rocket fire on Sderot, Israel had imposed a complete blockade. Five days later, Hamas detonated charges along the southern border wall. Bulldozer crews then completed the demolition job, punching a massive hole through which tens of thousands of Palestinians poured into Egypt. For days, Palestinians moved unhindered through the passage – a freedom they had not enjoyed since Israel's 1982 withdrawal from the Sinai. Exploiting this reprieve, they stocked up on essentials, including gas, food, cement, and clothing.[113]

The next month, the State Department swept aside the conditions on aid. During the earlier congressional debate, Rice had broadcast her opposition. In a joint letter to Speaker of the House Nancy Pelosi, she and Gates had stressed the importance of unrestricted foreign military financing for Egypt: "As a central pillar of our bilateral relationship with Egypt, U.S. military assistance is essential to our success in achieving our foreign policy objectives in the region. . . . Conditioning any portion of [foreign military funding] could cause grave damage to U.S. national security interests." They averred that Egypt had made progress in the areas flagged in the appropriations bill. Conceding that "much work remains to be done in promoting human rights, judicial reform, and border security in Egypt," Rice and Gates insisted that "withholding funds destined for the Egyptian military will *not* help achieve these goals."[114]

Even though the administration defended its military financing for Egypt as a plank of the larger security relationship, it often found the Egyptian army unhelpful. Despite its "modernization" under U.S. aid and training programs, the Egyptian military was primarily geared to fight a 1973-style war with Israel and defend the country's expansive territory. "Egypt is completely desert," explained Elkeshky. "So what is working [for] us is the tank. We need tanks, we need mobility. . . . We don't work in the city. If you work in the city it's . . . something [else]. . . . [We are] working in the desert. In the western desert, in the south, in the Sinai."[115] By contrast, the Pentagon had reoriented its doctrine not to defend territory from hostile armies but to govern it through "counterinsurgency."[116] The evolution of Operation Bright Star reflected the disconnect between the two militaries. After nearly three decades of joint exercises, the Egyptian military was still not interoperable with U.S. land and air forces.[117] From a peak in 1999 of 70,000 participating troops, the biennial war games comprised 34,000 soldiers in 2005 and 7,000 troops in 2007.[118]

U.S. officials considered Tantawi, who had led the Egyptian Armed Forces since 1991, to be "change-resistant," "uncomfortable with our shift to the post-9/11 GWOT [Global War on Terror]," and "mired in a post-Camp David military paradigm."[119] The field marshal bristled at cuts in the size of Bright Star and cherished a large-scale military tackling large-scale missions.[120] He had also been stunned by the 2007 conditionality bill. Even after the restrictions were waived, he objected to investing in counterterrorism at the expense of conventional forces and chafed at U.S. attempts to micromanage Egypt's antismuggling efforts.[121] Tantawi balked at foreign militaries playing any kind of tutelary role on Egyptian soil and resisted the introduction of new antismuggling monitoring systems. Elkeshky explained, "It's our sovereignty, our dignity, and I am not going to let you come to put up some equipment to observe my home, 24/7. You don't have this

right."[122] Only after Rice intervened would Tantawi accept a team
from the U.S. Army Corps of Engineers to assess the tunnels. The
estimated $23 million required for training, sensors, and robots for
probing underground would come out of existing U.S. military aid
allocations.[123] Already, those funds were stretched thin. The military
aid package had never been adjusted for inflation and had lost half
its real value since 1979. Moreover, the lion's share of the military
aid (73 percent) went to maintaining and upgrading current systems.
The Egyptian military was left with $351 million for new weapons
systems, which it often paid for over multiple years.[124] The reduction
of military aid in real terms, and in relative terms compared to what
Israel received, reflected the diminishing geostrategic importance of the
Egyptian army.

On February 29, 2008, Assistant Secretary of State John Negroponte invoked a built-in national waiver on the $100 million in
economic and military assistance that allowed the administration to
supersede the conditionality in cases affecting national security. An
accompanying letter explained that Egyptian support for U.S. diplomacy and military operations in the region made punitive actions
"counterproductive at a time in which we are asking the Government of Egypt to do more to move regional issues of mutual concern
in the right direction." Further, the aid restrictions threatened to sap
the "good will that our decades of partnership have built up" and
"force the U.S. government to choose between damaging our economic
assistance programs in Egypt or our mutually advantageous military
cooperation."[125] Democracy advocates who had lauded Bush's efforts
in Egypt in 2005 derided the 180-degree turn. "The Bush administration once was ready to express its dissatisfaction with Mr. Mubarak in
practical ways," opined the *Washington Post*. "Three years after Mr.
Bush promised the world's democratic reformers that the United States
would stand with them, the administration has so reversed itself that
it joins Mr. Mubarak in rejecting restrictions attached by Congress to
aid money."[126]

Conclusion

The second Bush term witnessed a rare attempt by Washington to
use the United States' unparalleled assistance to an autocratic ally

to change that regime's behavior. The move did not originate at the White House, however, and it was not intended to impose political reform or derail a Mubarak dynasty. Congress was pressuring Egyptian officials to ramp up their efforts against Hamas. Some of the same representatives who voted for conditionality had defended the Egyptian regime just a year earlier, and their positions were not inconsistent. After Palestinian voters produced a Hamas-led government in 2006, U.S. lawmakers feared Egyptians might replicate that outcome. In addition, many politicians on Capitol Hill considered Suleiman a useful ombudsman between the Palestinian factions. But after Hamas repelled Dahlan's coup attempt in 2007, stopping arms and resources from reaching Hamas became paramount. Representatives yanked the purse strings on U.S. aid to make the Egyptians fight smugglers more aggressively. They focused their ire on the Egyptian army, which seemed inept or unwilling to address U.S. and Israeli concerns about security along the Gaza Strip. Meanwhile, the Egyptian General Intelligence Services remained indispensable for antiterrorism and backchannel talks with the Palestinians.

Ironically, the U.S. president who had called for Egypt to lead the way toward Arab democracy came to Mubarak's defense. Bush and Rice had accepted the value of traditional U.S. diplomacy in the Middle East and could not afford to alienate Mubarak. Whereas they repudiated the United States' "sixty years" of cozying up with Middle Eastern dictators, in practice they reproduced that tradition. The Freedom Agenda found its targets through the periscope of U.S. national security: Arafat, Saddam Hussein, Hamas. The Bush White House never sought to remove pro-U.S. dictators in Egypt and other strategic locations.

5

Groundswell

While the Freedom Agenda receded, internal challenges to Mubarak escalated. This chapter analyzes how Egyptian politics grew more contentious during 2006–2011. As workers' actions spread, a "culture of protest" swept the country, and, eventually, millions took to the streets. The January 25 Revolution brought the Egyptian people to the fore of domestic policies and opened the prospect of a more equitable relationship between Cairo and Washington.

The potency of mass demonstrations against Mubarak raises important questions about the resilience of authoritarianism. In my prior book, for example, I maintained that changes from authoritarianism to democracy begin when elites defect from the ruling coalition.[1] In Egypt, core elites stood pat for weeks. Dr. Hossam Badrawi, a quintessential regime "soft-liner," later admitted he had favored the same limited constitutional changes advanced by Mubarak, Suleiman, and the White House; he never asked Mubarak to resign.[2] Such fealty speaks volumes, for although the Egyptian uprising did not deliver democratization – or even regime change – it demonstrated the power of "bottom-up" mass movements to influence otherwise complacent elites.[3]

Contrary to the image of a teetering regime, in many respects Mubarak's Egypt in winter 2010–2011 resembled the collision of massive repression and widespread discontent before the Autumn of Fury. The coercive apparatus was well equipped. Internally, the regime cohered. Although top security officials Suleiman and

Tantawi begrudged Gamal Mubarak, they did not obstruct his ascent or maneuver to seize power. Meanwhile, the opposition to Mubarak looked ineffectual. Egyptian workers commanded much larger constituencies than did Kefaya but they generally did not pay attention to the activists centered in Cairo. Labor instead focused energy on improving salaries and benefits, as well as on prying their unions away from government control. The two distinct streams of opposition were gaining strength, however. Workers denounced the regime's exploitive economic reforms, while Cairo-based dissidents slammed the succession scheme and police brutality. As the grievances accumulated through 2010, Mubarak and his lieutenants blithely persisted in rigging elections and preying on the populace.

Egypt's Malcontents

After 2005 Bush muted his calls for political reform in Egypt, while the Mubaraks prepared a hereditary succession. In March 2007, the regime again modified the Egyptian constitution to stage Gamal's future election to the presidency.

Thanks to the 2005 amendments, aspiring presidential candidates would need to belong to a licensed party with 5 percent of the seats in the two houses of parliament (the People's Assembly and the largely symbolic Consultative Assembly), or would have to collect signatures from 250 elected officials, including 90 parliamentarians and 140 members of local councils.[4] The NDP held hegemonic majorities throughout parliament, ran the parties' authorizing committee, and pervaded the relevant councils, making it very difficult for opposition figures to qualify. The skewed 2005 parliamentary elections, coupled with the postponement of municipal council polls in 2006, made the prospect virtually impossible. But if the bar was not lowered, only a single candidate, the ruling party's candidate, would appear on the ballot. A de facto plebiscite would be a huge embarrassment for a regime that had touted the introduction of multicandidate polls.

Amendments in 2007 made it easier for official opposition parties (the Wafd, Tagammu) to field presidential candidates, although licensed parties would have to hold a seat in one house of parliament and could only nominate members from their executive boards. For Egypt's most vibrant nonparty groups, therefore the barriers to entry remained insurmountable. The Muslim Brotherhood, Kefaya, and other nonlicensed groups would need to gather signatures in institutions run by the NDP. "The change will ostensibly facilitate more competitive presidential elections," the U.S. Embassy concluded, "while still protecting against any serious challenge to the NDP candidate."[5] In addition to rigging elections in Gamal's favor, the 2007 amendments reinforced the ability of the president to refer civilians to military courts, and enabled him to circumvent individual freedoms (of privacy and from arbitrary arrest) in terrorism-related cases. They also reduced the judiciary's electoral oversight power and hindered any effort by the Muslim Brotherhood to form a political party.[6]

In the middle of 2007, while the Mubaraks were plotting succession, Bush delivered a valediction for the Freedom Agenda. At Czernin Palace in Prague, the White House's democratic muse, Sharansky, gathered critics of authoritarianism from seventeen countries, including Saad Eddin Ibrahim from Egypt. At the occasion Bush remarked, "America pursues our freedom agenda in many ways, some vocal and visible, others quiet and hidden from view." He invoked Ayman Nour, along with "democratic dissidents" from Belarus, Burma (Myanmar), Cuba, and Vietnam, and he spoke privately with Ibrahim. Bush also announced that he had "asked Secretary Rice to send a directive to every U.S. ambassador in an unfree nation: Seek out and meet with activists for democracy. Seek out those who demand human rights."[7] In fact, U.S. diplomats already communicated regularly with local opposition figures. With respect to Egypt, neither Bush nor U.S. officials in the field would press Mubarak any harder about Nour and other prisoners. Just by meeting with Ibrahim on the side, however, Bush stoked Mubarak's suspicion that the White House desired a Ukraine-style regime change. At the advice of U.S. ambassador to Egypt Francis Ricciardone, who sensed Mubarak might retaliate, Ibrahim stayed abroad, entering a self-imposed exile that would last more than three years.[8]

Some of the Freedom Agenda's putative beneficiaries in Egypt bemoaned Bush's Prague speech for going too far. Ayman Nour's wife, Gameela Ismail, worried that by specifically mentioning her husband's case the U.S. president had reduced the chance of Nour winning an early medical release from prison.[9] Other Egyptians felt the U.S. president was not doing enough. In the fall of 2007, Bush hosted a group of democratic activists at the White House. Among them was Egyptian publisher Hisham Kassem, founder of the widely read independent daily *al-Misry al-Yom* (*The Egyptian Today*). According to Kassem, Bush asked about NDP reformists (an oxymoron in Kassem's view) and declared, "We give your country $2 billion a year in order to keep it stable and prevent it from turning into a theocracy." From 2003 through 2005, Kassem had celebrated the United States' relatively assertive stance toward Mubarak. He exited the meeting crestfallen: "[Bush's] more or less lack of interest in what is happening politically in Egypt left me without any doubt that this whole [democracy] program was over."[10]

After its *annus horribilis*, the Bush administration recognized Egypt as an ally against Hamas and other shared enemies. It also understood that the price of Arab cooperation was U.S. attention to the Israeli-Palestinian conflict. In Sharm El-Sheikh in January 2008, Bush praised Mubarak's support of the Annapolis meeting.[11] Ambassador Fahmy recalled that the trip went well, and Mubarak received Bush with greater warmth than he had displayed in past visits to Washington.[12] During a second trip to Sharm El-Sheikh, this time for the World Economic Forum, Bush asserted the Freedom Agenda would bring progress over the long term. Asked by a local talk-show host about the state of democracy in Egypt, Bush answered, "I would say fits and starts; good news and bad news. In other words, there's been some moments where it looked like Egypt was going to continue to lead the Middle East on the democracy movement, and there's [sic] been some setbacks."[13] "What you're beginning to see is new democracies," he told a U.S. journalist. "You'll see a Palestinian state. You'll see Iraq emerging. And it doesn't happen overnight. . . . The freedom movement is a challenge to a system that said the status quo is acceptable – when underneath was brewing all kinds of resentments."[14]

At the time, Egyptians vehemently rejected Bush's and Mubarak's policies. Hundreds of miles from the World Economic Forum, protesters in Cairo denounced both men. Islamists and liberals slammed Bush for devastating the region, and they railed at Mubarak for repressing his critics and abetting U.S. policies. At a Kefaya demonstration, one leftist explained: "We don't differentiate between the American administration and Mubarak's regime. They each serve the other."[15] The outcry showed that although bilateral relations had improved, discontent against Mubarak had grown. In the wake of the Freedom Agenda, Egyptian workers and Internet activists were confirming its precepts: The regime was not indefinitely stable. Without serious reforms, Mubarak could fall and be replaced by the Muslim Brotherhood or other forces hostile to U.S. strategy. Moreover, the liberal opposition that included Ibrahim and Nour was only part of the picture. A larger cohort of protesters came from blue-collar professions. Egyptian workers struggled with rising food prices and stagnant wages, for which they blamed the Nazif government and its neoliberal policies.

After a sluggish start in the early 1990s, structural adjustment had taken off. In the first twenty months after Mubarak appointed the Nazif cabinet in July 2004, private investors purchased eighty state-owned companies, 27 percent of the total sold since 1991.[16] Managers of the companies being sold often slashed labor costs – through layoffs, early retirements, and pension reductions – to entice buyers.[17] These measures aggravated workers who were already struggling against government exploitation.[18] Whereas during 1998–2003 there were an average of one hundred contentious labor actions each year, in 2004–2006 there were twice as many.[19] The defiance of Egyptian workers, however, led to a kind of entente between local unions and national political leaders. The regime would tolerate strikes that were technically illegal (not authorized by the government-controlled Egyptian Trade Union Federation) and often respond with negotiations rather than with repression.[20] In this context, of calibrated resistance to the exploitative sell-offs of state-owned industries, textile workers in the Delta town of Mahalla al-Kubra drew national attention.[21]

In December 2006, after the Nazif government broke a promise to provide a two-month salary bonus to workers at Misr [Egypt] Spinning and Weaving, 20,000 textile workers in Mahalla struck for three days.[22] For male and female workers, the supplemental income would have bridged the gap between their regular wages, last raised in 1984, and the costs of supporting their families. Demonstrators also called for independent union leadership at the local and national levels, not managers from the regime-controlled General Union of Textile Workers.[23] Mahalla showcased the struggle for workers' rights, and direct actions continued into 2007. The Egyptian government boasted its third straight year of 7 percent GDP growth, and the World Bank recognized Egypt for having the world's most improved investment climate.[24] Yet Egyptian labor staunchly opposed the practices that earned their government such accolades, and there were three times as many instances of working-class protest across the country as there had been in 2006.[25]

The workers' rights movement was rolling forward while Kefaya was losing steam. But the men and women of Mahalla did not share the goals of the Cairo-based group and were barely aware of its existence.[26] Egyptians fighting to improve labor conditions did not push a national political agenda, like Solidarity had in Poland, but instead worked locally on the problems of their industries.[27] Occasionally strike leaders situated their grievances in problems of political corruption and misrule by Mubarak, but criticisms of the regime were the exception.[28] The tendency was to focus on basic living conditions, which were deteriorating under the Nazif government.[29] Affordable bread had become increasingly difficult to obtain, and eleven people died of exhaustion or in violent scuffles while queuing for hours at government bakeries.[30] As the government selectively reduced subsidies, gasoline prices rose 30 percent in the summer of 2006. From 2005 to 2008, the cost of basic foodstuffs, including milk, cheese, eggs, and beans, shot up by 100 to 150 percent.[31] The gap between earnings and the cost of supporting a family pushed more and more blue- and white-collar employees into contentious politics.[32] In 2007–2008, more than a million Egyptians took part in this tsunami of collective action, the largest popular movement the Arab world had seen since World War II.[33]

Differences between the material campaigns of Mahalla residents and the political reform calls from Cairo activists were on display in April 2008. To advance negotiations with the management of Misr Spinning and Weaving, workers called for a general strike on April 6.[34] Two weeks before the general strike was scheduled to begin, a group of young political activists led by Israa Abdel Fatah, who had previously affiliated with Nour's al-Ghad party, called on Egyptians to stay home in solidarity with the Mahalla workers. She and her compatriots gathered supporters through Facebook (garnering 70,000 "friends"), text messaging, and flyers.[35] The elevation of the Mahalla dispute into a national cause brought atypical attention to the factory and, in the view of at least one Mahalla worker, sabotaged labor's strategy.[36] Regime security forces occupied the factory on April 2. Concerted pressure, plus a small number of concessions including "free transportation to and from work," convinced the local leaders to call off the general strike. In lieu of a work stoppage, however, Mahalla saw mass demonstrations on April 6 over a dearth of bread. In a blow to the regime's iconography, participants destroyed a billboard of President Mubarak and tore down posters for the NDP. When protests grew the following day, the Ministry of Interior clamped down, shooting dead one teenager, arresting more than three hundred people, and injuring hundreds more. Twenty-two protesters were sentenced to three to five years in jail by one of the regime's emergency courts.[37] The clash brought Nazif to visit Mahalla and forced concessions, including a one-month pay bonus and better distribution of bread.[38]

Back in Cairo, few harked to the call for a general strike.[39] Still, the Internet-based group had succeeded in alarming the regime. State security detained organizer Israa Abdel Fatah for two weeks, holding her incommunicado, and later held and tortured her fellow activist Ahmed Maher.[40] Undeterred by the public's disaffection, their group dubbed itself the Youth of April 6 and planned subsequent activities.[41] Rather than driving a new wave of opposition, however, the Youth of April 6 became one subset of Egyptian society inspired by – but not necessarily in harmony with – the workers' movement. Although its political impact was unclear, a "culture of protest" was sweeping Egypt.[42] Political activists and rights activists accounted for the plurality of contentious gatherings from late 2005 to early 2009, while workers were responsible for the second most common form of protests.[43] In addition to popular action, individual members of the media and intelligentsia decried political corruption and economic injustice. In late September, the outspoken editor-in-chief of *al-Dostour* newspaper, Ibrahim Eissa, was sentenced to two months in jail for earlier covering rumors that Mubarak was ill. Amid a national outcry over the case, Eissa received a presidential pardon on the October 6 holiday.[44]

Mubarak's top advisors did not act as if they considered the regime in crisis. Egyptian officials recalled the price riots and the dangers of popular unrest, but they treated rising inequality as an inevitable by-product of growth.[45] Mubarak offered periodic raises for government workers and instructed the military to produce more cheap bread. He did not, however, protect workers from the threats of privatization and rampant inflation. Nor did his ruling party loosen its grip. In April 2008, the NDP won more than 90 percent of seats in the municipal elections that had been postponed two years earlier. The next month, parliament extended the state of emergency for another two years.

The United States generally shared the regime's confidence. With a 1.4-million–strong security force at Mubarak's command – twice the number available under Sadat – the U.S. Embassy reasoned that "any kind of violent change of leader [was] unlikely." Mubarak had "systematically and 'legally' eliminated virtually all political opposition."[46] At the same time, comments cited in an embassy cable after the events of April 6, 2008, betrayed volatile undercurrents. Applauding the Mahalla workers, one man in the capital remarked, "God willing, such riots will occur in Cairo soon; the only thing stopping us is fear." Assessing such attitudes, the embassy noted that "widespread bitterness about spiraling prices, seething upset about government corruption, disdain for the Mubarak government's perceived pro-US and Israel posture, and working class economic woes ... bubble up in virtually every conversation." Still, embassy officials judged Mubarak's hold on power was not threatened: "Egypt's omnipresent security apparatus is ... a strong counter-balance to riots and demonstrations. We think it is possible that Egypt will witness further spasms of limited violence, but these are likely to be isolated and uncoordinated, rather than revolutionary in nature."[47]

Grievances abounded but there was no focal point to mount a serious challenge, wrote embassy personnel who canvassed Cairo coffee shops:

> While we heard much grousing about the Egyptian government, including pointed critiques of President Mubarak and his son Gamal, there was no indication that anyone had plans to do anything but complain. We picked up no hint of revolutionary fervor; no hushed whispers expressing admiration for an opposition figure or advocating any actual political change, or calling for a resort to violence. Egyptians are frustrated and embittered, but still seem characteristically quiescent and passive, willing to sit on the sidelines in a cafe and list the failings of the government, but not to attempt to do anything about it.[48]

Labor actions notwithstanding, the U.S. Embassy saw the Egyptian government as being on the right track: "Economic reform has been a success story, although Egypt still suffers from widespread and so far irremediable poverty affecting upwards of 35–40% of the population."[49]

To the White House, Egypt looked stable, or stable enough that it required no special assistance. Unlike the late 1970s and the early 1990s, when Carter and George H. W. Bush had pulled their Egyptian partners from the brink of economic catastrophe, Bush increased Cairo's fiscal burden. To avoid a third year of debating aid conditionality with Congress, the president sliced through the Gordian knot and halved economic support funds to $200 million.[50] Annually, Cairo would be paying Washington a larger amount, $350 million, to finance its debt to the United States. Foreign Minister Aboul Gheit raised the discrepancy with a visiting congressional delegation: "This hurts us, and between two allies, the poorer party should not be paying the richer country." He also contended, in the words of a U.S. embassy official, "that Egypt is a pillar of stability in the region, but will not be able to maintain that stability if the economy does not improve, jobs get created, and the bread subsidy continue[s] to get paid."[51] Another strain on Egypt's finances was the country's trade imbalance with the United States (its largest trading partner), which had more than doubled between 2006 and 2008, from $1.74 billion to $3.66 billion.[52]

War on Gaza

In the U.S.-Egyptian network, Suleiman continued to provide the most reliable operational link. In June 2008, he negotiated a six-month ceasefire between Israel and Hamas.[53] He also argued for ameliorating conditions in Gaza to boost Fatah's local popularity. "The Israelis must help Abbas," Suleiman informed the U.S. Embassy in Cairo, "by lifting their siege and giving security responsibility to the PA [Palestinian Authority], thereby giving the PA some credit." Speaking to a U.S. congressional delegation, he pledged that his agents would bolster Abbas, work more closely with Israeli officials, and continue seeking Shalit's release.[54] By August 2008, a "hotline" was keeping Suleiman's intelligence services and the Israeli

Ministry of Defense in daily contact. Reports from the U.S. embassy in Tel Aviv showed that Israelis relied increasingly on Suleiman over Mubarak, expressed concerns about the Egyptian president's declining health, and were "most comfortable with the prospect of Omar Suleiman" eventually succeeding the incumbent.[55]

That fall, the hope of politically isolating Hamas faded. The ceasefire had given Israelis a period of relative quiet, but it had also enabled Hamas to recuperate.[56] Meanwhile, time was running out for leaders in Israel, the Palestinian Authority, and the United States. Beset by corruption charges, Prime Minister Ehud Olmert had lost leadership of Israel's ruling Kadima Party to Foreign Minister Tzipi Livni in the summer of 2008. Unable to form her own government, Livni was forced to call new elections for February 10, 2009.[57] Abbas's four-year term as the elected president of the Palestinian Authority was ending on January 9, 2009. Amid the Fatah-Hamas rift Abbas was not expected to cede the position or to organize fresh elections. The expiration of his original term would reduce his leverage with Hamas.[58] But the most momentous leadership transition was happening in Washington. Bush would step aside on January 20, 2009, and Democratic president-elect Barack Obama was expected to be more attentive to the Palestinians.

The ceasefire between Hamas and Israel had been violated during its six-month period. On December 19, it officially ended. Militias in Gaza immediately increased their rocket attacks. Hamas entertained the possibility of another short-term ceasefire but continued holding Shalit. Rather than negotiate, Olmert's lame-duck government tried to dethrone Hamas through massive military force. Late in the morning of December 27, Israeli jets struck at dozens of sites in the Gaza Strip, including a police graduation ceremony in Arafat City, killing some 240 trainees.[59] Only a small number of the victims belonged to paramilitaries, meaning most of the dead were civilians, not "combatants." After the air campaign had gone on for a week, Israeli land forces entered the Gaza Strip and naval forces also fired on the territory from sea. Dubbed Operation Cast Lead, the campaign's professed goal was to degrade Gaza militias through disproportionate force. Israel destroyed tunnels, military installations, weapons depots, the homes of militants, and alleged launching sites, including some in heavily populated areas.[60]

Mubarak had hosted Foreign Minister Livni on December 25, and Egyptians suspected that he had foreknowledge of Israel's assault. In fact Israeli defense minister Ehud Barak later told the U.S. embassy in Tel Aviv that before beginning Operation Cast Lead he had floated the prospect of Fatah or the Egyptians taking over Gaza afterward. Abbas and Mubarak declined the invitation.[61] Once the operation was under way, Mubarak made an obligatory and unconvincing denunciation of Israel's actions.[62] Demonstrators across Egypt and the region slammed him for purporting to sympathize with the Palestinians under attack while keeping the border sealed and Gaza's inhabitants trapped.[63] More than 50,000 people gathered in Alexandria on Friday, January 9, to express solidarity with the people of Gaza while rebuking Israel and Mubarak. The size of the rally eclipsed even the Iraq War protests. A young woman who belonged to the April 6 Facebook group, Asmaa Mahfouz, posted an essay whose title asked her compatriots, "Are you all fed up, or what?"[64] The next Friday, nearly 30,000 Egyptians protested in different parts of the country.[65]

On January 18, two days before Obama's inauguration, Israel declared a unilateral ceasefire; within four days, the IDF had withdrawn all its ground forces.[66] The Palestinians had suffered tremendous losses. Israeli and Hamas officials counted just over 700 Palestinian combatants killed, while nongovernmental Palestinian and Israeli sources reported the deaths of an additional 678 to 708 Palestinian civilians. Three Israeli civilians died during the campaign, as well as ten IDF soldiers, four from friendly fire. As the embargo on Gaza continued, Egyptians did their best to convey essentials to the Palestinians whenever the regime opened the Rafah crossing.[67]

A New Beginning

Shortly before the 2008 U.S. presidential election, Gamal Mubarak griped to the new U.S. ambassador, Margaret Scobey, that U.S. policies toward Egypt and the region had harmed U.S.-Egyptian relations: "Our job has become much more difficult because of your decisions. I hope that the next president and administration reviews the past eight years and draws some lessons."[68] As it happened, Obama was eager to turn the page on the Freedom Agenda. Neither he nor his secretary of state, Hillary Clinton, would admonish Mubarak or other Arab allies. Through traditional diplomacy they would mend the bilateral relationship and treat Mubarak as a key participant in the pursuit of a two-state solution for Israel and Palestine.

Obama opened his foreign policy hoping to improve the United States' image in Muslim-majority states. To the delight of Egyptian officials, he made Mubarak's Egypt the centerpiece of this campaign.[69] Speaking before a packed auditorium at Cairo University on June 4, 2009, he called for "a new beginning between the United States and Muslims around the globe, one based on mutual interest and mutual respect," and he rejected interventionism. "Let me be clear: No system of government can or should be imposed by one nation by any other. That does not lessen my commitment, however, to governments that reflect the will of the people." In contrast to Rice's lecture at the American University in Cairo, he evoked freedom without juxtaposing the United States and Egypt. The closest he came to chiding Arab rulers was to say, "No matter where it takes hold, government of the people and by the people sets a single standard for all who would hold power: You must maintain your power through consent, not coercion." While gesturing toward democratic reform, Obama stressed the need for Middle East peace. In the longest section of the fifty-four-minute speech, he averred that "the situation between Israelis, Palestinians, and the Arab world" could only be resolved "through two states, where Israelis and Palestinians each live in peace and security." He then saddled both sides with responsibility for the conflict. Whereas Palestinians would need to reject violence, Israelis would have to stop building settlements in the West Bank.[70]

The presidential visit, which included tours of the pyramids at Giza and of Islamic Cairo, raised Egyptians' confidence in U.S. foreign policy. A public opinion survey conducted from mid-May to mid-June estimated that 42 percent of Egyptians expected Obama to "do the right thing in world affairs," up from 11 percent under Bush. Still, less than one in four of those polled expected Obama to "be fair in the Middle East," and the United States' approval in Egypt rose modestly, to 27 percent from 22 percent the prior year.[71] While ordinary Egyptians waited for Obama to follow words with deeds, Mubarak's adjutants gushed about the trip.[72] No U.S. leader since Carter had given Egypt such high-profile attention. Obama healed wounded egos and reestablished some of the trust that had eroded during Bush's tenure. In August, Mubarak reciprocated by visiting the United States for the first

time in more than four years.[73] At the White House, the presidents
dealt overwhelmingly with Israeli-Palestinian issues.[74] "For the first
almost year in office," observed Dunne, "they reverted to this kind
of 1990s policy, I thought, of 'Egypt helps us in the peace process,
Mubarak is our friend.'"[75]

Human rights concerns were not off the administration's agenda
completely, but they had receded from public view. Writing to Clinton
in February 2009, Ambassador Scobey encouraged the secretary to
raise the situations of Ayman Nour (who was in prison and ailing)
and Saad Eddin Ibrahim (still in self-imposed exile) with her Egyptian
counterpart:

> You should press Aboul Gheit hard on Nour and Ibrahim, and also
> urge the GOE to stop arresting other less prominent political activists.
> Nour's health is bad and he has served more than half his sentence;
> he deserves a humanitarian pardon. You may wish to lay down a
> marker for a future discussion on democratization and human rights
> concerns. You might note that although you and the President want
> to improve the relationship, Egypt could take some steps to remove
> these very volatile issues from the agenda.[76]

As it happened, Nour was released in February 2009, before Clinton
made her first visit to Egypt as secretary of state, in an unsubtle jab at
the Bush administration.[77]

U.S. and Egyptian officials also disagreed about the ideal amounts
and usage of U.S. assistance. With respect to economic support funds,
the Egyptian government refused to implement the FY 2009 aid program until the unilateral cuts imposed by Bush had been amended.
The Obama administration placated Mubarak's government by providing an additional $50 million of supplemental funding for FY
2009 and maintaining the funding level at $250 million for the fol-
lowing fiscal year.[78] Still concerned about their debt repayments to
Washington, Egyptians involved in aid discussions sought in vain to
establish an "endowment" that would eventually provide aid without
congressional oversight or intervention. Given that U.S. lawmakers
were unlikely to approve a measure that circumvented them, embassy
staff judged the idea "a nonstarter."[79]

For its part, the Egyptian regime balked at U.S. proposals to use
economic support funds to assist local civil society organizations.
Through MEPI and the State Department's Bureau of Democracy,

Human Rights, and Labor, the administration could fund organizations like the Ibn Khaldun Center that were registered as civil companies and not formally approved as NGOs by the Egyptian minister of social solidarity.[80] One embassy cable reported, for example, that an "unregistered NGO" had been "recently awarded a MEPI grant to organize an NGO workshop and prepare publications in advance of the 2010 Forum for the Future."[81] Subsequent to the Gina London incident with IRI, however, the flow of such funding had been sharply reduced. Organizations based outside of Egypt, like IRI and NDI, were hardest hit as U.S. government support for activities in Egypt fell from an estimated $9 million in FY 2008 to about $2 million in FY 2009. The amount of money reaching Egyptian organizations directly, as opposed to through subcontracts from foreign organizations, remained about the same, slightly less than $1 million during this period.[82]

The biggest problem for organizations that sought to expand their activities in Egypt was not the level of U.S. fiscal support but the political system in which they operated. Control over authorization and funding ultimately lay with Mubarak's security forces, not the Ministry of Social Solidarity, which formally presided over NGO licensing. When Tamara Cofman Wittes, the deputy assistant secretary for Near Eastern affairs, pointed out to Minister Ali El-Meselhi that his government frequently denied or ignored some NGO applications, he admitted that "The Minister of Interior and Egyptian Intelligence Services have the final say on NGO programs and NGO registration requests."[83] Just as the U.S. Congress was unlikely to adopt an endowment program that would undermine its power over U.S. aid, the Egyptian security apparatus would not enable funding for organizations that sought to expand dissent and autonomous political activity under Mubarak. Unregulated aid to Egyptian and foreign civil society organizations was a nonstarter.

The Ministry of Interior was doing far more than obstructing civil society groups. Headed since 1997 by Habib al-Adly, the ministry held an estimated 20,000 detainees without trial each year.[84] It employed more than a million people, not including informants, and its tentacles reached into universities, political parties, NGOs, and Egyptians' homes.[85] According to one NDP insider, security officials held Egyptian politics in a "clandestine chokehold."[86] The ministry's troops for crowd suppression included some 800,000 police as well as

450,000 in the CSF.[87] Between FY 2005 and FY 2007 its budget expanded from approximately $1.5 billion to nearly $2 billion.[88] U.S. commercial small arms and ammunition worth $744,000 were approved for sale to Egypt in FY 2009, and four times that amount the following fiscal year.[89] Total authorized commercial sales (across all categories) were $91 million in FY 2009 and $101 million in FY 2010, suggesting an uptick in the ministry's acquisitions.[90]

The Ministry of Defense overshadowed the Ministry of Interior in resources, but the utility of its purchases was often in question. In 2010, the Egyptian military commanded a budget of $4.5 billion. To the Pentagon's continuing disappointment, more than half of Tantawi's money went into maintaining a bulky fleet of land and air forces.[91] The field marshal resisted U.S. pleas to expand antismuggling operations along the Egypt-Gaza border. His motives, the embassy speculated, were to protect Egyptian sovereignty from outside interference and, equally important, to safeguard foreign military financing so that the Egyptian military could continue acquiring and sustaining its "M1A1 tanks and aircraft."[92]

Defense officials from the two countries regularly exchanged words about the appropriate evolution of the Egyptian armed forces. Representatives from the U.S. military hoped "to re-invent Bright Star," so that when the biennial war games reconvened in 2011 they could cover "full-spectrum operations," such as counterinsurgency, stability operations, and nation-building.[93] At one point, the deputy assistant secretary of defense for the Middle East, Colin Kahl, contended that Operation Desert Storm had been the last large-scale conventional war. Subsequently, by not retooling for twenty-first century conflicts, the Egyptian army had fallen behind.[94] Egyptian officers responded that they faced different security concerns than the United States; their forces needed to secure a large amount of territory, significant coastlines and borders, and the Suez Canal. The Egyptian military, they explained, needed a force large enough to deter or prevail in a potential conflict with Libya or Nile Basin countries. Egypt also had to maintain a strategic balance with Israel, and the officers complained that Israel was receiving two and a half times what Egypt got, not 50 percent more, as the "Camp David ratio" had established.[95]

With respect to the tunnels into Gaza, Tantawi saw smuggling as a product of the Israeli blockade, not insufficient security on Egypt's side of the border.[96] Although he impeded a U.S. proposal for

high-tech surveillance to interdict the smuggling, the Ministry of
Defense ultimately pursued a low-tech solution of its own.[97] In December 2009, the Egyptian army began implanting a subterranean steel
wall nearly five inches thick that ran from ten feet below the surface to
more than sixty feet down. Inside Egypt, the wall became a symbol of
the army's part in policing Gaza. Despite the controversy, U.S. officials
doubted the wall would curb smuggling. The steel sheets being used
were "basic construction-grade material that [could] be cut using a
tool like a blow torch."[98] Given Tantawi's methods, the Israelis and
Americans were thankful Suleiman was "disrupting arms smuggling
networks" beyond the immediate border.[99]

The cohesion of U.S.-Egyptian security cooperation was matched by
civil-military cooperation inside the Egyptian regime. Some observers
have argued the military had misgivings about presidential succession that threatened to split the regime from within. Writer Abdullah
al-Senawy later commented that "People who were close to the army
witnessed a silent uproar within the military over the rise of Gamal and
like-minded businessmen."[100] In addition, Suleiman once told U.S. officials he "detest[ed]" the idea of Gamal becoming president.[101] Yet during the period in question, 2005–2011, neither Tantawi nor Suleiman
took any steps to impede Gamal's political ascent. As reported by the
U.S. Embassy in 2008, the military was likely to back Gamal Mubarak
politically in exchange for additional patronage. "[S]enior military
officers would support Gamal if Mubarak resigned and installed him
in the presidency," U.S. officials forecast, "as it [was] difficult to
imagine opposition from these officers who depend[ed] on the president and defense minister for their jobs and material perks."[102]
In short, the bickering among high officials did not amount to a
schism. Crucially, neither the generals nor the rank and file were
expected to break from the regime without a crisis, which looked
unlikely.

The Alternative

The regime rigidly defended its foreign policies while its critics
remained fragmented. Journalist Magdy Hussein and two other
activists received prison sentences for illegally "infiltrating" the Gaza
Strip, through tunnels, to deliver aid to the Palestinians.[103] Natural gas

exports to Israel also evoked opposition but proceeded without interruption. The sales had begun in May 2008, reportedly at below-market
rates, and comprised 60 billion cubic feet per year.[104] The Youth of
April 6 invoked these issues and called for a strike on the first anniversary of its founding event. Once more, the public remained mute. "In
contrast to the mass protests against the Gaza war in December and
January," reported the U.S. Embassy, "the weak turnout on April 6
indicates that a divided opposition is unable to rally public support
for political and economic reforms within Egypt."[105] Labor-related
strikes and protests also failed to coalesce as a national force against
the regime.[106] In April 2009, however, property tax collectors won a
historic victory when, for the first time in more than fifty years, the
government recognized an independent union: the Independent General Union of Real Estate Tax Authority Workers. The achievement
was a milestone in the quest to pull labor away from the thrall of the
regime-controlled Egyptian Trade Union Federation.[107]

For activists hoping to build a broad movement against Mubarak,
Egypt's largest opposition movement, the Muslim Brotherhood,
proved an unreliable ally. The organization protested selectively, often
about foreign policy issues and seldom joined with April 6, Kefaya, and
other political reform advocates.[108] Without the Brotherhood at their
side, secular activists had difficulty drawing more than a few hundred
participants to their events.[109] When a fall 2009 conference held opposite the ruling party's convention attracted four hundred participants,
the U.S. Embassy deemed it a major feat for April 6 after a lackluster
year and a half. Still, the group's leader remained "pessimistic about
the movement's prospects to raise money and recruit new members for
future activities, such as those related to the upcoming elections."[110]

Presidential elections scheduled for 2011 offered the opposition a
chance to focus popular anger against the regime, for in that election or
the one after Gamal would most likely be the NDP's nominee. Gamal's
coterie defended the tortuous set of rules established in 2005 and 2007
as a "test of seriousness," comparable to qualification procedures in
France and Austria.[111] But the constitutional amendments required
would-be candidates to have support in the NDP-dominated parliament, all but guaranteeing only the NDP and its adjuncts would be
able to field candidates.[112] Miraculously, however, secular dissidents
discovered a compelling foil to Gamal. At the end of 2009 Mohamed

ElBaradei was set to complete his third and final term as director general of the International Atomic Energy Agency (IAEA). ElBaradei had been awarded a Nobel Peace Prize and enjoyed a sterling reputation for his career of international service. He topped the opposition's short list of possible presidential contenders. Moreover, the notion that he was ineligible for the presidency – he belonged to no Egyptian party – made the "test of seriousness" risible.

On December 4, 2009, days after departing the IAEA, ElBaradei wrote his supporters. He expressed his willingness to run as a national consensus candidate on the condition that such a bid reflected the wishes of a broad and diverse set of Egyptians. Before entering any such race, however, ElBaradei stipulated that presidential elections must be open to all Egyptians. With this demand he challenged the rules that prefigured a Mubarak dynasty and made their abrogation the prerequisite for a meaningful election.[113] The announcement thrilled April 6 and Kefaya.[114] Meanwhile, regime elites blithely defended the barriers to an ElBaradei candidacy. In a conversation with U.S. embassy staff, "NDP insider Mohamed Kamal... seemed unconcerned, saying ElBaradei should run 'if he qualifies' as a candidate."[115]

The opinions of Mubarak's cronies mattered little to ElBaradei's fans. In February, several thousand people swarmed Cairo International Airport to welcome him as he returned to Egypt. The bespectacled diplomat's quasi-candidacy had drawn crowds bigger than anything secular opposition leaders had organized on their own.[116] Soon ElBaradei was steering a National Coalition for Change, through which Web activists, liberals, Islamists, and leftists worked to open the elections.[117] He called for an end to the harsh restrictions on aspiring candidates, media access for all movements and candidates, judicial supervision of the elections, voting through national ID cards (not the corrupted voter registration system), enfranchisement of Egyptians living abroad, and a two-term limit on the presidency. Within days, tens of thousands had signed on.[118]

Paradoxically, a tragedy caused by abusive cops strengthened ElBaradei's coalition. On the evening of June 6, two plainclothes policemen entered an Alexandria Internet café and demanded a bribe from a twenty-eight-year-old entrepreneur named Khaled Said. It is widely held that the cops targeted Said because he had uploaded a video showing police officers pocketing confiscated drugs.[119] When

Said refused to be extorted, the cops assaulted him. They dragged him out of the café and continued bludgeoning him in a nearby apartment building, where witnesses say he perished from his injuries. News of the murder, along with grisly postmortem photos of Said's battered visage, spread virally. ElBaradei supporters organized a Facebook group called We Are All Khaled Said. Thousands marched in Said's memory, demanding accountability from the Ministry of Interior.[120] Charges were filed against the two suspected officers, but the trials were repeatedly delayed. Lack of accountability underscored the opposition's point. All Egyptians, not just the intelligentsia and political opposition, were imperiled by a brutal police force that was outside the law.[121] By the end of 2010, We Are All Khaled Said had nearly 350,000 members – a world of difference from the April 6 meeting a year before.[122]

ElBaradei's presence enabled independent activists to organize more openly than ever before during Mubarak's tenure. In fall 2010, his National Coalition for Change called for the opposition to boycott the legislative elections. The Muslim Brotherhood and most licensed parties initially ignored the call. But when the NDP cruised through victories in the first round of voting, the Muslim Brotherhood and several opposition groups joined the boycott. The elections produced a scandalous 97 percent majority for Mubarak's party.[123] Candidates who had withdrawn then began forming a shadow parliament that would delegitimize Mubarak's crooked legislature. The president mocked their initiative – "Let them amuse themselves" – but popular ire at his misrule was growing.[124]

Early in 2011 a deadly explosion underscored Mubarak's failure to protect anyone but his own entourage. Barely thirty minutes into the new year, shrapnel ripped through a group of parishioners leaving a midnight mass in Alexandria. The bomb killed more than twenty people, reportedly all of them Christians, and injured dozens more. Members of Egypt's Coptic Christian community, which numbered some 8 million, were horrified by the attack and outraged that Egyptian security forces had not prevented it. Mubarak's police had not only failed to intercept the bomber, they stood by after the blast as Christians and Muslims clashed in the surrounding area. Some Egyptians speculated that Mubarak and al-Adly had planned the bombing to stir sectarian conflict and obscure the regime's own failures.[125] If so, the attempt flopped. The New Year's bombing was the regime's last scandal before January 25.[126]

Egyptians seething over corruption, poverty, and repression found inspiration thirteen hundred miles away. On December 17, Tunisian police in the southern governorate of Sidi Bouzid had humiliated a young produce vendor named Mohamed Bouazizi. His wares confiscated, Bouazizi chose to light himself on fire rather than suffer another moment of indignity. The self-immolation provoked riots in Sidi Bouzid. Demonstrations soon spread to nearby regions. During the following weeks protests against economic conditions and the ruling elite swept northward toward the capital. On January 4, 2010, Bouazizi perished from his burns. On January 9, police began shooting demonstrators, an escalation that only brought more Tunisians into the streets.[127] Three days later, Turisian president Zine El Abidine Ben Ali ordered the Tunisian army to fire upon civilians, but General Rachid Ammar, the armed forces chief of staff, refused.[128] Instead of suppressing demonstrators, he protected them, inserting Tunisian troops between the police and the people. Throngs of protesters filled the boulevards of Tunis, demanding "Ben Ali, degage!" (Ben Ali, get out!). On January 14, the embattled despot fled into exile.[129] It was the first time since the end of the Cold War that a popular uprising had ousted an Arab dictator.

Tunisia became a lodestar for Egyptians. When copycat self-immolations began April 6 and We Are All Khaled Said turned frustration into action.[130] Online and in the streets, they announced a Day of Rage for January 25, a national holiday remembering Egyptian police who had resisted the British fifty-nine years earlier. In a four-minute online video, April 6 member Asmaa Mahfouz closed the movement's case: "We want our rights. We don't want anything else. This whole government is corrupt. The president is corrupt. State Security is corrupt.... Your turning out with us will matter, not just a little, but a lot.... I am going out on the twenty-fifth, and I will say 'no' to corruption and 'no' to the regime."[131] Tens of thousands joined her.

The Uprising

The Day of Rage evinced the newfound power of anti-Mubarak activists, but on January 25, 2011, the security state remained intact, and the Egyptian military and the U.S. government stood firmly behind

Mubarak. Consequently, when the uprising began, an emboldened social movement faced a strong regime.[132] Over the course of unrelenting protests, however, the White House and Egyptian generals shifted from unconditionally backing Mubarak, to supporting a handoff to Omar Suleiman, to finally accepting Mubarak's resignation.

Egyptians attending the Day of Rage called for Interior Minister al-Adly's resignation, a monthly minimum wage of 1,200 Egyptian pounds (approximately $215), repeal of the Emergency Law, dissolution of the current parliament, and a two-term limit on the presidency.[133] Evading police – the day's titular honorees – thousands converged on Tahrir Square. Meanwhile, analogous marches began in other Egyptian cities. By the early morning of January 26, CSF soldiers firing tear gas and rubber bullets had forced protesters in Tahrir to regroup.[134] During Wednesday and Thursday, organizers planned to resume their campaign in a Friday of Anger. Mubarak's resignation now topped their agenda.

The Obama administration initially perceived no threat to Mubarak's hold on power. On the Day of Rage, U.S. secretary of state Hillary Clinton called for restraint by all sides but did not rescind support for Mubarak: "Our assessment is that the Egyptian government is stable and is looking for ways to respond to the legitimate needs and interests of the Egyptian people."[135] In his State of the Union address the night of January 25, Obama referred to Ben Ali as a "dictator," but Vice President Joe Biden later balked at applying the same epithet to Mubarak.[136]

Early Friday morning, the Egyptian regime disabled Internet access and text messaging in the hope of disrupting the opposition. The move backfired, infuriating citizens who might otherwise have remained on the sidelines.[137] That afternoon, tens of thousands poured from prayer services at mosques, headed toward Tahrir, and chanted, "The people want to topple the regime!" Parallel marches across the country overwhelmed al-Adly's forces.[138] The Ministry of Interior retreated from bridges and intersections, and that night all of its agents withdrew.[139] The opposition had scored its greatest victory yet against the security apparatus.[140] Across the country protesters incinerated police stations and NDP offices.[141] Popular mobilization had frozen the Ministry of Interior in its tracks. "All of us were astonished," al-Adly later confessed. "The faces of the demonstrators showed how clear they were in challenging the regime and how much they hated it, how willing they were to resist with their bodies all attempts to divide them with truncheons and water cannons and all other tools. They outnumbered security forces by a million or more, a fact that shocked the Interior Ministry leaders and the president."[142]

By Friday evening, hundreds had died, while tens of thousands congregated in Tahrir.[143] The duration and size of the protests eclipsed the price riots of 1977. Egyptian military officers visiting Washington for an annual discussion of bilateral issues rushed back to Cairo.[144] But even after Egyptians from Alexandria to Suez had overcome violent attacks, the White House said only that it would be "reviewing" assistance – not severing or freezing aid – if repression resumed.[145] That evening, Mubarak made a ten-minute television appearance. He acknowledged demands for expanding democracy and reducing poverty, but he did not resign. Instead, he announced he would dismiss the current cabinet and form a new government. The autocrat continued to see himself saving the people from "chaos."[146] Afterward, Obama spoke with his counterpart for the first time since the uprising began and conveyed that the Egyptian president had "a responsibility to give meaning to those words [of the speech], to take concrete steps and actions that deliver on that promise."[147]

On Saturday, Mubarak appointed Suleiman as vice president and the White House's response took shape. Sunday morning, Clinton said that the administration supported an "orderly transition."[148] It would become the U.S. watchword for the remainder of the uprising. Reports show Obama wanted to ensure stability in Egypt while appearing to support gradual democratization. An "orderly transition" would ostensibly bring about liberalizing reforms, placate protesters and sustain a cornerstone of U.S. strategy. It would also reassure regional allies – mainly Israel and Saudi Arabia – who supported Mubarak. Although a junior faction within the White House, including presidential speechwriter Ben Rhodes and human rights advocate Samantha Power, favored positioning the United States behind the protesters, the top national security figures – Biden, Clinton, Defense Secretary Robert Gates, and National Security Advisor Thomas Donilon – argued against abandoning the regime. The transition they envisioned would shift power not to the opposition but to Suleiman.[149]

During the weekend, the Egyptian army had moved into the streets, filling the space left by the Ministry of Interior. The military remained aligned with the regime, however. As Clinton argued on Sunday talk shows for order and gradual change, Mubarak's airmen were swooping U.S. F-16s over Tahrir in a bid to frighten protesters. There is evidence that ground forces were also instructed to attack the demonstrators. One reporter witnessed tank commanders refusing to obey orders to fire upon demonstrators in the square. At this point, if there were any cracks in the chain of command, they appeared in the field, not between Mubarak and his generals.[150] On Monday, Mubarak replaced his cabinet, including Minister of Interior al-Adly, with a "security cabinet" of military men headed by Lieutenant General Ahmed Shafiq as prime minister.[151] The military, after flirting with force over the weekend, announced it would not fire upon peaceful demonstrators.[152] It soon became clear, however, that the absence of military force did not amount to the provision of military protection.

As the uprising celebrated its first week, more than a million people in the streets of Cairo insisted Mubarak leave office. The night of Tuesday, February 1, Mubarak made another partial concession in an evening television appearance: He would complete his current term of office, due to expire in September, but would not run in the next presidential election. During his remaining months in office, Mubarak pledged, he would oversee constitutional amendments that would open presidential elections and establish term limits. The speech won him a momentary reprieve, as some Egyptians embraced his vow to retire after September and live the rest of his days on Egyptian soil.[153] It also prompted a second – and final – call between the U.S. and Egyptian presidents.

If Mubarak remained at the helm of government until September, Obama reasoned, the demonstrations might continue for months. A crisp change was becoming necessary and in a tense conversation that lasted thirty minutes, Obama advised his counterpart that "orderly transition must be meaningful, it must be peaceful, and it must begin now."[154] This statement did not necessitate Mubarak's resignation – he could recede into the background while formally staying in office. The Egyptian ruler replied, "You don't understand the Egyptian culture and what would happen if I step down now." He also assured Obama the crisis would soon abate: "Let's talk in the next three or four days. . . . when we talk, you will find that I was right."[155] Frustrated by Mubarak's stubbornness, administration officials communicated with Suleiman and Egyptian military officers in the hope of turning Mubarak into a lame duck and accelerating a transition to the vice president.[156]

Mubarak's henchmen soon squandered any domestic goodwill his second speech might have garnered. The next day, thugs on horseback and camelback stampeded into Tahrir, lashing out at unarmed demonstrators. After this "Battle of the Camel," regime clients began shooting from rooftops and lobbing Molotov cocktails at the crowds below. More than a thousand people were injured during the two days of violence.[157] The attacks soured the public and strengthened activists' resolve to outlast Mubarak. As Prime Minister Shafiq unconvincingly promised that the assailants would be held accountable, the squatters of Tahrir hunkered behind barricades jerry-rigged during the fighting.[158] More than 100,000 people assembled for the Friday of Departure on February 4.

With Egypt's ruler on the ropes and its strategic role in jeopardy, anxiety gripped Washington. Congressional representatives unloaded their frustrations onto U.S. intelligence professionals, who purportedly had failed to notify U.S. policymakers of the threat to Mubarak. A February 3 Senate confirmation hearing for the principal deputy director of national intelligence turned into an audit about what the intelligence community had known and when.[159] Committee chair Senator Dianne Feinstein (D-CA) opened the proceedings by referring to the "instability and protests in the Middle East." The senator expressed "doubts" about "whether the intelligence community lived up to its obligations" to provide "timely intelligence analysis" to top policymakers at the White House, in the Department of State, and on Capitol Hill. She added, however, that the nominee, Stephanie O'Sullivan, was not among those at fault, because O'Sullivan had been serving in the higher echelons of the CIA since 2009, not in the field. Senator Ron Wyden (D-OR) had fewer qualms about grilling the nominee and twice asked when the president had been notified "that Egyptian street protestors were likely to threaten President Mubarak's hold on power." O'Sullivan answered, in general terms, that the intelligence community had long warned of "instability," including at the end of 2010, but had not known "what the triggering mechanism would be."[160]

The scramble for better intelligence obscured a core contradiction of White House and congressional policy toward Egypt. During calmer periods, policymakers had formulated U.S. national interests while ignoring Egyptian popular attitudes, yet when the groundswell occurred they expressed disbelief and wanted to have known when suppressed local views would crystallize into mass action. Describing shortfalls in intelligence gathering, Feinstein remarked to one journalist, "These events should not have come upon us with the surprise that they did.... There should have been much more warning.... Was someone looking at what was going on the Internet?"[161] But writers on Facebook and blogs were not harbingers, and the Internet was not a Rosetta Stone for deciphering Arab perspectives. New social media were fresh forums for expressing views that had been circulating in Egyptian discourse for decades. Intelligence professionals, politicians, and interested laypersons could readily learn that Mubarak ruled through repression and that his foreign policy served U.S. strategy while circumventing public opinion. Leaders in Washington, however, had opted not to harmonize their policies with Egyptian priorities or to seriously encourage Mubarak to do the same. As NSC staffers observed before Sadat's assassination, the balance had shifted long ago, from "'what is good for Egypt' to 'what is good for the U.S.'"[162] The yearning to subordinate the Egyptian masses rather than incorporate their interests into foreign policy appeared likely to outlast the crisis. Even in a moment of self-criticism, officials in Washington focused on the technical problems of intelligence gathering and analysis, rather than on the political gap between official U.S. interests and popular Egyptian goals. Calls for more "timely intelligence" implied U.S. officials should keep better tabs on opposition currents inside Egypt, not revamp their approach to the country and its rulers.

Having failed to eject the protesters violently, the regime tried to coax activists to leave. Vice President Suleiman started a dialogue with select opposition forces, including the Muslim Brotherhood but excluding ElBaradei. Unimpressed by the former intelligence chief's overtures, leaders of the January 25 movement rejected any negotiations before Mubarak resigned. Instead they favored a proposal by ElBaradei to form an independent "national salvation government," free from the influence of Mubarak and his cronies.[163]

The strategy of Mubarak and Suleiman, supported by the White House, looked like a cynical attempt by the Egyptian leadership to demobilize the opposition and regain control. Asked by a foreign journalist what else he could offer the demonstrators, Suleiman replied, "We can say only go home; we cannot do more than that. We cannot push them by force. Everybody has to go home. We want to have normal life. We don't want anybody in the streets. Go to work. Bring back once again the tourists. Go to the normal life. Save the economy of the country."[164] The Egyptian military reinforced Suleiman's call for protesters to "go home." On the Friday of Departure, Defense Minister Tantawi, who was in close contact with the Pentagon throughout the crisis, visited Tahrir and urged protesters to pack up.[165]

The Obama administration also preferred Suleiman's strategy to ElBaradei's proposal. Rather than endorsing a national salvation government, the White House deferred to the Egyptian constitution. Thanks to Hosni and Gamal Mubarak's amendments, however, that document provided no serious chance for the opposition to take power. According to the constitution, if Mubarak resigned, the speaker of the People's Assembly would serve as acting president until new elections were held within sixty days. The organizers of the uprising, however, did not recognize the parliament, much less its speaker, as legitimate. Moreover, the new election would be a one-party contest thanks to the "test of seriousness" that excluded all groups but the NDP from fielding a candidate.[166] Therefore, U.S. officials accepted that Mubarak would need to remain president while new electoral rules were written. To signal that he was gradually stepping down, however, Mubarak could cede his presidential powers to Suleiman while staying in office.[167]

The plan put Suleiman at the helm of an orderly transition. The second weekend of the uprising, Clinton portrayed the Egyptian vice president as steering the ship of state through turbulent waters: "There are forces at work in any society, and particularly one that is facing these kinds of challenges, that will try to derail or overtake the process to pursue their own specific agenda, which is why I think it's important to support the transition process announced by the Egyptian Government, actually headed by now-Vice President Omar Suleiman."[168] Later Clinton expressed confidence that Suleiman would reduce government repression and enable Egyptians to campaign freely. Asked by Michele Kelemen of National Public Radio if Suleiman was "reassuring" Clinton that he was "really doing things differently," Clinton replied, "Look, we have had numerous conversations with him and others, both the Vice President and I have spoken with him in the last several days. We hear that they are committed to this, and when we press on concrete steps and timelines, we are given assurance that that will happen."[169]

Suleiman's argument for returning Egypt to normal proved more compelling than repression or pseudo-liberalization. After nearly two weeks of protests, the regime had an opportunity to outlast the Tahrir tent city by portraying its critics as recalcitrant, unwilling to accept the vice president's reforms, and obstructing fellow citizens from resuming work. Yet, for a third time (after the Internet outage and the Battle of the Camel), Mubarak's heavy-handed tactics bolstered his opponents. On Monday, February 7, Google executive and We Are All Khaled Said organizer Wael Ghonim was released from ten days' detention. That evening, in a tearful appearance on satellite television, he recounted his story and partly apologized to the parents and families of those who had lost loved ones in the uprising. He argued, however, that ultimate responsibility lay with a regime that denigrated its citizens and held a young Egyptian man incommunicado without notifying his parents.[170] Ghonim's interview reminded viewers that the security state was alive and well, and it would continue threatening them if they retreated.[171] The interview gave a second wind to the uprising. In a rare convergence of political activism and workers' actions, the real estate tax collectors' union and three other labor organizations announced a strike supporting calls for Mubarak's resignation. Tens of thousands of workers "in textiles, military production, transportation, petroleum, cement, iron and steel, hospitals, universities, telecommunications, and the Suez Canal" then took part in strikes or protests.[172]

As organizers of the January 25 movement enjoyed new popular support and planned new marches, Obama and the Egyptian military looked for an extraconstitutional solution. Through Biden, the White House urged Suleiman to lift the state of emergency and signal a serious transition.[173] Instead of acceding to these requests, which could have potentially ended the crisis, Suleiman promised he would soon be delegated Mubarak's powers and made "de facto president."[174] Recognizing that Mubarak and Suleiman had failed to quell the uprising, the military moved toward assuming control. "At the beginning, we gave the presidential institution the full opportunity to manage events," SCAF members later revealed. "If it were able to succeed, nothing would have happened. We would have pulled our people back to the barracks. But they were incapable of responding to the events.... On Feb. 10, there were demonstrations that amounted to millions of people all over the country."[175]

That Thursday, the SCAF – Egypt's top twenty military officers – convened without President Mubarak in attendance. Issuing their first communiqué, councilmembers announced they would remain in session indefinitely and take appropriate measures to safeguard the nation and the achievements of the Egyptian people.[176] Elites in Egypt and the United States anticipated a decisive break – albeit without a presidential resignation – and signaled to demonstrators that their wait was nearly over. The chief of staff of the armed forces, Lieutenant General Sami Enan, visited Tahrir and communicated that the protesters' demands were about to be met.[177] Obama told an audience in Michigan, "We are witnessing history unfold – it is a moment of transformation that is taking place because the people of Egypt are calling for change."[178] Ghonim, who had achieved iconic status and seemed in the know, wrote on Twitter, "Mission accomplished. Thanks to all the brave young Egyptians."[179]

Their expectations raised, millions of Egyptians watched Mubarak give his third address since January 25. The opposition hoped for a resignation. The White House wanted a crisp handover to Suleiman. Mubarak gave neither. His speech reportedly defied the army's directions and reflected attempts by Gamal Mubarak to retard his father's exit.[180] The initial remarks showed he planned to remain in office until September. After rambling for fourteen minutes, Mubarak said he would transfer some "powers" of the presidency to Suleiman. The implications of the single sentence were unclear, buried in an address that meandered through self-eulogy, calls for patriotism, and the minutiae of constitutional reform.[181] As outraged viewers in Tahrir raised their shoes, Suleiman tried to reinforce Mubarak's message. In sepulchral tones he called on Egyptians to unite and act rationally, saying the youth of January 25 had succeeded in moving Egypt on the path to democracy. Without mentioning Mubarak's name, the would-be successor tried to portray the handoff as a done deal. He would honor the commitments of the political dialogue and of any subsequent talks as he oversaw the peaceful transition of power in coming months. Committees had been formed to oversee constitutional changes before new elections, and hence there was no need for protest. "Return to your homes and places of work," he intoned. The opposition geared up for another massive Friday rally.[182]

Bemused, the White House sought clarification: "The Egyptian people have been told that there was a transition of authority, but it is not yet clear that this transition is immediate, meaningful or sufficient.... The Egyptian government must put forward a credible, concrete and unequivocal path toward genuine democracy, and they have not yet seized that opportunity."[183] The night's events had crippled Suleiman's political standing and scotched the blueprint for an orderly transition. Faced with further escalation of the uprising or constitutional uncertainty, the Obama administration accepted the idea of the SCAF deposing Mubarak, suspending the constitution, and leading Egypt until new elections were organized.[184] Gates spoke with Tantawi Thursday night, their fifth conversation during the uprising.[185]

Shortly after noon on Friday, February 11, in a second communiqué, the SCAF vowed to end the state of emergency after current conditions passed, propose constitutional amendments that would open candidacy requirements, and execute clean and free presidential elections.[186] Mubarak and family were flown by helicopter from the Presidential Palace in Cairo to their compound in Sharm El-Sheikh. Soon after, tanks around the palace rotated their turrets away from the crowds assembled nearby.[187] At 6 P.M. local time, Suleiman spoke for thirty-five seconds on national television to announce that Mubarak had "relinquished" the office of the presidency and empowered the Supreme Council of the Armed Forces with "administering the country's affairs."[188] The SCAF then issued its third communiqué. In addition to saluting the recent martyrs (more than 850 people had been killed during the uprising), the council stated that legitimacy lay with the people and that it would soon announce the steps to come.[189] Obama hailed the shift: "The people of Egypt have spoken, their voices have been heard, and Egypt will never be the same."[190]

For two and a half weeks, the White House and the Egyptian generals had refrained from lending their weight to the opposition and, even when they did, their support was tactical. Participants in the uprising overwhelmed police, withstood Mubarak's thugs, drew support from workers, and made the plan for an "orderly transition" to Suleiman untenable. After proactively supporting the Egyptian ruler for decades, the White House and the SCAF reactively accepted his removal. While conducting a leadership change, however, U.S. and Egyptian officials safeguarded the regime. Months later, crowds in Tahrir would be demanding police reform and civilian sovereignty.

Conclusion

The road to Egypt's popularly celebrated "soft coup" was paved with the opposition's disunity, disappointment, and singular tenacity.[191] For years Kefaya and April 6 had labored in the political wilderness, holding audacious rallies that few people attended. Only when their campaigns dovetailed with the Muslim Brotherhood's causes, as in the 2006 protests for judicial independence and the 2009 demonstrations against Operation Cast Lead, had they drawn more than a few hundred into the streets. In 2010, however, they expanded their constituency as part of ElBaradei's coalition. Meanwhile Egyptian workers struggled for material improvements and generally ignored calls for action against the Mubaraks' succession schemes. Similarly, many Egyptians were concerned about rising prices on basic necessities but were not moved to participate in urban street protests. Terrible violence within Egypt, the murder of Khaled Said, and the Alexandria church bombing ratified the regime's abject failure at providing public safety and impelled Egyptians to mass action. Simultaneously, Tunisia offered a model of what should be done.

In social revolutions, dilapidated institutions and international pressure spur mass mobilization that leads to a radical overhaul of state and class structures.[192] The January 25 Revolution, or Egyptian uprising, differed in process and outcome. Egyptian protesters did not challenge a tottering and isolated state. Rather, they undermined Mubarak's otherwise dependable repressive organizations and foreign support network, and they derailed plans for a Mubarak-Suleiman handover. Yet when Egyptian officers – in close contact with the White House – pushed Mubarak aside, they circumscribed the revolt and safeguarded their position as political overseers. Policymakers in Washington would wring their hands over the United States' putative lack of intelligence about the threat to Mubarak. Once the immediate crisis had passed, however, they continued to see Egypt in terms of regional security, rather than local attitudes. During the first year after Mubarak fell, relations between the Obama administration and the SCAF would display a familiar mix of public tension and unwavering strategic cooperation.

Conclusion

In 2009, a Council on Foreign Relations study speculated that if new leaders took power in Egypt, "Washington would no longer be able to rely on Cairo to undertake initiatives that are profoundly unpopular with the Egyptian people."[1] U.S. presidents from Carter to Obama have counted on their Egyptian counterparts to do the "profoundly unpopular." Since 1979, U.S. and Egyptian leaders have advanced U.S. strategic goals in the Middle East (namely, Israeli security and U.S. influence in the Persian Gulf) while forestalling democracy in Egypt. Public discourse and internal deliberations show top decision makers interested in political reform and this book does not charge individuals in either government with hypocrisy. But the promotion of democracy and other altruistic aims has come second to a strategic vision that depends on autocratic continuity. Bilateral peace between Egypt and Israel required Sadat to rule with an iron fist while shackling Egyptian dissidents. Authoritarianism kept public opinion in check and held Egypt's position in the United States' strategic framework.

Two years after the Council on Foreign Relations paper, popular protests threatened to raise Egyptians' interests above U.S. security demands. The January 25 Revolution showed that the hypothetical threat of a potential electoral victory by the Muslim Brotherhood misconstrued Washington's dilemma. On one hand, conservative Islamic rule did not preclude alignment with U.S. geostrategy. The United States worked closely with the orthodox Kingdom of Saudi Arabia. In Egypt, the United States' "problem" was not with Islam but with the people. *Democratically* elected governments, whether they were led by Islamists or secularists, could review Egypt's relations with its allies. Therefore the specter of "one man, one vote, one time" mattered less to U.S. primacy than did the prospect of repeated voting and new foreign policies.[2]

When Egyptians marked the first anniversary of their uprising, democracy and major policy changes remained elusive. After two decades of political decline, the Egyptian military suddenly occupied the helm of national power. Over the short term, Field Marshal Tantawi and the generals would rule; beyond that they hoped to preserve veto power over civilian governments. The stakes were high. Any democratically elected government could threaten the military's independent income stream from its enclave in the economy. Its manufacturing and export revenues were subsidized by conscripted labor, U.S. aid, and government spending that had historically been exempt from taxation and parliamentary oversight.[3] Within a short time the presiding military council had proved just as heavy-handed as Mubarak.

This conclusion assesses developments in Egypt during the remainder of 2011 and discusses the comparative lessons from Tunisia and other sites of major uprisings. I then distill the implications of this study. Even as tireless activists ensured Egypt would be more contentious than in decades, the struggle for democracy remained arduous. The prospect that authoritarianism in Egypt would outlast Mubarak owed to domestic and international factors, foremost among them the Egyptian military's dominance and its robust alliance with the world's sole superpower. As the Egyptian military sought to retain power, the U.S. government preferred having a pliable ally in Cairo.

Post-Mubarak Authoritarianism

Whereas the Tunisian military eschewed politics, the armed forces in other Arab states were invested in their countries' regimes. In Egypt, popular rule threatened the officers who backstopped authoritarianism and who controlled a part of the economy. Rather than stepping aside, the members of the SCAF made themselves interim leaders. Instead of receding into the wings of a civilian-led democracy, the junta hunkered down.

After February 11, protesters converged on Tahrir most Friday afternoons. Young members of April 6, We Are All Khaled Said, the January 25 movement, ElBaradei's alliance, the Muslim Brotherhood, and several liberal groups formed the Youth of the Revolution Coalition.[4] The Coalition fought to hold the government accountable and erase Mubarak's legacy – with intermittent success. On February 3, the military council replaced Prime Minister Ahmed Shafiq, a holdover from Mubarak's last cabinet, with Essam Sharaf, a popular civilian.[5] In March the coalition celebrated when the public prosecutor remanded Hosni Mubarak and his two sons into police custody for crimes committed during Mubarak's tenure. That summer the three men went on trial. Mubarak was charged with ordering police to shoot demonstrators with live ammunition during the uprising and with profiting from underpriced natural gas sales to Israel. Gamal and Alaa were accused of accepting villas in Sharm El-Sheikh in exchange for facilitating underpriced land purchases.[6]

Although the revolutionary youth scored tactical victories, the SCAF set the national agenda. While exposing Mubarak's coterie, acting-president Tantawi and his fellow officers protected the presidency, the police, and themselves. The military leaders did not need to resurrect the security state – it had never disappeared – and they blocked their opponents from dismantling it. While the SCAF shuffled personnel and allowed politicized trials, it preserved the authoritarian system. The junta did not allow Egyptians to overturn the 1971 constitution; it did not reform the Ministry of Interior; and in autumn 2011, when tens of thousands rallied against Tantawi, it did not cede power to civilians.

When Mubarak resigned, the SCAF suspended the constitution and began directing the transition. The military leaders designated a committee of jurists to write constitutional amendments that would enable parliamentary elections within six months and presidential polls before the end of the year. They tapped Tarek El-Bishry, a legal guru and Mubarak critic, to head the committee.

On February 26, the committee proposed amending seven articles of the constitution and eliminating an eighth. The changes ameliorated autocratic elements of the 1971 constitution and established a framework for fresh elections. They restricted the president to two four-year terms and loosened candidacy requirements. Presidential candidates who did not hail from parties with a parliamentary presence would need 30,000 signatures, including at least 1,000 each from fifteen of Egypt's twenty-seven governorates. The amendments also eliminated antiterrorism provisions and they required that a president extending the state of emergency beyond six months would need to pass the measure in a public referendum.⁷ The committee's proposal scheduled parliamentary and presidential elections before the end of 2011. The elected bodies would select delegates to a one-hundred-member constituent assembly, which would write a new constitution. These changes, however, did not preclude another authoritarian chief executive ruling Egypt. Sadat and Mubarak had overridden term limits. Further, the president still commanded extraordinary powers, while the parliament and the judiciary remained weak.

The constitutional proposals divided Egypt's political organizations into two camps. Liberals and leftists favored scrapping the 1971 constitution and they wanted more time to build public support. Their alternative was for a committee of experts to write a new constitution, after which elections would be held no earlier than spring 2012. This process, they maintained, would help new groups catch up to the recognized parties, the Muslim Brotherhood and the NDP. (Although the former ruling party was in disarray – and a court would dissolve it in April 2011 – the NDP provided a bank of seasoned candidates with significant local networks.)

Islamists, including the Muslim Brotherhood and Salafists, endorsed the constitutional measure. (Salafists advanced a more stringent interpretation of Islam than the Muslim Brotherhood. They had not participated as a bloc in elections under Mubarak.) The current constitution included article 2, which set the principles of Islamic jurisprudence as the main basis of Egyptian law, and Egypt's Islamists did not want to tamper with that provision. They also expected to fare well in elections. (Under newly reformed party registration procedures, the Muslim Brotherhood later won recognition for an official political wing, the Freedom and Justice Party [FJP].⁸ Salafists formed their own parties, including the Nour [Light] Party.) Whereas the liberal-leftist camp wanted more time and more change in the constitution, the Islamists were comfortable with elections later in the year and a conservative approach to constitutional reform.

On March 19, 18 million people queued to vote on the amendments in the first free and fair election of the Egyptian republic. Seventy-seven percent approved the measure, a thunderous signal of the Islamists' popularity.[9] The 23 percent "no" vote signaled that the Youth of the Revolution Coalition did not dominate the polls as it did in Tahrir. Soon after the results came in, however, the SCAF validated liberals and leftists' concerns of antidemocratic rule. On March 30, the generals issued a sixty-three-article "interim constitutional declaration" that superseded both the autocratic 1971 constitution and the approved constitutional amendments.[10] Similar to the 1971 constitution in spirit, the declaration enumerated individual rights but did not provide mechanisms for guaranteeing them.[11] Rather than deriving its power from the people, the SCAF treated the Egyptian public as an audience to manipulate or ignore.

After first announcing that sovereignty lay with the people, the SCAF behaved as an autocratic cabal, selectively meeting civilians and unilaterally issuing decrees.[12] When workers went on strike for stable employment and a living wage, the junta and state media vilified labor actions as "special interest" plots that impeded the revolution. On March 23, the government of prime minister Essam Sharaf banned contentious collective actions that threatened commerce. Violators faced a year's imprisonment and a 500,000 Egyptian-pound fine (about $84,000, whereas the monthly minimum wage was a little more than $200).[13] Although the SCAF repeatedly pledged to lift the state of emergency when circumstances permitted, the draconian strictures on public life remained operative.[14] Some SCAF members proposed reserving in the Egyptian constitution a political role for the military.[15]

Mubarak was behind bars but his institutions kept running. The SCAF retained Mubarak's propaganda arm, the Ministry of Information, and his coercive instruments. The dreaded internal police, State Security, resurfaced as "National Security." Family members of those killed in the uprising pushed in vain for the SCAF to hold their loved ones' assailants accountable. Instead of addressing the public's concerns, the junta answered their critics with censorship, detentions, and police raids.[16] The SCAF expanded military trials against civilians and, in its first six months in power, referred more than 10,000 civilians to military courts. Asmaa Mahfouz was threatened with a military trial before a massive outcry prompted the SCAF to release her.[17]

Thousands of other dissidents lingered in legal purgatory or faced military tribunals. Meanwhile, Mubarak's clan and his closest associates appeared in conventional criminal courts, with tighter evidentiary and procedural standards than Egypt's military justice system.

When it came to Coptic rights and security, the SCAF crossed the line from benign dictatorship to lethal misrule. The popularity of Islamists concerned Egyptian Copts. Their worries grew as groups began burning churches and assaulting Christian communities across Egypt. Copts beseeched the SCAF to intervene and protect their places of worship, but to no avail. On Sunday, October 9, after the recent arson of a church in Aswan, a large group of Copts and non-Coptic supporters marched toward the Maspero building, home of the Egyptian Television and Radio Union, the state broadcast service, to denounce the SCAF's complicity in anti-Coptic violence. Before they could reach the building, army vehicles plowed through the demonstrators. State television then claimed protesters were initiating violence and incited viewers to reinforce the army. While the Copts and their Muslim colleagues tried to regroup, thugs on nearby rooftops began barraging them with projectiles. Twenty-seven civilians died in the "Maspero massacre."

The SCAF defended itself by saying some soldiers had panicked. Rather than punishing those troops, the junta incarcerated thirty-one of the demonstrators and slated them for military trials.[18] Unashamed by the violence against civilians, Tantawi and his fellow officers announced they intended to retain power through elections for parliament (eventually set to proceed in stages between November and March) and the presidency, which could occur as late as 2013. El-Bishry called the move a "violation of the constitutional declaration" that he had helped author.[19]

The luster of military rule was fading. In early spring of 2011, 88 percent of Egyptians polled thought the military was playing a positive role in events and 90 percent approved of Tantawi. But polling in late October of the same year showed that most Egyptians no longer saw the army as an ally. More than two-fifths of respondents contended the SCAF was subverting the "gains of the revolution."[20]

Defiant, the SCAF tightened the constitutional process in the coming months. At the beginning of November, Deputy Prime Minister Ali El-Selmy presented a list of "supra-constitutional principles" to govern the transition period. The "El-Selmy document," as the list of principles came to be known, proved more controversial than did the articles of the March 30 Constitutional Declaration. It freed the military from future budget oversight by parliament and, in a stunning power grab, stipulated that 80 percent of the hundred-member constituent assembly charged with writing the new constitution would have to conform to quotas set by the SCAF. For example, fifteen would have to be university professors, and another fifteen would hail from the professional syndicates. In such a system, old regime loyalists could find their way onto the body writing Egypt's supposedly democratic constitution. The two houses of parliament, the People's Assembly and the Consultative Assembly, would independently choose only twenty members of the constituent assembly, diluting the already modest influence of elected MPs.[21]

Secularists and Islamists were outraged. The Youth of the Revolution Coalition rejected any attempt to concentrate power in the military. Members of the Muslim Brotherhood and Salafist groups objected to any measures that would weaken the parliament they expected to dominate. El-Selmy met with representatives from Egypt's major parties and movements to try and mollify them, but his document would, by default, structure future discussions. Unsatisfied, Islamists, liberals, and leftists brought tens of thousands (some estimates claimed hundreds of thousands) to Tahrir Square on Friday, November 18: The Friday of Protecting Democracy. Their partisans demanded the SCAF renounce the El-Selmy document, allow presidential elections no later than mid-May 2012, and relinquish power. After the initial day of protest, however, this alliance fragmented along familiar lines. The Muslim Brotherhood (and its political wing, the FJP) opposed the articles in the El-Selmy document that gave the SCAF powers that belonged with parliament, including the authority to choose 80 percent of the constitutional assembly.[22] But youth activists outside of the Muslim Brotherhood advocated a more radical break. They wanted the SCAF to cede power immediately, before elections. These activists, working without Brotherhood support, then mounted the largest popular challenge yet to the SCAF.

This second uprising grew from a relatively small sit-in on Saturday, November 19, the day after the Friday of Protecting Democracy. Participants sought compensation for the victims and families of civilians injured or killed in the eighteen-day revolt against Mubarak. Police tried to disperse the gathering, at which point thousands more joined the sit-in. By nightfall it had become an insurrection. In scenes reminiscent of late January, protesters pushed back the Central Security Forces.[23] The next week, tents and field hospitals checkered the square, while dissidents withstood clouds of tear gas and volleys of live ammunition. Supporters of their cause demonstrated in Alexandria, Assiut, and other parts of the country. More than three dozen civilians were killed and more than a thousand injured before the SCAF addressed the violence.

Speaking on national television Tantawi refused the crowds' core demand, that he resign, and he insisted parliamentary elections begin on schedule, on Monday, November 28. He also pledged that the armed forces sought no political role after the transition and, in a quasi-concession, he moved presidential elections up to June 2012. The shift to earlier presidential polls suggested the SCAF would leave power within a year, but it narrowed the window for constitutional debate. Under one timetable, members of the constitutional assembly would have only a single month, from April 10 until May 10, to draft the new constitution. Under such time constraints, drafters of Egypt's next political system would likely defer to prior SCAF texts like the March 30 Constitutional Declaration and the El-Selmy document.[24]

After Tantawi addressed the country, tear gas blanketed Tahrir and protesters again clashed with police. The military barricaded the street leading from the square to the nearby Ministry of Interior to prevent activists from marching on the ministry. While central Cairo remained on edge, though, millions of other Egyptians accepted Tantawi's plan, if not the sentiment behind it. The quickest path to civilian government – if not civilian rule – was voting. Elections would bring a sense of normality to the country, even if it also meant normalizing the military's extraordinary powers.

Elections for the People's Assembly were staggered across three stages, each covering nine of the country's twenty-seven governorates. Two-thirds of the 498 seats at stake would be filled proportionally through party lists. The other third would be decided among individual candidates. Another ten MPs would be appointed by acting-president Tantawi. More than half of registered voters participated in the first stage. Most of them supported Islamists. Results showed the

Freedom and Justice Party would control a plurality of seats and Salafists would form the second largest bloc. Liberals and leftists, now clustered around two coalitions, the Egyptian Bloc and the much smaller Revolution Continues Alliance, struggled to win a tenth of contested seats.

Foreign Relations

Mubarak had fancied himself saving Egypt from Iranian-style theocracy, but Egyptians hoped to emulate Ankara, not Tehran. In fall 2011, two-fifths of Egyptians said that they preferred candidates like Prime Minister Erdogan and a political system like Turkey's.[25] When it came to foreign affairs, the democratic government of Turkey respected its allies while advancing its own interests. Likewise, a democratic Egypt could pursue foreign policies that diverged from its partners' priorities. Very little divergence occurred, however, thanks to the SCAF, which foiled diplomatic innovation and suppressed domestic dissent. Like its approach to constitutional reform, the ruling military council managed public attitudes on foreign policy rather than answering them. Although the junta and its emissaries periodically criticized Israeli and U.S. actions, they did not realign Egypt or contest Washington's regional strategy.

Despite continuity in Egyptian policies overall, Israeli and U.S. officials worried about the unrest simmering beneath military rule. Their responses echoed debates during the Freedom Agenda about the best way to stabilize the Egyptian regime. Some favored overt authoritarianism; others advocated limited reforms that would help the SCAF retain control. Israeli prime minister Benjamin Netanyahu warned that the Arab Spring had unleashed antidemocratic forces; the White House and State Department said Tantawi needed to normalize Egyptian public life by lifting the state of emergency and reducing attacks on civilian demonstrators.

After Mubarak, Egypt's relations with Israel were punctuated by moments of tension. Even though Egyptian "hard" power threatened Israel less than in 1973, a democratic Egypt could exercise more "soft" power than Sadat or Mubarak wielded.[26] With a meaningful legislature, Egyptians, like their Israeli counterparts, could cite local opinion as the anchor of foreign policy. "If we do it right, we will be under the same pressures that everybody is under in a democratic country," said Ambassador Nabil Fahmy. He described the potential shift:

> When we would say, 'The Israelis need to go back to the 1967 borders,' [American officials] would say, 'Well, the Israelis have a coalition government, and there is this small, minute, political party that is way off the wall here but holds the seat in some subcommittee.' Well, we have it too. So yes, you are going to see a much more assertive Egypt, an Egypt that is not less concerned with strategic objectives – they won't change – but much more concerned with immediate short-term things [related to domestic politics].[27]

For local sentiments to become regional influence, however, leaders would need to advance the public's preferences rather than their own ideas.

During its first days in power, the SCAF pledged to uphold Egypt's international obligations. While 54 percent of Egyptians surveyed said the treaty with Israel should be annulled (while 36 percent favored maintaining it), the military command recognized peace with Israel as a strategic necessity.[28] At the same time, the officers could use domestic uncertainty to their advantage abroad. Egypt had weathered its most serious crisis in thirty years. The military could guarantee the peace treaty would not be scrapped. Such radical possibilities, however remote, buttressed the junta's position. Like Mubarak after Sadat's assassination, Tantawi enjoyed an opportunity to adjust Egyptian foreign policies while staying within the bounds of the post-1979 Egyptian-Israeli relationship.

The main shifts the SCAF oversaw concerned the Palestinians, the Gaza Strip, and the Sinai Peninsula. In May, Murad Muwafi, Suleiman's successor as head of the General Intelligence Services, brokered a Fatah-Hamas reconciliation deal. That month, the SCAF also reopened the Rafah border crossing. Both steps drew domestic applause, although no more than five hundred Palestinians were allowed into Egypt on any given day (creating a four-week-long queue by the end of summer) and the Palestinian accord mimicked a text designed by Suleiman.[29] With respect to the Sinai, the Egyptian government had long contended it needed a larger military presence there. Saboteurs reinforced that argument. Between February 5 and November 10, they targeted the pipeline delivering gas to Israel (as well as

Jordan) seven times, forcing lengthy suspensions of the flow of gas.[30] In response Israel acceded to Egypt, stationing 10,000 troops in the Peninsula and 4,000 at the border.[31]

Added border security did not stop a lethal encounter between Israeli and Egyptian military forces. In August, Arab gunmen killed eight Israelis in a series of coordinated attacks. When Israeli troops pursued the attackers they killed five Egyptian soldiers inside the Sinai. Thousands protested around the Israeli embassy in Cairo. The SCAF demanded an apology from Israel, but affirmed the peace treaty was safe.[32] On Friday, September 9, demonstrators breached the wall outside the high-rise housing the Israeli embassy and stormed inside. Egyptian officials again vowed to honor their country's international agreements and ensure the safety of foreign officials. This stance matched broader public sentiments. Despite the drama in Cairo, only one in three Egyptians favored the radical step of abrogating the peace treaty.[33]

Even with the SCAF sustaining Egypt's international alignment, Israel and the United States had alienated the Egyptian public and people across the Arab world. On September 23, Palestinian president Mahmoud Abbas asked the United Nations to recognize Palestine as a member state. The proposal failed to win a majority on the UN Security Council and, if it had, would have faced a promised U.S. veto. The blow to the Palestinian Authority reinforced regional skepticism. Two years after Obama's Cairo speech, most Arabs had little confidence in the U.S.-led peace process. Respondents in five Arab states (Egypt, Jordan, Lebanon, Morocco, and the United Arab Emirates) saw Israeli security (44 percent) and control over oil (53 percent) driving U.S. foreign policy. Two thirds supported a two-state solution along the pre-1967 War borders, but a majority believed such peace was unattainable. Fifty-nine percent viewed the United States unfavorably, and most (52 percent) identified Israeli-Palestinian peace as the best way to improve their view of Washington.[34]

In light of these attitudes, democracy in Egypt threatened to increase diplomatic pressure on Israel and criticisms of U.S. policies. During the November demonstrations in Tahrir, Netanyahu said the Arab uprisings had birthed an "anti-Western, anti-liberal, anti-Israeli and anti-democratic wave."[35] Obama did not want to see a hostile government take root on the Nile either. But he also saw risks if Egypt changed too slowly. Thus the White House sought to preserve military control overall while preventing a popular revolution. While declaring a pro-democracy policy, Obama and his national security team defended military aid against congressional efforts to apply conditionality and mildly urged the Egyptian army to reduce repression. Much like the Freedom Agenda, this "new chapter in American diplomacy" purported to break the mold; in actuality it repackaged old priorities.[36]

On May 19, Obama spoke to employees of the State Department and invited guests about the Arab uprisings. He depicted a region in which the only route to justice was through revolution: "In too many countries, a citizen like that young vendor [Bouazizi] had nowhere to turn – no honest judiciary to hear his case . . . no free and fair election where he could choose his leader." The task for U.S. foreign policy, he averred, would be to help end such desperation and build a better future. In language that recalled Bush's 2003 National Endowment for Democracy speech, Obama pivoted from the failed approaches of the past to a vision that balanced ideals and interests:

> For decades, the United States has pursued a set of core interests in the region: countering terrorism and stopping the spread of nuclear weapons; securing the free flow of commerce and safe-guarding the security of the region; standing up for Israel's security and pursuing Arab-Israeli peace. We will continue to do these things, with the firm belief that America's interests are not hostile to people's hopes; they're essential to them. . . . Yet we must acknowledge that a strategy based solely upon the narrow pursuit of these interests will not fill an empty stomach or allow someone to speak their mind.

If the United States continued to rank security ahead of democracy, U.S. relations with the Arab world would deteriorate. Moreover, in the long run, these autocracies would shatter: "The status quo is not sustainable. Societies held together by fear and repression may offer the illusion of stability for a time, but they are built upon fault lines that will eventually tear asunder."[37]

Although posing as an iconoclast, Obama offered no end to the despotism Washington had enabled. "It will be the policy of the United States to promote reform across the region," he vowed, "and to support transitions to democracy." He continued, saying, "That effort begins in Egypt and Tunisia, where the stakes are high – as Tunisia was at the vanguard of this democratic wave, and Egypt is both a longstanding partner and the Arab world's largest nation." Supporting transitions, however, would not mean withdrawing U.S. support from the Egyptian regime. Obama preferred to discuss new economic programs rather than cut U.S. aid to the Egyptian security state. His proposals comprised additional loans and mandates for neoliberal reform, measures that, if accepted, would likely exacerbate poverty.[38] The president said nothing about reducing weapons sales or military aid for nondemocratic regimes. On Bahrain he blandly urged "dialogue" between battered oppositionists and a kingdom armed by the United States and backed to the hilt by the United States' biggest client in the Persian Gulf, Saudi Arabia.[39] Whether Arab autocracies were unsustainable or not, the United States looked ready to prop them up as long as possible.[40]

After fretting about intelligence failures during the Egyptian uprising, U.S. lawmakers continued seeing U.S.-Egyptian relations and U.S. aid to Egypt through the prism of Israeli security. The chairwoman of the House Foreign Relations Committee, Ileana Ros-Lehtinen (R-FL), sought to ensure that U.S. military assistance affirmed the United States' "unwavering support for . . . Israel, especially" through the two countries' "close relationship and cooperation on missile defense" and by preserving Israel's "Qualitative Military Edge" over neighboring states. And, because the Egyptian uprising had opened the prospect that the Muslim Brotherhood, other Islamist groups, or non-Islamist critics of the United States could take power electorally, the committee also "condition[ed] U.S. assistance to Egypt, Lebanon, Yemen and the Palestinian Authority" to ensure that U.S. citizens' dollars would not go to "groups that seek to undermine U.S. policies, interests, and allies."[41] In similar fashion, the House Foreign Appropriations Subcommittee linked military aid to Egypt's posture toward Israel. "We have placed restrictions on our aid to Egypt," commented Chairwoman Kay Granger (R-TX) when the subcommittee convened to mark up the fiscal year 2012 State and Foreign Operations Appropriations bill. "The Egyptians have been a key strategic ally and we value our military-to-military relationship," she remarked, but "we will continue to support the Egyptian government as they go through its transition with the conditions that they will fully honor their treaty with Israel, end the smuggling tunnels, and make sure a new government is not aligned with terrorist organizations."⁴² These were arguments about preventing Egyptian hostility toward Israel, not about fostering democracy. The White House continued rejecting conditionality but affirmed its commitment to Israeli defense. Obama increased military aid to Israel, reinforcing the country's already dominant strategic position.⁴³

Periodic tensions over aid did not rupture bilateral ties between Washington and Cairo. The SCAF even allowed foreign "observers" or "witnesses" to attend the parliamentary elections, a decision Obama hailed.⁴⁴ Relations between the U.S. government and the Egyptian people, however, remained frosty. More Egyptians viewed the United States unfavorably (79 percent) than five years earlier (75 percent), although a majority favored sustaining or strengthening relations.⁴⁵

U.S. and Egyptian interests would never match perfectly, Fahmy believed, but they would overlap significantly: "And that's enough to have a solid relationship. That's exactly what you have with your allies."⁴⁶ "It's an international game," said Muslim Brotherhood spokesman Essam El-erian "[Before the uprising,] it was between intelligence and government and military. Now the people are in the game."⁴⁷ As the locus of Egyptian politics shifted from the square to parliament, it remained to be seen how much "the people" would influence the U.S.-Egyptian alliance. Signs suggested that the ruling military junta would not allow popular sentiments to impede U.S.-Egyptian cooperation. When initial results of the legislative elections favored candidates from the FJP and the Nour Party, the SCAF assured foreign journalists that parliament's power would be limited to ensure that elected politicians did not endanger "Egypt's economy and security and relations with [the] international community."⁴⁸

Egypt amid the Arab Uprisings

Of the major Arab uprisings of 2011, only Tunisia's swung the country sharply from authoritarianism to representative government. Although only four weeks separated the downfall of Ben Ali and Mubarak, twelve months later the two countries appeared decades apart in terms of civilian authority and representative government. A less militarized and less strategically pivotal Arab country, Tunisia advanced rapidly toward electoral democracy while Egyptians labored under SCAF rule.

This pattern extends across the Middle East. Tunisians changed not only a leader but a regime, in large part because the Tunisian military did not pursue a political role and was not a major geostrategic ally of the West. By contrast, in countries where the military was as dominant as it has been in Egypt, if not more so – such as Libya and Syria – uprisings stretched into protracted internal conflicts. Furthermore, where genuine revolution threatened military and security cooperation, as in Bahrain and Yemen, the United States hedged its bets rather than side with the opposition.

Juxtaposed with Egypt, Tunisia's healthy tradition of civil-military relations offered a more propitious starting point for democratization. With a president-for-life, corrupt elections, and massive domestic policing, Ben Ali's regime resembled Egypt under Mubarak. But these features belied a political community poised to govern. Tunisia's founder, Habib Bourguiba, did not have a background in armed struggle, and he kept the military small and removed from national politics.[49] Even after Ben Ali pushed aside Bourguiba in a 1987 coup, the uniformed military never numbered more than 35,000 soldiers. (The combined police and security forces were four times as large.)[50] Because the Tunisian military had not become invested in national politics, Ben Ali overreached when he called on them to rescue his regime in 2011. Army chief Rachid Ammar refused Ben Ali's order to fire on unarmed demonstrators in the town of Kasserine, replying that the military would not shoot the people but would instead deploy troops to calm the situation.[51] The Tunisian army then moved into Tunis, separating protesters from the police. The head of the presidential guard, Ali Seriati, ushered Ben Ali out of the country in a bid to take power himself. Ammar allowed Ben Ali to flee, then captured Seriati. The general "made it clear that neither he nor the military had any intention of playing any political role beyond protecting . . . the Tunisian public . . . and ensuring the formation of a civilian-led democracy."[52]

In a second wave of mass protest, Tunisian political parties and civil society organizations pushed to elect a transitional government and constitutional assembly. After Ben Ali went into exile, a wave of Tunisian oppositionists returned from theirs. Led by Ennahda (Renaissance), Tunisia's foremost Islamist movement, these and other grassroots movements demanded a completely new government, free from members of the old regime. In caravans they ferried supporters from the countryside to the capital for a mass sit-in on the government's doorstep. The uprising was known as Kasbah 2 because it took place in the historic quarter of Tunis and was the sequel to the anti–Ben Ali protests. On February 27, Prime Minister Mohamed Ghannouchi, a Ben Ali appointee, bowed to popular pressure and resigned. Four days later, interim Prime Minister Béji Caïd Essebsi announced that new elections would be held for a National Constituent Assembly that would write a fresh constitution and form an interim government until a second round of elections could be carried out under the new system.[53]

The concessions opened the opposition's path to power. A small set of committees representing an array of social and political forces led the transition. Foremost among them was the 150-member High Commission for the Fulfillment of Revolutionary Goals, Political Reform, and Democratic Transition, which included "representatives from 12 political parties, 18 civil society organizations, including trade unions, professional associations, and human rights NGOs."[54] The commission created an inclusive electoral system of proportional representation that virtually guaranteed no single party would win a majority of seats in the Assembly.[55] On October 23, 2011, more than half of all eligible Tunisians cast ballots in a free, fair, and meaningful election. Ennahda won 41 percent of seats in the National Constituent Assembly and formed a coalition government with two leftist parties. On November 22, assembly members began working on a new constitution.

If Tunisians were blessed with a military that was less entangled in politics than the Egyptian armed forces, they benefited secondarily from the fact that their country mattered less to the United States than did Egypt. Washington and Tunis had cooperated on security affairs, principally counterterrorism, but Tunisia was never a regional powerhouse, nor did it pose a strategic challenge to Israel.[56] Tunisia was also not a major oil exporter, like neighboring Libya, and it did not control a strategic chokepoint, like Egypt with the Suez Canal. These traits distinguished the medium-size Mediterranean country from its more pivotal neighbors and help explain the United States' comparably subdued reaction.

The Tunisian uprising caught the Obama administration off guard. On January 14, shortly before Ben Ali left his country, the White House equivocally asked "all parties to maintain calm and avoid violence, and...[for] the Tunisian government to respect human rights, and to hold free and fair elections in the near future that reflect the true will and aspirations of the Tunisian people."[57] After the protesters had triumphed Obama positioned the United States on their side, declaring on January 25, "The will of the people proved more powerful than the writ of a dictator. And tonight, let us be clear: The United States of America stands with the people of Tunisia, and supports the democratic aspirations of all people."[58]

Obama's tardy salute to the foes of a pro-U.S. regime prefigured the U.S. response to upheaval in Egypt and other Arab states: Amid the crisis the administration would urge calm – and by implication a return to the undemocratic status quo – but if opposition forces forced the ruler out, U.S. officials would extol the victory as if they had been seeking democratic change all along. Until events broke in one direction or the other, Washington sought to demobilize protesters and restabilize allied regimes. This pattern became clear during the eighteen-day uprising against Mubarak, and it reemerged in the months that followed as the White House sought to minimize the damage to U.S. interests from other Arab uprisings.

Just as the overthrow of Ben Ali in Tunisia inspired Egyptians, the revolt against Mubarak emboldened protest movements across the Arab world. In late January, demonstrators in Yemen and Syria began calling for Presidents Ali Abdullah Saleh and Bashar al-Asad to step down. These campaigns expanded when Egyptians celebrated Mubarak's resignation on February 11, 2011. Approximately one week later, Libyans and Bahrainis rose up against their rulers. By early March, insurrections gripped four Arab nations. Significantly, none of the leaders in question fell as quickly as Ben Ali or Mubarak had. Regimes responded to the second phase of the Arab Spring with much heavier levels of violence than Egyptian and Tunisian protesters had faced. The Bahraini opposition was physically crushed by the kingdom's own security forces and a Saudi-led Gulf Cooperation Council invasion force.[59] Muammar Qadhafi launched uninhibited military assaults upon armed rebels until March 19, when NATO forces imposed a UN-authorized "no-fly zone." The action, which grew to include active support on the ground as well as from the air, enabled the opposition to push back against Qadhafi's forces and topple the regime in October. At the end of 2011, foreign militaries had not intervened in Yemen and Syria. In November, Saleh belatedly accepted a Gulf Cooperation Council deal to relinquish his office in exchange for immunity from prosecution. The Yemeni president had ruled for thirty-three years; violent rifts between his regime and its opponents continued after he resigned. In Syria, Asad's regime killed thousands, fighting first unarmed protesters and then organized militias.

Implications

Briefly it looked as if the Arab uprisings would topple durable autocracies and the literature that investigated them in one blow. A year after Tunisians blanketed the streets, though, three-quarters of the region's regimes remained intact, and democracy champions in Egypt, Libya, and Yemen faced an uphill climb. Much *had* changed: New groups opposing corruption and repression strove to institutionalize political accountability. The inception of dynamic social movements, however, did not equate to the fall of old political orders. As the dust settled, authoritarian regimes that initially appeared brittle had withstood the strongest regional challenge in decades and looked resilient once more.

When regimes survived they reinforced prior theories of robust authoritarianism – theories that had seemed analytically bankrupt when the revolts first erupted.[60] In particular, elite unity remained a major force in authoritarian continuity and, conversely, elite cleavages mattered immensely for regime change.[61] The contrast between democratizing Tunisia, on one side, and still-autocratic Egypt, Syria, and Yemen, on the other, underscored the pivotal role of General Ammar. In the absence of high-level fragmentation, the opposition removed leaders but did not replace them with its own people. As Egyptian activist and political scientist Rabab El-Mahdi put it, "In a revolution, you would assume that the revolutionaries take over power, and this is something we haven't seen."[62]

Regime cohesion, however, also spotlights the impact of activists who challenged sturdy states. Rather than waiting for intraregime fissures, Egyptian organizers moved against a strong regime with superpower support. Only when the opposition made "orderly transition" untenable on February 10 did the United States, in communication with the SCAF, accede to Mubarak's resignation and an extraconstitutional transition. Hence, popular mobilization, while not overturning the Egyptian political system in a revolutionary sense, forced influential participants to shift their positions.

The interplay of domestic dissidents, local elites, and foreign patrons in the Arab uprisings pushes the frontier of research on the role of international forces in authoritarianism. In the post–Cold War era, Susan Hyde has observed a norm toward election monitoring that fits general expectations of a liberalizing trend in foreign affairs. An international preference for foreign observers at election time puts rulers in a bind: They must permit delegations and risk constraining their chance of manipulating results, or be branded as antidemocrats.[63] The normative push for election monitoring should be especially strong when the regime in question works closely with the West. Curiously, Mubarak always refused monitors.[64] The SCAF eventually accepted them under the face-saving guise of election "followers" or "witnesses," but only for polls that did not threaten the military's authority.[65] The history of the U.S.-Egyptian alliance helps explain why Egypt, while wedded to Washington in terms of aid and geostrategy, resisted election observation.

Even as liberal norms toward election monitoring spread globally, policy makers in Washington and Cairo followed countervailing *security* norms. Hence, far from disproving the importance of norms in shaping regime behavior, the U.S.-Egyptian relationship reveals an alternative set of values. These values presuppose the suppression of popular sovereignty, they run counter to publicly professed liberalism, and they shape the goals of U.S. and Egyptian officials. Security norms also help to explain why, in the case of Egypt, the United States' unparalleled linkage to and leverage over an autocratic ally has not brought Egyptians closer to democracy. Tens of billions of dollars in assistance go only part of the way toward explaining why the United States was so invested in an "orderly transition." What has mattered for the U.S.-Egyptian alliance more than the dollars, the artillery, and the latest generation of vehicles is the political superstructure through which the support flows: U.S. and Egyptian officials worked to block coups and revolts; they colluded to protect the Egyptian government's international alignment; and they accepted U.S. primacy within a mutually advantageous accord.

This pattern suggests scholars and practitioners need to rethink their approach to authoritarianism. Rather than being bounded within the juridical borders of nation-states, authoritarianism is co-constituted by actors from different governments. These officials collaborate to advance common interests and act upon shared subjects. In such cases, foreign powers are not sanctioning or promoting abuses of power from afar; they are producing those practices from within.

Transnational authoritarianism is a companion to the pro-democratic "linkage" and "leverage" studied by Levitsky and Way. The authors' landmark work on competitive authoritarianism measures linkage as connections between the United States and other countries through trade, travel, communication, and regular government cooperation. They identify leverage as vulnerability to democratizing pressure.[66] Further, they argue that the strategic importance of countries like Egypt limits this vulnerability.[67] The issue at hand, however, is not that Egypt would resist democratizing pressure *were it applied by the United States*, but rather that such efforts – on behalf of the public and against the government – have been absent. As I noted in the Introduction, in the conventional sense of Levitsky and Way's main concepts, during the post–Cold War era no autocracy has been more linked to and more leveraged by the United States than Egypt. Rather than prying open the Egyptian regime, however, Washington has preserved it. Whereas Way postulates that "autocrats who rely less on U.S. support would seem to have a freer hand [than Mubarak] to deal with opposition," hundreds died while the White House and Egyptian army banked on Mubarak and Suleiman restoring order.[68]

At the same time, while the U.S.-Egyptian relationship exhibits forms of leverage and linkage that impede democratization, post-Mubarak politics may come to resemble the kinds of *competitive* authoritarianism that Levitsky and Way saw proliferating in the 1990s. This shift would entail the end of supermajorities for a single party and the rise of more robust opposition movements. Rather than the viselike grip of the Mubarak era, Egyptians would then experience freer-but-still-flawed voting and localized thuggery, while an unelected security elite remained the ultimate authority.[69]

Consequently, the main lessons from Egypt in 2011 are in tension but not in contradiction. Egyptian organizers demonstrated they could surmount repression and compel the Egyptian army and foreign patrons to shift positions. Hence mass challengers can provoke leadership changes, even when the regime has not lost foreign support or split from within. Yet a blend of domestic coercion and international support continue to carry authoritarian regimes through extraordinary crises. Initial developments in post-Mubarak Egypt bear out this observation.

On a conceptual level, this project joins efforts by theorists and practitioners to advance beyond the teleological framework of "transitions" that sets all countries on a course toward Western-style democracy.[70] One fruitful response has been the literature on robust authoritarianism and hybrid regimes. Such studies try to identify the forces that help nondemocratic regimes stay in power.[71] While intellectually provocative and often insightful, however, the latest generation of scholarship on authoritarianism actually closely resembles the transition paradigm. The conceptual apparatus of transition scholarship implies that there are conveyor belts carrying countries toward a common democratic outcome. Rather than rejecting the tenets of such thinking, most authoritarianism studies instead try to explain why the conveyor belt has paused or rolled backward. The Arab uprisings implied the belt had resumed forward movement. If students and practitioners continue to place democracy and authoritarianism on a linear continuum, the conveyor-belt approach will retain a certain utility. Still, the struggle of Egyptians against Sadat and Mubarak also entailed substantive political demands that the concepts of democratic transitions do not capture.

From the Autumn of Fury through the January 25 Revolution, Egyptians have questioned what foreign and domestic issues are open to public comment and what subjects Egyptian citizens are expected to take for granted as the sole domain of government. This post–Camp David conflict represented a Gramscian "war of position," a battle over ideas.[72] In this fight for hegemony, the Egyptian regime has been physically fierce and ideologically frail. Periodically Egyptian critics of Sadat's initiative have gained the upper hand in shaping what Egypt's "normal" stance toward the United States and Israel should be. Critics of the bilateral peace with Israel faulted Sadat for pushing the treaty through via a rigged legislature and phony referendum. Twenty-five years later, groups that stood in solidarity with the second Palestinian intifada formed the vanguard against Mubarak and dynastic succession.

The oppositionists who lambasted Sadat and Mubarak for jeopardizing national sovereignty and squandering Egypt's regional influence showed foreign policy was a domestic issue. Therefore, this book strongly endorses long-running efforts in political science to ensure that professional subfield partitions do not obstruct rigorous analysis.[73] In the case of the U.S.-Egyptian alliance, distinctions between "international" and "domestic" forces fragment processes that are better understood holistically. The coming years will determine whether Egyptian protest movements and broader societal constituencies will create a government that is procedurally democratic at home and substantively representative abroad. In the meantime, academic approaches that separate a supposedly external sphere of foreign affairs (about international trade and wars) from an internal realm of domestic politics (about elections and presidential authority) will reveal more about conventions in political science than about contentious politics in Egypt.

The implications of this account for the policy making community relate not to aid programs and conditionality initiatives, but to the worldview that underpins them. Any serious discussion of U.S. democracy promotion in Egypt must first question the U.S. priorities that relegate popular sovereignty in Egypt to a second-order concern. Advocates of political reform have written of using the U.S.-Egyptian military relationship to leverage concessions in the area of democracy. Historically, U.S. policy makers have done the reverse, selectively invoking democracy to influence Egyptian diplomacy and security operations. To reorder this equation, leaders in Washington would need to reconsider how they approach Egypt in the Middle East. Here the Tunisian uprising is instructive. The less the Egyptian military and its chief foreign sponsor in Washington try to mold Egyptian internal politics and the more they accept the goals and priorities of the Egyptian masses, the faster Egyptian organizations will be able to construct their own version of the Tunisian model.

In the absence of a strategic overhaul that renounces the Carter Doctrine and other interventionist strains of U.S. military and intelligence policy, talk of political conditionality will remain a tool for pressuring Egypt to fall in line with U.S. designs. Even then, this hierarchical discourse will be circumscribed by the codependence of U.S.

and Egyptian officials. It follows that U.S. decision makers will only embrace democracy in Egypt if they rely less on the Egyptian regime. Strategically divesting from Egyptian authoritarianism would entail a lower level of security cooperation and a downward adjustment of U.S. goals, so that they do not hinge on the preservation of a nondemocratic government in Cairo.

How might such a shift occur? One scenario would be to put U.S. strategic policy in genuine dialogue with mainstream views in the Arab world. If U.S. officials took Egyptian public opinion seriously as they formulated their goals in the Middle East (rather than assuming the aims first and trying to mold local views afterward), they would harmonize U.S. policy with Egyptians generally and reduce their need for autocratic partners. If the United States then rescinded its behind-the-scenes support for the bastions of authoritarianism in Egypt, bilateral relations might gradually resemble U.S. ties with Turkey since the rise of the Justice and Development Party (AKP) to power in 2002. In the U.S.-Turkish relationship, two allies agree on many issues, but they also have differences of opinion that reflect each government's domestic constituents. One material symptom of such a shift would be reshaping U.S. aid to respond to the needs Egyptians have articulated – such as forgiving the debt to Washington that Mubarak accumulated.

Close

During his first years administering Egypt, Evelyn Baring (Lord Cromer) observed "a hybrid form of government," short of annexation, "to which no name can be given, and for which . . . there is no precedent."[74] Cromer soon embraced this synthesis, which continued long beyond his tenure as viceroy (1883–1907). The United Kingdom's dominion over Egypt lasted until the Free Officers took power in July 1952 and would rank among the most durable modern nondemocratic regimes. In comparison, the U.S.-Egyptian alliance, which the Egyptian-Israeli Peace Treaty of 1979 sealed, has not entailed the formal authority Britain exercised within Egyptian territory. Up through the uprising of 2011, however, the bilateral relationship between U.S. and Egyptian officials promoted shared elite interests over popular opposition with an effectiveness that rivaled the British protectorate.

Of course, as the preceding chapters have shown, the bilateral relationship evolved over time. In the 1970s and 1980s, U.S. and Egyptian officials worked to thwart the Soviet Union, maintain peace between Egypt and Israel, and expand the United States' capacity to intervene in the Persian Gulf. After the Cold War, Washington depended on Cairo for intelligence on Islamist militants and saw Egypt less as a strategic asset. Until the Egyptian army seized control on February 11, 2011, Suleiman was a more central figure in the U.S.-Egyptian alliance than Tantawi.

The uprising of 2011 opened a new phase in U.S.-Egyptian relations but did not crack the security alliance between the two governments. Thanks to the SCAF and its friends abroad, Mubarak's resignation has yet to vindicate the struggle that brought it about. Rather than delivering a watershed, the leadership transition has resembled the aftermath of Sadat's assassination, when officials tweaked Egyptian domestic and foreign policies while reproducing authoritarianism.

Notes

Introduction

1. Memo, Chris Shoemaker to Zbigniew Brzezinski, 9/20/80, NLC-10–31-6-24-4, Jimmy Carter Library (hereafter, JCL), Remote Access Capture [hereafter, RAC] Project; Photograph, n.d., "9/6–12/80" folder, Box 31, NSA-Brzezinski Material, JCL.

2. Skocpol, *States and Social Revolutions.*

3. In a prior book, I accounted for the persistence of Egyptian authoritarianism and electoral hegemony by showing that the institutions of ruling parties sustained elite cohesion. The present book maintains the basic argument that elites only make concessions under duress. At the same time, it recognizes the considerable (but still provisional) success of the Egyptian uprising and seeks to provide an integrated consideration of elite and popular forces. On elites and electoral dominance, see Brownlee, *Authoritarianism in an Age of Democratization.*

4. The United States has not only sought to ensure that Israel's borders are not violated, but has also helped Israel maximize its influence in the original Palestine mandate area and the remainder of the Levant (Lebanon, Syria, Jordan). For U.S. policymakers, therefore, supporting "Israeli security" has entailed promoting Israel's political and military predominance in its subregion.

5. See Brownlee, "Authoritarianism after 1989," 44–49.

6. The causal effects of U.S. policy do not function like a light switch, increasing or decreasing authoritarianism mechanistically. They are "constitutive:" They have been part of what constitutes authoritarianism in Egypt. Katzenstein, *Culture of National Security,* 5, 22.

7. For more than a century, Washington has intervened in the domestic politics of other countries to foil perceived threats to U.S. security or

advance other core interests. On this tradition, Williams's *Tragedy of American Diplomacy* remains the locus classicus.

8. Boix, "Democracy, Development, and the International System;" Fukuyama, "End of History;" Narizny, "Anglo-American Primacy and the Global Spread of Democracy."

9. Carothers, *In the Name of Democracy*; Muravchik, *Exporting Democracy*; Smith, *America's Mission*; Whitehead, "International Aspects of Democratization;" and Barany and Moser, *Is Democracy Exportable?*

10. Huntington, *Third Wave*.

11. Schmitz, *United States and Right-Wing Dictatorships*; Snyder, "Explaining Transitions from Neopatrimonial Dictatorships;" and Herman and Chomsky, *Manufacturing Consent*.

12. Quoted in Schlesinger, *A Thousand Days*, 704–705.

13. These developments occurred under the shadow of Kennedy's Alliance for Progress, an initiative that portrayed the advance of freedom in Latin America as the best ward against communism.

14. Kirkpatrick, "Dictatorships and Double Standards," 34–45.

15. The first wave of democratization took place in the nineteenth century, the second in the first half of the twentieth century. The third wave began in Portugal in April 1974 with a military coup that preceded the first freely elected government in decades. Huntington, *Third Wave*.

16. The oil reserves of Saudi Arabia have long been recognized by the State Department as a "a stupendous source of strategic power, and one of the greatest material prizes of world history." Although seldom grasped conceptually (much less admitted publicly) by those defending it, the United States' post-1973 fixation on the Persian Gulf centers on access to the wealth itself, rather than on controlling the oil or ensuring it flows freely. Oil reached the United States through non-Arab suppliers in late 1973. It was an open question, however, to whom the money from oil sales would flow. Since the 1970s, the principal method of "extracting" the capital of the Gulf into American coffers has been arms sales. Miller, *Search for Security*, 144; and Vitalis, "Closing of the Arabian Oil Frontier."

17. Acemoglu and Robinson, *Economic Origins of Dictatorship and Democracy*, 41; Levitsky and Way, "Rise of Competitive Authoritarianism," 61.

18. Bunce and Wolchik, *Defeating Authoritarian Leaders*.

19. Wollack, "Democracy Promotion in the Age of Obama," *Foreign Policy Forum*, September 21–22, 2009, http://www.foreignpolicyi.org/advancing-and-defending-democracy/democracy-promotion-the-bush-doctrine-in-the-age-of-obama, accessed January 11, 2011.

20. On benevolent and antidemocratic norms, see Finnemore and Sikkink, "International Norm Dynamics and Political Change;" and Vitalis, "Making Racism Invisible."

21. See, among others, Ayubi, *Over-stating the Arab State*; Kassem, *In the Guise of Democracy*; Ross, "Does Oil Hinder Democracy?"; Posusney, "Enduring Authoritarianism;" Herb, "No Representation without Taxation?;" Peters and Moore, "Beyond Boom and Bust;" and Stepan, "'Arab' Electoral Gap."

22. Bellin, "Robustness of Authoritarianism;" and Hudson, "After the Gulf War," 408.

23. Levitsky and Way, *Competitive Authoritarianism*.

24. Levitsky and Way treat strategic considerations as mitigating American leverage (defined as "vulnerability to democratizing pressure"). My approach differs in two main respects. First, I do not take strategic interests as a fixed exogenous variable, instead showing how Washington became invested in Egyptian authoritarianism over time. It follows that I also leave open the prospect that those interests may change in response to international developments or domestic events within Egypt. Second, rather than inferring that a country's strategic importance means it is not susceptible to "democratizing pressure," I argue that America has not *applied* significant democratizing pressure and instead has done the opposite, bolstering authoritarianism through material and political support.

25. By "regime" I mean a structure of authority, rules, practices, and personnel that may be directed by one individual (Sadat, Mubarak) but extends beyond that person. See Fishman, "Rethinking State and Regime."

26. Klare, *American Arms Supermarket*, 112; and Yergin, *The Prize*, 626.

27. Tyler, *World of Trouble*, 125; and Memorandum, Henry A. Kissinger – the Shah of Iran, July 24, 1973, 5:00 – 6:40 P.M., National Security Archive, http://www.gwu.edu/~nsarchiv/NSAEBB/NSAEBB265/index.htm, accessed September 24, 2010.

28. Klare, *American Arms Supermarket*, 108.

29. "U.S. Military Sales to Iran," Subcommittee on Foreign Assistance, U.S. Senate Committee on Foreign Relations, 94th Congress, 2nd session (July 1976), iii.

30. "Jimmy Carter: Champion for Human Rights," *American Experience: Presidents*, http://www.pbs.org/wgbh/amex/presidents/video/carter_13_qt.html#v288, accessed September 24, 2010.

31. Memo, Shoemaker to Brzezinski (NLC-10–31-6–24-4); and Photograph, n.d., "9/6–12/80" folder, Box 31.

32. Harold Brown, "Carter Doctrine," 23.

33. Bronson, *Thicker Than Oil*, 263n4.

34. Dunne, "Integrating Democracy Promotion;" Dunne, "Freedom Agenda;" and Cook, "Arab Reform."

35. Mayer, *Dark Side*; and Grey, *Ghost Plane*.

36. One instance of "exceptionalizing" the standard work of U.S. and Egyptian security forces was Vice President Dick Cheney's reference to working

on the "dark side" in the wake of the September 11, 2001, attacks. The phrase "dark side" implies that practices such as extraordinary rendition and torture occur rarely, and that the norm is more humanitarian. "Interview with Vice President Dick Cheney," *Meet the Press*, September 16, 2001.

37. Specifically, the U.S.-Egyptian partnership represents a "network-as-actor." Unlike preexisting "networks-as-structures," which operate as constraints on their members, networks-as-actors arise through the intentional effort of multiple parties to pursue shared interests. See Keck and Sikkink, *Activists Beyond Borders*, as well as Kahler, "Networked Politics;" Eilstrup-Sangiovanni, "Varieties of Cooperation;" and Sikkink, "Power of Networks." To the extent that the U.S.-Egyptian alliance promotes authoritarianism rather than democracy, it can be classified as a "dark network," albeit a network between governments, not vigilante organizations. Raab and Milward, "Dark Networks as Problems." My approach also draws on Mitchell, "Limits of the State."

38. Gerges, *America and Political Islam*.

39. Edward P. Djerejian, "The US and the Middle East in a changing world," U.S. Department of State Dispatch, June 8, 1992, http://heinonline.org/HOL/LandingPage?collection=journals&handle=hein.journals/dsptch5&div=246&id=&page=, accessed November 3, 2009.

40. Bellin, "Robustness of Authoritarianism;" and Brownlee, "Neopatrimonial Regimes."

41. Bueno de Mesquita, Smith, Siverson, and Morrow, *Logic of Political Survival*.

42. O'Donnell and Schmitter, *Transitions from Authoritarian Rule*, 19.

43. Jackson, *Quasi-States*; and Lustick, "Absence of Middle Eastern Great Powers."

44. "Interview with Hermann Frederick Eilts," 37.

45. Brownlee, "Hereditary Succession," 602.

46. Springborg, "The President and the Field Marshal," 4–11, 14–16, 42.

47. Quinlivan, "Coup-Proofing," 131–165.

48. Stork, "Bailing out Sadat," 8–11.

49. Skocpol, *States and Social Revolutions*.

50. These claims are testable and falsifiable, both at the level of the paired comparison of 1981 and 2011 and in terms of the effects of U.S. involvement on the Egyptian regime over time. For a useful treatment of the difference U.S. influence made on human rights in Latin America, particularly Guatemala, see Sikkink, *Mixed Signals*, 210–211. On standards of evidence in historical analysis, see Fisher, *Historians' Fallacies*; Trachtenberg, *Craft of International History*; and the book review forums of H-Diplo: http://www.h-net.org/~diplo/roundtables/.

51. Scholars have identified similar patterns in the Jordanian-Israeli peace. Brand, "Political Liberalization in Jordan;" and Yom and Al-Momani, "Authoritarian Regime Stability."

Chapter 1: Peace before Freedom

1. Portions of this chapter originally appeared in Brownlee, "Peace Before Freedom," and are reproduced here by permission.
2. See, for example, Quandt, *Camp David*; and Telhami, *Power and Leadership*.
3. For works on U.S.-Egyptian relations during Nasser's presidency, see Alterman, *Egypt and American Foreign Assistance*; Aronson, *From Sideshow to Center Stage*; Copeland, *Game of Nations*; Meyer, *Egypt and the United States*; and Weinbaum, *Egypt and U.S. Economic Aid*.
4. Burns, *Economic Aid*, 2.
5. Ibid., 23, 51.
6. Ibid., 126.
7. Ibid., 121.
8. Ibid., 17.
9. Ibid., 160.
10. Ibid., 74.
11. Ibid., 173.
12. Copeland, *Game of Nations*, 89.
13. Beattie, *Egypt during the Nasser Years*, 122–123.
14. Raymond Baker, *Egypt's Uncertain Revolution*, 99. See also Sirrs, *Egyptian Intelligence Services*, 59–60, 72, 84, 87.
15. Springborg, *Mubarak's Egypt*, 101.
16. "Kalamat al-ra'is Gamal Abdel Nasser fi iftitah dawr al-ina'qad al-khamis li majlis al-umma" [Speech of President Gamal Abdel Nasser on the opening of the fifth session of the national assembly], November 23, 1967, http://nasser.bibalex.org/Speeches/browser.aspx?SID=1224, accessed July 15, 2010.
17. Beattie, *Egypt during the Nasser Years*, 214–215; and Said, *Al-intiqal al-dimuqrati al-muhtajaz*, 6.
18. Abdalla, *Student Movement and National Politics*, 149–153.
19. "Bayan ra'is Gamal Abdel Nasser illa al-umma: Bayan March 30" [Statement of President Gamal Abdel Nasser to the Nation, Statement of March 30], March 30, 1968, http://nasser.bibalex.org/Speeches/browser.aspx?SID=1234, accessed July 15, 2010.
20. Sirrs, *Egyptian Intelligence Services*, 112–113.
21. Said, *Al-intiqal al-dimuqrati al-muhtajaz*, 6; Dekmejian, *Egypt under Nasir*, 309; and Hamrush, *Thawrat 23 Yulio*, 246.
22. Ibrahim, "Domestic Developments in Egypt," 24; and Cooper, *Transformation of Egypt*, 140. In Sadat's memoirs, he deplored Nasser's

apparatus: "Instances were rife of men...who spied on their own kin just like the Fascist regimes." Sadat, *In Search of Identity*, 209.

23. Sadat, *In Search of Identity*, 224.
24. Nathan Brown, *Rule of Law in the Arab World*, 95–96; Moustafa, *Struggle for Constitutional Power*, 69–74; and Said, *Al-intiqal al-dimuqrati al-muhtajaz*, 7.
25. Singerman, "Politics of Emergency Rule," 29–30.
26. Ismail Fahmy, *Negotiating for Peace*, 8.
27. Ambassador Alfred Leroy Atherton, ADST Oral History.
28. Quandt, *Peace Process*, 96; and Kissinger, *Years of Upheaval*, 201.
29. Ismail Fahmy, *Negotiating for Peace*, 6.
30. Kissinger, *Years of Upheaval*, 205.
31. Ibid., 196.
32. Petersen, *Decline of the Anglo-American Middle East*, 30; and Little, *American Orientalism*, 139.
33. National Security Council memorandum, "U.S. Strategy toward the Soviet Union in the Middle East," September 14, 1973, NLC-25-70-16-5-5, JCL, RAC Project.
34. Atherton, ADST Oral History.
35. Fahmy, interview.
36. Seale, *Asad*.
37. Ismail Fahmy, *Negotiating for Peace*, 58–61.
38. Atherton, ADST Oral History; and Quandt, *Peace Process*, 104–120.
39. Quandt, *Peace Process*, 120–124.
40. Kissinger, *Years of Upheaval*, 636–646.
41. Ibid., 640.
42. Eilts, ADST Oral History.
43. Quandt, *Peace Process*, 153–154.
44. Atherton, ADST Oral History.
45. Memo, Cyrus Vance to Jimmy Carter, "Sadat Visit: The Military Supply Issue," March 25, 1977, NLC-128-11-19-1-6, JCL, RAC Project.
46. Stork, "Bailing Out Sadat," 8–11; and Sharp, "Egypt," 31–32.
47. Sinai II also entailed a written U.S. commitment to Israel not to negotiate with the PLO until it accepted UNSC resolutions 242 and 338 and recognized Israel's right to exist – a provision that, while subject to different interpretations, would shape Arab-Israeli peacemaking for years to come. "Interim Agreement between Israel and Egypt," September 1, 1975, http://www.ibiblio.org/sullivan/docs/SinaiII.html (August 10, 2011); Eilts, ADST Oral History; Atherton, ADST Oral History; Quandt, *Peace Process*, 162–170; and Kissinger, *Years of Upheaval*, 456.
48. Telhami, *Power and Leadership*, 99.
49. "Suez Is Busy with Traffic Again, but Fewer Tankers Use the Canal," *New York Times*, June 12, 1977.
50. Waterbury, *Egypt*.

51. Sadat, "Tasks of the Stage: Or, a Comprehensive Civilisation Strategy," from the October Paper, April 1974, p. 54; Raymond Baker, *Egypt's Uncertain Revolution*, 135; and Cooper, *Transformation of Egypt*, 89.
52. Economic reform never progressed as far as the October Paper envisaged. Seven years after Sadat introduced neoliberal privatization, public spending as a share of GDP had risen from less than 50 percent to more than 60 percent. Soliman, *Autumn of Dictatorship*, 39.
53. Waterbury, *Egypt*, 221; Raymond Baker, *Egypt's Uncertain Revolution*, 144–145; Cooper, *Transformation of Egypt*, 91–115; and McLaughlin, "Infitah in Egypt," 885–906.
54. Cooper, *Transformation of Egypt*, 115.
55. Ibid., 118–119.
56. Raymond Baker, *Egypt's Uncertain Revolution*, 167.
57. Ibid., 168.
58. National Security Council study draft, "NSSM 238: US Policy toward the Persian Gulf," September 18, 1976, NLC-25-72-3-2-0, JCL, RAC Project.
59. Telhami, *Power and Leadership*, 96.
60. "Soviet-Egyptian Treaty of Friendship and Cooperation," May 27, 1971, English translation, http://www.sadat.umd.edu/archives/correspondence/AAAC%20Egyptian-Soviet%20Friendship%20Treaty%205.27.71.pdf, accessed January 19, 2010; Stork, "Carter Doctrine," 29.
61. Raymond Baker, *Egypt's Uncertain Revolution*, 139–140.
62. Memo, Cyrus Vance to Carter, NLC-128–11-19-1-6.
63. Stork, "Bailing out Sadat."
64. Stork, "Carter Doctrine," 29.
65. Cooper, *Transformation of Egypt*, 122.
66. Beattie, *Egypt during the Sadat Years*, 311n315.
67. Cooper, *Transformation of Egypt*, 236.
68. Raymond Baker, *Egypt's Uncertain Revolution*, 165–167.
69. Burns, *Economic Aid and American Policy*, 186.
70. Cooper, *Transformation of Egypt*, 240.
71. Raymond Baker, *Egypt's Uncertain Revolution*, 166.
72. Stork and Reachard, "Chronology: U.S.-Egypt Military Relationship," 27; Cooper, *Transformation of Egypt*, 236; and Beattie, *Egypt during the Sadat Years*, 208.
73. Heikal, *Autumn of Fury*; and Ibrahim, "Domestic Developments in Egypt," 25.
74. Beattie, *Egypt during the Sadat Years*, 213.
75. "Kalamat al-ra`is Mohammed Anwar al-Sadat fi liqa'ihi bi a`adaa' al-majlis al-a'la lil-jamia't" [Speech of President Mohammed Anwar al-Sadat in his meeting with members of the higher council for universities], January 30, 1977, http://sadat.bibalex.org/speeches/browser.aspx?SID=539, accessed January 29, 2010.

76. "Al-ra'is Anwar al-Sadat ya`lan fi khitab ham lil-sha`b" [President Anwar al-Sadat announces in a speech guardianship for the people], *Al-Akhbar*, February 4, 1977, 3–4, 7; and Aulas, "A Very Strange Peace," 29.

77. Raymond Baker, *Egypt's Uncertain Revolution*, 155.

78. Memo, Vance to Carter, NLC-128–11-19-1-6, JCL, RAC Project.

79. That same month, the State Department licensed New York–based Jonas Aircraft and Arms Company to sell the Egyptian Ministry of the Interior 100,000 tear- and pepper-gas grenades, over six times what Egypt had acquired the prior year and a sturdy cache for future riot control. Klare and Arnson, *Supplying Repression*.

80. Jimmy Carter, "Inaugural Address," January 20, 1977, http://www .presidency.ucsb.edu/ws/index.php?pid=6575, accessed January 20, 2011; and Jimmy Carter, "Address at the commencement exercises at the University of Notre Dame," May 22, 1977, http://www.presidency .ucsb.edu/mediaplay.php?id=7552&admin=39, accessed January 20, 2011.

81. "Presidential Review Memorandum/NSC 28: Human Rights," August 15, 1977, NLC-132-44-6-1-9, JCL, RAC Project.

82. Dessouki, "Egyptian Foreign Policy since Camp David," 106.

83. Thomas W. Lippmann, "Massive U.S. Aid Flowing to Egypt," *Washington Post*, June 20, 1977.

84. Klare, *American Arms Supermarket*, 264–265.

85. Raymond Baker, *Egypt's Uncertain Revolution*, 143.

86. Carter, *Keeping Faith*, 292–293, 295.

87. Letter, Carter to Sadat, October 21, 1977, Jimmy Carter Library (hereafter, JCL), http://www.jimmycarterlibrary.gov/documents/camp david25/cda04.pdf, accessed January 18, 2011.

88. Carter, *Keeping Faith*, 296.

89. Eilts, ADST Oral History.

90. "Khitab al-ra'is Anwar al-Sadat fi iftitah dawrat al-ina`qad al-thani li majlis al-sha`b" [Speech of President Anwar al-Sadat on the opening of the second session of the People's Assembly], November 9, 1977, http://sadat.bibalex.org/speeches/browser.aspx?SID=641, accessed January 18, 2011.

91. Ibrahim, "Domestic Developments in Egypt," 26.

92. Eilts, ADST Oral History.

93. Sobel, *Peace-Making in the Middle East*, 165.

94. Memo, Alfred L. Atherton to Cyrus Vance, December 6, 1977, NLC-SAFE 17 B-6–31-7-7, JLC, RAC Project.

95. Ibrahim, "Domestic Developments in Egypt," 27; Dessouki, "Egyptian Foreign Policy since Camp David," 96.

96. Ibrahim, "Domestic Developments in Egypt," 27.

97. Hinnebusch, "Children of the Elite," 546.

98. Memo, Alfred L. Atherton to Cyrus Vance, November 28, 1977, NLC-SAFE 39 B-35–5-3-4, JCL, RAC Project.

99. Memo, the White House, November 17, 1977, NLC-1-4-4-50-7, JCL, RAC Project.
100. Quandt, interview.
101. Carter, *Keeping Faith*, 300; Quandt, *Peace Process*, 193; and Carter, *White House Diary*, 164.
102. Carter, *White House Diary*, 146–147.
103. Quandt, *Peace Process*, 195.
104. Ibid., 169; and Quandt, *Peace Process*, 195.
105. Memo, Harold Brown to Zbigniew Brzezinski, April 16, 1977, NLC-6-17-9-18-9, JCL, RAC Project; Memo, Cyrus Vance to Jimmy Carter, May 28, 1977, Brzezinski Material, "Egypt 4–6/77," Box 17, JCL; Memo, the White House, "Sadat is to be informed that President Carter has given approval for taking steps to work out a maintenance program for Egyptian MIGs," August 20, 1977, NLC-1-3-4-35-5, JCL, RAC Project.
106. Vance to Carter, NLC-128-11-19-1-6, JCL, RAC Project.
107. Briefing Paper, the Department of State, "The Military Supply Relationship," 9/15/77 (sic), NLC-5-3-9-2-2, JCL, RAC Project; and Quandt, *Peace Process*, 196.
108. Memo, "Middle East/Persian Gulf Arms Supply," January 19, 1977, NLC-15-31-4-1-6, JCL, RAC Project; and Memo, William B. Quandt to Zbigniew Brzezinski, January 26, 1978, NLC-10-8-4-6-2, JCL, RAC Project.
109. Bronson, *Thicker than Oil*, 143.
110. Letter, Carter to Sadat, May 16, 1978, and Letter, Sadat to Carter, May 17, 1978, both in NSA-Brzezinski Material, "Egypt: President Anwar al-Sadat, 1–12/78," Box 5, JCL.
111. Bronson, *Thicker than Oil*, 143.
112. Raymond Baker, *Egypt's Uncertain Revolution*, 143; and Carter, *Keeping Faith*, 311.
113. Simone Mundesir, "Sadat and Democracy," *Arab Report*, February 14, 1979, 9.
114. Christopher S. Wren, "98% Endorse Sadat's Curbs," *New York Times*, May 23, 1978.
115. *Middle East Journal*, "Chronology: February 16, 1978–May 15, 1978," 160; and *Middle East Journal*, "Chronology: May 16, 1978–August 15, 1978," 460–461.
116. Memo, Harold H. Saunders to Cyrus Vance, June 8, 1978, "Analysis of Arab-Israeli Developments No. 475, June 8, 1978," NLC-17-143-4-7-4, JCL, RAC Project.
117. The stance also provided a study in contrasts when Carter, the following month, stood up to Dominican Republic President Joaquin Balaguer. For the strategically marginal Caribbean nation, Carter rejected electoral malfeasance, warning, "The degree of our country's support for the Dominican Government will depend upon the integrity of the election

process." With respect to Egypt, strategic cooperation mattered more
than calling out Sadat for his stilted plebiscites. Memo, David Aaron to
Carter, May 18, 1978, and memo, Aaron to Cyrus Vance, May 19, 1978,
both in NSA-Brzezinski Material, "Dominican Republic 1/77–1/81," Box
17, JCL.

118. Central Intelligence Agency, "Human Rights Performance: January
1977–July 1978," September 1, 1978, NLC-28–17-15-9-8, JCL, RAC
Project; and Memo, David Aaron to Gary Sick, August 7, 1978, NLC-
25–139-6–6-9, JCL, RAC Project.

119. Quandt, *Peace Process*, 197.

120. Sobel, *Peace-Making in the Middle East*, 221.

121. Telhami, "Evaluating Bargaining Performance," 630.

122. Dayan, *Breakthrough*, 154.

123. Eilts, ADST Oral History.

124. For a critique of the literature that emphasized Sadat's personality, see
Karawan, "Sadat and the Egyptian-Israeli Peace Revisited," 249–266.

125. Carter, *White House Diary*, 225.

126. Carter, *Keeping Faith*, 322.

127. Kamel, *Camp David Accords*, 290.

128. Quandt, interview.

129. Kamel, *Camp David Accords*, 308.

130. Carter, *Keeping Faith*, 356. Sadat's advisors, Carter recorded in his journal, "always try to harden his position to accommodate the feelings of
the Arab leaders in other countries." Carter, *White House Diary*, 234.

131. Carter, *Keeping Faith*, 358; see also Kamel, *Camp David Accords*, 149.

132. Weizman, *Battle for Peace*, 165–166.

133. Ibid., 342.

134. Kamel, *Camp David Accords*, 341.

135. Carter, *Keeping Faith*, 383; and Kamel, *Camp David Accords*, 372.

136. Carter, *White House Diary*, 237.

137. Quandt, *Camp David*, 236, 258.

138. Eilts, ADST Oral History.

139. Brzezinski, *Power and Principle*, 274.

140. Quandt, interview.

141. Kamel, *Camp David Accords*, 357.

142. Carter, *We Can Have Peace*, 35.

143. Part of the concern from the Israeli delegation was that removal of settlers in the Sinai Peninsula would set a precedent for withdrawing them
elsewhere, such as in the Golan Heights. Carter, *White House Diary*,
232.

144. Ibid., 225, 231.

145. Weizman, *Battle for Peace*, 372; Carter, *Keeping Faith*, 312; and
Brzezinski, *Power and Principle*, 270. Sadat would also need to gain
his parliament's imprimatur. This step did not imply an equivalent

amount of political wrangling on the Egyptian side; Sadat's party held more than three-quarters of seats in the legislature, and the institution had historically reflected the preferences of the president. See Dayan, *Breakthrough*, 180; and Kamel, *Camp David Accords*, 356.

146. Carter, *Keeping Faith*, 362, 380, 394; and Carter, *White House Diary*, 227.

147. Atherton, ADST Oral History.

148. Kamel, *Camp David Accords*, 363–368.

149. Atherton, ADST Oral History.

150. Carter, *Keeping Faith*, 405.

151. Quandt, interview.

152. Letter, Sadat to Carter, April 24, 1978, photocopy provided to author.

153. Ibid.

154. Cable, "Analysis of Arab-Israeli Developments: No. 567," September 22, 1978, NLC-SAFE 17 B-13-72-4-7, JCL, RAC Project.

155. Quandt, introduction to *Middle East*, 7; Eilts, ADST Oral History.

156. Minutes, Policy Review Committee Meeting, February 1, 1979, NLC-15-32-4-7-9, JCL, RAC Project.

157. John M. Goshko, "Sadat Seeking Arms, Broader Pro-West Role," *Washington Post*, February 21, 1979. Carter's public remarks were more subdued. See John M. Goshko, "Carter on Regional Stability: A Vision of Mideast at Peace," *Washington Post*, February 23, 1979; Evening News, broadcast by NBC, February 17, 1979, Television News Archive, Vanderbilt University, accessed January 14, 2010.

158. Brzezinski, *Power and Principle*, 277.

159. Brown, interview. The deal would also help the Pentagon's bottom line. In Iran, the Ayatollah Khomeini had cancelled some $8 to $10 billion worth of U.S. arms requested by the shah. Klare, *American Arms Supermarket*, 133.

160. Memo, Brzezinski to Carter, February 1, 1979, NLC-17-82-2-10-0, JCL, RAC Project; and Brown, interview.

161. Carter, *Keeping Faith*, 426.

162. Brzezinski, *Power and Principle*, 283.

163. Quandt, *Camp David*, 302.

164. Carter, *Keeping Faith*, 417, emphasis added.

165. Ibid., 422–425.

166. Ibid., 425.

167. Klare, *American Arms Supermarket*, 142–143.

168. Memo, Walter F. Mondale to Thomas P. O'Neill, April 9, 1979, WHCF, Subject File, "CO45 Executive 1/1/79–6/30/79," Box Co-24, JCL.

169. Quandt, *Peace Process*, 234–235.

170. Klare, *American Arms Supermarket*, 144.

171. Christopher S. Wren, "Egypt, Cut Off from Saudi Funds, Is Likely to Seek Increase in U.S. Arms Aid," *New York Times*, May 22, 1979; and

Graham Hovey, "U.S. Puts Off Jet Sale to Egypt after Saudis Delay on Paying Costs," *New York Times*, July 7, 1979.

172. Sadat's need for foreign armaments reflected an old concern of the Egyptian elite. "The army is a basic factor in Egyptian life," Nasser remarked in 1955. "Our revolution was stimulated in the army by a lack of equipment. If our officers feel we still have no equipment, they will lose faith in the government." Burns, *Economic Aid and American Policy*, 8.

173. Marvin Howe, "Arabs Deeply Split, Bar Stronger Steps against U.S., Egypt," *New York Times*, March 29, 1979.

174. Stanley Reed, "Peace Treaty Blues in Egypt," *Arab Report*, May 9, 1979.

175. "Egypt Assembly Approves Pact," *Los Angeles Times*, April 11, 1979; and Aulas, "A Very Strange Peace," 19.

176. Christopher S. Wren, "Sadat Sets April 9 Vote on Peace Pact," *New York Times*, April 12, 1979.

177. The same referendum began the process of creating a second parliamentary body (the Consultative Assembly) and a supreme council overseeing the press. Anwar Sadat, "Bayan al-ra'is Muhammad Anwar al-Sadat illa al-umma" [Statement of President Muhammed Anwar al-Sadat to the Nation], April 11, 1979, http://sadat.bibalex.org/Speeches/browser.aspx?SID=819, accessed February 2, 2010; and Thomas W. Lippman, "Egyptians Vote on Treaty with Israel," *Washington Post*, April 19, 1979.

178. Evening News, broadcast by NBC, April 19, 1979.

179. "Egypt Votes and Sadat's Sitting Pretty," *Montreal Gazette*, June 7, 1979.

180. Thomas W. Lippman, "Victory by Sadat's Party Strengthens his Control," *Washington Post*, June 11, 1979; and Aulas, "A Very Strange Peace," 18–19.

181. Stanley Reed, "Sadat Stage-Manages the Elections," *Arab Report*, June 6, 1979; and Waterbury, *Egypt of Nasser and Sadat*, 371.

182. Stanley Reed, "Sadat Does It Again," *Arab Report*, June 20, 1979; and Heikal, *Autumn of Fury*, 104, 207.

183. Beattie, *Egypt under Sadat*, 242.

184. General Saad El-Din El-Shazli, army chief of staff during the October War, denounced the treaty as one man's pact: "If Carter and Begin think they will achieve peace in the Middle East through this treaty they are delusional. The treaty is tied to Sadat personally; if Sadat falls, the treaty falls with him." "Al-salam al-surr bayn misr wa isra'il" [The Bitter Peace Between Egypt and Israel], *Al Jazeera*, originally broadcast March 26, 2009, http://www.aljazeera.net/NR/exeres/4BD91528-3DEB-40FF-B3BB-A0CE5F27FAF9, accessed January 15, 2010. Begin's minister of defense shared this view: "The dangers facing the first agreement [the bilateral peace treaty] hinge on Sadat. In the whole Camp David mosaic, Sadat constitutes the key link whose fracture would lead to disintegration of the entire chain." Weizman, *Battle for Peace*, 376.

185. Carter, *White House Diary*, 371.
186. Memo, David E. Mark to Harold H. Saunders, January 4, 1980, NLC-SAFE 17 D-24-18-4-3, JCL, RAC Project.
187. Memo, Brzezinski to Carter, January 9, 1980, NLC-33-6-2-8-9, JCL, RAC Project.
188. Jimmy Carter, "State of the Union Address," January 23, 1980, http://www.jimmycarterlibrary.gov/documents/speeches/su80jec.phtml, accessed January 21, 2010.
189. Stork and Reachard, "Chronology," 31.
190. Carter, *Keeping Faith*, 508.
191. Memo, Peter Tarnoff to Brzezinski, January 5, 1980, NSA-Brzezinski Material, "Egypt, 12/79–1/80," Box 19, JCL; and Cable, Secretary of State to Embassy Cairo, January 25, 1980, NLC-16-120-3-23-3, JCL, RAC Project.
192. Minutes, Special Coordination Committee Meeting, May 29, 1980, NLC-12-48-1-5-0, JCL, RAC Project.
193. Memo, Harold Brown to Carter, May 2, 1980, NLC-12-44-7-22-9, JCL, RAC Project; Minutes, Special Coordination Committee Meeting, August 4, 1980, NLC-12-45-7-10-1, JCL, RAC Project; and Memo, Brzezinski to Carter, September 2, 1980, NLC-7-32-9-12-7, JCL, RAC Project.
194. Memo, Carl R. Smith to Leslie G. Denend, June 16, 1980, NSA-Brzezinski Material, "Egypt, 6/80," Box 19, JCL; and unauthored diagram, NSA-Brzezinski Material, "Egypt, 6/80," Box 19, JCL.
195. Memo, William Odom to Brzezinski, November 26, 1980, NLC-10-33-3-12-8, JCL, RAC Project; Memo, Odom to Brzezinski, December 3, 1980, NLC-SAFE 17 A-33-88-1-2, JCL, RAC Project; and Memo, Chris Shoemaker to Odom, December 17, 1980, NLC-31-121-7-58-3, JCL, RAC Project.
196. Richard Halloran, "U.S. Troops, Taking Off for Egypt, Get Some Advice on Camel Drivers," *New York Times*, November 12, 1980; Special to the *New York Times*, "Americans Fly Into 'Battle' in Egypt in Swirls of Dust," *New York Times*, November 19, 1980; and Richard Halloran, "U.S. Troops Get Lessons in Desert Warfare in Egypt," *New York Times*, December 15, 2010.
197. Christopher S. Wren, "Israel Lowers Flag over Another Part of Sinai and Egyptians Take Over," *New York Times*, September 26, 1979.
198. Youssef M. Ibrahim, "U.S. Stake in Egypt Rests on One Man – Anwar el-Sadat," *New York Times*, March 30, 1980.
199. Memo, Harold Saunders to Cyrus Vance, March 19, 1980, NLC-5-4-1-16-4, JCL, RAC Project; and memo, David Aaron to Carter, April 3, 1980, NLC-25-118-2-1-1, JCL, RAC Project.
200. In reply, Bandar expressed Saudi Arabia's readiness to "recognize Israel's right to exist within approximately the borders of 1967" at the right

moment. Memorandum of conversation, April 9, 1980, NLC-128-4-2-9-4, JCL, RAC Project.

201. Ibid.
202. Beinin, "Cold Peace," 5.
203. William B. Quandt, "May 26: Now What?" *Washington Post*, May 26, 1980.
204. Raymond Baker, *Egypt's Uncertain Revolution*, 168.
205. "Sadat Gets Overwhelming Mandate, Egypt Reports," *New York Times*, May 24, 1980; "98.9% of Egyptians Vote to Allow Sadat as Many Terms as He Wants," *Los Angeles Times*, May 24, 1980.
206. Sid-Ahmed, "Shifting Sands of Peace," 75; Waterbury, *Egypt of Nasser and Sadat*, 372; and Kienle, *Grand Delusion*, 19.
207. Robert Fisk, "Why the Red Major Sees Democracy Ebbing from Egypt," *London Times*, April 10, 1980.
208. Raymond Baker, "Sadat's Open Door," 383–384; and Waterbury, *Egypt of Nasser and Sadat*, 372–373.
209. Memo, Robert Hunter and Gary Sick to Brzezinski, September 12, 1980, NLC-25-144-5-7-3, JCL, RAC Project.
210. Sobel, *Peace-Making in the Middle East*, 165.
211. Ibrahim, "Domestic Developments in Egypt," 41–42.
212. Reagan, *An American Life*, 290.
213. Ronald Reagan, "Toasts of President Reagan and President Anwar el-Sadat of Egypt at the State Dinner," August 5, 1981, http://www.presidency.ucsb.edu/ws/index.php?pid=44148, accessed February 3, 2010; Ibrahim, "Domestic Developments in Egypt," 26.
214. El-Sayed, "Egyptian Attitudes toward the Palestinians," 39.
215. Sabri, *Al-Sadat*, 166.
216. "Sadat to Be Premier, Promises Reforms," *Los Angeles Times*, May 15, 1980.
217. Sabri, *Al-Sadat*, 165.
218. Springborg, *Mubarak's Egypt*, 101.
219. Ibrahim, "Domestic Developments in Egypt," 25.
220. Murphy, *Passion for Islam*, 62–63.
221. Dessouki, "Egyptian Foreign Policy since Camp David," 98; and Ibrahim, "Domestic Developments in Egypt," 33–34.

Chapter 2: Mubarak's War on Terrorism

1. Woodward, *Veil*, 352.
2. Atherton, ADST Oral History.
3. Ibrahim, "Domestic Developments in Egypt," 31.
4. Billed as a one-year measure, the state of emergency was renewed twelve months later and then repeatedly, remaining in operation through Hosni Mubarak's tenure. William E. Farrell, "Egypt after Sadat," *New York Times*, October 7, 1981; and Charles Richards, "Overseas

News: Emergency 'Precaution' in Egypt," *Financial Times*, October 5, 1982.

5. Singerman, "Politics of Emergency Rule," 30.
6. William E. Farrell, "Mubarak, in Tears at Swearing-In, Tells Egyptians, 'This Is My Fate,'" *New York Times*, October 15, 1981.
7. "Egypt Reports 2,500 Arrests," *Washington Post*, December 21, 1981.
8. Wright, *Looming Tower*, 57–67.
9. Henry Tanner, "Egypt Dismisses 134 in the Army Suspected of 'Extremist Leanings,'" *New York Times*, October 20, 1981.
10. Memo, Peter Tarnoff to Zbigniew Brzezinski, January 5, 1980, NSA-Brzezinski Material, "Egypt, 12/79–1/80," Box 19, JCL; Cable, Secretary of State to Embassy Cairo, January 25, 1980, NLC-16-120-3-23-3, JCL, RAC Project.
11. Muammar Qadhafi was a major buyer of Soviet arms and had a penchant for meddling in nearby countries, such as Chad – an intervention Sadat had thwarted. An early 1981, U.S. intelligence estimate credited Sadat with "quietly bleeding Qadhafi at his most vulnerable point – his overextension in Chad and the danger this poses for him at home." Woodward, *Veil*, 90.
12. Henry Tanner, "Haig Says the U.S. Is Ready to Speed Arms Aid to Egypt," *New York Times*, October 12, 1981; "Egypt to Get Weapons Faster," *Reuters News Agency*, February 10, 1982.
13. Reagan, *An American Life*, 419–420; and Bernard Gwertzman, "Reagan to Offer Israel and Egypt More Military Aid," *New York Times*, February 1, 1982.
14. Jeremy M. Sharp, "Egypt: Background and U.S. Relations," *CRS Report for Congress*, February 4, 2011, 34.
15. Leslie H. Gelb, "The Mideast Arms Race: New Weapons, Old Fears," *New York Times*, January 24, 1982; and Leslie H. Gelb, "Amid Israeli Armed Might, Arabs Look to U.S.," *New York Times*, January 25, 1982.
16. Department of Defense Security Assistance Agency, *Fiscal Year Series as of September 30, 1998* (Washington, DC: Deputy for Financial Management Comptroller DSAA, 1998), 96, obtained from the Web site of the Federation of American Scientists http://www.fas.org.
17. Leslie H. Gelb, "Amid Israeli Armed Might, Arabs Look to U.S.;" "US-Egypt: Crumbling Alliance?" *Washington Report on Middle East Affairs*, May 17, 1982, http://www.wrmea.com/backissues/051782/820517002.htm, accessed November 8, 2010.
18. "Remarks of President Reagan and President Mohamed Hosni Mubarak of Egypt Following Their Meetings," February 4, 1982, http://www.reagan.utexas.edu/archives/speeches/1982/20482b.htm, accessed November 9, 2010.
19. William E. Farrell, "Egypt's Chief Turns from Diplomacy to Economics," *New York Times*, February 11, 1982.

20. William E. Farrell, "Mubarak's Time of Testing," *New York Times Magazine*, January 31, 1982.
21. David K. Shipler, "Israelis Say Mubarak Is Not Welcome unless He Will Visit Jerusalem," *New York Times*, March 1, 1982; and "Mubarak Postpones Israel Trip," *Globe and Mail*, March 2, 1982.
22. By the spring of 1982, the United States had nearly resolved a logistical challenge to Israel's pullout – the need for an international observation force as required by the treaty. The Soviet Union had blocked the planned deployment of a UN force to monitor Egyptian and Israeli force deployments, leaving it to the White House to develop an alternative. A protocol agreed to in 1981 allowed for a separate multinational force and observers that would assume the monitoring function on a permanent basis. The initial multinational force comprised troops from the Ninety-Second Airborne, as well as Latin American, European, Australian, and Fijian soldiers. "About the Multinational Force and Observers," http://www.mfo.org/aboutus.php, accessed February 8, 2011; and Atherton, ADST Oral History.
23. William E. Farrell, "Cairo Affirms Vow on Peace Process," *New York Times*, April 19, 1982.
24. In 1989 international arbiters ruled in favor of the Egyptian claim on Taba. Alan Cowell, "Israel Gives Disputed Resort to Egypt," *New York Times*, March 16, 1989.
25. "Fanaticism Stalks Yamit's Last Days," *Globe and Mail*, April 22, 1982.
26. Shlaim, *Iron Wall*, 399–400. The moment presaged similar trauma twenty-three years later when Sharon himself would preside over the forcible removal of Israeli settlers from the Gaza Strip.
27. Dessouki, "Egyptian Foreign Policy since Camp David," 98; Aly, "Egypt," 73, 88–89; and Shultz, *Turmoil and Triumph*, 95.
28. Ibrahim, "Domestic Developments in Egypt," 33.
29. Atherton, ADST Oral History.
30. Ibrahim, "Domestic Developments in Egypt," 19.
31. An official commission found that Sharon, as the senior officer in charge of the area and civilian safety, bore "personal responsibility" for the killings. "Report of the Commission of Inquiry into the Events at the Refugee Camps in Beirut (The Kahan Commission)," February 8, 1983, http://www.jewishvirtuallibrary.org/jsource/History/kahan.html, accessed August 15, 2011.
32. Atherton, ADST Oral History; "Interview with Hermann Frederick Eilts," 32; and William E. Schmidt, "Egyptians Bitter over Beirut Killings, Have Second Thoughts about Israel," *New York Times*, September 29, 1982.
33. William Safire, "Turning Back Fanatics," *New York Times*, November 6, 1983; Shultz, *Turmoil and Triumph*, 233–234; Quandt, *Peace Process*, 258; John M. Goshko, "Gemayel Shuttering 'Window of Opportunity' for U.S.," *Washington Post*, February 17, 1984; and Atherton, ADST Oral History. It took four years before Mubarak reposted the

ambassador, and that move followed a breakthrough in talks over Taba. "Israeli President Meets New Egyptian Envoy," *New York Times*, September 24, 1986.

34. Veliotes, ADST Oral History.
35. Randal, *Tragedy of Lebanon*, 274.
36. Thomas L. Friedman, "Counting the Casualties in Beirut and Beyond," *New York Times*, April 24, 1983.
37. Quandt, *Peace Process*, 258–259.
38. After Algeria resumed its ties with Egypt in November 1988, only Lebanon, Libya, and Syria remained disconnected from Mubarak's government. Bahgat Badie, "Egypt and Algeria Restore Full Diplomatic Relations," *Reuters News*, November 24, 1988.
39. Marr, *Egypt at the Crossroads*, xix; and Ahmed Shawki, "Arab Ministers Elect Egypt's Abdel-Maguid as Arab League Chief," *Reuters News*, May 15, 1991.
40. Veliotes, ADST Oral History.
41. Leslie H. Gelb, "U.S. Said to Increase Arms Aid for Afghan Rebels," *New York Times*, May 4, 1983; Coll, *Ghost Wars*, 66; Bronson, *Thicker Than Oil*, 171–172, 196n13; and Woodward, *Veil*, 99.
42. "It seemed that at least once a week," recalled Veliotes, "there was a new, Libyan-inspired plot to kill officials of the Egyptian government, or me, or bomb the Embassy." In the case of the embassy bomb attack, Egyptian intelligence penetrated the plot, conducted an elaborate simulation to let the conspirators think it was going forward, and then exposed Qadhafi's hand. Veliotes, ADST Oral History; and Veliotes, interview.
43. Woodward, *Veil*, 470.
44. Ibid., 472, 475–476.
45. Veliotes, interview. The following spring Reagan, without Egyptian cooperation, ordered U.S. bombers to strike the Libyan ruler's headquarters. Sleeping in a tent nearby, Qadhafi survived the de facto assassination attempt. The background to the attack was as follows: On March 22, 1986, U.S. forces baited Qadhafi into a four-day skirmish over the "line of death" he had conjured across the Gulf of Sidra. Two weeks later, Libyan-backed militants bombed a West German nightclub, killing one U.S. serviceman and a Turkish civilian and injuring hundreds more. Reagan then ordered the assault. Declaring that the United States had struck a "preemptive" blow against "Qadhafi's reign of terror," he informed a prime-time U.S. audience that Qadhafi had miscalculated: "He counted on America to be passive. He counted wrong.... I said that we would act with others if possible, and alone if necessary, to ensure that terrorists have no sanctuary anywhere. Tonight, we have." Woodward, *Veil*, 510–515; Shultz, *Turmoil and Triumph*, 680; and "President Reagan's Address to the Nation on U.S. Air Strike against Libya," April 14, 1986, http://www.youtube.com/watch?v=13xx1J5FdNE&feature=related, accessed February 19, 2010.

46. Coll, *Ghost Wars*, 138.
47. Gerald Boyd, "Out of Captivity," *New York Times*, July 1, 1985; Tony Walker, Nora Boustany, David Lennon, and Reginald Dale, "US Hostages on Flight to Freedom," *Financial Times*, July 1, 1985; and Reginald Dale, "After the US Hostage Crisis: Why the Story Is Far from Over," *Financial Times*, July 2, 1985.
48. Masha Hamilton, "PLO Bombing Is Warning to Terrorists," *Associated Press*, October 1, 1985.
49. Arthur Max, "Egyptian Soldier Fatally Shoots Seven People," *Associated Press*, October 5, 1985.
50. Veliotes, ADST Oral History.
51. Veliotes, interview; and Veliotes, ADST Oral History.
52. Reagan, *An American Life*, 508.
53. Woodward, *Veil*, 477.
54. Nicholas Veliotes, ADST Oral History; and Shultz, *Turmoil and Triumph*, 669–675.
55. Shultz, *Turmoil and Triumph*, 675.
56. Veliotes, ADST Oral History.
57. Veliotes, interview.
58. Judith Miller, "Fire, not Bullets, Reported to Kill Most Victims on Hijacked Plane," *New York Times*, November 28, 1985.
59. The five original MNNAs were Australia, Egypt, Israel, Japan, and South Korea. As the club of MNNA expanded and the United States sought to placate nearby countries not given the same standing, top officials downplayed the material benefits of MNNA status. Fielding a question in 1998 about Argentina becoming a MNNA (the only Latin American country yet to do so), Secretary of Defense William Cohen answered, "[T]his was just a – really a gesture on the part of the United States.... It does not convey any major status and should not be construed as such." Likewise when Pakistan – but not India – was designated a MNNA in 2004, Secretary of State Colin Powell explained that such allies have "greater access to... excess defense [articles] and property that we might have. In some instances it is more symbolic than practical. I don't know if Pakistan, whether they'll be able to take great advantage of it. But it is just a sign of the strength of the relationship." In short, U.S. arms merchants remained the main beneficiaries of waiving purchasing restrictions and guaranteeing loans for major buyers of U.S. weaponry. David B. Ottaway, "Shamir Indicates Israel Wants NATO Ally Status," *Washington Post*, February 20, 1987; "Fact Sheet – Major Non-NATO Ally (MNNA) Status for Thailand," *Thai News Service*, November 4, 2003; Andrew Prosser, "U.S. Arms Transfers to America's Newest 'Major Non-NATO Ally,'" Center for Defense Information, April 30, 2004, http://www.cdi.org/program/issue/document.cfm?DocumentID=2194&IssueID=116&StartRow=1&ListRows=10&appendURL=&Orderby=

DateLastUpdated&ProgramID=39&issueID=116, accessed May 19, 2010; and "DoD News Briefing," Office of the Assistant Secretary of Defense (Public Affairs), May 22, 1998, http://web.archive.org/web/20041118044622/http://www.defense.gov/transcripts/1998/t05271998_t522enrt.html, accessed May 19, 2010.

60. Atherton, ADST Oral History; Veliotes, ADST Oral History.

61. Veliotes, ADST Oral History.

62. Atherton, ADST Oral History.

63. After the Cold War ended, Egyptian officers happily received antiquated M-60 tanks that had flanked the Iron Curtain. Wisner, interview.

64. Atherton, ADST Oral History.

65. David B. Ottaway, "Mubarak Orders Price Rollbacks to Quell Violence near Alexandria," *Washington Post*, October 2, 1984.

66. Quandt, *United States and Egypt*, 36n33.

67. Richards, "Dilatory Reform," 68–73; Richards and Waterbury, *Political Economy of the Middle East*, 248–249.

68. Richards and Waterbury, *Political Economy of the Middle East*, 249; and Richards, "Dilatory Reform," 74.

69. Jeremy M. Sharp, "Egypt: Background and U.S. Relations," *CRS Report for Congress*, February 4, 2011, 34; and Atherton, ADST Oral History.

70. Wisner, interview.

71. Richards, "Dilatory Reform," 67; and Richards and Waterbury, *Political Economy of the Middle East*, 249.

72. Richards and Waterbury, *Political Economy of the Middle East*, 248–249.

73. William C. Mann, "Rumor Sparked Egyptian Riots, but Economics Fed the Flames," *Associated Press*, March 2, 1986; Barbara Rosewicz and Gerald F. Seib, "Egypt Finds Calm after Storm, Backs Mubarak," *Wall Street Journal*, March 3, 1986.

74. Christopher Dickey, "Mubarak Ends Curfew in Cairo: Riots May Have Enhanced Defense Minister's Standing," *Washington Post*, March 9, 1986; John Kifner, "Egypt's Army Praised in Quelling Riots, but for Mubarak, Crisis Is Not Over," *New York Times*, March 9, 1986; and Springborg, *Mubarak's Egypt*, 101–102.

75. Springborg, "The President and the Field Marshal," 4–6.

76. "Mubarak Flexes Muscle by Ousting Defense Minister," *Associated Press*, April 15, 1989; Patrick E. Tyler, "Mubarak Reassigns Key Deputy," *Washington Post*, April 16, 1989; Anthony Walker, "Defense Supremo Dumped in Bloodless, Bureaucratic Coup," *Sydney Morning Herald*, April 17, 1989; and Tony Walker, "Mubarak Disarms More Than Defense Chief: Removal of His Number Two Is a Puzzling, and Risky, Move," *Financial Times*, April 18, 1989.

77. Mustafa, "The 1995 Elections," 27.

78. Brownlee, *Authoritarianism in an Age of Democratization*, 125.

79. Eberhard Kienle has noted that opposition rallies during this period tended not to revolve around local political rights but instead reflected "nationalist fervor, directed generally against Israel or the United States." Demonstrations against the Israeli response to the intifada signified how "foreign policy" issues have been a leading domestic issue. Kienle, *Grand Delusion*, 90.

80. Michael Ross, "Egyptian-Israeli Ties under New Strain," *Los Angeles Times*, January 10, 1988.

81. Barbara Slavin, "U.S-Egyptian Ties on the Upswing," *St. Petersburg Times*, May 22, 1987; "Egypt Satisfied with Paris Club Accords That Reschedules $12 Billion of Its Debt," *Wall Street Journal*, May 26, 1987; "President Mubarak Arrives in Washington on 27 January for a Visit That Will Be Dominated by Strategic and Policy Issues," *Middle East Economic Digest*, January 23, 1988; Barbara Slavin, "Egypt's Mubarak to Press U.S. on Middle East Role," *St. Petersburg Times*, January 25, 1988; "Egypt Starts Crucial Economic Review with IMF," *Reuters News*, June 8, 1988; Tony Walker, "Egypt Debt Crunch Worries US Officials," *Financial Times*, November 24, 1988; David B. Ottaway, "U.S. Withholds $230 Million from Egypt," *Washington Post*, March 8, 1989; "Egypt Caught in Fiscal Tight Spot," *Congressional Quarterly Weekly Report*, April 8, 1989; "IMF Deals Gives New Lease of Life," *Middle East Economic Digest*, July 14, 1989; "U.S. Thaws Aid to Egypt," *Washington Post*, August 18, 1989; Quandt, *United States and Egypt*, 44; and Richards, *Dilatory Reform*, 67.

82. Soliman, *Autumn of Dictatorship*, 102.

83. Richards, "Dilatory Reform," 65; and Richards and Waterbury, *Political Economy of the Middle East*, 249.

84. Mitchell, "America's Egypt," 20–21.

85. Seddon, "Politics of Adjustment," 100.

86. Springborg, *Mubarak's Egypt*, 104–105, 109.

87. Bush and Scowcroft, *World Transformed*, 61.

88. The prologue to Operation Desert Shield involved escalating disagreements between the U.S. and Iraqi governments over Hussein's treatment of local dissidents and foreign journalists. Bush and Scowcroft, *World Transformed*, 305–306.

89. Ibid., 310–311.

90. Cable, April Glaspie to the Secretary of State, July 25, 1990, http://www.margaretthatcher.org/document/0DFD0DDB2BA34EF59F2570CE7EEE 03C8.pdf, accessed February 22, 2011.

91. Bush and Scowcroft, *World Transformed*, 313, 318–319.

92. Ibid., 313.

93. Ibid., 340.

94. Ibid., 344.

95. "US Congress Drafting Special Law to Forgive Egypt's Military Debts,"
Middle East Economic Digest, November 2, 1990; "Bush Signs Bill
Forgiving Egypt's Military Debt," *Reuters News*, November 6, 1990;
"Gulf Countries Write Off Debts," *BBC Monitoring Service: Middle
East*, November 6, 1990; and Bush and Scowcroft, *World Transformed*,
360, 372–374.
96. Bush and Scowcroft, *World Transformed*, 411–412.
97. Ibid., 441–442.
98. Quandt, *Peace Process*, 302.
99. Bush and Scowcroft, *World Transformed*, 441–442.
100. The eventual benefit was somewhat reduced when the IMF failed in 1994
to certify Egypt's compliance with mandated reforms, leaving $4 billion
of debt still on the books. Richards and Waterbury, *Political Economy
of the Middle East*, 250; and Steven Greenhouse, "Half of Egypt's $20.2
Billion Debt Being Forgiven by U.S. and Allies," *New York Times*, May
27, 1991.
101. Richards, "Dilatory Reform," 68.
102. Quandt, *Peace Process*, 310–311; and Tyler, *World of Trouble*, 390–393.
103. According to then U.S. ambassador to Cairo Robert Pelletreau, during
the conference Baker approached Egyptian foreign minister Amr Moussa
for help interceding with the Syrians, at which point Mubarak telephoned
al-Assad and helped orchestrate the first face-to-face meeting between the
Israelis and Syrians. Pelletreau, interview.
104. Atherton, ADST Oral History.
105. James Baker, "Looking Back on the Middle East."
106. Barton Gellman, "Keeping the U.S. First: Pentagon Would Preclude a
Rival Superpower," *Washington Post*, March 11, 1992; and Patrick E.
Tyler, "U.S. Strategy Plan Calls for Insuring No Rivals Develop," *New
York Times*, March 8, 1992.
107. Djerejian, "The US and the Middle East in a Changing World."
108. In the autumn of 1992, Harvard University professor Samuel Huntington wrapped America's nascent anti-Islamic foreign policy in the
mantle of scholarly knowledge. To a packed audience in Washington,
Huntington conjured a geopolitical map demarcated not by contemporary interests but by atavistic identities. The United States and fellow descendants of "Western Christianity," he averred, should constrain
"the military strength of Confucian and Islamic states" in the immediate
term while working to coexist with them in the long run. Titled "The
Clash of Civilizations," his lecture (elaborated in print over subsequent
years) provided a seductive conceptual framework for U.S. strategists –
its power regularly reinforced by the formulaic assertions of top officials that no such conflict existed. Samuel P. Huntington, Excerpts from
"Clash of Civilizations," delivered at the American Enterprise Institute,

October 20, 1992, http://www.aei.org/issue/29196, accessed February 22, 2011. Video available at http://wn.com/clash_of_civilizations, accessed February 22, 2011.

109. Murphy, *Passion for Islam*, 77–79.
110. Brownlee, "Unrequited Moderation," 477.
111. Murphy, *Passion for Islam*, 80.
112. Ibrahim, "The Changing Face of Egypt's Islamic Activism," 38–41.
113. Tyler, *World of Trouble*, 399–401.
114. Sirrs, *Egyptian Intelligence Service*, 169–170. While Mubarak expanded Egyptian security agencies, he shrank the active military to 500,000, nearly half its strength in 1973. Springborg, *Mubarak's Egypt*, 99, 125n1.
115. Springborg, *Mubarak's Egypt*, 176n19.
116. Ibid., 35–37.
117. "Mubarak Wins Third Term," *Agence France-Press*, October 5, 1993.
118. William J. Clinton, "Address Before a Joint Session of Congress on the State of the Union," January 25, 1994, http://www.presidency.ucsb.edu/ws/index.php?pid=50409, accessed February 23, 2011.
119. Coll, *Ghost Wars*, 259.
120. Martin Indyk, "The Clinton Administration's Approach to the Middle East," address delivered at the Washington Institute for Near East Policy, Washington, DC, May 18, 1993, http://www.washingtoninstitute.org/print.php?template=C07&CID=61, accessed February 19, 2011.
121. Indyk, "Back to the Bazaar," 77–78.
122. Kepel, *Jihad*, 292.
123. Sirrs, *Egyptian Intelligence Service*, 171.
124. That fall, in a somber postlude to Mubarak's brush with death, an Israeli who bitterly opposed the peace process assassinated Yitzhak Rabin. To attend Rabin's funeral, the Egyptian president made his first and only trip to Israel. Clinton, *My Life*, 678–679.
125. Egyptian National Committee, *Taqrir al-lajna al-wataniyya al-misriya*.
126. El-Ghobashy, "Metamorphosis of the Muslim Brothers," 382.
127. Kienle, *Grand Delusion*.
128. Ibid., 98–101.
129. Ibid., 118.
130. Yosi Melman, "The General's Cold Peace," *Haaretz.com*, January 20, 2009, http://www.haaretz.com/print-edition/features/the-general-s-cold-peace-1.268497, accessed September 14, 2011.
131. Salah, *Waqa`a sanawat al-jihad*, 139–144.
132. Gerges, "End of the Islamist Insurgency."
133. Presidential Decision Directive/NSC-39, "U.S. Policy on Counterterrorism."
134. Grey, *Ghost Plane*, 136; and "Staff Statement No. 5," *National Commission on Terrorist Attacks Upon the United States (9/11 Commission)*, n.d.

http://govinfo.library.unt.edu/911/staff_statements/staff_statement_5 .pdf, accessed March 20, 2012.

135. In February 1995, the Federal Bureau of Investigation rendered Ramzi Yousef from Pakistan to the United States. Yousef was subsequently convicted of murder for his 1993 role in planting the bombs in the garage of the World Trade Center. Wright, *Looming Tower*, 201–203, 230–233.

136. U.S. House Committee on Foreign Affairs, "Extraordinary Rendition," 15, 36.

137. Jane Mayer, "Outsourcing Torture," *New Yorker*, February 14, 2005, http://www.newyorker.com/archive/2005/02/14/050214fa_fact6? printable=true, accessed March 4, 2010.

138. Peter Bergen and Katherine Tiedemann, "Disappearing Act: Rendition by the Numbers," *Mother Jones*, March 3, 2008; and Mayer, *Dark Side*, 113.

139. Grey, *Ghost Plane*, 141.

140. U.S. House Committee on Foreign Relations, *Extraordinary Rendition*, 36.

141. Grey, *Ghost Plane*, 141–142; and Mayer, "Outsourcing Torture."

142. Grey, *Ghost Plane*, 144.

143. Zayat, *Road to al-Qaeda*, 31.

144. Grey, *Ghost Plane*, 144.

145. Tyler, *World of Trouble*, 487–488.

146. Sirrs, *Egyptian Intelligence Services*, 177.

147. Grey, *Ghost Plane*, 144–146; and Tyler, *World of Trouble*, 510–511.

148. Clinton, *My Life*, 740–741, 925–992; Bronson, *Thicker Than Oil*, 229–230; Fahmy, interview.

149. Kurtzer, interview.

150. No'am Amit, "The Puppet Master," *Ma'ariv* [FBIS translation], May 2, 2003, http://www.fas.org/irp/world/egypt/sulayman.html, accessed May 2, 2011.

151. "In the battalion, of course, we don't have our armed forces with 100 percent the American equipment. So as I mentioned before, we have 52 percent American, and the other is Russian. So in the battalion we used two systems." Elkeshky, interview.

152. The country also made $366.5 million in commercial purchases, including hand grenades, small arms, rifles, police equipment, riot control chemicals, and explosives. See the Web site of the Federation of American Scientists: http://www.fas.org.

153. "First Joint U.S.-Egyptian Military Exercises in Three Years," *Associated Press*, November 10, 1993; John West, "Egypt, U.S. in First War Games since Gulf War," *Reuters News*, November 12, 1993.

154. Susan Sevareid, "Cohen Oversees War Games in Egypt," *AP Online*, October 22, 1999.

155. William S. Cohen, "DOD News Brief: Bright Star Exercise, El-Omayid, Egypt," October 25, 1999, http://www.defenselink.mil/transcripts/transcript.aspx?transcriptid=340, accessed October 27, 2008.
156. Harb, "The Egyptian Military in Politics," 285–286.
157. Richards, "Dilatory Reform," 72–73.
158. Ray Bush, *Economic Crisis*, 30–31.
159. Richards and Waterbury, *Political Economy of the Middle East*, 250–251.
160. Richards, "Dilatory Reform," 76–77.
161. Marr, *Egypt at the Crossroads*, xxv.
162. See Hellman, "Winners Take All."
163. Basheer, "Egyptian State in Transition," 10.
164. Richards and Waterbury, *Political Economy of the Middle East*, 251.
165. Indyk, "Back to the Bazaar," 78.
166. Kurtzer, interview.
167. Jeremy M. Sharp, "Egypt: Background and U.S. Relations," *CRS Report for Congress*, February 4, 2011, 26.
168. "Mubarak Awarded Honorary Doctorate from George Washington University," June 29, 1999, http://www2.sis.gov.eg/En/Politics/Presidency/President/Speeches/000001/040105020000000000072.htm, accessed October 26, 2010.

Chapter 3: The Succession Problem

1. Cook, "Arab Reform," 91–92.
2. Heydemann, *Upgrading Authoritarianism*, 18; Wittes and Yerkes, *What Price Freedom?*
3. Wittes, *Freedom's Unsteady March*, 97.
4. Dunne, interview.
5. Welch, interview.
6. While most Arab allies of the United States eschewed Operation Enduring Freedom completely, Egypt opened the El Salam field hospital in Bagram, Afghanistan, in the summer of 2003. With plywood construction reminiscent of *M*A*S*H*, El Salam gave pediatric and primary care to Afghan civilians. Brian Mockenhaupt, "The Doctor's War," *Atlantic*, October 2009, http://www.theatlantic.com/magazine/print/2009/10/the-doctor-8217-s-war/7659/, accessed March 17, 2010; Yun-Hua Fan, "El Salam Egyptian Field Hospital," *Army*, May 2010; Liam Fox, "We Must Not Be Left to Fight Alone," *Sunday Telegraph*, October 28, 2007; "Egyptian Field Hospital Re-opened," *Pajhwok Afghan News*, January 8, 2009; "Egyptian Hospital in Afghanistan Provides Care, Changes Attitude," *Department of Defense Documents*, October 7, 2008; "Nations Team Up to Train Afghan Doctors," *Department of Defense Documents*, November 17, 2008; and "Program Builds Better Health Care System in Afghanistan," *States News Service*, February 19, 2009.

7. Quandt, *Peace Process*, ix.

8. On Powell's position at a September 13, 2001, national security meeting, Feith writes: "We should also get Palestinian-Israeli diplomacy going, [Powell] advised, 'so we can show we remain engaged.'" Feith, *War and Decision*, 13.

9. Ibid., 89.

10. Feith, interview.

11. Ibid.

12. U.S. House Committee on Foreign Relations, "Review of U.S. Assistance Programs to Egypt," 17.

13. "Foreign Military Training and DoD Engagement Activities of Interest: Joint Report to Congress," Department of State, March 2002, http://www.state.gov/t/pm/rls/rpt/fmtrpt/2002/10723.htm, accessed May 18, 2010.

14. Colin L. Powell, "Remarks with Egyptian Minister of Foreign Affairs Ahmed Maher," September 26, 2001, http://avalon.law.yale.edu/sept11/powell_brief21.asp, accessed December 5, 2010.

15. Mamdouh Habib, who was sent from Pakistan to Egypt and Guantanamo before eventually being repatriated to Australia, reported that Suleiman personally oversaw his torture and interrogation. Habib, *My Story*, 112–115; and Antony Lowenstein, "Exclusive: Mamdouh Habib Interview on New US/Israeli Egyptian Pet Omar Suleiman," *Antony Lowenstein blog*, http://antonyloewenstein.com/2011/02/11/exclusive-mamdouh-habib-interview-on-new-usisraeli-egyptian-pet-omar-suleiman, accessed May 29, 2011.

16. Grey, *Ghost Plane*, 28–36; and Hersh, *Chain of Command*, 53–55.

17. Isikoff and Corn, *Hubris*, 119–123; John D. Rockefeller IV and Carl Levin, letter to Vice Admiral Lowell E. Jacoby, director, Defense Intelligence Agency, October 18, 2005, http://levin.senate.gov/newsroom/supporting/2005/DIAletter.102605.pdf, accessed May 14, 2010; and Michael Hirsh, John Barr, and Daniel Klaidman, with Michael Isikoff, Mark Hosenball, and Tamara Lipper, "A Tortured Debate," *Newsweek*, June 21, 2004.

18. U.S. Senate Select Committee on Intelligence, "Report on Iraq's WMD Programs," 81.

19. Ibid., 78–79, 79n206, 82, 107; Office of Senator Carl Levin, "Administration Statements About Iraqi–al Qaeda Links," n.d., http://levin.senate.gov/newsroom/supporting/2005/adminstmts.IraqalQaeda.110605.pdf, accessed May 14, 2010; and Office of Senator Carl Levin, "Administration Statements on Iraq Training al Qa'ida in Chemical and Biological Weapons," n.d., http://www.fas.org/irp/news/2005/11/adminstmts.CBW.110605.pdf.

20. George W. Bush, *Decision Points*, 398.

21. Dunne, interview.

22. Doran, "Is Palestine the Pivot?;" Douglas J. Feith, "Strategy and the Idea of Freedom," November 24, 2003, http://www.heritage.org/Research/Lecture/Strategy-and-the-Idea-of-Freedom-by-Douglas-J-Feith, accessed November 17, 2010.

23. Writes Feith in his memoirs, "As I saw it, curing poverty and solving the Arab-Israeli conflict were worthy goals even aside from the war on terrorism, and the US government would pursue them in any event. But in practice such talk of 'root causes' tended to produce paralysis rather than motivate action against terrorist extremist ideology." *War and Decision*, 170.

24. Office of the Press Secretary, "President Bush Welcomes President Mubarak to the White House," March 5, 2002, http://georgewbush-whitehouse.archives.gov/news/releases/2002/03/20020305–18.html, accessed December 10, 2010.

25. In a commencement address delivered to West Point graduates that June, Bush averred: "The requirements of freedom apply fully to Africa and Latin America and the entire Islamic world. The peoples of the Islamic nations want and deserve the same freedoms and opportunities as people in every nation. And their governments should listen to their hopes." Office of the Press Secretary, "President Bush Delivers Graduation Speech at West Point," June 1, 2002, http://georgewbush-whitehouse.archives.gov/news/releases/2002/06/20020601-3.html, accessed December 7, 2010.

26. Fahmy, interview.

27. Dunne, interview.

28. Office of the Press Secretary, "President Bush Meets with Egyptian President Mubarak," June 8, 2002, http://georgewbush-whitehouse.archives.gov/news/releases/2002/06/20020608-4.html#, accessed December 7, 2010. Days earlier, Mubarak had articulated a similar position to the *New York Times*. Patrick E. Tyler and Neil MacFarquhar, "Mubarak to Press Bush on a State for Palestinians," *New York Times*, June 4, 2002.

29. Office of the Press Secretary, "Bush Meets with Mubarak."

30. Douglas Frantz and James Risen, "A Secret Iran-Arafat Connection Is Seen Fueling the Mideast Fire," *New York Times*, March 24, 2002.

31. George W. Bush, *Decision Points*, 401.

32. Sharansky, "Democracy for Peace."

33. Sharansky had spent nine years in a Soviet prison before being released, at the pinnacle of Reaganite anticommunism, and resettling in Israel. Sharansky bridged the Cold War and the War on Terror; few were so qualified to claim democracy advanced U.S. interests and human freedom. Speaking earlier at a conference organized by the American Enterprise Institute, Sharansky argued that Bush should no longer recognize Arafat's leadership and instead begin a post–World War II-style trusteeship for the occupied territories. He then pressed his case in extended face-to-face

meetings with Vice President Cheney and Wolfowitz, telling them: "Arafat has to go. A terrorist regime has to go. Then there can be an opportunity for a state." Dan Ephron and Tamara Lipper with Daniel Klaidman, "Sharansky's Quiet Role: What Pushed Bush to Demand That Arafat Must Go?" *Newsweek*, July 15, 2002; Jonathan Rosenblum, "A Vision in Tatters," *Jerusalem Post*, June 20, 2003; and Connie Bruck, "Back Roads," *New Yorker*, December 15, 2003.

34. Office of the Press Secretary, "President Bush Calls for New Palestinian Leadership," June 24, 2002, http://georgewbush-whitehouse.archives .gov/news/releases/2002/06/20020624-3.html, accessed September 14, 2011.

35. Bush's address linking Palestinian democracy and statehood can be viewed, retrospectively, as the opening of the Freedom Agenda, although Deputy Secretary of State Richard Armitage stated, "It wasn't seen as that at the time," and the State Department could point to the call for a Palestinian state as a positive step. Armitage, interview.

36. The Rose Garden speech evoked images of planting democracy in Baghdad. As one journalist mused: "[T]he president's blunt ultimatum to the Palestinians raised a tantalizing question. What if the United States were as serious about saving the Arabs from corrupt autocrats and radical Islam as it once was about saving the world from communism? What if the tools of the cold war ... were put to use to promote Arab democracy and moderation?" Interviewees for the piece favored reprising Cold War democracy-promotion methods, like the Helsinki conference of 1975, and earlier practices from postwar Japan and Germany. Susan Sachs, "How to Rig a Democracy," *New York Times*, June 30, 2002; and Max Boot, "George W. Bush: The 'W' Stands for Woodrow," *Wall Street Journal*, July 1, 2002.

37. "George W. Bush Participates in a Roundtable with Young Professionals," *Political Transcripts by Federal Document Clearing House*, February 23, 2005.

38. For example, asked in the spring if "the President [was] thinking about using the same metrics for Egypt" that he prescribed for future aid to the Palestinian Authority, the White House spokesman answered, "[W]hat is universal and will be consistent ... is that nations follow a rule of law, that nations are transparent, that nations have democratic institutions. And that will be the formula that the United States will follow in its pursuit of aid programs around the world, and Egypt fulfills those requirements." Press Briefing by Ari Fleischer, March 25, 2002, http://www.presidency.ucsb.edu/ws/index.php?pid=62550, accessed December 11, 2010.

39. By winter 2004–2005, Sharansky had become Bush's muse on matters of democracy: "If you want a glimpse of how I think about foreign policy read Natan Sharansky's book [*The Case for Democracy*] ... I think it

will help . . . explain a lot of the decisions that you'll see being made – you've seen made and will continue to see made." He called Sharansky's treatise "part of my presidential DNA" and "a part of all policy." In his memoirs, Bush mentions how his view of the United States meshed with Sharansky's philosophy: "In one memorable passage, Sharansky describes a fellow Soviet dissident who likened a tyrannical state to a soldier who constantly points a gun at a prisoner. Eventually, his arms tire and the prisoner escapes. I considered it America's responsibility to put pressures on the arms of the world's tyrants. Making that goal a central part of our foreign policy was one of my most consequential decisions as president." "Excerpts: Bush to Remain 'Committed' to War on Terror," *Washington Times*, January 11, 2005; Elisabeth Bumiller, "Bush's Book Club Picks a New Favorite," *New York Times*, January 21, 2005; and George W. Bush, *Decision Points*, 398.

40. "Activist Released from Jail," *Globe and Mail*, August 11, 2000.
41. "Egyptian Human Rights Activist Goes back on Trial Tuesday," *Agence France-Presse*, January 15, 2001.
42. "Court Convicts Human Rights Activists of Charges Including Tarnishing Egypt's image," *Associated Press Newswires*, May 21, 2001.
43. Nadia Abou El-Magd, "U.S.-Egyptian Activist Released from Prison, Pending Retrial," *Associated Press Newswires*, February 7, 2002.
44. Tyler and MacFarquhar, "Mubarak to Press Bush on a State for Palestinians."
45. Jane Perlez, "U.S. Regards Egypt as Key To Peace Deal In the Mideast," *New York Times*, August 27, 2000; and "Clinton Leaves Egypt after Mideast Talks," *Reuters News*, August 29, 2000.
46. Nadia Abou El-Magd, "Egyptian Academic Convicted Again: U.S. 'Disappointed' by Ruling," *Associated Press Newswires*, July 29, 2002.
47. "Mr. Mubarak's Challenge," *Washington Post*, July 30, 2002; and "The Shame of Egypt," *New York Times*, July 31, 2002.
48. Thomas L. Friedman, "Bush's Shame," *New York Times*, August 4, 2002.
49. Jackson Diehl, "The Silence Signal: Why Bush Must Speak to Muslims," *Washington Post*, August 5, 2002.
50. Peter Slevin, "Bush, in Shift on Egypt, Links New Aid to Rights," *Washington Post*, August 15, 2002; and Christopher Marquis, "U.S., Protesting Rights Leader's Sentence, Halts New Aid to Egypt," *New York Times*, August 16, 2002.
51. Explained Ambassador Welch, "I don't think there was an expectation it [the supplemental funding] would get through Congress." Welch, interview. For one interpretation of the measure at the time, see Brownlee, "Decline of Pluralism," 13.
52. "World: In Brief," *Washington Post*, December 4, 2002. The next March, he and twenty-six co-defendants were fully acquitted. Nadia Abou

El-Magd, "Egyptian-American Rights Activist Acquitted," *Associated Press Newswires*, March 18, 2003.

53. Peter Slevin and Glenn Kessler, "U.S. to Seek Mideast Reforms: Programs Aim to Foster Democracy, Education, Markets," *Washington Post*, August 12, 2002.

54. Armitage, interview.

55. Haass, "Toward a Greater Democracy."

56. Bronson, *Thicker than Oil*, 240.

57. MEPI started with an FY 2002 budget of $29 million, which expanded to $100 million in FY 2003 and dropped to $89.5 million in FY 2004. U.S. Department of State and the Broadcasting Board of Governors, Office of the Inspector General, "Report of Inspection," 3–4; Colin L. Powell, "The U.S.-Middle East Partnership Initiative: Building Hope for the Years Ahead," *Remarks made at The Heritage Foundation*, December 12, 2002, http://www.heritage.org/research/lecture/the-us-middle-east-partnership-initiative, accessed December 10, 2010; U.S. Government Accounting Office, "Foreign Assistance," 9, 14; McInerney, "President's Budget Request for 2009,"11; and Glenn Kessler and Robin Wright, "Realities Overtake Arab Democracy Drive: Autocratic Allies and Israeli-Palestinian Conflict Sometimes Block U.S. Efforts," *Washington Post*, December 3, 2003.

58. Powell, "The U.S.-Middle East Partnership Initiative."

59. Welch, interview.

60. Ten of Bush's appointees had signed a 1998 letter advocating Washington "change the regime in Baghdad": Elliott Abrams, Richard Armitage, John Bolton (under secretary for arms control and international security affairs), Paula Dobriansky (under secretary of state for global affairs), Douglas Feith, Zalmay Khalilzad (senior director for Southwest Asia, Near East, and North African affairs at the National Security Council), Richard Perle (chairman of the Defense Policy Board Advisory Committee), Peter Rodman (assistant secretary of defense for international affairs), Donald Rumsfeld, and Paul Wolfowitz. Feith, *War and Decision*, 196; Committee for Peace and Security in the Gulf, "Open Letter to the President," February 19, 1998, http://www.iraqwatch.org/perspectives/rumsfeld-openletter.htm, accessed December 4, 2010.

61. E. J. Dionne Jr., "In Search of a War Rationale," *Washington Post*, August 16, 2002; and Gause, *International Relations of the Persian Gulf*, 229–231.

62. "'Moral Case' for Deposing Saddam," *BBC World Edition*, August 15, 2002, http://news.bbc.co.uk/2/hi/americas/2193426.stm, accessed December 10, 2010.

63. Office of the Press Secretary, "President's Remarks at the United Nations General Assembly," September 12, 2002, http://www.whitehouse.gov/news/releases/2002/09/print/20020912-1, archived January 23, 2008.

64. "If an American road to a calmer situation in Palestine does in fact exist, it runs through Baghdad." Doran, "Palestine, Iraq, and American Strategy," 22.

65. Armitage, interview.

66. Later analysis of pre-Iraq war intelligence published by the U.S. Senate revealed al-Libi's was the sole testimony ever given a modicum of weight: "The other reports of possible al-Qa'ida CBW [chemical and biological weapons] training from Iraq were never considered credible by the Intelligence Community." U.S. Senate Select Committee on Intelligence, "Report on Iraq's WMD Programs," 82.

67. Ibid.

68. For example, al-Libi's coerced confession surfaced in Powell's February 5, 2003, address to the UN Security Council. The next day, Bush intoned from the Roosevelt Room that "Iraq has also provided al Qaeda with chemical and biological weapons training." Speaking on NBC's *Meet the Press*, Vice President Cheney declared, "We know that he has a long-standing relationship with various terrorist groups, including the al-Qaeda organization." Ibid., 78–79, 79n206, 82, 107; Office of Senator Carl Levin, "Administration Statements About Iraqi–al Qaeda Links;" Office of Senator Carl Levin, "Administration Statements on Iraq Training al Qa'ida in Chemical and Biological Weapons."

69. Office of the Press Secretary, "President Says Saddam Hussein Must Leave Iraq within 48 Hours," March 17, 2003, http://georgewbush-white house.archives.gov/news/releases/2003/03/20030317-7.html, accessed December 12, 2010.

70. Formally known as the "Coalition for the Immediate Disarmament of Iraq," the group comprised thirty countries that had pledged support to the war or postwar effort: Afghanistan, Albania, Australia, Azerbaijan, Colombia, the Czech Republic, Denmark, El Salvador, Eritrea, Estonia, Ethiopia, Georgia, Hungary, Iceland, Italy, Japan, Latvia, Lithuania, Macedonia, the Netherlands, Nicaragua, Philippines, Poland, Romania, Slovakia, South Korea, Spain, Turkey, the United Kingdom, and Uzbekistan. "Willing Countries in Coalition Listed," *Associated Press Newswires*, March 18, 2003. A plurality of Turkish MPs present voted to provide overland access (264–251-19), but the measure failed for lack of majority support. Gordon and Trainor, *Cobra II*, 115.

71. "Eight More U.S. Warships Cross Egypt's Suez Canal ahead of Looming War in Iraq," *Associated Press Newswires*, March 15, 2003; "Six Ships Enter Suez Canal on Way to Iraq War," *Reuters News*, March 27, 2003. In his memoirs, Bush writes that about 15,000 troops, half of the division, would have been sent into Iraq through Turkey. George W. Bush, *Decision Points*, 250.

72. In the first months of the Obama presidency, Egyptian distrust of the United States returned to pre-Iraq War levels (14 percent favorable versus 78 percent unfavorable). Zogby and Zogby, *Arab Opinions*, 8.

73. Telhami, "View from the Arab World."
74. In the wake of the march, the U.S. embassy and Egyptian government established permanent checkpoints on the streets abutting the embassy compound. The security clampdown eliminated casual foot traffic in the surrounding area, and visitors took to referring to the neighborhood as the "Green Zone," after the outsized U.S. compound in Baghdad.
75. Amira Howeidy, "A Day at 'Hyde Park,'" *Al-Ahram Weekly On-line*, March 27–April 2, 2003, http://weekly.ahram.org.eg/2003/631/eg8.htm, accessed December 12, 2010; and Schemm, "Egypt Struggles to Control Protests."
76. "Statement by David Kay on the Interim Progress Report on the Activities of the Iraq Survey Group (ISG) before the House Permanent Select Committee on Intelligence, the House Committee on Appropriations, Subcommittee on Defense, and the Senate Select Committee on Intelligence," October 2, 2003, http://www.fas.org/irp/cia/product/dkay100203.html, accessed December 15, 2010.
77. "Bush: Saddam Was 'Danger to the World,'" *Agence France Presse*, October 3, 2003.
78. Feith, *War and Decision*, 475–477.
79. "The objective I propose," Reagan had said then, "is quite simple: to foster the infrastructure of democracy, the system of a free press, unions, political parties, universities, which allows a people to choose their own way to develop their own culture, to reconcile their own differences through peaceful means." "Address to Members of the British Parliament," June 8, 1982, http://www.reagan.utexas.edu/archives/speeches/1982/60882a.htm, accessed December 15, 2010.
80. Office of the Press Secretary, "Remarks by the President at the 20th Anniversary of the National Endowment for Democracy," Washington, DC, November 6, 2003, http://www.whitehouse.gov/news/releases/2003/11/print/20031106-3.html, accessed December 8, 2004.
81. Ibid.
82. Mubarak's tenure in office and the absence of a clear second-in-command may not have been coincidental. With no clear successor beneath him, the Egyptian president mitigated the chance for rival power centers like those that had initially bedeviled Sadat.
83. Nadia Abou El-Magd, "Interruption in Egyptian President's Speech to Parliament Focuses Attention on Succession," *Associated Press Newswires*, November 19, 2003.
84. In the Reagan administration, Abrams had argued for democratic change in the Southern Cone of Latin America. He later described his enthusiasm when he was tapped to head the Bureau of Human Rights and Humanitarian Affairs at the State Department: "Human Rights! This was what American foreign policy should be all about; this was what separated us from the Communist world. Here was a chance for me to make a real contribution, explaining to the Left that any serious human rights policy

had to be strongly anti-Communist, and to the Right that fighting right-
wing – as well as Communist – dictatorships must be a matter of principle for the United States." *Undue Process*, 4. On Abrams's work
shifting U.S. policy toward authoritarian regimes from Haiti to Chile,
see Carothers, *In the Name of Democracy*, and Shultz, *Turmoil and
Triumph*.

85. Office of the Press Secretary, "Statement by the Press Secretary," June
    28, 2001, http://georgewbush-whitehouse.archives.gov/news/releases/
    2001/06/20010628-12.html, accessed December 4, 2010.

86. Abrams, "Israel and the 'Peace Process.'"

87. Abrams, interview.

88. Ibid.

89. Office of the Spokesman, "A Performance-Based Roadmap to a
    Permanent Two-State Solution to the Israeli-Palestinian Conflict,"
    U.S. Department of State, April 20, 2003, http://web.archive.org/web/
    20030513213010/http://www.state.gov/r/pa/prs/ps/2003/20062.htm,
    accessed January 22, 2010.

90. Israel Ministry of Foreign Affairs, "Address by Ariel Sharon at the
    Fourth Herzliya Conference," December 18, 2003, http://www.mfa.gov
    .il/MFA/Government/Speeches+by+Israeli+leaders/2003/Address+by+
    PM+Ariel+Sharon+at+the+Fourth+Herzliya.htm, accessed December
    26, 2010; Migdalovitz, "Israel's Disengagement from Gaza," 1–2.

91. Fahmy, interview.

92. Abrams, interview.

93. Ibid.

94. Fahmy, interview.

95. Ibid.

96. George W. Bush, *Decision Points*, 402–403.

97. Steve Holland, "Mubarak Tells Bush of Serious Concerns on Iraq,"
    Reuters News, April 12, 2004; Dana Milbank and Peter Slevin,
    "Bush Qualifies Praise for Israeli Plan: Gaza Pullout Won't Replace
    'Road Map,'" *Washington Post*, April 13, 2004; and Khaled Dawoud,
    "Another Start," *Al-Ahram Weekly On-line*, April 15–21, 2004, http://
    weekly.ahram.org.eg/2004/686/eg1.htm, accessed July 28, 2010.

98. Office of the Press Secretary, "President Bush, Egyptian President
    Mubarak Meet with Reporters," April 12, 2004, http://georgewbush-
    whitehouse.archives.gov/news/releases/2004/04/20040412-3.html,
    accessed March 10, 2010.

99. Office of the Press Secretary, "Joint Statement by President George
    W. Bush and President Mohamed Hosny Mubarak," Crawford, Texas,
    April 12, 2004, http://georgewbush-whitehouse.archives.gov/news/
    releases/2004/04/20040412-4.html, accessed May 23, 2011.

100. Barry Schweid, "Sharon's Plan for Gaza Puts Bush on Spot," *Associated
     Press Newswires*, April 10, 2004; and "Profile: Egyptian President Hosni

Mubarak Visits President Bush in Crawford, Texas," *NPR: All Things Considered*, April 12, 2004.

101. Office of the Press Secretary, "President Bush Commends Israeli Prime Minister Sharon's Plan," April 14, 2004, http://georgewbush-whitehouse .archives.gov/news/releases/2004/04/20040414–4.html#, accessed July 27, 2010; and Office of the Press Secretary, "Letter from President Bush to Prime Minister Sharon," April 14, 2004, http://georgewbush-whitehouse.archives.gov/news/releases/2004/04/20040414–3.html, accessed July 27, 2010.

102. Hillal, interview.

103. Sonni Efron and Megan K. Stack, "Arab Leaders Blast the U.S.," *Los Angeles Times*, April 16, 2004; Dina Ezzat, "Seismic Shift," *Al-Ahram Weekly On-line*, April 22–28, 2004, http://weekly.ahram.org .eg/2004/687/fr1.htm, accessed July 28, 2010; John C. Henry, "Mubarak Advises Steady Withdrawal after June 30: U.S. Credibility at Risk, He Says at Rice Event," *Houston Chronicle*, April 15, 2004; and John C. Henry, "Mubarak Urges U.S. to Be Fair in Mideast: 'Shocked' by Bush Policy Shift on Israel," *Houston Chronicle*, April 16, 2004.

104. "Arabs Hate U.S. More Than Ever, Egypt's Mubarak," *Reuters News*, April 20, 2004.

105. Amira Howeidy, "Bush to Balfour," *Al-Ahram Weekly On-line*, April 15–21, 2004, http://weekly.ahram.org.eg/2004/686/fr3.htm, accessed July 28, 2010; Dina Ezzat, "Danger Zone," *Al-Ahram Weekly On-line*, April 22–28, 2004, http://weekly.ahram.org.eg/2004/687/eg1.htm, accessed July 28, 2010; Hassan Nafaa, "An Unacceptable Invitation," *Al-Ahram Weekly On-line*, April 22–28, 2004, http://weekly.ahram .org.eg/2004/687/op61.htm, accessed July 28, 2010; and Mohamed Sid-Ahmed, "The Second Balfour Declaration," *Al-Ahram Weekly On-line*, April 22–28, 2004, http://weekly.ahram.org.eg/2004/687/op5.htm, accessed July 28, 2010.

106. Blaydes, *Elections and Distribution*, 204.

107. Abrams, interview.

108. Fahmy, interview.

109. Abrams, interview.

110. Schenker, interview.

111. Zogby and Zogby, *Impressions of America 2004*, 3.

112. U.S. Government Accountability Office, "Security Assistance," 17; and Jeremy Sharp and Christopher M. Blanchard, "Post-War Iraq: Foreign Contributions to Training, Peacekeeping, and Reconstruction," *CRS Report for Congress*, September 25, 2007.

113. "Interview with Egyptian Prime Minister Ahmed Nazif," *Meet the Press*, May 15, 2005.

114. U.S. Department of State, "Antiterrorism Assistance Program," 30, 33.

115. U.S. Department of State, Bureau of Democracy, Human Rights, and Labor, "Egypt: Country Reports on Human Rights Practices," February 25, 2004, http://www.state.gov/g/drl/rls/hrrpt/2003/27926.htm, accessed May 24, 2010.

116. Armitage, interview.

117. "Saudi Arabia and Egypt Joint Statement," February 24, 2004, http://www.mofa.gov.sa/Detail.asp?InSectionID=4317&InNewsItem ID=44285, accessed December 21, 2010.

118. "Mubarak: Al-sahafiyun al-masriyun kanu wa la zalu lisan halat al-ummah," [Mubarak: Egyptian Journalists Were and Continue to give voice to the Nation's Situation], *Al-Ahram*, February 24, 2004, http://www.ahram.org.eg/Archive/2004/2/24/INVE1.HTM, accessed December 21, 2010; and "Mubarak: Al-islah darura hatmiyah sharitah in yanba` min al-dakhl," [Mubarak: Reform is an imperative that must come from the inside], *Al-Ahram*, February 26, 2004, http://www.ahram.org.eg/Archive/2004/2/26/FRON2.HTM, accessed December 21, 2010.

119. Guy Dinmore, "US Plans for 'Greater Mideast' Sees Key Role for G8 Summit," *Financial Times*, February 27, 2004; Robin Wright, "U.S. Readies Push for Mideast Democracy Plan," *Washington Post*, February 28, 2004; "A Higher Standard," *Jerusalem Post*, March 8, 2004; and Barbara Slavin, "U.S. Toning Down Goals for Mideast," *USA Today*, May 27, 2004.

120. "A Creaking Partnership: The Transatlantic Alliance," *Economist*, June 5, 2004.

121. G-8, "Partnership for Progress;" and Ottaway, "Broader Middle East."

122. Niveen Wahish and Yasmine El-Rashidi, "Hardware Spot for CIT Whiz," *Al-Ahram Weekly On-line*, July 15–21, 2004, http://weekly.ahram.org.eg/2004/699/eg3.htm, accessed January 2, 2011; and Shaden Shehab, "The Cabinet's New Look," *Al-Ahram Weekly On-line*, July 15–21, 2004, http://weekly.ahram.org.eg/2004/699/eg1.htm, accessed January 2, 2011.

123. El-Mahdi, "Enough!," 1018.

124. Gamal Essam El-Din, "Space to Say 'No' to the President," *Al-Ahram Weekly On-line*, December 16–22, 2004, http://weekly.ahram.org.eg/2004/721/eg4.htm, accessed January 2, 2011; and El-Ghobashy, "Egypt Looks Ahead."

125. Dina Shehata, "Al-harakat al-ihtijajiyah al-jadidah fi misr," 12.

126. Shehata, interview.

127. Way, "Kuchma's Failed Authoritarianism," 131–145; and Bunce and Wolchik, "Favorable Conditions and Electoral Revolution," 5–18.

128. George W. Bush, *Decision Points*, 430.

129. Yasser Arafat had passed away in November 2004. Steven Erlanger, "Hoping Democracy Can Replace an Icon," *New York Times*, November 14, 2004; and Chomsky, *Interventions*, 166.

130. In the spring of 2005, Lebanese demonstrators also forced Syria to withdraw its forces from their country. The "Cedar Revolution" brought down the pro-Syrian government and opened the way for Lebanon's first government independent of foreign domination in nearly three decades.

131. Office of the Press Secretary, "President Sworn-In to Second Term," January 20, 2005, http://www.whitehouse.gov/news/releases/2005/01/print/20050120-1.html, accessed January 21, 2005.

132. Office of the Press Secretary, "State of Union Address," February 2, 2005, http://georgewbush-whitehouse.archives.gov/news/releases/2005/02/20050202-11.html, accessed September 14, 2011.

133. When Bush and Mubarak spoke by phone at the end of January 2005, the White House's foci on regional security had not changed. A journalist inquired whether Bush used the call to advise Egyptians to "open themselves to competitive elections?" Press Secretary Scott McClellan responded that the "brief" calls focused on Iraq and the Palestinian Authority, where competitive voting had recently taken place. Office of the Press Secretary, "Press Briefing by Scott McClellan," January 31, 2005.

134. "Personnel Announcement," *White House Press Releases and Documents*, February 2, 2005.

135. Elisabeth Cheney, "Interview," http://www.carnegieendowment.org/files/Interview.pdf, accessed November 15, 2010.

136. At her confirmation hearing, the secretary of state invoked Sharansky in distinguishing between "free societies" and "fear societies." Said Rice, "The world should really apply what Nathan Sharansky called the town square test. If a person cannot walk into the middle of the town square and express his or her views without fear of arrest, imprisonment and physical harm, then that person is living in a fear society. And we cannot rest until every person living in a fear society has finally won their freedom." "Transcript: Confirmation Hearing of Condoleezza Rice," January 18, 2005, http://www.nytimes.com/2005/01/18/politics/18TEXT-RICE.html?pagewanted=print, accessed January 4, 2011.

137. Guy Dinmore and Daniel Dombey, "Rice 'Will Take Lead on US Policy in Mideast,'" *Financial Times*, January 18, 2005.

138. Abrams, interview.

139. Tuàymah, *Jumhuriyat Al Mubarak*.

140. Cable, US Embassy in Cairo to Secretary of State, "CODEL Pelosi's March 19–20 Visit to Cairo," March 23, 2005, 05CAIRO2280, http://wikileaks.org/cable/2005/03/05CAIRO2280.html, accessed August 30, 2011.

141. Joel Brinkley and David E. Sanger, "Lacking Details, U.S. Is Cautious on Egypt's Plan for Open Vote," *New York Times*, February 27, 2005.

142. "President Discusses War on Terror," Speech at National Defense University, March 8, 2005, http://www.whitehouse.gov/news/releases/2005/03/print/20050308-3.html, accessed March 8, 2005.

143. Steve Coll, "Islamic Activists Sweep Saudi Council Elections," *Washington Post*, April 24, 2005.

144. Welch, interview.

145. Fahmy, interview.

146. Neil MacFarquhar, "Mubarak Pushes Egypt to Allow Freer Elections," *New York Times*, February 27, 2005.

147. Abrams, interview.

148. Gamal Essam El-Din, "Day of Reckoning," *Al-Ahram Weekly Online*, May 26–June 1, 2005, http://weekly.ahram.org.eg/2005/744/fr1.htm, accessed April 20, 2010; Amira Howeidy, "Reading the Signs," *Al-Ahram Weekly Online*, May 26–June 1, 2005, http://weekly.ahram.org.eg/2005/744/fr2.htm, accessed April 20, 2010; and Gihan Shahine, "'The One You Know'?" *Al-Ahram Weekly Online*, May 26–June 1, 2005, http://weekly.ahram.org.eg/2005/744/eg1.htm, accessed April 20, 2010.

149. Independent accounts attested to low attendance, while official turnout was recorded as 53.6 percent, with 82.9 percent voting in favor.

150. Office of the Press Secretary, "President and South African President Mbeki Discuss Bilateral Relations," June 1, 2005, http://georgewbush-whitehouse.archives.gov/news/releases/2005/06/20050601.html, accessed March 10, 2010.

151. Gamal Essam El-Din, "Maverick MP Detained," *Al-Ahram Weekly On-line*, February 3–9, 2005, http://weekly.ahram.org.eg/2005/728/eg2.htm, accessed January 4, 2011.

152. Daniel Williams, "Mubarak Rival Loses Freedom Bid," *Washington Post*, May 19, 2006.

153. Glenn Kessler, "Rice Drops Plan for Visit to Egypt," *Washington Post*, February 26, 2005.

154. Sarah El Deeb, "Egyptian Opposition Charged with Forgery," *Associated Press Newswire*, March 22, 2005.

155. Rice's speech marked the "apogee" of the administration's discussions of democracy in Egypt. Abrams, interview.

156. "Secretary Rice Urges Democratic Change in the Middle East," *State Department Press Releases and Documents*, June 20, 2005.

157. Paul Schemm and Farah Stockman, "U.S. Prods Arab Allies on Democratic Change," *Boston Globe*, June 21, 2005.

158. Maggie Michael, "Iraq's Neighbors Pledge to End Baghdad's Diplomatic Isolation by Sending Ambassadors," *Associated Press Newswire*, June 22, 2005.

159. Christine Hauser, "Al Qaeda of Iraq Says It Killed Envoy," *International Herald Tribune*, July 8, 2005.

160. International Crisis Group, "Egypt's Sinai Question," 1.

161. Alexander, "Mubarak in the International Arena," 144.

162. Migdalovitz, "Israel's Disengagement from Gaza," 2.

163. Cable, Embassy Cairo to Department of State, "PDAS Liz Cheney's September 28 Meeting with Gamal Mubarak," October 11, 2005, 05CAIRO7782, http://wikileaks.ch/cable/2005/10/05CAIRO7782.html, accessed January 5, 2011.

164. Central Elections Committee – Palestine, "Presidential Elections Final Results," n.d., http://www.elections.ps/admin/pdf/Presidential_ Elections_Final_Results.pdf, accessed June 2, 2010; and "Mubarak Confirms Plans for Cabinet Reshuffle Following Re-election," *Agence France-Presse*, September 28, 1999. By contrast, Palestinian Authority president Mahmoud Abbas had won with 62.5 percent in January 2005.

165. Office of the Press Secretary, "Statement on President Congratulating Egyptian President Mubarak on Election," September 10, 2005, http://georgewbush-whitehouse.archives.gov/news/releases/2005/09/ 20050919-11.html, accessed March 9, 2010.

166. Krasner, interview.

167. Cable, Embassy Cairo to Department of State, "PDAS Liz Cheney's September 28 Meeting with Gamal Mubarak," October 11, 2005.

168. Dan Murphy, "Egypt Holds a More-Transparent Vote," *Christian Science Monitor*, November 10, 2005; Mona El-Nahhas, "Hardly a Sore Loser," *Al-Ahram Weekly On-line*, November 17–23, 2005, http://weekly.ahram.org.eg/2005/769/eg5.htm, accessed May 11, 2010.

169. Independent Committee for Elections Monitoring, *Testimony for History*, 65.

170. Analysts at one Washington think tank later claimed: "American funding enabled local groups to implement their ideas and effectively challenge the authority of the new regime-appointed electoral commissions." The main election-monitoring group, however, chronicled its own failure to stop the Interior Ministry from warping the vote count or preventing Egypt's election commission from ratifying the fraudulent result. Wittes and Yerkes, "What Price Freedom?," 19; and Independent Committee for Elections Monitoring, *Testimony for History*, 42, 46, 50, 59, 63.

171. Mona El-Nahhas, "Will It Be Different This Time?" *Al-Ahram Weekly On-line*, December 8–14, 2005, http://weekly.ahram.org.eg/2005/772/ eg6.htm, accessed May 11, 2010.

172. Abeer Allam, "Government Suspected in Attacks During Egyptian Vote," *New York Times*, November 21, 2005.

173. Independent Committee for Elections Monitoring, *Testimony for History*, 7, 51.

174. Ibid., 39, 45.

175. Mohamed Sid-Ahmed, "After the Elections," *Al-Ahram Weekly On-line*, December 15–21, 2005, http://weekly.ahram.org.eg/2005/773/op3.htm, accessed May 11, 2010.
176. Independent Committee for Elections Monitoring, *Testimony for History*, 7.
177. Dan Murphy and Sameh Naguib, "Egypt's Islamists Arrested but Gain Seats," *Christian Science Monitor*, November 22, 2005; Mohamed Sid-Ahmed, "Israel and Egypt's Elections," *Al-Ahram Weekly On-line*, December 1–7, 2005. http://weekly.ahram.org.eg/2005/771/op3.htm, accessed May 11, 2010; and Mustafa El-Menshawy, "Change in Tactics," *Al-Ahram Weekly On-line*, December 8–14, 2005, http://weekly.ahram.org.eg/2005/772/eg7.htm, accessed May 11, 2010.
178. Sean McCormack, "Daily Press Briefing," December 1, 2005, http://2001-2009.state.gov/r/pa/prs/dpb/2005/57539.htm, accessed May 11, 2010.
179. Cable, U.S. Embassy in Cairo to Secretary of State, "Scenesetter for FBI Director Mueller's Visit to Cairo," November 29, 2005, 05CAIRO8938, http://wikileaks.ca/cable/2005/11/05CAIRO8938.html, accessed August 30, 2011.
180. Gerges, *America and Political Islam*; Nadia Aboul El-Magd, "U.S. Official Urges Egypt on Democracy," *Associated Press Newswire*, September 29, 2005; Guy Dinmore, "Dismay for US as Elections Benefit Islamists," *Financial Times*, November 12, 2005.
181. William Wallis, "Jailing of Nour puts Egypt Links with US at Risk," *Financial Times*, December 27, 2005.
182. "Hosni Mubarak's Democracy," *New York Times*, December 29, 2005.
183. Office of the Press Secretary, "Statement on Conviction of Egyptian Politician Ayman Nour," December 24, 2005, http://georgewbush-whitehouse.archives.gov/news/releases/2005/12/20051224-1.html, accessed May 12, 2010. In February 2009, less than a month after Bush left office and ten months before the end of the full sentence, Nour was freed without apology or explanation.
184. Cable, U.S. Embassy in Cairo to Secretary of State, "Scenesetter for the Vice President's Visit to Egypt," December 12, 2005, http://www.aftenposten.no/spesial/wikileaksdokumenter/article4018096.ece, accessed August 25, 2011.
185. Ibid.
186. Excerpt of untitled cable from U.S. Embassy in Cairo to Mueller, January 29, 2006, 06CAIRO493, http://wikileaks.org/cable/2006/01/06CAIRO493.html, accessed August 30, 2011.

Chapter 4: Gaza Patrol

1. Electoral data come from the Central Elections Commission – Palestine Web site, http://www.elections.ps/template.aspx?id=291, accessed

June 8, 2010. On the electoral process, see National Democratic Institute, *Final Report*, 2–3; and "Palestinian Elections: Trip Report by Former U.S. President Jimmy Carter," The Carter Center, January 30, 2006, http://www.cartercenter.org/news/documents/doc2287.html?printer Friendly=true, accessed June 7, 2010.

2. Voters also chose candidates from district lists. At the district level, Hamas's margin of victory over Fatah was slightly wider, 6 percentage points, helped by strong support in urban areas and refugee camps. Gunning, *Hamas in Politics* 26, 148.

3. U.S. Department of State, "Foreign Terrorist Organizations," http://www.state.gov/j/ct/rls/other/des/123085.htm, accessed March 28, 2012.

4. Ibid., 153.

5. Terence Hunt, "Bush Says U.S. Won't Deal with Hamas," *Associated Press Newswire*, January 26, 2006.

6. Ibid.

7. This account draws on the leaked internal UN memo written by the secretary-general's envoy to the Palestinian Authority from May 2005 until May 2007. Alvaro de Soto, "End of Mission Report," May 2007, pp. 3–22, http://image.guardian.co.uk/sys-files/Guardian/documents/2007/06/12/DeSotoReport.pdf, accessed September 14, 2011.

8. International Crisis Group, "Israel/Palestine/Lebanon," 7, 7n34.

9. U.S. Government, *National Security Strategy*, 4–5.

10. Ibid., 5.

11. Schenker, interview.

12. Abrams, interview.

13. A dissenting view within the administration was that Hamas should have been allowed to govern for its elected term and the experience of administering public services would have moderated the movement over time. Interviews.

14. Supporting Kirkpatrick's view, Feith contended: "[T]he friendly authoritarian regimes that America deals with will liberalize over time.... Communists or fascists or Islamist governments that are philosophically hostile to democracy are much less likely to evolve democratically." Feith, interview.

15. Excerpt of cable from U.S. Embassy in Cairo, "FBI Director Mueller's Visit to Egypt," February 15, 2006, 06CAIRO941, http://wikileaks.zeira.org/cable/2006/02/06CAIRO941.html, accessed September 2, 2011.

16. "Rice Kicks off Mideast Tour with Egypt Talks," *Agence France Presse*, February 21, 2006; "Rice Acknowledges Egypt's Democratic Advances, Despite Setbacks," *America.gov*, February 21, 2006, http://www.america.gov/st/washfile-english/2006/February/20060221185045ndyblehso.7834436.html, accessed July 29, 2010; and Neil King Jr. and Yasmine

el-Rashidi, "Mixed Message: In Volatile Mideast, U.S. Finds a Use for Old Autocrats," *Wall Street Journal*, August 8, 2006.

17. U.S. House Committee on Foreign Relations, "United States Policy toward the Palestinians," 5.

18. U.S. House Committee on Foreign Relations, "Review of U.S. Assistance Programs to Egypt," 16.

19. As Israel became more successful at foiling suicide bombings, Palestinian militant groups expanded their use of rockets. In 2003, rockets fired constituted over 50 percent of attacks on Israeli targets. From 2005 through 2007, they made up over 90 percent of such attacks. Pedahzur, *Israeli Secret Services*, 138–139.

20. International Crisis Group, "Israel/Palestine/Lebanon," i, 2–3, 5–6, 20; United Nations Security Council, "Report on the Implementation of Resolution 1701."

21. Nir Rosen, "Anatomy of a Civil War," *Boston Review*, November/ December 2006, http://www.newamerica.net/publications/articles/2006/ anatomy_of_a_civil_war_4405, accessed April 17, 2009; Rosen, *Aftermath*, 27, 32, 70–71.

22. For civilians, 2006 would be the bloodiest year of the war, with 27,925 reported deaths. By the end of the year, 3,255 service members from the international coalition had died, 872 of them in the prior twelve months. Database, *Iraq Body Count* Web site, http://www .iraqbodycount.org/database/, accessed April 24, 2011; and "Iraq Coalition Military Fatalities by Year," *Iraq Coalition Casualty Count* Web site, http://icasualties.org, accessed April 24, 2011.

23. Office of the Press Secretary, "President Bush and Russian President Putin Participate in Press Availability," July 15, 2006, http://www .whitehouse.gov/news/releases/2006/07/20060715-1.html, accessed June 11, 2007.

24. Pew Global Attitudes Project, *America's Image Slips*; and Program on International Policy Attitudes, "World Public Says Iraq War Has Increased Global Terrorist Threat," February 28, 2006, http://www .worldpublicopinion.org/pipa/articles/international_security_bt/172.php? nid=&id=&pnt=172&lb=btvoc.

25. International Crisis Group, "Israel/Palestine/Lebanon," 9.

26. Ibid., 6.9–10, 12–13; and United Nations Security Council, "Report on the Interim Force."

27. International Crisis Group, "Israel/Hizbollah/Lebanon," 1.

28. Israeli Ministry of Foreign Affairs, "Israel-Hizbullah Conflict: Victims of Rocket Attacks and IDF Casualties," http://www.mfa.gov.il/MFA/ Terrorism-+Obstacle+to+Peace/Terrorism+from+Lebanon-+ Hizbullah/Israel-Hizbullah+conflict-+Victims+of+rocket+attacks+and +IDF+casualties+July-Aug+2006.htm, accessed August 25, 2011.

29. "Secretary Rice Holds a News Conference," *CQ Transcripts Wire*, July 21, 2006, http://www.washingtonpost.com/wp-dyn/content/

article/2006/07/21/AR2006072100889.html, accessed April 24, 2011.

30. Tim Butcher, "The Children Went to Sleep Believing They Were Safe," *Daily Telegraph*, July 31, 2006, http://www.telegraph.co.uk/news/1525271/The-children-went-to-sleep-believing-they-were-safe.-And-then-Israel-targeted-them-as-terrorists.html, accessed August 26, 2011; and Human Rights Watch, "Israel/Lebanon: Qana Death Toll at 28," August 1, 2006, http://www.hrw.org/en/news/2006/08/01/israellebanon-qana-death-toll-28, accessed August 26, 2011.

31. Cable, U.S. Embassy to Secretary of State, "Revenge, Revenge, Revenge! Expel the American Ambassador," August 6, 2006, 06CAIRO4675, http://www.scoop.co.nz/stories/WL0607/S00371.htm, accessed September 2, 2011.

32. Cable, U.S. Embassy to Secretary of State, "July 26 Demonstrations," July 27, 2006, 06CAIRO4611, http://wikileaks.org/cable/2006/07/06CAIRO4611.html, accessed September 2, 2011; Cable, U.S. Embassy to Secretary of State, "Increasing Egyptian Anger about Lebanon," July 31, 2006, 06CAIRO4680, http://wikileaks.org/cable/2006/07/06CAIRO4680, accessed September 2, 2011; Roula Khalaf and William Wallis, "Arab Leaders Fear Fall-out from Spread of Anti-US Feeling," *Financial Times*, July 28, 2006; "Mubarak: Any Attempt to Drag Egypt into an Irrational and Illogical Conflict Is Unacceptable," *Egypt State Information Service*, July 29, 2006, http://www.sis.gov.eg/En/Story.aspx?sid=24672, accessed May 20, 2011; "Rallies across Mideast Show Support for Hezbollah," *Dow Jones International News*, August 4, 2006; Michael Slackman, "War News from Lebanon Gives Egyptians a Mirror of Their Own Desperation," *New York Times*, August 6, 2006; Nadia Abou El-Magd, "Nearly a Month into Lebanon Fighting, Arab Anger at Their Governments Grows," *Associated Press Newswires*, August 7, 2006; King and El-Rashidi, "In Volatile Mideast, U.S. Finds a Use for Old Autocrats;" and "Egypt's and Arab Stance on Lebanon 'Identical' Foreign Minister," *BBC Monitoring Middle East*, August 9, 2006.

33. Cable, U.S. Embassy in Cairo to Secretary of State, "Egyptian Liberals Predict Momentum for Reform Will Be Set Back by Lebanon Crisis," August 9, 2006, 06CAIRO4899, http://wikileaks.org/cable/2006/08/06CAIRO4899.html, accessed September 2, 2011.

34. Press release, "Security Council Unanimously Calls for End to Hostilities between Hizbollah, Israel," United Nations Security Council, August 11, 2006, http://www.un.org/News/Press/docs/2006/sc8808.doc.htm, accessed March 28, 2012.

35. International Crisis Group, "Israel/Hizbollah/Lebanon," 1.

36. International Crisis Group, "Israel/Palestine/Lebanon," 6, 20; and United Nations Security Council, "Report on the Implementation of Resolution 1701."

37. Welch, interview.
38. Ibid.
39. Inboden, interview.
40. Ibid.
41. Dunne, interview.
42. "Egypt's Municipal Elections Postponed, Ruling Party Changes," *Arab Reform Bulletin*, February 19, 2006, http://www.carnegieendowment .org/arb/?fa=show&article=20985, accessed April 21, 2011.
43. "Crackdown on Egyptian Judges, Press, Muslim Brothers," *Arab Reform Bulletin*, March 19, 2006, http://www.carnegieendowment.org/arb/ ?fa=show&article=20963, accessed April 21, 2011; Human Rights Watch, "Egypt: Troops Smother Protests, Detain Activists," May 5, 2006, http://www.hrw.org/en/news/2006/05/05/egypt-troops-smother-protests-detain-activists, accessed April 21, 2011; and Shehata and Stacher, "Brotherhood Goes to Parliament."
44. Dina Shehata, "Al-harakat al-ihtijajiyah al-jadidah fi misr," 12.
45. Cable, Embassy Cairo to Secretary of State, "Actions Louder Than Words: Gamal Mubarak and the Presidency," April 3, 2006, 06CAIRO2010, http://files.vpro.nl/wikileaks/cable/2006/04/06CAIRO2010.html. The cable mentioned Minister of Defense Tantawi in passing but deemed him "frail and without any political ambition."
46. Salah Nasrawi, "Al-Jazeera: Mubarak's Son Met Secretly with Top White House Officials," *Associated Press Newswire*, May 15, 2006; and Peter Baker, "Mubarak's Son Met with Cheney, Others; Secret Visit Came after Cairo Unrest," *Washington Post*, May 16, 2006.
47. Office of the Press Secretary, "President Discusses Democracy in Iraq with Freedom House," March 29, 2006, http://georgewbush-whitehouse .archives.gov/news/releases/2006/03/20060329-6.html, accessed March 11, 2010.
48. Gamal was comfortable on economic matters and circumspect about political reform. "Turn [from economics] to politics," recalled Abrams, "and the answers and the body language change. If you ask about freedom of the press or freedom of speech...he is careful, and he is not voluble, and he is presumably worried about saying anything that can be used against him or his father." Abrams, interview.
49. Inboden, interview.
50. Cable, U.S. Embassy in Cairo to Secretary of State, "Presidential Succession in Egypt," May 14, 2007, 07CAIRO1417, http://www.cable gatesearch.net/cable.php?id=07CAIRO1417.
51. Abrams, interview.
52. Cable, U.S. Embassy in Cairo to Secretary of State, "Scene-setter for Deputy Secretary Zoellick's Visit to Egypt," May 16, 2006, 06CAIRO2933, http://cablesearch.org/cable/view.php?id=06 CAIRO2933&hl=, accessed September 2, 2011.

53. Cable, Embassy Cairo to Secretary of State, "Actions Louder Than Words."

54. The same cable called Hosni Mubarak "indispensable...on Israel/ Palestine and Sudan, while helping also on Iraq, Syria, and Lebanon." Cable, U.S. Embassy in Cairo to Secretary of State, "Scenesetter for Deputy Secretary Zoellick's Visit to Egypt," May 16, 2006, o6CAIRO2933, accessed September 2, 2011.

55. The Israeli press reported Suleiman's security work made him an acceptable if not favored candidate among top Israeli officials: "Suleiman is viewed as a pragmatic and realistic statesman who believes that fighting terror and stabilizing and bringing peace to the Middle East is an Egyptian interest. The State of Israel benefits from this view and the ceaseless efforts he has been making to implement it, even as chief of intelligence." No'am Amit, "The Puppet Master," *Ma'ariv* [FBIS translation], May 2, 2003, http://www.fas.org/irp/world/egypt/sulayman.html, accessed May 2, 2011.

56. Baraq Ravid, "HAMAS Must Be Toppled," *Ma'ariv*, October 25, 2006, GMP20061025739002, accessed April 12, 2011.

57. Burns, *Economic Aid*, 2.

58. According to Welch, political events in Egypt had complicated free trade talks, but the Bush administration was unlikely to pursue them anyway: "Even if you had not had [Ayman Nour's case], this [free-trade agreement (FTA)] would have been a problematic issue...[T]o this day, there hasn't been any change in the number of FTAs in the Arab Middle East, and we generally have concluded FTAs with countries with which we do not trade...there's a large context, and those who say that [Nour] was the only reason would have to explain why in the Egypt case, now [late 2010] that that reason is gone, there is no revival of the effort, and number two, why didn't it proceed elsewhere? There's no FTA with Tunisia. There's no FTA with Qatar." Welch, interview.

59. Fahmy, interview; and cable, U.S. Embassy in Cairo to Secretary of State, "Scenesetter for the Vice President's Visit to Egypt," November 29, 2005, o5CAIRO8938, http://wikileaks.ca/cable/2005/11/05CAIRO8938.htm, accessed September 2, 2011.

60. Press release, U.S. Embassy in Cairo, Egypt, "United States Awards Six Grants to Civil Society Groups Working to Advance Democracy in Egypt," March 3, 2005, http://web.archive.org/web/20060103051224/ http://egypt.usembassy.gov/pa/pro30305.htm, accessed June 1, 2010. The unprecedented move originated in an amendment introduced the previous December. Office of Senator Sam Brownback, "Brownback's Iran, North Korea, Egypt Provisions Pass Senate in Omnibus Spending Bill," news release, December 1, 2004, http://brownback.senate.gov/ pressapp/record.cfm?id=228667, accessed June 14, 2010; and Conference Report 108–792, FY 2005 Omnibus Appropriations, P.L. 108–447, FY 2005 (2004), p. 993.

61. Despite the furor that erupted, MEPI funding to Egyptian NGOs was paltry. During FYs 2002–2005, nearly a third of all MEPI funding went to Arab governments or official agencies. Meanwhile, the NGO sector (including entities that "benefited" persons outside of government) comprised 11 percent of the initiative's beneficiaries. In per-capita terms, programs in Egypt constituted a negligible portion. In MEPI's first years, only $800,000, or less than 2 percent of obligations for the Arab world, went to Egypt, approximately one cent for every Egyptian. Morocco received over fifty times that amount per capita, and Jordan's MEPI funding averaged $1.30/person. Wittes and Yerkes, *What Price Freedom*, 20; U.S. Government Accounting Office, "Foreign Assistance," 15.

62. Anne Gearan, "Mideast Democracy Summit Ends with No Deal," *Associated Press Newswire*, November 12, 2005; and Robin Wright, "U.S. Goals Are Thwarted at Pro-Democracy Forum," *Washington Post*, November 13, 2005.

63. Sherine Bahaa, "Waiting for Plan B," *Al-Ahram Weekly On-line*, November 17–23, 2005, http://weekly.ahram.org.eg/2005/769/re9.htm, accessed May 25, 2010.

64. "Egypt Tells U.S. Institute to Suspend Work," *Reuters News*, June 4, 2006; "U.S. Democracy Institute Asked to Shut Down All Operations," *Daily News Egypt*, June 5, 2006, http://www.dailystaregypt.com/article.aspx?ArticleID=1776, accessed April 21, 2011; "Egypt Tells US Institute to Halt Activities," *Agence France Presse*, June 5, 2006; Ahmed al-Khamisi, "Gina London: Tarsad adaqq al-raghbat" [Gina London: Most closely covering the desires (of civil society)], *Droob.com*, June 16, 2006, http://www.doroob.com/archives/?p=8924, accessed April 21, 2011; and Penny Parker, "Woman Back in Town after Fleeing Egypt as 'Spy,'" *Rocky Mountain News*, January 20, 2007.

65. U.S. House Committee on Appropriations, "Foreign Operations Report."

66. Ibid.

67. Vicki Allen, "U.S. House Committee Backs Full Aid to Egypt," *Reuters News*, May 25, 2006.

68. U.S. Congress, "Foreign Operations, Export Financing, and Related Programs Act, 2007."

69. Ibid., H3538–H3539.

70. Ibid., H3539–H3540.

71. Ibid., H3540.

72. Ibid., H3540–H3541.

73. Dan Morgan, "House Rejects Cut in Military Aid to Egypt," *Washington Post*, July 16, 2004, http://www.washingtonpost.com/wp-dyn/articles/A53129-2004Jul15.html, accessed April 24, 2011.

74. U.S. Congress Votes Database, http://projects.washingtonpost.com/congress/109/house/2/votes/236/, accessed April 20, 2011.

75. Amr Hamzawy and Michael McFaul, "Giving up on the 'Liberty Doctrine': The U.S. and Egypt," *International Herald Tribune*, July 4, 2006.

76. Jan Fallström, "Ce qui s'est vraiment passé à Gaza" [What really happened in Gaza], *Jeune Afrique*, 23–29 September 2007, 32–35; David Rose, "The Gaza Bombshell," *Vanity Fair*, April 2008, http://www.vanityfair.com/politics/features/2008/04/gaza200804, accessed February 23, 2010; International Crisis Group, "After Mecca," i.
77. Cam Simpson and Neil King, Jr., "Dangerous Territory: With Aid, U.S. Widens Role in Palestinian Crisis," *Wall Street Journal*, January 12, 2007.
78. Fallström, "Ce qui s'est vraiment passé à Gaza;" Rose, "Gaza Bombshell;" and International Crisis Group, "After Mecca," i.
79. Avi Issacharoff and Amos Harel, "Fatah to Israel: Let Us Get Arms to Fight Hamas," *Ha'aretz*, June 7, 2007, http://www.haaretz.com/misc/article-print-page/fatah-to-israel-let-us-get-arms-to-fight-hamas-1.222473?trailingPath=2.169%2C2.225%2C2.226%2C, accessed May 3, 2011.
80. Fallström, "Ce qui s'est vraiment passé à Gaza;" and Rose, "Gaza Bombshell."
81. International Crisis Group, "After Gaza," i.
82. Shim'on Schiffer, "Israel to Egyptians: Renew Negotiations with HAMAS on Gil'ad Shalit's Release," *Yediot Aharanot*, July 29, 2007, GMP20070729754003, accessed April 12, 2011.
83. Once again, the Bush administration objected in a letter to the committee: "Military assistance is critical to our strategic partnership with Egypt and has contributed to a broad range of U.S. objectives in the region. Such a restriction will undermine the U.S. relationship with Egypt and send the wrong message to this important ally in the region." "Statement of Administration Policy," H.R. 2764 (State, Foreign Operations, and Related Programs Appropriations Act), 2008. "Consolidated Appropriations Act, 2008," P.L.110–161, 521.
84. Rep. Lantos, *Congressional Record* 153 (June 21, 2007): H6914.
85. U.S. Congress Votes Database, "Vote 535," 110th Congress (June 21, 2007), http://projects.washingtonpost.com/congress/110/house/1/votes/535/, accessed May 4, 2011; ibid., "Vote 542," June 22, 2007, http://projects.washingtonpost.com/congress/110/house/1/votes/542/, accessed May 4, 2011.
86. Jeremy Sharp, "The Egypt-Gaza Border and Its Effect on Israeli-Egyptian Relations," *CRS Report for Congress*, February 1, 2008; and International Crisis Group, "Ruling Palestine I."
87. In the same meeting, he also gave a seldom-reported critique of U.S. policy: "The Americans have not been listening to us in the last two or three years. Everything that we've told them, all our warnings, have materialized on the ground. It's happened to them in Iraq, where they are losing to the extremists; they made a big mistake in Lebanon as well, they didn't understand the correct solution, didn't go in the right direction, don't understand what is happening, think that democratization is the answer to everything." Ben Kaspit, "Umar Sulayman: Israel Holding Up

Shalit Deal," *Ma'ariv*, July 10, 2007, GMP20070710741006, accessed April 12, 2011.

88. International Crisis Group, "Ruling Palestine I," 1.

89. Abraham Rabinovich, "Hamas Fighters Strengthening Border Defense," *Washington Times*, November 2, 2007; Sharp, "Egypt-Gaza Border;" and International Crisis Group, "Ruling Palestine I."

90. Cable, U.S. Embassy in Cairo to Federal Bureau of Investigation, "Scenesetter for FBI Deputy Director John Pistole," October 30, 2007, 07CAIRO3155, http://wikileaks.org/cable/2007/10/07CAIRO3155.html, accessed September 2, 2011.

91. In 2004, Egypt discovered 20 tunnels, in 2005, 25; 2006, 73; and 2007, 119. Sharp, "Egypt-Gaza Border," 7.

92. Elkeshky, interview.

93. Cable, U.S. Embassy in Tel Aviv to Secretary of State, "DAS Danin and DASD Kimmitt Discuss Gaza Smuggling with ISA Chief Diskin," November 9, 2007, 07TELAVIV3258, http://wikileaks.org/cable/2007/11/07TELAVIV3258.html, accessed September 2, 2011.

94. Cable, U.S. Embassy in Cairo to Secretary of State, "Repairing Egyptian Israeli Communications," December 17, 2007, 07CAIRO3503, http://wikileaks.org/cable/2007/12/07CAIRO3503.html, accessed September 2, 2011.

95. Nathan Guttman, "Threat to Cut U.S. Aid Opens Rift with Egypt," *The Forward*, January 11, 2008, http://www.forward.com/articles/12443/, accessed April 24, 2011.

96. Steven Erlanger, "Israel Urges Egypt to Act against Hamas," *New York Times*, November 9, 2007; and "Israeli MP Urges US to Freeze Aid to Egypt over Support for Hamas," *BBC Monitoring Middle East*, November 12, 2007.

97. Jim Lobe, "U.S.: Congress Approves Military Spending, Doubles Aid Funding," *Inter Press Service*, December 21, 2007.

98. The text read: "Of the funds appropriated by this Act under the heading 'Foreign Military Financing Program' or under the heading 'Economic Support Fund' that are available for assistance for Egypt, $100,000,000 shall not be made available for obligation until the Secretary of State certifies and reports to the Committees on Appropriations that the Government of Egypt has taken concrete and measurable steps to – (1) adopt and implement judicial reforms that protect the independence of the judiciary; (2) review criminal procedures and train police leadership in modern policing to curb police abuses; and (3) detect and destroy the smuggling network and tunnels that lead from Egypt to Gaza. (b) Not less than 45 days after enactment of this Act, the Secretary may waive subsection (a) if the Secretary determines and reports to the Committees on Appropriations that such waiver is in the national security interest of the United States." "Consolidated Appropriations Act, 2008," 521.

99. Guttman, "Threat to Cut U.S. Aid Opens Rift with Egypt."
100. Office of the Press Secretary, "President Bush Discusses the Middle East," July 16, 2007, http://georgewbush-whitehouse.archives.gov/news/releases/2007/07/print/20070716-7.html, accessed May 5, 2011.
101. Abrams, interview.
102. Fahmy, interview.
103. Prime Minister Ehud Olmert assured Israelis, "Other than the increase in aid, we received an explicit and detailed commitment to guarantee Israel's qualitative advantage over other Arab states." "Israeli PM announces 30 Bln Dollar US Defence Aid," *Agence France Presse*, July 29, 2007.
104. David S. Cloud, "U.S. Set to Offer Huge Arms Deal to Saudi Arabia," *New York Times*, July 28, 2007; Robin Wright, "U.S. Plans New Arms Sales to Gulf Allies," *Washington Post*, July 28, 2007; Lolita C. Baldor and Anne Gearan, "Rice, Gates Calm Nervous Arab Leaders," *Associated Press Newswire*, July 29, 2007; and "UK Report Mulls US Motives for Arms Deals with Egypt, Saudi Arabia," *BBC Monitoring Middle East*, August 1, 2007; Stockholm International Peace Research Institute, *Yearbook 2008*, 297.
105. Gamal Mubarak actually harbored hopes of extracting the economic assistance package from the political process in Washington by creating a binational "endowment" from which funds would be disbursed annually. In 2007, the Bush administration chose not to pursue the idea, but it would continue to circulate in aid discussions for years. The glaring obstacle to such a plan was that it would immediately be opposed by the U.S. lawmakers it was designed to circumvent. Cable, U.S. Embassy in Cairo to Secretary of State, "Gamal Mubarak Advisor Discusses Egypt's Assistance Package," August 29, 2007, 07CAIRO2669, http://www.wikileaks.ch/cable/2007/08/07CAIRO2669.html, accessed September 2, 2011.
106. Andrew England, "Peace Process Gives Cairo Central Role," *Financial Times*, December 10, 2007.
107. Ibrahim, interview.
108. Cable, U.S. Embassy in Cairo to Secretary of State, "Repairing Egyptian Israeli Communications," 07CAIRO3503, http://www.telegraph.co.uk/news/wikileaks-files/egypt-wikileaks-cables/8309336/REPAIRING-EGYPTIAN-ISRAELI-COMMUNICATIONS.html, accessed March 28, 2012.
109. "Political Parties Reject Setting Conditions on US Aid to Egypt," *IPR Strategic Information Database*, December 29, 2007; "Major News Items in Leading Egyptian Newspapers," *Xinhua News Agency*, December 31, 2007; and "Egypt Refuses to Link U.S. Aid to Any Conditions," *Xinhua News Agency*, December 31, 2007.
110. Dan Williams, "Israel's Barak Makes Fence-Mending Visit to Egypt," *Reuters News*, December 26, 2007.

111. Guttman, "Threat to Cut U.S. Aid Opens Rift with Egypt."
112. Sharp, "Egypt-Gaza Border," 10.
113. International Crisis Group, "Ruling Palestine I," 19–20.
114. Robert M. Gates and Condoleezza Rice, "Letter to the Honorable Nancy Pelosi, Speaker of the House of Representatives," October 3, 2007, emphasis in original, photocopy obtained by author.
115. Elkeshky, interview.
116. Brownlee, "Imagining the Next Occupation."
117. Cable, U.S. Embassy in Cairo to Secretary of State, "Scenesetter for General Petraeus' Visit to Egypt," 08CAIRO2543, http://cables.mrkva .eu/cable.php?id=184168, accessed March 28, 2012.
118. *A Partnership for Peace, Stability and Progress: Egypt's FY 2007 Request for Military Assistance*, n.d., 4, photocopy of white paper obtained by author; "Paratroopers from Five Nations Jump in 'Bright Star,'" *US Fed News*, November 19, 2007.
119. Cable, U.S. Embassy in Cairo to White House, "Scenesetter for MINDEF Tantawi's Visit to the U.S.," March 16, 2008, 08CAIRO524, http://wikileaks.org/cable/2008/03/08CAIRO524.html; and Cable, US Embassy in Tel Aviv to Secretary of State, "IDF Deputy Chief of Staff Discusses Gaza Operation," February 19, 2009, 09TELAVIV422, http://www.wikileaks.ch/cable/2009/02/09TELAVIV422.html, accessed September 2, 2011.
120. Cable, U.S. Embassy in Cairo to Secretary of State, "Demarche Delivered on Possible Violation of Retransfer, End-Use, and Security Obligations," September 25, 2008, 08CAIRO2100, http://www .wikileaks.ch/cable/2008/09/08CAIRO2100.html, accessed September 2, 2011.
121. Cable, U.S. Embassy in Cairo to Secretary of State, "Update: Egypt Increases Countersmuggling Efforts," October 13, 2008, 08CAIRO2175, http://wikileaks.ch/cable/2008/10/08CAIRO2175.html, accessed September 2, 2011.
122. Elkeshky, interview.
123. Cable, U.S. Embassy in Cairo to Secretary of State, "Repairing Egyptian Israeli Communications."
124. *A Partnership for Peace*, 4.
125. Memo, Jeffrey D. Feltman to John D. Negroponte, February 28, 2008, electronic copy provided to author.
126. "Ms. Rice's Retreat," *Washington Post*, March 11, 2008, http://www .washingtonpost.com/wp-dyn/content/article/2008/03/10/ AR2008031002669.html, accessed May 7, 2011.

Chapter 5: Groundswell

1. Brownlee, *Authoritarianism in an Age of Democratization*.
2. "Hossam Badrawi: 'I didn't see it coming,'" *Cairo Review of Global Affairs* 1 (Spring 2011): 80–81.

3. Initial commentary on Mubarak's downfall implied an incoherent and ineffectual regime, a portrait at odds with the evidence presented here. See Gause, "Why Middle East Studies Missed;" Marc Lynch, "U.S. Public Diplomacy and the Arab Uprisings," Foreignpolicy.com [blog], April 21, 2011, http://lynch.foreignpolicy.com/posts/2011/04/13/us_public_diplomacy_and_the_arab_uprisings, accessed July 9, 2011; Masoud, "Road to and from Liberation Square," 21, 24–25; Lucan Way, "Some Thoughts on Authoritarian Durability in the Middle East," The Monkey Cage [blog], February 21, 2011, http://themonkeycage.org/blog/2011/02/21/some_thoughts_on_authoritarian/, accessed July 9, 2011.

4. Stacher, "Anatomy of Succession," 312; and Egypt State Information Service, "Political Reform in Egypt," n.d., http://www.sis.gov.eg/en/LastPage.aspx?Category_ID=204, accessed June 1, 2010.

5. Cable, U.S. Embassy in Cairo to Secretary of State, "Presidential Succession in Egypt," May 14, 2007, 07CAIRO1417, http://test.cablegatewiki.org/index.php?title=07CAIRO1417, accessed August 30, 2011.

6. Brown, Dunne, and Hamzawy, *Egypt's Controversial Constitutional Amendments*, 1–3.

7. Office of the Press Secretary, "President Bush Visits Prague, Czech Republic, Discusses Freedom," White House, June 5, 2007, http://georgewbush-whitehouse.archives.gov/news/releases/2007/06/20070605-8.html, accessed May 4, 2011.

8. Ibrahim, interview.

9. Cable, U.S. Embassy in Cairo to Secretary of State, "Egypt: Reaction To President Bush's Prague Speech," June 7, 2007, 07CAIRO1727, http://www.superkuh.com/library/Wikileaks/cable/2007/06/07CAIRO1727.html, accessed August 30, 2011.

10. Alaa Shahine, "Interview – Egyptian Activist Sees Liberals Abandoned by US," *Reuters News*, October 9, 2007.

11. Office of the Press Secretary, "President Bush Meets President Hosni Mubarak of Egypt," January 16, 2008, http://georgewbush-whitehouse.archives.gov/news/releases/2008/01/20080116-2.html, accessed May 10, 2011.

12. Fahmy, interview.

13. Office of the Press Secretary, "Interview of the President by Mona Shazli, Dream TV, Egypt," May 12, 2008, http://georgewbush-whitehouse.archives.gov/news/releases/2008/05/20080512-12.html, accessed May 11, 2011. At the World Economic Summit, the occasion of that visit, Bush refrained from naming Mubarak's critics but still raised the "plight of political prisoners in this region," "democratic activists who are intimidated or repressed," and "dissidents whose voices are stifled." Having received a copy of the speech beforehand, Mubarak abstained from attending. Bush reciprocated the snub by skipping Mubarak's opening address. Office of the Press Secretary, "Bush Attends World

Economic Forum," May 18, 2008, http://georgewbush-whitehouse
.archives.gov/news/releases/2008/05/print/20080518-6.html, accessed
May 10, 2011; and Magdi Abdelhadi, "Jibes Highlight Bush-
Mubarak Rift," *BBC News*, May 20, 2008, http://news.bbc.co.uk/2/hi/
7410669.stm, accessed May 10, 2011.

14. Office of the Press Secretary, "Interview of the President by Richard
    Engel, NBC News," May 18, 2008, http://georgewbush-whitehouse
    .archives.gov/news/releases/2008/05/20080518-8.html,
    accessed May 11, 2011.

15. Mohamed El-Sayed, "Unwelcome Visit," *Al Ahram Weekly On-line*,
    January 17–23, 2008, http://weekly.ahram.org.eg/2008/880/eg7.htm,
    accessed May 11, 2011.

16. Farah, *Egypt's Political Economy*, 50, cited in Samer Shehata, *Shop Floor Culture*, 259.

17. Beinin, "Popular Social Movements."

18. Posusney, "Irrational Workers."

19. El-Mahdi, "`Umal al-mahalla," 147.

20. Beinin, "Workers' Social Movement," 183, 200.

21. El-Mahdi, "`Umal al-mahallah," 147.

22. Ibid., 158.

23. Beinin and El-Hamalawy, "Egyptian Textile Workers."

24. Paul Schemm, "Egypt's Workers Squeezed by Prices Turn to Strikes," *Associated Press Newswire*, September 29, 2007.

25. Data are from the Web site of the Land Center for Human Rights, http://www.lchr-eg.org/, accessed May 8, 2011.

26. El-Mahdi, "`Umal al-mahalla," 155.

27. Beinin, "Workers' Social Movement," 183.

28. Ibid., 195; and Beinin, "Militancy of Mahalla al-Kubra."

29. Seyam, "Kharitat al-ihtijajat al-selmiya fi misr," 61.

30. Samer Shehata, *Shop Floor Culture*, 279n59.

31. Ibid., 260–261.

32. Beinin and El-Hamalawy, "Strikes in Egypt Spread."

33. Beinin, "Labor Protest Politics."

34. E-mail correspondence with Joel Beinin, August 4, 2011.

35. Dina Shehata, "Al-harakat al-ihtijajiyah al-shababiya,"261.

36. El-Mahdi, "`Umal al-mahalla," 165.

37. Beinin, "Workers' Social Movement," 199.

38. Beinin, "Undermining Mubarak," 5–6.

39. Beinin and Vairel, "Afterword," 249.

40. "April 6 Strike Kicks Off a Year of Protests," *Daily News Egypt*, December 23, 2008. Records later retrieved from State Security headquarters showed that the internal police monitored Abdel Fatah and her colleagues obsessively, scrutinizing mundane communications for hidden meanings. Hannah Allam and Mohannad Sabry, "Egypt Faces New Turmoil: Looted State Security Files," *McClatchy Newspapers*, March 7, 2011.

41. Dina Shehata, "Al-harakat al-ihtijajiyah al-shababiya," 261.

42. Seyam, "Kharitat al-ihtijajat al-selmiya fi misr,"55.

43. Nearly one in four workers who joined in contentious collective action was from the textiles sector. Ibid., 56.

44. "Presidential Pardon for Egyptian Journalist," *Associated Press Newswire*, October 6, 2008.

45. "The Best of Times…the Worst of Times," *Al Ahram WeeklyOnline*, December 27, 2007–January 2, 2008, http://weekly.ahram.org .eg/2007/877/economy.htm, accessed May 10, 2011.

46. Cable, U.S. Embassy in Cairo to Secretary of State, "Egypt in Transition: Sadat and Mubarak," September 23, 2007, 07CAIRO2871, http://wikileaks.org/cable/2007/09/07CAIRO2871.html, accessed August 30, 2011.

47. Cable, U.S. Embassy to Secretary of State, "Mahalla Riots: Isolated Incident or Tip of an Iceberg?" April 16, 2008, 08CAIRO0783, http://www.cablegatesearch.net/cable.php?id=08CAIRO783, accessed August 30, 2011.

48. Cable, U.S. Embassy in Cairo to Secretary of State, "The View from the Ahwa: The Talk of Town in Cairo's Myriad Cafes," October 28, 2008, 08CAIRO2266, http://www.superkuh.com/library/Wikileaks/ cable/2008/10/08CAIRO2266.html, accessed August 30, 2011.

49. Cable, U.S. Embassy to Secretary of State, "Scenesetter for General Petraeus' Visit to Egypt," December 21, 2008, 08CAIRO2543, http://wikileaks.org/cable/2008/12/08CAIRO2543.html, accessed August 30, 2011.

50. U.S. Senate Committee on Appropriations, "Department of State, Foreign Operations, and Related Appropriations Bill, 2009," 110th Congress, 2nd session (2008): 46.

51. Cable, U.S. Embassy in Cairo to Secretary of State, "CODEL Ackerman Meetings with Mubarak, Suleiman," July 7, 2008, 08CAIRO1416, http://wikileaks.org/cable/2008/07/08CAIRO1416.html.

52. Jeremy M. Sharp, "Egypt: Background and U.S. Relations," *CRS Report for Congress*, February 4, 2011, 22.

53. Alain Navarro, "Egypt Back in Diplomatic Saddle with Gaza Deal," *Agence France Presse*, June 18, 2008.

54. Cable, U.S. Embassy in Cairo to Secretary of State, "CODEL Ackerman Meetings with Mubarak, Suleiman," 08CAIRO1416, accessed August 30, 2011.

55. Cable, U.S. Embassy in Tel Aviv to Secretary of State, "Defense Minister Barak's Discussions in Egypt," August 29, 2008, 08TELAVIV1984, http://www.wikileaks.ch/cable/2008/08/08TELAVIV1984.html, accessed August 30, 2011.

56. Ibid.; and Yossi Melman, "The General's Cold Peace," *Haaretz*, January 20, 2009, http://www.haaretz.com/print-edition/features/the-general-s-cold-peace-1.268497, accessed July 11, 2011.

57. Israeli Ministry of Foreign Affairs, "Elections in Israel – February 2009," http://www.mfa.gov.il/MFA/History/Modern+History/Historic+Events/ Elections_in_Israel_February_2009.htm, accessed May 11, 2011.
58. International Crisis Group, "Palestine Divided," 7.
59. International Crisis Group, "Ending the War in Gaza," 4.
60. Human Rights Watch, "Deprived and Endangered: Humanitarian Crisis in the Gaza Strip," January 2009, http://www.hrw.org/sites/ default/files/related_material/2009_OPT_MENA.PDF, accessed August 27, 2011.
61. Cable, U.S. Embassy in Tel Aviv to Secretary of State, "Codels Casey and Ackerman Meet with Defense Minister Barak," June 2, 2009, 09TELA-VIV1177, http://wikileaks.ch/cable/2009/06/09TELAVIV1177.html, accessed August 30, 2011.
62. "Egypt's Mubarak Meets with Israeli FM on Palestinian-Israeli Calm," *Xinhua News Agency*, December 25, 2008; and Sakher Abu El Oun, "At Least 225 Dead as Israel Hammers Hamas-Run Gaza," *Agence France Presse*, December 27, 2008.
63. Heba Saleh and Andrew England, "Arab States Squirm as Anger Rises," *Financial Times*, December 29, 2008; Andrew England, "Egypt's Consulate in Aden Attacked," *Financial Times*, December 31, 2008; Roula Khalaf, "Egyptian Balancing Act Falls Victim to Crisis," *Financial Times*, January 6, 2009; and Andrew England, "Protests Sweep Arab World," *Financial Times*, January 5, 2009.
64. Samantha M. Shapiro, "Revolution, Facebook-Style," *New York Times Magazine*, January 25, 2009, http://www.nytimes.com/2009/01/ 25/magazine/25bloggers-t.html?pagewanted=print, accessed May 17, 2011.
65. Omar Sinan, "Mideast Protesters Demand Israeli Gaza Withdrawal," *Associated Press Newswire*, January 9, 2009; and "Some 30,000 Egyptians Demonstrate against Gaza War," *Agence France Presse*, January 16, 2009.
66. International Crisis Group, "Gaza's Unfinished Business," 18–19.
67. "Hamas Admits Higher Casualties among Fighters in Gaza War," *Agence France Presse*, November 1, 2010; and United Nations Human Rights Council, "Report on the Gaza Conflict," September 25, 2009, 10–11, 253–255. In April 2011, the chair of the Fact-Finding Mission, Justice Richard Goldstone, announced that in light of subsequent investigation by the Israeli government, he no longer supported the report's most incendiary charge that Israel had deliberately targeted civilians. He accepted Hamas and Israeli casualty figures. His three co-investigators stood by the group's original findings. See, Richard Goldstone, "Reconsidering the Goldstone Report on Israel and War Crimes," *Washington Post*, April 1, 2011, http://www.washingtonpost.com/ opinions/reconsidering-the-goldstone-report-on-israel-and-war-crimes/

2011/04/01/AFg111JC_print.html, accessed May 16, 2011; and
Hina Jilani, Christine Chinkin, and Desmond Travers, "Goldstone
Report: Statement Issued by Members of UN Mission on Gaza War,"
Guardian, April 14, 2011, http://www.guardian.co.uk/commentisfree/
2011/apr/14/goldstone-report-statement-un-gaza?CMP=twt_gu,
accessed May 16, 2011.

68. Cable, U.S. Embassy to Secretary of State, "Gamal Mubarak on Economic
Issues and the Bilateral Relationship," October 20, 2008, 08CAIRO2224,
http://wikileaks.org/cable/2008/10/08CAIRO2224.html, accessed August
30, 2011.

69. Cable, U.S. Embassy in Cairo to Secretary of State, "Senior Egyptian
Official Welcomes Recent POTUS Comments," January 27, 2009,
09CAIRO145, http://www.telegraph.co.uk/news/wikileaks-files/egypt-
wikileaks-cables/8327101/SENIOR-EGYPTIAN-OFFICIAL-
WELCOMES-RECENT-POTUS-COMMENTS.html, accessed July 12,
2011; Michele Dunne, "A Message for Mubarak," *Washington Post*,
August 17, 2009; Saad Eddin Ibrahim, "The President and the Arab
Status Quo," *Wall Street Journal*, August 18, 2009; Elliott Abrams,
"Who Cares About Human Rights?" *Weekly Standard*, August 20, 2009;
and Jackson Diehl, "The Deflated Arab Hopes for Obama," *Washington
Post*, November 30, 2009.

70. Office of the Press Secretary, "A New Beginning," http://www.whitehouse
.gov/the-press-office/remarks-president-cairo-university-6–04-09,
accessed November 22, 2010.

71. Pew Global Attitudes Project, *Confidence in Obama Lifts U.S.
Image*.

72. Cable, U.S. Embassy in Cairo to Secretary of State, "Egypt's Speaker
of the Peoples Assembly on Prospects for Dissolution," July 13, 2009,
09CAIRO1333, http://www.telegraph.co.uk/news/wikileaks-files/egypt-
wikileaks-cables/8327252/EGYPTS-SPEAKER-OF-THE-PEOPLES-
ASSEMBLY-ON-PROSPECTS-FOR-DISSOLUTION.html, accessed
July 12, 2011.

73. Mubarak had originally been scheduled to visit Washington before
Obama's Cairo speech but had postponed the visit because of the sudden
death of his grandson, the eldest son of Alaa Mubarak.

74. Kori Schulman, "President Mubarak of Egypt at the White House,"
White House Blog, August 19, 2009, http://www.whitehouse.gov/blog/
President-Mubarak-of-Egypt-at-the-White-House, accessed June 14,
2011.

75. Dunne, interview.

76. Cable, U.S. Embassy in Cairo to Secretary of State, "Scenesetter for
Requested Egyptian Fm Aboul Gheit Meeting with the Secretary,"
February 9, 2009, 09CAIRO231, http://wikileaks.zakulisa.org/cable/
2009/02/09CAIRO231.html, accessed August 30, 2011.

77. Cable, U.S. Embassy in Cairo to Secretary of State, "Ayman Nour's Release," February 19, 2009, 09CAIRO300, http://wikileaks.zakulisa.org/cable/2009/02/09CAIRO300.html, accessed August 30, 2011.

78. Cable, U.S. Embassy in Cairo to Secretary of State, "Scenesetter for President Mubarak's Visit to Washington," May 19, 2009, 09CAIRO874, http://www.wikileaks.org/cable/2009/05/09CAIRO874.html, accessed August 30, 2011; and Cable, U.S. Embassy in Cairo to Secretary of State, "Scenesetter For Deputy Secretary Lew's February 15–16 Visit," February 4, 2010, 10CAIRO159, http://wikileaks.discipulosdopinguim.com.br/cable/2010/02/10CAIRO159.html, accessed August 30, 2011.

79. Cable, U.S. Embassy in Cairo to Secretary of State, "GOE Proposes New Model for Economic Assistance," September 3, 2009, 09CAIRO1725, http://www.wikileaks.ch/cable/2009/09/09CAIRO1725.html, accessed August 30, 2011; Cable, U.S. Embassy in Cairo to Secretary of State, "Request for Guidance on GOE Economic Assistance Proposal," September 3, 2009, 09CAIRO1727, http://www.wikileaks.ch/cable/2009/09/09CAIRO1727.html, accessed August 30, 2011.

80. Wittes, interview.

81. Cable, U.S. Embassy in Cairo to Secretary of State, "Ambassador, Human Rights Activist Discuss Secretary's Speech, Elections, Succession," December 17, 2009, 09CAIRO2323, http://wikileaks.electric-castle.net/cable/2009/12/09CAIRO2323.html, accessed August 30, 2011.

82. McInerney, "Federal Budget and Appropriations for 2011," 26.

83. Cable, U.S. Embassy in Cairo to Secretary of State, "DAS Wittes Engages GOE, Civil Society on Elections, Naga Hammadi, Democracy Promotion," February 4, 2010, 10CAIRO163, http://www.wikileaks.ch/cable/2010/02/10CAIRO163.html, accessed August 30, 2011.

84. Saad Eddin Ibrahim, "Egypt's Unchecked Repression," *Washington Post*, August 21, 2007; and Singerman, "Politics of Emergency Rule."

85. Ibrahim, "Egypt's Unchecked Repression;" and International Crisis Group, "Popular Protest in North Africa," 1n6.

86. Hala Mustafa, "Ending the Silent War in Egypt," *Washington Post*, December 24, 2005, http://www.washingtonpost.com/wp-dyn/content/article/2005/12/23/AR2005122301065_pf.html, accessed July 9, 2010.

87. Qandil, *Al-ayam al-akhirah*, 63.

88. "The general's budget," *Arabawy* [blog], November 29, 2006, http://www.arabawy.org/2006/11/29/adlys-budget/, accessed June 25, 2011.

89. During the 1990s the ministry acquired thousands of handguns with tens of thousands of rounds, as well as tens of thousands of tear gas canisters, from U.S. arms merchants. Although procurement data for the following decade are unavailable, the sale of approved arms suggests equal if not greater amounts of weaponry and equipment going to Egypt. Federation of American Scientists, Database on Small Arms Shipments.

90. Ibid., U.S. Department of State, "Report [on] Direct Commercial Sales Authorization 2009," 10, 107; U.S. Department of State, "Report [on] Direct Commercial Sales Authorization 2010," 10, 111.
91. "Defense Budget (Egypt)," *Jane's*, March 3, 2011, http://articles.janes .com/articles/Janes-Sentinel-Security-Assessment-North-Africa/Defence–budget-Egypt.html, accessed July 11, 2011; Egyptian Ministry of Defense, "United States-Egyptian Military Cooperation," 5; and El-Keshky, interview.
92. Cable, U.S. Embassy in Cairo to Secretary of State, "Scenesetter for General Schwartz," March 31, 2009, 09CAIRO549, http://wikileaks .nl/cable/2009/03/09CAIRO549.html, accessed August 30, 2011.
93. Ibid.; Cable, U.S. Embassy in Cairo to Secretary of State, "Sinai Update: Counter Smuggling and Floods," February 9, 2010, 10CAIRO177, http://www.wikileaks.ch/cable/2010/02/10CAIRO177.html, accessed August 30, 2011.
94. Cable, U.S. Embassy in Cairo to Secretary of State, "DASD Kahl Meeting with Egyptian Military Officials," February 28, 2010, 10CAIRO257, http://www.telegraph.co.uk/news/wikileaks-files/egypt-wikileaks-cables/8326780/DASD-Kahl-Meeting-with-Egyptian-Military-Officials.html, accessed August 30, 2011.
95. Ibid.
96. Cable, U.S. Embassy in Cairo to Secretary of State, "Lt. General North Discusses Gaza, Piracy, and Military Cooperation with MOD Officials," February 23, 2009, 09CAIRO327, http://www.telegraph.co.uk/news/ wikileaks-files/egypt-wikileaks-cables/8327050/LT-GENERAL-NORTH-DISCUSSES-GAZA-PIRACY-AND-MILITARY-COOPERATION-WITH-MOD-OFFICIALS.html, accessed August 30, 2011.
97. Cable, U.S. Embassy in Cairo to Secretary of State, "Scenesetter for General Schwartz," 09CAIRO549, March 31, 2009, http://wikileaks .ch/cable/2009/03/09CAIRO549.html, accessed August 30, 2011.
98. Cable, U.S. Embassy in Cairo to Secretary of State, "Egypt: Counter Smuggling Update," December 20, 2009, 09CAIRO2325, http://wikileaks.ch/cable/2009/12/09CAIRO2325.html, accessed August 30, 2011.
99. Cable, U.S. Embassy in Cairo to Secretary of State, "Counter Smuggling Update: Egypt Increases Efforts," July 16, 2009, 09CAIRO1377, http://dazzlepod.com/cable/09CAIRO1377/, accessed August 30, 2011; and U.S. Embassy in Tel Aviv to Secretary of State, "IDF Deputy Chief of Staff Discusses Gaza Operation," February 19, 2009, 09TELAVIV422, http://www.wikileaks.ch/cable/2009/02/09TELAVIV422.html, accessed August 30, 2011.
100. Ahmed Zaki Osman, "Powerhouse and Powerbrokers: A Profile of Egypt's Military," *Al-Misry Al-Yawm* [English edition], February 16,

2011, http://www.almasryalyoum.com/en/print/320687, accessed June 28, 2011.

101. Cable, U.S. Embassy in Cairo to Secretary of State, May 13, 2007, 07CAIRO1417, http://www.wikileaks.ch/cable/2007/05/09CAIRO1417.html, accessed August 30, 2011.

102. Cable, U.S. Embassy in Cairo to Secretary of State, "Academics See the Military in Decline but Retaining Strong Influence," September 23, 2008, 08CAIRO2091, http://www.telegraph.co.uk/news/wikileaks-files/egypt-wikileaks-cables/8327036/ACADEMICS-SEE-THE-MILITARY-IN-DECLINE-BUT-RETAINING-STRONG-INFLUENCE.html, accessed July 12, 2011.

103. Cable, U.S. Embassy in Cairo to Secretary of State, "GOE Releases Egyptian-German Blogger, Cracks Down," February 11, 2009, 09CAIRO255, http://wikileaks.zakulisa.org/cable/2009/02/09CAIRO255.html, accessed August 30, 2011.

104. "Egyptian Court Bans Natural Gas Exports to Israel," *Haaretz.com*, November 18, 2008, http://www.haaretz.com/news/egyptian-court-bans-natural-gas-exports-to-israel-1.257429, accessed August 30, 2011.

105. Cable, U.S. Embassy in Cairo to Secretary of State, "April 6 Strike and Protests Fizzle into a Non-Event," April 7, 2009, 09CAIRO591, http://www.wikileaks.ch/cable/2009/04/09CAIRO591.html, accessed August 30, 2011.

106. Cable, U.S. Embassy in Cairo to Secretary of State, "Egyptian Labor Activism as a Political Force," December 15, 2009, 09CAIRO2301, http://www.wikileaks.ch/cable/2009/12/09CAIRO2301.html, accessed August 30, 2011.

107. Beinin, "Workers' Social Movement," 198.

108. Abdel-Moneim Mahmoud, "Habib: Gaza madkhalina lil-islah wa sanusharak bi tashri'iyyat 2010 [Habib: Gaza is our entryway to reform; we will participate in the 2010 legislative elections], *Islam-Online*, February 8, 2009, http://www.islamonline.net/servlet/Satellite?c=ArticleA_C&pagename=Zone-Arabic-News/NWALayout&cid=1233567710742, accessed February 21, 2009.

109. Shapiro, "Revolution, Facebook-Style."

110. Cable, U.S. Embassy in Cairo to Secretary of State, "April 6 Holds Parallel NDP Conference despite Alleged GOE Interference," November 17, 2009, 09CAIRO2155, http://www.telegraph.co.uk/news/wikileaks-files/egypt-wikileaks-cables/8326948/APRIL-6-HOLDS-PARALLEL-NDP-CONFERENCE-DESPITE-ALLEGED-GOE-INTERFERENCE.html, accessed July 14, 2011.

111. "Panel Discussion on Egypt's Parliamentary Elections Held by VOA," *Voice of America* broadcast, November 17, 2011, http://www.voanews.com/mp3/voa/special-events/Egypt_Votes_Challenges_and_Prospects.mp3, accessed July 14, 2011.

112. Cable, U.S. Embassy in Cairo to Secretary of State, "Egypt: Political Activists Suggest Change Unlikely to Come in Elections," October 19, 2009, 09CAIRO1977, http://orianomattei.blogspot.com/2011/06/wikileaks-viewing-cable-09cairo1977.html, accessed July 13, 2011.
113. "ElBaradei yantadhar mabai`ah al-misriyin" [ElBaradei awaits Egyptians' endorsement], *Al-Shorouk*, December 4, 2009, http://www.shorouknews.com/ContentData.aspx?id=159188, accessed July 14, 2011.
114. Cable, U.S. Embassy to Secretary of State, "Can Kifaya Regain Lost Momentum?" December 17, 2009, 09CAIRO2308, http://www.telegraph.co.uk/news/wikileaks-files/egypt-wikileaks-cables/8326906/EGYPT-CAN-KIFAYA-REGAIN-LOST-MOMENTUM.html, accessed July 14, 2011.
115. Cable, U.S. Embassy in Cairo to Secretary of State, "El Baradei's 'Conditioned' Presidential Run," December 10, 2009, 09CAIRO2279, http://www.telegraph.co.uk/news/wikileaks-files/egypt-wikileaks-cables/8326915/EGYPT-EL-BARADEIS-CONDITIONED-PRESIDENTIAL-RUN.html, accessed July 14, 2011.
116. Cable, U.S. Embassy in Cairo to Secretary of State, "Activists Prepare for El-Baradei's Arrival; Detainees," February 18, 2010, 10CAIRO215, http://www.telegraph.co.uk/news/wikileaks-files/egypt-wikileaks-cables/8326800/ACTIVISTS-PREPARE-FOR-EL-BARADEIS-ARRIVAL-DETAINEES-RELEASED.html, accessed July 14, 2011; and Cable, U.S. Embassy in Cairo to Secretary of State, "El Baradei Returns to Cairo," February 18, 2010, 10CAIRO237, http://www.telegraph.co.uk/news/wikileaks-files/egypt-wikileaks-cables/8326789/El-Baradei-Returns-to-Cairo.html, accessed July 14, 2011.
117. Marwa Awad, "Egypt's ElBaradei to Lead Coalition Seeking Change," *Reuters*, February 24, 2010, http://www.reuters.com/article/2010/02/24/us-egypt-elbaradei-opposition-idUSTRE61N4UX20100224, accessed July 14, 2011.
118. Ahmed Fathi, "Khamsin alf tuqia` `ala biyan ElBaradei fi tisa`a ayam" [Fifty thousand signatures on El Baradei's declaration in nine days], *Al-Shorouk*, July 16, 2010, http://www.shorouknews.com/ContentData.aspx?id=267786, accessed July 14, 2011.
119. Beinin and Vairel, "Afterword," 243.
120. Egyptian novelist Alaa Al Aswany later called Khaled Said's case highly significant: "The people became angry, like never before." "Narrating the Revolution," 89.
121. Cable, U.S. Embassy in Cairo to Secretary of State, "Scenesetter for A/S Posner's January 12–15 Visit to Cairo," January 6, 2010, 10CAIRO47, http://wikileaks.org/cable/2010/01/10CAIRO47.html, accessed August 30, 2011; and Shehata, interview.

122. Gamal Essam El-Din, "In Support of Khaled Said," *Al Ahram Weekly On-line*, July 1–7, 2010, http://weekly.ahram.org.eg/2010/1005/eg6 .htm, accessed July 14, 2011; and Abeya Bakry, "Not All Bad?" *Al Ahram Weekly On-line*, December 30, 2010–January 6, 2011, http://weekly.ahram.org.eg/2010/1029/fe2.htm, accessed July 14, 2011.

123. El-Ghobashy, "Praxis of the Egyptian Revolution."

124. "Khaleehum yetsalo.... Mubarak yestahayn bi sha'bihi... al-barliman al-mowaza" [Let them amuse themselves.... Mubarak mocks his own people... the parallel parliament], December 19, 2010, http://www.youtube.com/watch?v=lvK1nqh3-0I, accessed September 14, 2011. Likewise indifferent, the prior fall Gamal had laughed off a question from an Egyptian journalist about facing members of the Muslim Brothers, Kefaya, or April 6 in a public debate. "Al su'al aladhi ahraj Gamal Mubarak" [The question that embarrassed Gamal Mubarak], November 10, 2009, http://www.youtube .com/watch?v=qoZsdRP9aQc&feature=related, accessed September 14, 2011.

125. Borzou Daragahi and Amro Hassan, "Coptic Church Bombing in Egypt Is Latest Assault on Mideast Christians," *Los Angeles Times*, January 1, 2011, http://articles.latimes.com/2011/jan/01/world/la-fg-egypt-church-attack-20110102, accessed July 15, 2011; Abigail Hauslohner, "After Bombing, Egypt's Christians Worship and Worry," *Time*, January 3, 2011, http://www.time.com/time/world/article/ 0,8599,2040491,00.html, accessed July 15, 2011.

126. Issandr El-Amrani, "Confronting Egypt's Dangerous Decline," *POMED Policy Brief*, January 6, 2011.

127. Beinin and Vairel, "Afterword," 240.

128. Margaret Coker, "Tunisia Taps Interim Rulers, Lauds Army," *Wall Street Journal*, January 18, 2011.

129. Chomiak and Entelis, "Making of North Africa's Intifadas."

130. International Crisis Group, "Popular Protest in the Middle East," 2.

131. "Meet Asmaa Mahfouz and the vlog that Helped Spark the Revolution," http://www.youtube.com/watch?v=SgjIgMdsEuk&feature=player_ embedded, accessed July 15, 2011.

132. El-Ghobashy, "Praxis of the Egyptian Revolution."

133. International Crisis Group, "Popular Protest in the Middle East," 2–3; and Beinin and Vairel, "Afterword," 242.

134. El-Ghobashy, "Praxis of the Egyptian Revolution."

135. "US Urges Restraint in Egypt, Says Government Stable," *Reuters*, January 25, 2011, http://af.reuters.com/article/topNews/idAFJOE70O0 KF20110125, accessed July 16, 2011.

136. "Biden: Mubarak Is Not a Dictator, but People Have a Right to Protest," *PBS Newshour*, January 27, 2011, http://www.pbs.org/ newshour/bb/politics/jan-june11/biden_01-27.html, accessed July 16,

2011; and Office of the Press Secretary, "Remarks by the President in State of Union Address," January 25, 2011, http://www.whitehouse .gov/the-press-office/2011/01/25/remarks-president-state-union-address, accessed July 16, 2011.

137. International Crisis Group, "Popular Protest in the Middle East," 4.
138. Fathi, *Kan fi murah thawrah*, 23–24.
139. El-Ghobashy, "Praxis of the Revolution."
140. International Crisis Group, "Popular Protest in the Middle East," 4.
141. Ibid., 5.
142. El-Ghobashy, "Praxis of the Revolution."
143. Ibid., 12.
144. Elkeshky, interview.
145. Office of the Press Secretary, "Press Briefing by Press Secretary Robert Gibbs," January 28, 2011, http://www.whitehouse.gov/the-press-office/ 2011/01/28/press-briefing-press-secretary-robert-gibbs-1282011, accessed July 18, 2011.
146. "President Hosni Mubarak's Speech, January 28 (Arabic)," http://www .youtube.com/watch?v=nE5wuvCyjNM, accessed July 18, 2011.
147. "US Raises Pressure on Mubarak as Egypt Protests Rage," *Reuters News*, January 28, 2011; "Digest of Other White House Announcements," *Daily Compilation of Presidential Documents*, January 28, 2011; and "Remarks on the Situation in Egypt," *Daily Compilation of Presidential Documents*, January 28, 2011.
148. Mark Landler, "Clinton Calls for 'Orderly Transition' to Greater Freedom in Egypt," *New York Times*, January 31, 2011.
149. Peter Nicholas and Christi Parsons, "Obama's Advisors Split on When and How Mubarak Should Go," *Los Angeles Times*, February 10, 2011, http://articles.latimes.com/2011/feb/10/world/la-fg-obama-team-20110210, accessed July 19, 2011; and Helene Cooper, Mark Landler, and David E. Sanger, "Policy Rift Muddled U.S. Signals about the Departure of Mubarak," *New York Times*, February 13, 2011.
150. Robert Fisk, "As Mubarak Clings on . . . What Now for Egypt?" *Independent*, February 11, 2011, http://www.independent.co.uk/opinion/ commentators/fisk/robert-fisk-as-mubarak-clings-on-what-now-for-egypt-2211287.html, accessed July 13, 2011.
151. Scott Shane and David D. Kirkpatrick, "Military Caught between Mubarak and Protesters," *New York Times*, February 10, 2011.
152. Anthony Shadid, "Mubarak Won't Run Again, but Stays: Obama Urges a Faster Shift of Power," *New York Times*, February 2, 2011.
153. International Crisis Group, "Popular Protest in the Middle East," 8.
154. David E. Sanger, "As Mubarak Digs In, Complications for U.S. Policy," *New York Times*, February 6, 2011.
155. "Mubarak: If I Resign Today There Will be Chaos," *ABC News*, February 3, 2011, http://abcnews.go.com/International/egypt-abc-news-

christiane-amanpour-exclusive-interview-president/story?id=12833673 &page=2, accessed July 19, 2011; and Helene Cooper et al., "Policy Rift Muddled U.S. Signals."

156. Helene Cooper, Mark Landler, and Mark Mazzetti, "Sudden Split Recasts Foreign Policy," *New York Times*, February 3, 2011.

157. Ryan Lucas and Paul Schemm, "Cairo's Anti-Mubarak Activists Bruised, Battered, Sleep-Deprived and Hungry," *Associated Press*, February 5, 2011.

158. Shokr, "Eighteen Days of Tahrir," 16, 18.

159. Greg Miller, "Senators Question Intelligence Agencies' Anticipation of Egypt Uprising," *Washington Post*, February 4, 2011, http://www .washingtonpost.com/national/senators-question-intelligence-agencies-anticipation-of-egypt-uprising/2011/02/03/ABk2O5E_story.html, accessed November 13, 2011.

160. Senate Select Committee on Intelligence, *Nomination of Stephanie O'Sullivan*.

161. Kimberly Dozier, "Criticism from White House and Lawmakers Aimed at Intelligence on Unrest in Tunisia and Egypt," *Associated Press Newswire*, February 4, 2011.

162. Memo, Robert Hunter and Gary Sick to Brzezinski, September 12, 1980, NLC-25-144-5-7-3, JCL, RAC Project.

163. "ElBaradei: Mubarak Must Go," *CBS News*, January 30, 2011, http://www.cbsnews.com/video/watch/?id=7319276n, accessed July 19, 2011.

164. "'This Week's Transcript: Crisis in Egypt," *ABC News*, February 6, 2011, http://abcnews.go.com/ThisWeek/week-transcript-crisis-egypt/ story?id=12851408&page=5, accessed July 20, 2011.

165. David D. Kirkpatrick and David E. Sanger, "Egypt Officials Seek to Nudge Mubarak Out," *New York Times*, February 5, 2011; and Craig Whitlock and Greg Jaffe, "Where Egypt Military's Loyalties Lie Remains Unclear," *Washington Post*, February 5, 2011, http:// www.washingtonpost.com/wp-dyn/content/article/2011/02/04/ AR2011020407140_pf.html, accessed July 18, 2011.

166. Tarek Masoud, "An Exit Plan for Mubarak," *New York Times*, February 3, 2011.

167. Charles Levinson, Matt Bradley, Jonathan Weisman, and Adam Entous, "Turmoil in Egypt: Regime Seeks an Exit for Mubarak," *Wall Street Journal*, February 5, 2011.

168. U.S. Department of State, "Question and Answer Session at the Munich Security Conference," February 5, 2011, http://www.state.gov/ secretary/rm/2011/02/156045.htm, accessed July 18, 2011.

169. Hillary Rodham Clinton, "Interview with Michele Kelemen of NPR."

170. "Egypt Activist Wael Ghonim Tells TV Station: 'I Am No Hero' – Video," http://www.guardian.co.uk/world/video/2011/feb/08/egypt-activist-wael-ghonim-google-video, accessed July 20, 2011.

171. Human Rights Watch, "Egypt: Investigate Arrests of Activists, Journalists," February 9, 2011, http://www.hrw.org/en/news/2011/02/09/egypt-investigate-arrests-activists-journalists, accessed July 20, 2011; and Amnesty International, "Egyptian Military Urged to Halt Torture of Detainees," February 17, 2011, http://www.amnesty.org/en/news-and-updates/egyptian-military-urged-halt-torture-detainees-2011–02-17, accessed July 20, 2011.

172. Beinin and Vairel, "Afterword," 247.

173. Office of the Vice President, "Readout of the Vice President's Call with Egyptian Vice President Omar Soliman," February 8, 2011, http://www.whitehouse.gov/the-press-office/2011/02/08/readout-vice-presidents-call-egyptian-vice-president-omar-soliman, accessed July 21, 2011; and Kareem Fahim and David D. Kirkpatrick, "Labor Actions in Egypt Boost Protests," *New York Times*, February 10, 2011.

174. David D. Kirkpatrick and David E. Sanger, "A Tunisian-Egyptian Link That Shook Arab History," *New York Times*, February 14, 2011.

175. "Egyptian Generals Speak about the Revolution, Elections," *Washington Post*, May 18, 2011, http://www.washingtonpost.com/world/middle-east/egyptian-generals-speak-about-revolution-elections/2011/05/16/AF7AiU6G_print.html, accessed May 26, 2011.

176. "Al-bayan al-thani lil-majlis al-a`la lil-quwat al-musallaha al-masriyya fi 11 febrayir 2011" [Second statement from the Egyptian Supreme Council of the Armed Forces on February 11, 2011], http://www.youtube.com/watch?v=yscNSMqLICw&feature=related, accessed July 21, 2011.

177. Scott Shane and David D. Kirkpatrick, "Military Caught between Mubarak and Protesters," *New York Times*, February 11, 2011.

178. "US President Obama's Statement on Egypt," February 10, 2011, http://egypt.usembassy.gov/tr100211.html, accessed July 20, 2011.

179. Wael Ghonim (Ghonim), Twitter, February 10, 2011, http://twitter.com/#!/Ghonim/status/35722406748233728, accessed July 20, 2011.

180. Ahmed Eleiba, "Army and Presidency at Odds Says Former Intelligence Official," *Ahramonline* [English], February 11, 2011, http://english.ahram.org.eg/NewsContent/1/64/5417/Egypt/Politics-/Army-and-presidency-at-odds–says-former-intellige.aspx, accessed July 21, 2011; and "Gamal Mubarak behind Leader's Surprise Attempt to Retain Power," *Associated Press*, February 13, 2011, http://www.theaustralian.com.au/news/world/gamal-mubarak-behind-leaders-surprise-attempt-to-retain-power/story-e6frg6so-1226005194176?from=public_rss, accessed July 21, 2011.

181. "Khitab al-ra'is Mubarak" [The address of President Mubarak], February 10, 2011, http://www.youtube.com/watch?v=t140C_XLOkI, accessed July 20, 2011.

182. "VP Omar Soliman Speech," February 10, 2011, http://www.youtube.com/watch?v=VXoJTUBaCNg, accessed July 20, 2011.

183. Office of the Press Secretary, "Statement of President Barack Obama on Egypt," February 10, 2011, http://www.whitehouse.gov/the-press-office/2011/02/10/statement-president-barack-obama-egypt, accessed July 21, 2011.

184. Kirkpatrick and Sanger, "Tunisian-Egyptian Link."

185. Charles Levinson, Margaret Coker, Matt Bradley, Adam Entous, and Jonathan Weisman, "Fall of Mubarak Shakes Middle East," *Wall Street Journal*, February 12, 2011.

186. "Al-bayan al-thani lil-majlis al-aʿla lil-quwat al-musallaha al-masriyya [The second communique of the Egyptian Supreme Council of the Armed Forces]."

187. "'Egypt Is Free' after Mubarak Quits," *CNN*, February 11, 2011, http://news.blogs.cnn.com/2011/02/11/egypt-unrest-protesters-begin-18th-day-of-demonstrations, accessed July 21, 2011.

188. "Egyptian President Mubarak Steps Down (Omar Soliman Announcement)," http://www.youtube.com/watch?v=weskzq8PYzc&feature=related, accessed July 21, 2011.

189. "Al-biyan al-thalith lil-quwat al-musallaha baʾd tatahi al-raʾis Mubarak" [The third statement from the armed forces after the resignation of President Mubarak], February 11, 2011, http://www.youtube.com/watch?v=JXrfT-YVHiI&feature=related, accessed July 21, 2011.

190. Office of the Press Secretary, "Remarks by the President on Egypt," February 11, 2011, http://www.whitehouse.gov/the-press-office/2011/02/11/remarks-president-egypt, accessed July 21, 2011.

191. Ellis Goldberg, "Mubarak without Mubarakism: Why Egypt's Military Will Not Embrace Democracy," *Foreign Affairs.com*, February 11, 2011, http://www.foreignaffairs.com/articles/67416/ellis-goldberg/mubarakism-without-mubarak?page=show, accessed July 22, 2011.

192. Skocpol, *States and Social Revolutions*.

Conclusion

1. Steven Cook, "Political Instability in Egypt," *Contingency Planning Memorandum No. 4*, Council on Foreign Relations, 2009, p. 2.

2. Edward P. Djerejian, "The US and the Middle East in a Changing World," U.S. Department of State Dispatch, June 8, 1992.

3. Harb, "Egyptian Military in Politics," 285–287.

4. Salma Shukrallah, "Egypt Revolution Youth Form National Coalition," *Ahramonline* [English], February 9, 2011, http://english.ahram.org.eg/~/NewsContent/1/64/5257/Egypt/Politics-/Coalition-of-The-Revolutions-Youth-assembled.aspx, accessed November 26, 2011.

5. Steve Hendrix and William Wan, "Egyptian Prime Minister Ahmed Shafiq Resigns ahead of Protests," *Washington Post*, March 4, 2011,

http://www.washingtonpost.com/wp-dyn/content/article/2011/03/03/
AR2011030305118.html, September 12, 2011.

6. Gamal Essam El-Din, "Mubarak's Trial to Shift into High Gear," *Al Ahram Weekly On-line*, August 18–24, 2011, http://weekly.ahram.org.eg/2011/1061/eg5.htm, accessed September 12, 2011.

7. Nathan Brown and Michelle Dunne, "Egypt's Draft Constitutional Amendments Answers Some Questions and Raises Others," Carnegie Endowment for International Peace Web site, March 3, 2011, http://egyptelections.carnegieendowment.org/2011/03/03/egypt's-draft-constitutional-amendments-answer-some-questions-and-raise-others, accessed November 26, 2011; and "Army Council Issues Statement on Constitutional Amendments," Egypt State Information Service, February 27, 2011, http://www.sis.gov.eg/En/Story.aspx?sid=53903, accessed November 26, 2011.

8. Kristen Chick, "Muslim Brotherhood Officially Enters Egyptian Politics," *Christian Science Monitor*, June 8, 2011, http://www.csmonitor.com/World/Middle-East/2011/0608/Muslim-Brotherhood-officially-enters-Egyptian-politics, accessed September 12, 2011.

9. Pew Global Attitudes Project, *Egyptians Embrace Revolt Leaders*, 36.

10. Masoud, "Road to (and from) Liberation Square," 28.

11. Nathan J. Brown and Kristin Stilt, "A Haphazard Constitutional Compromise," *Carnegie Endowment for International Peace* Web site, April 11, 2011, http://carnegie-mec.org/publications/?fa=43533#, accessed November 27, 2011; Government of Egypt, "Constitutional Declaration," http://www.cabinet.gov.eg/AboutEgypt/Constitutional Declaration_e.pdf, accessed November 27, 2011.

12. The military had sullied its reputation during the uprising, when military police replaced the Ministry of Interior as regime enforcers, rounded up demonstrators, and tortured civilians. Amnesty International, "Egyptian Military Urged to Halt Torture of Detainees," February 17, 2011, http://www.amnesty.org/en/news-and-updates/egyptian-military-urged-halt-torture-detainees-2011-02-17, accessed September 13, 2011; and Amnesty International, "Egyptian Women Forced to Take 'Virginity Tests,'" March 23, 2011, http://www.amnesty.org/en/news-and-updates/egyptian-women-protesters-forced-take-'virginity-tests'-2011-03-23, accessed September 13, 2011.

13. Hesham Sallam, "Striking back at Egyptian workers," *Middle East Report* 259 (Summer 2011), http://merip.org/mer/mer259/striking-back-egyptian-workers, accessed June 30, 2011.

14. Evan Hill, "Scorecard: Egypt's Army and the Revolution," *Al Jazeera*, June 30, 2011, http://english.aljazeera.net/news/middleeast/2011/06/201162912484856932.html, accessed September 13, 2011; and Wael Eskandar, "SCAF Balance Sheet at a Glance," *Ahramonline*,

August 29, 2011, http://english.ahram.org.eg/News/19938.aspx, accessed September 13, 2011.

15. Leila Fadel, "Egypt's Generals May Maintain Large Role in Governance," *Washington Post*, July 17, 2011, http://www.washingtonpost.com/world/middle-east/egypts-generals-may-maintain-large-role-in-governance/2011/07/14/gIQAlZgxJI_print.html, accessed September 14, 2011.

16. Amnesty International, *Broken Promises*, 6.

17. "Egypt's SCAF Drop Charges against Asmaa Mahfouz and Loai Nagati," *Ahramonline*, August 18, 2011, http://english.ahram.org.eg/NewsContent/1/64/19218/Egypt/Politics-/Egypts-SCAF-drop-charges-against-Asmaa-Mahfouz-and.aspx, accessed September 13, 2011; and Malika Bilal, "Egypt: An Incomplete Revolution," *Al Jazeera*, August 19, 2011, http://english.aljazeera.net/indepth/features/2011/08/20118196543 8805396.html, accessed September 13, 2011.

18. Mariz Tadros, "Egypt's Bloody Sunday," *Middle East Report Online*, October 13, 2011, http://www.merip.org/mero/mero101311, accessed November 21, 2011; and "The Maspero Massacre: What Really Happened" (Video), *Jadaliyya*, November 11, 2011, http://www.jadaliyya.com/pages/index/3103/the-maspero-massacre_what-really-happened-(video), accessed November 21, 2011.

19. David D. Kirkpatrick, "Egypt's Military Expands Power, Raising Alarms," *New York Times*, October 14, 2011, http://www.nytimes.com/2011/10/15/world/middleeast/egypts-military-expands-power-raising-alarms.html?pagewanted=all, accessed November 27, 2011.

20. Pew Global Attitudes Project, *Egyptians Embrace Revolt Leaders*, 30, 32; and Shibley Telhami, "2011 Arab Public Opinion Survey," Web site of the Anwar Sadat Chair for Peace and Development, November 23, 2011, http://sadat.umd.edu/, accessed November 25, 2011.

21. "Al-nus al-kaml li wathiqat al-duktur ali al-salmi lil mabadi' fuq al-dusturiyah" [The complete text of the document of supra-constitutional principles], *An Arab Citizen* blog, November 3, 2021, http://anarabcitizen.blogspot.com/2011/11/blog-post.html, accessed November 27, 2011.

22. The document also referenced a yet-to-be-created National Defense Council, which would exercise authority on security matters and further shorten parliament's political reach. "Mi'at min al-misriyin yatjamm`un fi al-tahrir ihtijajan `ala wathiqat al-salmi" [Hundreds of Egyptians gather in Tahrir to protest the El-Selmy document], *Al-Arabiya*, November 17, 2011,   http://www.alarabiya.net/articles/2011/11/17/177757.html, accessed November 27, 2011.

23. David D. Kirkpatrick and Liam Stack, "Violent Protests in Egypt Pit Thousands against Police," *New York Times*, November 19, 2011, http://www.nytimes.com/2011/11/20/world/middleeast/violence-erupts-in-cairo-as-egypts-military-cedes-political-ground.html?_r=1&ref=daviddkirkpatrick&pagewanted=all, accessed November 27, 2011.

24. On a late-night talk show, the leader of the Wafd Party, Sayed Badawi, conceded as much. Registration of presidential candidates would begin on April 15, more than a month before the new constitution was ratified or rejected by referendum. The criteria for candidacy, he stated casually, would therefore be those set by the SCAF's constitutional declaration – not the rules of the new constitution. *Al-`asharah masa'an*, satellite TV broadcast, November 16, 2011.
25. Telhami, "2011 Arab Public Opinion Survey."
26. Kearn, "Hard Truths about Soft Power;" and Nye, *Bound to Lead.*
27. Nabil Fahmy, "A More Assertive Arab Foreign Policy," 110.
28. Pew Global Attitudes Project, *Egyptians Embrace Revolt Leaders*, 33.
29. Gregg Carlstrom, "End of Summer Brings Bigger Backlogs at Rafah," *Al Jazeera English*, September 9, 2011, http://english.aljazeera.net/indepth/features/2011/09/201199212421157988.html, accessed September 11, 2011; "Nus al-maqtarhat al-misriyyah al-muqaddima li al-fasa'il al-falastiniyyah litahqiq al-musallahah" [Text of the Egyptian proposals presented to the Palestinian factions to achieve reconciliation], Al Zaytouna Centre for Studies and Consultations, September 14, 2009, http://www.alzaytouna.net/arabic/?c=129&a=98706, accessed September 11, 2011; and Mahmoud Khalouf, "Tafasil al-itifaq al-musallahah wa ma tadminhu min tafahamat" [Details of the reconciliation agreement and its underpinnings], *Wafa Palestine News and Info Agency*, June 5, 2011, http://www1.wafa.ps/arabic/index.php?action=detail&id=104599, accessed September 11, 2011. Later that year, Egypt facilitated a swap that freed Gilad Shalit in exchange for Israel releasing more than a thousand Palestinian prisoners. "Israeli Soldier Gilad Shalit Released by Hamas into Egyptian Custody," *Telegraph*, October 18, 2011, http://www.telegraph.co.uk/news/worldnews/middleeast/israel/8833144/Israeli-soldier-Gilad-Shalit-released-by-Hamas-into-Egyptian-custody.html, accessed November 28, 2011.
30. Amro Hassan, "Egypt: Pipeline Blast Halts Gas Exports to Israel, Jordan," *Associated Press*, April 27, 2011; Amro Hassan, "Egypt: Nearly 20 Alleged Gas Pipeline Saboteurs Arrested," *Associated Press*, August 17, 2011; and Ola Galal and Calev Ben-David, "Egypt's Gas Pipeline to Israel, Jordan Hit by Explosions," *Business Week*, November 11, 2011, http://www.businessweek.com/news/2011-11-11/egypt-s-gas-pipeline-to-israel-jordan-hit-by-explosions.html, accessed November 15, 2011.
31. Amy Teibel, "Calls to Raise Israel-Egypt Treaty Troop Limits," *Associated Press*, August 28, 2011.
32. Heba Afify and Isabel Kershner, "A Long Peace Is Threatened in Israel Attack," *New York Times*, August 19, 2011; and David D. Kirkpatrick and Isabel Kershner, "Nations Race to Defuse Crisis between Egypt and Israel," *New York Times*, August 20, 2011.

33. Telhami, "2011 Arab Public Opinion Survey."

34. Ibid.

35. David Blair, "Arab Spring 'Anti-Democratic' Says Benjamin Netanyahu," *Telegraph*, November 24, 2011, http://www.telegraph.co.uk/news/worldnews/middleeast/israel/8913577/Arab-Spring-anti-democratic-says-Benjamin-Netanyahu.html, accessed November 29, 2011.

36. Office of the Press Secretary, "Remarks by the President on the Middle East and North Africa," State Department, Washington, DC, May 19, 2011, http://www.whitehouse.gov/the-press-office/2011/05/19/remarks-president-middle-east-and-north-africa, accessed September 13, 2011.

37. Ibid.

38. Austin Mackell, "The IMF versus the Arab Spring," *Guardian*, May 25, 2011, http://www.guardian.co.uk/commentisfree/2011/may/25/imf-arab-spring-loans-egypt-tunisia?CMP=twt_gu, accessed September 13, 2011.

39. Office of the Press Secretary, "Remarks by the President," May 19, 2011, http://www.whitehouse.gov/the-press-office/2011/05/19/remarks-president-middle-east-and-north-africa, accessed November 9, 2011.

40. Limited self-reflection also characterized a later speech by Clinton. Citing "the refusal to change" as "the greatest single source of instability in today's Middle East," she forecast: "If – over time – the most powerful political force in Egypt remains a roomful of unelected officials, they will have planted the seeds for future unrest, and Egyptians will have missed a historic opportunity." She did not specify how the White House and State Department would reduce their strategic reliance on Egypt's ill-fated junta. Office of the Spokesperson, U.S. Department of State, "Clinton at National Democracy Institute's Awards Dinner," November 7, 2011, http://translations.state.gov/st/english/texttrans/2011/11/20111108084112suo.1240002.html, accessed November 9, 2011.

41. "Ros-Lehtinen Opening Statement at Markup of Foreign Relations Authorization Act," July 20, 2011, press release, Committee on Foreign Relations, http://foreignaffairs.house.gov/press_display.asp?id=1922, accessed November 29, 2011.

42. "Chairwoman Granger Opening Remarks on FY 2012 State and Foreign Operations Bill at Subcommittee Markup," press release, Committee on Appropriations, July 27, 2011, http://appropriations.house.gov/News/DocumentSingle.aspx?DocumentID=253956, accessed November 29, 2011.

43. In a policy address that pushed back against conditionality proposals, Andrew Schapiro, assistant secretary at the Department of State's Bureau of Political-Military Affairs, stated: "The Obama Administration is proud to carry on the legacy of robust U.S. security assistance for Israel. Indeed, we are carrying this legacy to new heights at a time when Israel needs

our support to address the multifaceted threats it faces. Despite these budget constrained times our commitment is unshakeable. For Fiscal Year 2012, the Administration requested more than $3 billion in security assistance funding specifically for Israel, the largest such request in U.S. history." Andrew J. Schapiro, "Ensuring Israel's Qualitative Military Edge," remarks delivered at the Washington Institute for Near East Policy, November 4, 2011, http://www.state.gov/t/pm/rls/rm/176684.htm, accessed November 29, 2011.

44. Office of the Press Secretary, "Readout of the President's Call with Egyptian Field Marshal Tantawi," October 24, 2011, http://www.whitehouse.gov/the-press-office/2011/10/24/readout-president-s-call-egyptian-field-marshal-tantawi, accessed November 12, 2011.
45. Pew Global Attitudes Project, *Egyptians Embrace Revolt Leaders*, 30, 35.
46. Fahmy, interview.
47. El-Erian, "Rise of the Brothers," 98.
48. Heba Fahmy, "SCAF Statements to Foreign Press Irk Freedom and Justice Party," *Daily News Egypt*, December 9, 2011.
49. Kamrava, "Military Professionalization," 78n39.
50. Schraeder and Redissi, "Ben Ali's Fall," 6.
51. Samy Ghorbal, "Rachid Ammar, homme fort de la Tunisie: 'L'armée ne tire pas,'" *Rue89*, January 16, 2011, http://www.rue89.com/2011/01/16/larmee-ne-tire-pas-lhomme-fort-de-la-tunisie-est-general-185923, accessed November 25, 2011.
52. Schraeder and Redissi, "Ben Ali's Fall," 13–14.
53. Graham Usher, "That Other Tunisia," *The Nation*, September 12, 2011, 31–33.
54. McCurdy, *Guide to the Tunisian Elections*, 1.
55. Carey and Reynolds, "Impact of Election Systems," 40–41.
56. Cable, U.S. Embassy in Tunis to Secretary of Defense, "Tunisian Defense Minister Grira Looking Forward to JMC," February 9, 2010, 10TUNIS101, http://cablesearch.org/cable/view.php?id=10TUNIS101&hl=origin%3ATunis+, accessed November 25, 2011.
57. White House, "Statement by the President on Events in Tunisia," January 14, 2011, http://www.whitehouse.gov/the-press-office/2011/01/14/statement-president-events-tunisia, accessed November 8, 2011.
58. Office of the Press Secretary, "Remarks by the President in State of Union Address," January 25, 2011, http://www.whitehouse.gov/the-press-office/2011/01/25/remarks-president-state-union-address, accessed July 16, 2011.
59. Scheherezade Faramarzi, "Clampdown in Bahrain," *The Nation*, September 12, 2011, 41–42.
60. Bellin, "Robustness of Authoritarianism;" and Posusney and Angrist, *Authoritarianism in the Middle East*.

61. Brownlee, *Authoritarianism in an Age of Democratization*; Goldstone et al., "Global Model;" and O'Donnell and Schmitter, *Transitions from Authoritarian Rule.*

62. "The Evolution of Arab Revolution," *Empire* [broadcast program], April 22, 2011, http://www.youtube.com/watch?v=QxY87ZkT6l8, accessed July 12, 2011.

63. Hyde, "Observer Effect in International Politics."

64. Hyde, *Pseudo-Democrat's Dilemma*, 85–86, 123–124.

65. Omar Halawa, "As Egypt Rejects International Election Monitors, Rights Advocates Fear Fraud," *Al-Masry Al-Yom* [English], July 21, 2011, http://www.almasryalyoum.com/en/node/479258, accessed July 24, 2011; and Carter Center, "Carter Center Announces International Delegation for Egypt's Parliamentary Elections," press release, November 14, 2011.

66. Levitsky and Way, *Competitive Authoritarianism*, 372–375.

67. Ibid., 41.

68. Lucan Way, "Some Thoughts on Authoritarian Durability in the Middle East," *The Monkey Cage* [blog], February 21, 2011, http://themonkeycage.org/blog/2011/02/21/some_thoughts_on_authoritarian/, accessed December 14, 2011.

69. Levitsky and Way, "Rise of Competitive Authoritarianism."

70. Carothers, "End of the Transition Paradigm."

71. On the Middle East, see, among others, Brownlee, *Authoritarianism in an Age of Democratization*; Jamal, *Barriers to Democracy*; Heydemann, *Upgrading Authoritarianism*; Lust-Okar, *Structuring Conflict in the Arab World*; Posusney and Angrist, *Authoritarianism in the Middle East*; and Schlumberger, *Debating Arab Authoritarianism.*

72. Gramsci, *Selections from the Prison Notebooks*; Ayubi, *Over-stating the Arab State*; and Lustick, "Hegemony and the Riddle of Nationalism," 340. Arguably the January 25 Revolution opened a "war of maneuver" over state institutions. After a moment of seemingly open-ended struggle in the spring of 2011, that institutional battle tipped in favor of the previously dominant Egyptian armed forces and broader security apparatus.

73. Gourevitch, "Second Image Reversed;" Putnam, "Diplomacy and Domestic Politics;" and Werner, Davis, and Bueno de Mesquita, "Dissolving Boundaries."

74. Marquess of Zetland, *Lord Cromer*, 117; and Arendt, *Origins of Totalitarianism*, 213.

Sources

Government Archives

Jimmy Carter Library, Atlanta, GA.

Interviews by the Author

Elliott Abrams, Deputy National Security Advisor for Global Democracy Strategy (2005–2009), November 15, 2010, Washington, DC.

Ahmed Aboul Gheit, Egyptian Foreign Minister (2004–2011), March 23, 2011, Cairo, Egypt.

Richard Armitage, Deputy Secretary of State (2001–2005), March 9, 2011, Arlington, VA.

Harold Brown, Secretary of Defense (1977–1981), October 5, 2010, Washington, DC.

J. Scott Carpenter, Deputy Assistant Secretary of State for Near Eastern Affairs (2004–2007), November 18, 2010, Washington, DC.

Jackson Diehl, Member of the *Washington Post* editorial board, November 30, 2010, Washington, DC.

Michele Dunne, National Security Staff Director for Egypt and North Africa (2002–2003), October 19, 2010, Washington, DC.

Major General Mohamed Elkeshky, Egyptian Defense Attaché in Washington, DC (2009–), May 6, 2011, Washington, DC.

Nabil Fahmy, Egyptian Ambassador to the United States (2000–2008), March 21, 2011, Cairo, Egypt.

Douglas Feith, Under Secretary of Defense for Policy (2001–2005), December 1, 2010, Washington, DC.

Ali El Dean Hillal, Minister of Youth (1999–2004) and Professor of Political Science at Cairo University, March 20, 2011, Cairo, Egypt.

Saad Eddin Ibrahim, Founder of the Ibn Khaldun Center for Development, November 17, 2010, Hamilton, NJ.

William Inboden, Senior Director for Strategic Planning on the National Security Council (2005–2007), December 17, 2010, Austin, TX.

Stephen Krasner, Director of the Office of Policy Planning at the U.S. Department of State (2005–2007), November 15, 2010, phone.

Daniel Kurtzer, U.S. Ambassador to Egypt (1997–2001), U.S. Ambassador to Israel (2001–2005), October 26, 2010, Princeton, NJ.

Haynes Mahoney, Public Affairs Officer, U.S. Embassy in Cairo (2005–2011), March 20, 2011, Cairo, Egypt.

Hala Mustafa, member of the National Democratic Party and Higher Policies Secretariat (2002–2006), March 22, 2011, Cairo, Egypt.

Wael Nawara, Secretary General of the Ghad Party (2003–2011), March 21, 2011, Cairo, Egypt.

Robert Pelletreau, U.S. Ambassador to Egypt (1991–1994), Assistant Secretary for Near Eastern Affairs (1994–1997), November 3, 2010, Washington, DC.

William Quandt, member of the National Security Council (1972–1974, 1977–1979), November 16, 2010, Charlottesville, VA.

Francis Ricciardone, U.S. Ambassador to Egypt (2005–2008), October 18, 2010, and December 3, 2010, Washington, DC.

Maj. Gen. (ret.) Mohamed Kadry Said, Military Affairs Analyst, Al-Ahram Center for Political and Strategic Studies, March 20, 2011, Washington, DC.

David Schenker, Levant Country Director, Office of the Secretary of Defense (2002–2006), November 18, 2010, Washington, DC.

Dina Shehata, member of Kefaya, researcher at the Al-Ahram Center for Strategic and International Studies, March 22, 2011, Cairo, Egypt.

Nicholas Veliotes, U.S. Ambassador to Egypt (1984–1986), November 11, 2010, Washington, DC.

C. David Welch, U.S. Ambassador to Egypt (2001–2005), Assistant Secretary of State for Near Eastern Affairs (2005–2008), December 9, 2010, phone.

Frank G. Wisner, U.S. Ambassador to Egypt (1986–1991), December 6, 2010, New York.

Tamara Cofman Wittes, Deputy Assistant Secretary of State for Near Eastern Affairs (2009–2012), January 24, 2011, Washington, DC.

Other Interviews

Al-Aswany, Alaa. "Narrating the Revolution." *Cairo Review of Global Affairs* 1 (Spring 2011): 88–93.

Atherton, Alfred Leroy, Jr. Interview. Association for Diplomatic Studies and Training ADST Oral History, Summer 1990. http://memory.loc.gov/cgi-bin/query/r?ammem/mfdip:@field%28DOCID+mfdip2004atho1%29. Accessed April 11, 2012.

Bush, George W. "Interview of the President by Mona Shazli, Dream TV, Egypt." Office of the Press Secretary. May 12, 2008. http://georgewbush-whitehouse.archives.gov/news/releases/2008/05/20080512-12.html. Accessed May 11, 2011.

——. "Interview of the President by Richard Engel, NBC News." May 18, 2008. http://georgewbush-whitehouse.archives.gov/news/releases/2008/05/20080518-8.html. Accessed May 11, 2011.

Cheney, Elizabeth. "Interview." http://www.carnegieendowment.org/files/Interview.pdf. Accessed November 15, 2010.

Cheney, Richard. "Interview with Vice President Dick Cheney." *Meet the Press*, September 16, 2001.

Clinton, Hillary Rodham. "Interview with Michele Kelemen of NPR." *National Public Radio,* February 6, 2011. http://www.state.gov/secretary/rm/2011/02/156050.htm. Accessed July 20, 2011.

Eilts, Hermann Frederick. "A Candid View of the Middle East: An Interview with Hermann Frederick Eilts." *Fletcher Forum: A Journal of International Affairs.* 7, no. 1 (Winter 1983): 27–48.

——. Interview. Association for Diplomatic Studies and Training ADST Oral History, August 12, 1988. http://memory.loc.gov/cgi-bin/query/r?ammem/mfdip:@field%28DOCID+mfdip2004eil01%29. Accessed April 11, 2012.

El-Erian, Essam. "Rise of the Brothers." *Cairo Review of Global Affairs* 1, no. 1 (Spring 2008), http://www.aucegypt.edu/gapp/cairoreview/pages/articleDetails.aspx?aid=31. Accessed April 15, 2012.

Nazif, Ahmed. "Interview with Egyptian Prime Minister Ahmed Nazif." *Meet the Press,* May 15, 2005.

Published Sources

Abdalla, Ahmed. *The Student Movement and National Politics in Egypt.* London: Al-Saqi, 1985.

Abrams, Elliott. *Undue Process: A Story of How Political Differences Are Turned into Crime.* New York: Free Press, 1993.

——. "Israel and the 'Peace Process.'" In *Present Dangers: Crisis and Opportunity in American Foreign and Defense Policy,* ed. Robert Kagan and William Kristol, 221–240. San Francisco: Encounter, 2000.

Alexander, Anne. "Mubarak in the International Arena." In *Egypt: The Moment of Change,* ed. Rabab El-Mahdi and Philip Marfleet, 136–150. London: Zed, 2009.

Alterman, Jon B. *Egypt and American Foreign Assistance, 1952–1956: Hopes Dashed.* New York: Palgrave Macmillan, 2002.

Aly, Abdel Monem Said. "Egypt: A Decade after Camp David." In *The Middle East: Ten Years after Camp David,* ed. William B. Quandt, 63–93. Washington, DC: Brookings Institution, 1988.

Amnesty International. *Broken Promises: Egypt's Military Rulers Erode Human Rights.* London: Amnesty International, 2011.

Arendt, Hannah. *The Origins of Totalitarianism.* New York: Harcourt, Brace, 1951.

Aronson, Geoffrey. *From Sideshow to Center Stage: U.S. Policy toward Egypt, 1946–1956.* Boulder, CO: Lynne Rienner, 1986.

Aulas, Marie-Christine. "A Very Strange Peace." *MERIP Reports* 82 (November 1979): 18–21.

Ayubi, Nazih. *Over-stating the Arab State: Politics and Society in the Middle East.* London: I. B. Tauris, 1995.

Baker III, James A. "Looking Back on the Middle East: James A. Baker III." *Middle East Quarterly* (September 1994). http://www.meforum.org/233/looking-back-on-the-middle-east-james-a-baker-iii. Accessed February 23, 2011.

Baker, Raymond William. *Egypt's Uncertain Revolution under Nasser and Sadat.* Boston: Harvard University Press, 1978.

———. "Sadat's Open Door: Opposition from Within." *Social Problems* 28, no. 4 (April 1981): 378–384.

Barany, Zoltan, and Robert G. Moser, eds. *Is Democracy Exportable?* New York: Cambridge University Press, 2009.

Basheer, Tahseen. "The Egyptian State in Transition." In *Egypt at the Crossroads*, ed. Phebe Marr. Washington, DC: National Defense University Press, 1999.

Beattie, Kirk J. *Egypt during the Nasser Years.* Boulder, CO: Westview, 1994.

———. *Egypt during the Sadat Years.* New York: Palgrave, 2000.

Beinin, Joel. "The Cold Peace." *MERIP Reports* 129 (January 1985): 3–10.

———. "Popular Social Movements and the Future of Egyptian Politics." *Middle East Report Online*, 10 March 2005. http://www.mafhoum.com/press7/231S24.htm. Accessed March 28, 2005.

———. "The Militancy of Mahalla al-Kubra." *Middle East Report Online*, 29 September 2007. http://www.merip.org/mero/mero092907. Accessed May 9, 2011.

———. "Labor Protest Politics and Worker Rights in Egypt." February 18, 2010. http://www.carnegieendowment.org/files/0218_transcript_egypt_labor_protests.pdf. Accessed May 9, 2011.

———. "A Workers' Social Movement on the Margin of the Global Neoliberal Order: Egypt, 2004–2009." In *Social Movements, Mobilization, and Contestation in the Middle East and North Africa*, ed. Joel Beinin and Frédéric Vairel, 181–201. Palo Alto, CA: Stanford University Press, 2011.

Beinin, Joel, and Hossam El-Hamalawy. "Egyptian Textile Workers Confront the New Economic Order." *Middle East Report Online*, March 25, 2007. http://www.merip.org/mero/mero032507. Accessed May 9, 2011.

———. "Strikes in Egypt Spread from Center of Gravity." *Middle East Report Online*, May 9, 2007. http://www.merip.org/mero/mero050907. Accessed May 9, 2011.

Beinin, Joel, and Frédéric Vairel. "Afterword: Popular Uprisings in Tunisia and Egypt." In *Social Movements, Mobilization, and Contestation in the Middle East and North Africa*, ed. Joel Beinin and Frédéric Vairel, 237–254. Palo Alto, CA: Stanford University Press, 2011.

Bellin, Eva. "The Robustness of Authoritarianism in the Middle East: Exceptionalism in Comparative Perspective." *Comparative Politics* 36, no. 2 (2004): 139–157.

Blaydes, Lisa. *Elections and Distribution in Mubarak's Egypt*. New York: Cambridge University Press, 2010.

Boix, Carles. "Democracy, Development, and the International System." *American Political Science Review* 105, no. 4 (November 2011): 809–828.

Brand, Laurie A. "The Effects of the Peace Process on Political Liberalization in Jordan." *Journal of Palestine Studies* 28, no. 2 (Winter 1999): 52–67.

Bronson, Rachel. *Thicker than Oil: America's Uneasy Partnership with Saudi Arabia*. New York: Oxford University Press, 2006.

Brown, Harold. "What the Carter Doctrine Means to Me." *MERIP Reports* 90 (September 1980): 20–23.

Brown, Nathan J., Michele Dunne, and Amr Hamzawy. *Egypt's Controversial Constitutional Amendments*. Washington, DC: Carnegie Endowment for International Peace, 2007.

Brown, Nathan. *The Rule of Law in the Arab World: Courts in Egypt and the Gulf*. New York: Cambridge University Press, 1997.

Brownlee, Jason. " . . . And Yet They Persist: Explaining Survival and Transition in Neopatrimonial Regimes." *Studies in Comparative International Development* 37, no. 3 (Fall 2002): 35–63.

———. "The Decline of Pluralism in Mubarak's Egypt." *Journal of Democracy* 13, no. 4 (October 2002): 6–14.

———. "Hereditary Succession in Modern Autocracies." *World Politics* 59, no. 4 (July 2007): 595–628.

———. *Authoritarianism in an Age of Democratization*. New York: Cambridge University Press, 2007.

———. "Imagining the Next Occupation." *Middle East Report* 249 (Winter 2008): 8–11.

———. "Unrequited Moderation: Credible Commitments and State Repression in Egypt." *Studies in Comparative International Development* 45, no. 4 (December 2010): 468–489.

———. "Authoritarianism after 1989: From Regime Types to Transnational Processes." *Harvard International Review* (Winter 2010): 44–49.

———. "Peace Before Freedom: Diplomacy and Repression in Sadat's Egypt." *Political Science Quarterly* 126, no. 4 (2011–2012): 641–668.

Brownlee, Jason, and Joshua Stacher. "Change of Leader, Continuity of System: Nascent Liberalization in Post-Mubarak Egypt." *APSA-CD* 9, no. 2 (May 2011): 1, 4–9.

Brzezinski, Zbigniew. *Power and Principle: Memoirs of the National Security Advisor, 1977–1981*. New York: Farrar, Strauss and Giroux, 1983.

Bueno de Mesquita, Bruce, Alastair Smith, Randolph M. Siverson, and James Morrow. *The Logic of Political Survival*. Boston: MIT Press, 2003.

Bunce, Valerie, and Sharon L. Wolchik. "Favorable Conditions and Electoral Revolution." *Journal of Democracy* 17, no. 4 (October 2006): 5–18.

———. *Defeating Authoritarian Leaders in Post-Communist Countries*. New York: Cambridge University Press, 2011.

Burns, William J. *Economic Aid and American Policy toward Egypt, 1995–1981*. Albany: State University of New York Press, 1985.

Bush, George W. *Decision Points*. New York: Crown, 2010.

Bush, George H. W., and Brent Scowcroft. *A World Transformed*. New York: Knopf, 1998.

Bush, Ray. *Economic Crisis and the Politics of Reform in Egypt*. Boulder, CO: Westview, 1999.

Carey, John M., and Andrew Reynolds. "The Impact of Election Systems." *Journal of Democracy* 22, no. 4 (October 2011): 36–47.

Carothers, Thomas. *In the Name of Democracy: U.S. Policy towards Latin America in the Reagan Years*. Berkeley: University of California Press, 1993.

Carter, Jimmy. *Keeping Faith: Memoirs of a President*. Fayetteville: University of Arkansas Press, 1995.

———. *We Can Have Peace in the Holy Land: A Plan That Will Work*. New York: Simon and Schuster, 2009.

———. *White House Diary*. New York: Farrar, Straus and Giroux, 2010.

Chomiak, Laryssa, and John Entelis. "The Making of North Africa's Intifadas." *Middle East Report* 259 (Summer 2011): 8–15.

Chomsky, Noam. *Interventions*. San Francisco: City Lights, 2007.

Clinton, William J. *My Life*. New York: Knopf, 2004.

Coll, Steve. *Ghost Wars: The Secret History of the CIA, Afghanistan, and bin Laden, from the Soviet Invasion to September 10, 2001*. New York: Penguin, 2004.

Cook, Steven A. "The Right Way to Promote Arab Reform." *Foreign Affairs* 84, no. 2 (March–April 2005): 91–102.

Cooper, Richard. *The Transformation of Egypt*. Baltimore: Johns Hopkins University Press, 1982.

Copeland, Miles, Jr. *The Game of Nations: The Amorality of Power Politics*. New York: Simon and Schuster, 1970.

Dayan, Moshe. *Breakthrough: A Personal Account of the Egypt-Israel Peace Negotiations*. New York: Knopf, 1981.

Dekmejian, R. Hrair. *Egypt under Nasir: A Study in Political Dynamics*. Albany: State University of New York Press, 1971.

Dessouki, Ali E. Hillal. "Egyptian Foreign Policy since Camp David." In *The Middle East: Ten Years after Camp David*, ed. William B. Quandt, 94–110. Washington, DC: Brookings Institution, 1988.

Doran, Michael Scott. "Palestine, Iraq, and American Strategy." *Foreign Affairs* 82, no. 1 (January–February 2003): 19–33.

Dunne, Michele. "Integrating Democracy Promotion into U.S. Middle East Policy." *Carnegie Papers* 50 (October 2004).

Egyptian Ministry of Defense. "United States–Egyptian Military Cooperation: A Partnership for Peace, Stability and Progress." The White Paper, FY 2011, Egyptian Ministry of the Defense office, Washington, D.C.

Egyptian National Committee. *"Taqrir al-lajna al-wataniyya al-misriyya `an intikhabat 1995 al-barlamaniyya"* [Report of the Egyptian National Committee on the 1995 Parliamentary Elections]. Cairo: Ibn Khaldun Center for Development Studies, 1995.

Eilstrup-Sangiovanni, Mette. "Varieties of Cooperation: Government Networks in International Security." In *Networked Politics: Agency, Power, and Governance*, ed. Miles Kahler, 194–227. Ithaca, NY: Cornell University Press, 2007.

El-Ghobashy, Mona. "Egypt Looks Ahead to Portentous Year." *MERIP Online*, February 2, 2005. http://www.merip.org/mero/mero020205.html. Accessed January 3, 2005.

———. "The Metamorphosis of the Egyptian Muslim Brothers." *International Journal of Middle East Studies* 37 (2005): 373–395.

———. "The Praxis of the Egyptian Revolution." *MERIP Reports* 258 (Spring 2011). http://www.merip.org/mer/mer258/praxis-egyptian-revolution. Accessed July 28, 2011.

El-Mahdi, Rabab. "'Umal al-mahalla: Intilaq harakat 'umaliyya jadida" [The workers of Mahalla: The Launch of a new Worker's Movement]. In *'Adat al-siyasa: Al-harakat al-ihtijajiyah al-jadidah fi misr* [The return of politics: The new protest movements in Egypt], ed. Dina Shehata, 45–69. Cairo: Al Ahram Center for Political and Strategic Studies, 2008.

———. "Enough! Egypt's Quest for Democracy." *Comparative Political Studies* 42, no. 8 (August 2009): 1011–1039.

El Sayed Said, Mohammed. *Al-intiqal al-dimuqrati al-muhtajaz fi Misr* [The blocked democratic transition in Egypt]. Cairo: Merit, 2006.

El-Sayed, Mustapha K. "Egyptian Popular Attitudes toward the Palestinians Since 1977." *Journal of Palestine Studies* 18, no. 4 (Summer 1989): 37–51.

Fahmy, Ismail. *Negotiating for Peace in the Middle East*. Cairo: American University in Cairo Press, 1983.

Fahmy, Nabil. "A More Assertive Arab Foreign Policy." *Cairo Review of Global Affairs* 1, no. 1 (Spring 2011): 101–111.

Farah, Nadia Ramsis. *Egypt's Political Economy: Power Relations in Development*. Cairo: American University in Cairo Press, 2009.

Fathi, Mohamed. *Kan fi murah thawrah* [There was once a revolution]. Cairo: Dar al-Oktub lil-nashr wa al-tawzi'a, 2011.

Federation of American Scientists. Database on Small Arms Shipments from the US, 1990–2000. http://www.fas.org/programs/ssp/asmp/factsand figures/smallarms.html. Accessed July 4, 2011.

Feith, Douglas J. *War and Decision: Inside the Pentagon at the Dawn of the War on Terrorism.* New York: Harper, 2008.

Finnemore, Martha, and Kathryn Sikkink. "International Norm Dynamics and Political Change." *International Organization* 52, no. 4 (Fall 1998): 887–917.

Fisher, David Hackett. *Historians' Fallacies: Toward a Logic of Historical Thought.* New York: Harper and Row, 1970.

Fishman, Robert M. "Rethinking State and Regime: Southern Europe's Transition to Democracy." *World Politics* 42, no. 3 (April 1990): 422–440.

Fukuyama, Francis. "The End of History." *National Interest* 16, no. 4 (Summer 1989): 3–18.

G-8. "Partnership for Progress and a Common Future with the Region of the Broader Middle East and North Africa." June 9, 2004. http://web.archive.org/web/20040623045032/www.g8usa.gov/d_060904c.htm. Accessed April 16, 2010.

Gause, F. Gregory, III. *International Relations of the Persian Gulf.* New York: Cambridge University Press, 2009.

Gerges, Fawaz A. *America and Political Islam: Clash of Cultures or Clash of Interests?* New York: Cambridge University Press, 1999.

———. "The End of the Islamist Insurgency in Egypt? Costs and Prospects." *Middle East Journal* 54, no. 4 (2000): 592–612.

Goldstone, Jack A., Robert H. Bates, David L. Epstein, Ted Robert Gurr, Michael B. Lustik, Monty G. Marshall, and Jay Ulfelder. "A Global Model for Forecasting Political Instability." *American Journal of Political Science* 54, no. 1 (January 2010): 190–208.

Gordon, Michael R., and Bernard E. Trainor. *Cobra II: The Inside Story of the Invasion and Occupation of Iraq.* New York: Pantheon, 2006.

Gourevich, Peter. "The Second Image Reversed: The International Sources of Domestic Politics." *International Organization* 32, no. 4 (Autumn 1978): 881–912.

Gramsci, Antonio. *Selections from the Prison Notebooks.* London: Lawrence and Wishart, 1971.

Grey, Stephen. *Ghost Plane: The True Story of the C.I.A. Torture Program.* New York: St. Martin's Press, 2006.

Gunning, Jeroen. *Hamas in Politics: Democracy, Religion, Violence.* New York: Columbia University Press, 2009.

Haass, Richard N. 2002. "Toward a Greater Democracy in the Muslim World." Council on Foreign Relations, December 4, 2002. http://www.cfr.org/religion-and-politics/towards-greater-democracy-muslim-world/p5283. Accessed January 14, 2012.

Habib, Mamdouh. *My Story: The Tale of a Terrorist Who Wasn't.* Carlton North, Victoria, Australia: Scribe, 2008.

Hamrush, Ahmad. *Thawrat 23 Yulio: Al-Juz Al-Thalith* [The July 23 Revolution: Part Three]. Cairo: Al-Hi'a al-Misriyya Al-'Ama lil-Kitab, 1993.

Harb, Imad. "The Egyptian Military in Politics: Disengagement or Accommodation?" *Middle East Journal* 57, no. 2 (Spring 2003): 269–290.

Heikal, Mohammed. *Autumn of Fury: The Assassination of Sadat.* London: Andre Deutsch, 1983.

Hellman, Joel. "Winners Take All: The Politics of Partial Reform in Post-communist Transitions." *World Politics* 50, no. 2 (January 1998): 203–234.

Herb, Michael. 2005. "No Representation without Taxation? Rents, Development and Democracy." *Comparative Politics* 37, no. 3 (April 2005): 297–316.

Herman, Edward S., and Noam Chomsky. *Manufacturing Consent: The Political Economy of Mass Media.* New York: Pantheon, 1988.

Hersh, Seymour M. *Chain of Command: The Road from 9/11 to Abu Ghraib.* New York: Harper Collins, 2004.

Heydemann, Steven. *Upgrading Authoritarianism in the Arab World.* Washington, DC: Brookings Institution, 2007.

Hinnebusch, Raymond. "Children of the Elite: Political Attitudes of the Westernized Bourgeoisie in Contemporary Egypt." *Middle East Journal* 36, no. 4 (Autumn 1982): 535–561.

Hudson, Michael. "After the Gulf War: Prospects for Democratization in the Arab World." *Middle East Journal* 45, no. 3 (Summer 1991): 407–426.

Huntington, Samuel P. *The Third Wave: Democratization in the Late Twentieth Century.* Norman: University of Oklahoma Press, 1991.

Hyde, Susan D. "The Observer Effect in International Politics: Evidence from a Natural Experiment." *World Politics* 60, no. 1 (October 2007): 37–63.

———. *The Pseudo-Democrat's Dilemma: Why Election Observation Became an International Norm.* Ithaca, NY: Cornell University Press, 2011.

Ibrahim, Saad Eddin. "Domestic Developments in Egypt." In *The Middle East: Ten Years after Camp David*, ed. William B. Quandt, 19–62. Washington: Brookings Institution, 1988.

———. "The Changing Face of Egypt's Islamic Activism." In *Egypt at the Crossroads*, ed. Phebe Marr, 29-45. Washington, DC: National Defense University Press, 1999.

———. "Israel/Hizbollah/Lebanon: Avoiding Renewed Conflict." Middle East Report No. 59 (November 1, 2006), International Crisis Group, Beirut/Jerusalem/Amman/Brussels.

———. "Egypt's Sinai Question." Middle East/North Africa Report No. 61 (January 30, 2007), International Crisis Group, Cairo/Brussels.

————. "After Mecca: Engaging Hamas." Middle East/North Africa Report No. 62 (February 28, 2007), International Crisis Group, Amman/Jerusalem/Brussels.

————. "After Gaza." Middle East/North Africa Report No. 68 (August 2, 2007), International Crisis Group, Amman/Jerusalem/Gaza/Brussels.

————. "Ruling Palestine I: Gaza Under Hamas." Middle East/North Africa Report No. 73 (March 19, 2008), International Crisis Group, Gaza/Jerusalem/Brussels.

————. "Palestine Divided." Middle East Briefing No. 25 (Update brief, December 17, 2008), International Crisis Group, Ramallah, Gaza, Brussels.

————. "Ending the War in Gaza." Middle East Briefing No. 26 (January 5, 2009), International Crisis Group, Gaza City/Ramallah/Jerusalem/Brussels.

————. "Gaza's Unfinished Business." Middle East/North Africa Report No. 85 (April 23, 2009), International Crisis Group, Gaza City/Ramallah/Jerusalem/Washington, DC/Brussels.

————. "Popular Protest in North Africa and the Middle East I: Egypt Victorious?" Middle East/North Africa Report No. 101 (February 24, 2011), International Crisis Group, Cairo/Brussels.

Independent Committee for Electoral Monitoring (ICEM). *A Testimony for History: Monitoring the 2005 Egyptian Parliamentary Elections.* Cairo: Ibn Khaldun Center for Development Studies, 2005.

Indyk, Martin. "Back to the Bazaar." *Foreign Affairs* 81, no. 1 (January–February 2002): 75–88.

International Crisis Group. "Israel/Palestine/Lebanon: Climbing Out of the Abyss." Middle East/North Africa Report No. 57 (July 25, 2006), International Crisis Group, Amman/Beirut/Jerusalem/Brussels.

Isikoff, Michael, and David Corn. *Hubris: The Inside Story of Spin, Scandal, and the Selling of the Iraq War.* New York: Crown, 2006.

Jackson, Robert H. *Quasi-States, Sovereignty, International Relations, and the Third World.* New York: Cambridge University Press, 1990.

Jamal, Amaney. *Barriers to Democracy: The Other Side of Social Capital in Palestine and the Arab World* Princeton, NJ: Princeton University Press, 2007.

Kahler, Miles. "Networked Politics: Agency, Power, and Governance." In *Networked Politics: Agency, Power, and Governance,* ed. Miles Kahler, 1–22. Ithaca, NY: Cornell University Press, 2009.

Kamel, Mohamed Ibrahim. *The Camp David Accords: A Testimony by Sadat's Foreign Minister.* London: Keegan Paul, 1986.

Kamrava, Mehran. "Military Professionalization and Civil-Military Relations in the Middle East." *Political Science Quarterly* 115, no. 1 (Spring 2000): 67–92.

Karawan, Ibrahim A. "Sadat and the Egyptian-Israeli Peace Revisited." *International Journal of Middle East Studies* 26, no. 2 (May 1994): 249–266.

Kassem, Maye. *In the Guise of Democracy: Governance in Contemporary Egypt.* Ithaca, NY: Ithaca Press, 1999.

Katzenstein, Peter J. Introduction to *The Culture of National Security,* ed. Peter J. Katzenstein, 1–32. New York: Columbia University Press, 1996.

Kearn, David W., Jr. "The Hard Truths about Soft Power." *Journal of Political Power* 4, no. 1 (April 2011): 65–85.

Keck, Margaret E., and Kathryn Sikkink. *Activists Beyond Borders: Advocacy Networks in International Politics.* Ithaca, NY: Cornell University Press, 1998.

Kepel, Giles. *Jihad: The Trail of Political Islam.* Boston: Belknap Press of Harvard University, 2002.

Kienle, Eberhard. *A Grand Delusion: Democracy and Economic Reform in Egypt.* London: I.B. Tauris, 2001.

Kirkpatrick, Jeane. "Dictatorships and Double Standards." *Commentary* 68, no. 5 (November 1979): 34–45.

Kissinger, Henry. *Years of Upheaval.* New York: Little, Brown, 1982.

Klare, Michael T. *American Arms Supermarket.* Austin: University of Texas at Austin Press, 1984.

Klare, Michael T., and Cynthia Arnson. *Supplying Repression: U.S. Support for Authoritarian Regimes Abroad.* Washington, DC: Institute for Policy Studies, 1981.

Levitsy, Steven, and Lucan A. Way. "The Rise of Competitive Authoritarianism." *Journal of Democracy* 13, no. 2 (April 2002): 51–65.

———. *Competitive Authoritarianism: Hybrid Regimes after the Cold War.* New York: Cambridge University Press, 2010.

Little, Douglas. *American Orientalism: The United States and the Middle East since 1945.* Chapel Hill: University of North Carolina Press, 2008.

Lustick, Ian S. "The Absence of Middle Eastern Great Powers: Political 'Backwardness' in Historical Perspective." *International Organization* 51, no. 4 (Autumn 1997): 653–683.

———. "Hegemony and the Riddle of Nationalism." In *Ethnic Conflict and International Politics in the Middle East,* ed. Leonard Binder, 332–359. Gainesville: University of Florida Press, 1999.

Lust-Okar, Ellen. *Structuring Conflict in the Arab World: Incumbents, Opponents, and Institutions.* New York: Cambridge University Press, 2005.

Marquess of Zetland. *Lord Cromer.* London: Hodder and Stoughton, 1932.

Marr, Phebe. *Egypt at the Crossroads: Domestic Stability and Regional Role,* ed. Phebe Marr. Washington, DC: National Defense University, 1999.

Masoud, Tarek. "The Road to and from Liberation Square." *Journal of Democracy* 22, no. 3 (July 2011): 20–34.

Mayer, Jane. *The Dark Side: The Inside Story of How the War on Terror Turned into a War on American Ideals.* New York: Doubleday, 2008.

McCurdy, Daphne. *A Guide to the Tunisian Elections.* Washington, DC: Project on Middle East Democracy, 2011.

McInerney, Stephen. "The President's Budget Request for Fiscal Year 2009: Democracy, Governance, and Human Rights in the Middle East." Project on Middle East Democracy, May 2008.

———. "The Federal Budget and Appropriations for Fiscal Year 2011: Democracy, Governance and Human Rights in the Middle East." Project on Middle East Democracy, April 2010.

McLaughlin, Gerald T. "Infitah in Egypt: An Appraisal of Egypt's Open Door Policy for Foreign Investment." *Fordham Law Review* (January 1978): 885–906.

Meyer, Gail E. *Egypt and the United States: The Formative Years.* Cranbury, NJ: Associated University Presses, 1980.

Migdalovitz, Carol. "Israel's Disengagement from Gaza." CRS Report for Congress, September 16, 2005.

Miller, Aaron David. *Search for Security: Saudi Arabian Oil and American Foreign Policy, 1939–1949.* Chapel Hill: University of North Carolina Press, 1980.

Mitchell, Timothy. "America's Egypt: Discourse of the Development Industry," *Middle East Report* 169 (March–April 1991): 18–34, 36.

———. "The Limits of the State: Beyond Statist Approaches and Their Critics." *American Political Science Review* 85, no. 1 (March 1991): 77–96.

Moustafa, Tamir. *The Struggle for Constitutional Power: Law, Politics, and Economic Development in Egypt.* New York: Cambridge University Press, 2007.

Muravchik, Joshua. *Exporting Democracy: Fulfilling America's Destiny.* Washington, DC: AEI Press, 1992.

Murphy, Caryle. *Passion for Islam: Shaping the Modern Middle East: The Egyptian Experience.* New York: Scribner, 2002.

Mustafa, Hala. *"al-intikhabat al-barlamaniya 1995 fi siyaq al-tatawur al-siyasi al-misri"* [The 1995 Elections in the Context of Egyptian Political Development]. In *al-intikhabat al-barlamaniya fi misr 1995* [The Parliamentary Elections in Egypt, 1995], ed. Hala Mustafa, 15–34. Cairo: Al-Ahram Center for Strategic and International Studies, 1997.

Narizny, Kevin. "Anglo-American Primacy and the Global Spread of Democracy: An International Genealogy," *World Politics* 64, no. 2 (April 2012), 341–373.

National Democratic Institute. *Final Report on the Palestinian Legislative Council Elections January 25, 2006.* Washington, DC: National Democratic Institute for International Affairs, 2006.

Nye, Joseph S., Jr. *Bound to Lead: The Changing Nature of American Power.* New York: Basic, 1991.

O'Donnell, Guillermo, and Phillipe Schmitter. *Transitions from Authoritarian Rule: Tentative Conclusions about Uncertain Democracies.* Baltimore: Johns Hopkins University Press, 1986.

Ottaway, Marina. "The Broader Middle East and North Africa Initiative: A Hollow Victory for the United States." *Arab Reform Bulletin* 2, no. 6 (June 2004). http://carnegie-mec.org/publications/?fa=1559. Accessed January 14, 2012.

Pedahzur, Ami. *The Israeli Secret Services and the Struggle against Terrorism.* New York: Columbia University Press, 2009.

Peters, Anne Mariel, and Pete W. Moore. "Beyond Boom and Bust: External Rents, Durable Authoritarianism, and Institutional Adaptation in the Hashemite Kingdom of Jordan." *Studies in Comparative International Development* 44, no. 3 (Summer 2009): 256–285.

Petersen, Tore T. *The Decline of the Anglo-American Middle East, 1961–1969: A Willing Retreat.* Portland, OR: Sussex Academic Press, 2006.

Pew Global Attitudes Project. *America's Image Slips, but Allies Share US Concerns over Iran, Hamas.* Washington, DC: Pew Research Center, 2006.

———. *Confidence in Obama Lifts U.S. Image around the World.* Washington, DC: Pew Research Center, July 23, 2009. http://pewglobal.org/2009/07/23/confidence-in-obama-lifts-us-image-around-the-world./<τπ/> Accessed August 29, 2011.

———. *Egyptians Embrace Revolt Leaders, Religious Parties and Military as Well.* Washington, DC: Pew Research Center, April 25, 2011. http://pewresearch.org/pubs/1971/egypt-poll-democracy-elections-islam-military-muslim-brotherhood-april-6-movement-israel-obama. Accessed January 14, 2012.

Posusney, Marsha Pripstein. "Irrational Workers: The Moral Economy of Labor Protest in Egypt." *World Politics* 46, no. 1 (October 1993): 83–120.

———. "Enduring Authoritarianism: Middle East Lessons for Comparative Theory." *Comparative Politics* 36, no. 2 (January 2004): 127–138.

Posusney, Marsha Pripstein, and Michele Penner Angrist, eds. *Authoritarianism in the Middle East: Regimes and Resistance.* Boulder, CO: Lynne Rienner, 2005.

Putnam, Robert D. "Diplomacy and Domestic Politics: The Logic of Two-Level Games." *International Organization* 42, no. 3 (Summer 1988): 427–460.

Qandil, Abdel-Halim. *Al-ayam al-akhira* [The final days]. Cairo: Dar al-thaqafah al-jadida, 2008.

Quandt, William B. *Camp David: Peacemaking and Politics.* Washington, DC: Brookings Institution, 1986.

———. *The United States and Egypt: An Essay on Policy for the 1990s.* Washington, DC: Brookings Institution, 1990.

———, ed. *The Middle East: Ten Years after Camp David.* Washington, DC: Brookings Institution, 1988.

————. *Peace Process: American Diplomacy and the Arab-Israeli Conflict since 1967*. Berkeley: University of California Press, 2001.

Quinlivan, James. "Coup-Proofing: Its Practice and Consequences in the Middle East." *International Security* 24, no. 2 (Autumn 1999): 131–165.

Raab, Jorg, and H. Brinton Milward. "Dark Networks as Problems." *Journal of Public Administration Research and Theory* 13, no. 4 (2003): 413–439.

Randal, Jonathan. *The Tragedy of Lebanon: Christian Warlords, Israeli Adventurers, and American Bunglers*. London: Chatto and Windus, 1983.

Reagan, Ronald. *An American Life*. New York: Simon and Schuster, 1990.

Richards, Alan. "Dilatory Reform vs. Making a Break for the Market." In *Egypt at the Crossroads*, ed. Phebe Marr, 65–92. Washington, DC: National Defense University Press, 1999.

Richards, Alan, and John Waterbury. *A Political Economy of the Middle East*. Boulder, CO: Westview, 2008.

Rosen, Nir. *Aftermath: Following the Bloodshed of America's War in the Muslim World*. New York: Nation Books, 2010.

Ross, Michael L. "Does Oil Hinder Democracy?" *World Politics* 53, no. 3 (2001): 325–361.

Sabri, Moussa. *Al-Sadat: Al-haqiqah wa al-usturah* [Sadat: The reality and the legend]. Cairo: Al-maktab al-misri al-hadith, 1985.

Sadat, Anwar. *In Search of Identity: An Autobiography*. New York: Harper and Row, 1979.

Salah, Mohammed. *Waqa'a sanawat al-jihad: rihlat al-afghan al-arab* [The Reality of the Jihad Years: The Journey of the Afghan Arabs]. Cairo: Khulud Lil-Nashr, 2001.

Schemm, Paul. "Egypt Struggles to Control Anti-War Protests." *Middle East Report Online*. March 31, 2003. http://www.merip.org/mero/mero033103.html. Accessed December 12, 2010.

Schlesinger, Arthur M., Jr. *A Thousand Days: John F. Kennedy in the White House*. New York: Fawcett Premier, 1965.

Schlumberger, Oliver. *Debating Arab Authoritarianism: Dynamics and Durability in Nondemocratic Regimes*. Palo Alto, CA: Stanford University Press, 2007.

Schmitz, David F. *Thank God They're on Our Side: The United States and Right-Wing Dictatorships, 1921–1965*. Chapel Hill: University of North Carolina Press, 1999.

Schraeder, Peter J., and Hamadi Redissi. "Ben Ali's Fall." *Journal of Democracy* 22, no. 3 (July 2011): 5–19.

Seale, Patrick. *Asad: The Struggle for the Middle East*. Berkeley: University of California Press, 1990.

Seddon, David. "The Politics of Adjustment: Egypt and the IMF, 1987–1990." *Review of African Political Economy* 47 (Spring 1990): 95–104.

Seyam, Emad. "Kharitat al-ihtijajat al-selmiya fi misr: Mu'ashrat awliya 'ala tikhallaq mujtama' madani min noa' jadid" [Mapping peaceful protests in Egypt: First indicators of the creation of a new kind of civil society]. In *'Adat al-siyasa: Al-harakat al-ihtijajiyah al-jadidah fi misr* [The return of politics: The new protest movements in Egypt], ed. Dina Shehata, 49–75. Cairo: Al Ahram Center for Political and Strategic Studies, 2010.

Sharansky, Natan. "Democracy for Peace." In *Essential Essays, No. 1*. Washington, DC: American Enterprise Institute, 2002.

Shehata, Dina. "Al-harakat al-ihtijajiyah al-jadidah fi misr" [The new protest movements in Egypt]. In *'Adat al-siyasa: Al-harakat al-ihtijajiyah al-jadidah fi misr* [The return of politics: The new protest movements in Egypt], ed. Dina Shehata, 11–20. Cairo: Al Ahram Center for Political and Strategic Studies, 2010.

———. "Al-harakat al-ihtijajiyah al-shababiya: Shabab min ajl al-taghir wa harakat al-tadamin was shabab sit abril" [Youth Protest Movements: Youth for Change, The Solidarity Movement, and the Youth of 6th April]. In *'Adat al-siyasa: Al-harakat al-ihtijajiyah al-jadidah fi misr* [The return of politics: The new protest movements in Egypt], ed. Dina Shehata, 245–275. Cairo: Al Ahram Center for Political and Strategic Studies, 2010.

Shehata, Samer. *Shop Floor Culture and Politics in Egypt*. Cairo: American University Press, 2010.

Shehata, Samer, and Joshua Stacher. "The Brotherhood Goes to Parliament." *Middle East Report* 240 (Fall 2006). http://www.merip.org/mer/mer240/shehata_stacher.html. Accessed February 27, 2009.

Shlaim, Avi. *The Iron Wall: Israel and the Arab World*. New York: W. W. Norton, 2001.

Shokr, Ahmed. "The 18 Days of Tahrir." *Middle East Report* 258 (Spring 2011): 14–19.

Shultz, George P. *Turmoil and Triumph: My Years as Secretary of State*. New York: Scribner, 1993.

Sid-Ahmed, Mohamed. "Shifting Sands of Peace in the Middle East." *International Security* 5, no. 1 (Summer 1980): 53–79.

Sikkink, Kathryn. *Mixed Signals: U.S. Human Rights Policy and Latin America*. Ithaca, NY: Cornell University Press, 2004.

———. "The Power of Networks in International Politics." In *Networked Politics: Agency, Power, and Governance*, ed. Miles Kahler, 228–248. Ithaca, NY: Cornell University Press, 2009.

Singerman, Diane. "The Politics of Emergency Rule in Egypt." *Current History* 101 (January 2002): 29–35.

Sirrs, Owen. *History of the Egyptian Intelligence Services*. New York: Routledge, 2011.

Skocpol, Theda. *States and Social Revolutions*. New York: Cambridge University Press, 1979.

Smith, Tony. *America's Mission: The United States and the Worldwide Struggle for Democracy in the Twentieth Century*. Princeton, NJ: Princeton University Press, 1995.

Snyder, Richard. "Explaining Transitions from Neopatrimonial Dictatorships." *Comparative Politics* 24, no. 4 (July 1992): 379–399.

Sobel, Lester A. *Peace-Making in the Middle East*. New York: Facts on File, 1980.

Soliman, Samer. *The Autumn of Dictatorship: Fiscal Crisis and Political Change in Egypt under Mubarak*. Palo Alto, CA: Stanford University Press, 2011.

Springborg, Robert. "The President and the Field Marshal: Civil-Military Relations in Egypt Today." *MERIP Reports* 147 (July–August 1987): 4–11, 14–16, 42.

———. *Mubarak's Egypt: Fragmentation of the Political Order*. Boulder, CO: Westview, 1988.

Stacher, Joshua. "The Anatomy of Succession." *Review of African Political Economy* 35, no. 2 (2008): 301–314.

Stepan, Alfred. "An 'Arab' More than 'Muslim' Electoral Gap." With Graeme Robertson. *Journal of Democracy* 14, no. 3 (July 2003): 30–44.

Stockholm International Peace Research Institute (SIPRI). *Yearbook 2008: Armaments, Disarmament, and International Security*. New York: Oxford University Press, 2008.

Stork, Joe. "Bailing out Sadat." *MERIP Reports* 56 (April 1977): 8–11.

Stork, Joe, and Danny Reachard. "Chronology: U.S.-Egypt Military Relationship." *MERIP Reports* 90 (September 1980): 29–32.

———. "The Carter Doctrine and US Bases in the Middle East." *MERIP Reports* 90 (September 1980): 3–14, 32.

Telhami, Shibley. *Power and Leadership in International Bargaining: The Path to the Camp David Accords*. New York: Columbia University Press, 1990.

———. "Evaluating Bargaining Performance: The Case of Camp David." *Political Science Quarterly* 107, no. 4 (Winter 1992–1993): 629–653.

———. "A View from the Arab World: A Survey in Five Countries." Washington, DC: Brookings Institution, 2003.

Trachtenberg, Mark. *The Craft of International History: A Guide to Method*. Princeton, NJ: Princeton University Press, 2006.

Tu'aymah, Muhammad. *Jumhuriyat Al Mubarak [The Mubarak Family's Republic]*. Cairo: Dar al-thaqafa al-jadida, 2010.

Tyler, Patrick E. *A World of Trouble: The White House and the Middle East from the Cold War to the War on Terror*. New York: Farrar, Straus, Giroux, 2009.

United Nations Human Rights Council. "Report of the United Nations Fact-Finding Mission on the Gaza Conflict." September 25, 2009. http://www.unhcr.org/refworld/docid/4ac1dd252.html. Accessed May 16, 2011.

United Nations Security Council. "Report of the Secretary-General on the Implementation of Security Council Resolution 1701." 2006. http://www .un.int/wcm/webdav/site/lebanon/shared/documents/RESOLUTION% 201701/Second%20Report.pdf. Accessed April 23, 2011.

———. "Report of the Secretary-General on the United Nations Interim Force in Lebanon." 2006. http://domino.un.org/unispal.NSF/fd807e 46661e3689852570d00069e918/87e2508779d8ec83852571b6004c761f. Accessed April 23, 2011.

U.S. Congress. "Foreign Operations, Export Financing, and Related Programs Act, 2007." *Congressional Record* 152, no. 72 (June 8, 2006), H3537–H3538.

U.S. Department of State. "The Antiterrorism Assistance Program: Report to Congress for Fiscal Year." Washington, DC, 2005.

———. "Report by the Department of State Pursuant to Section 655 of the Foreign Assistance Act of 1961, as Amended: Direct Commercial Sales Authorization for Fiscal Year 2009." Washington, DC: Government Printing Office, n.d.

———. "Report by the Department of State Pursuant to Section 655 of the Foreign Assistance Act of 1961, as Amended: Direct Commercial Sales Authorization for Fiscal Year 2010." Washington, DC: Government Printing Office, n.d.

U.S. Department of State and the Broadcasting Board of Governors, Office of the Inspector General. "Report of Inspection: Review of Middle East Partnership Initiative Coordination and Implementation." Report Number ISP-I-06–18. March 2006.

U.S. Government. *The National Security Strategy of the United States of America*. Washington, DC: The White House, March 2006. http://www. au.af.mil/au/awc/awcgate/nss/nss_mar2006.pdf. Accessed April 11, 2012.

U.S. Government Accounting Office. "Foreign Assistance: Middle East Partnership Initiative Offers Tools for Supporting Reform, but Project Monitoring Needs Improvement." 2005. Report no. GAO-05–711.

———. "Security Assistance: State and DOD need to Assess How the Military Financing Program for Egypt Achieves U.S. Foreign Policy and Security Goals." April 2006. Report Number GAO-06–437.

U.S. House Committee on Appropriations. "Foreign Operations, Export Financing, and Related Programs Report." 109th Congress, 2nd session. April 4, 2006.

U.S. House Committee on Foreign Relations. "United States Policy toward the Palestinians in the Aftermath of Parliamentary Elections." 109th Congress, 2nd session. March 2, 2006.

———. "Review of U.S. Assistance Programs to Egypt: Hearing before the Subcommittee on the Middle East and Central Asia of the Committee on International Relations of the House of Representatives." 109th Congress, 2nd session. May 17 and June 21, 2006.

————. "Extraordinary Rendition in U.S. Counterterrorism Policy: The Impact on Transatlantic Relations: Joint Hearing before the Subcommittee on International Organizations, Human Rights, and Oversight and the Subcommittee on Europe of the House of Representatives." 110th Congress, 1st session. April 17, 2007.

U.S. Senate Select Committee on Intelligence. "The Nomination of Stephanie O'Sullivan to Be the Principal Deputy Director of National Intelligence: Hearing before the Senate Select Committee on Intelligence." 112th Congress, 1st session February 3, 2011. http://www.dni.gov/testimonies/20110203_testimony_osullivan.pdf. Accessed November 14, 2011.

U.S. Senate Select Committee on Intelligence. "Report on Postwar Findings About Iraq's WMD Programs and Links to Terrorism and How They Compare with Prewar Assessments, together with Additional Views." 109th Congress, 2nd session. September 8, 2006.

Vitalis, Robert. "The Closing of the Arabian Oil Frontier and the Future of Saudi-American Relations." *MERIP Reports* 204 (July–September 1997): 15–21, 25.

————. "The Graceful and Generous Liberal Gesture: Making Racism Invisible in American International Relations." *Millennium: Journal of International Studies* 29, no. 2 (2000): 331–356.

Waterbury, John. *Egypt: Burdens of the Past, Options of the Future.* Bloomington: Indiana University Press, 1978.

————. *The Egypt of Nasser and Sadat: The Political Economy of Two Regimes.* Princeton, NJ: Princeton University Press, 1983.

Way, Lucan A. "Kuchma's Failed Authoritarianism." *Journal of Democracy* 16, no. 2 (April 2005): 131–145.

Weinbaum, Marvin G. *Egypt and the Politics of U.S. Economic Aid.* Boulder, CO: Westview, 1986.

Weizman, Ezer. *The Battle for Peace.* New York: Bantam, 1981.

Werner, Suzanne, David Davis, and Bruce Bueno de Mesquita. "Dissolving Boundaries: Introduction." *International Studies Review* 5, no. 4 (December 2003): 1–7.

Whitehead, Laurence. "International Aspects of Democratization." In *Transitions from Authoritarian Rule: Comparative Perspectives,* ed. Guillermo O'Donnell, Phillipe Schmitter, and Laurence Whitehead, 3–46. Baltimore: Johns Hopkins University Press, 1986.

Williams, William Appleman. *The Tragedy of American Diplomacy.* Cleveland, OH: World Publishing, 1959.

Wittes, Tamara. *Freedom's Unsteady March: America's Role in Building Arab Democracy.* Washington, DC: Brookings Institution, 2008.

Wittes, Tamara, and Sarah Yerkes. *"What Price Freedom?" Assessing the Bush Administration's Freedom Agenda.* Washington, DC: Brookings Institution, 2006. http://www.brookings.edu/fp/saban/analysis/wittes20060901.htm. Accessed March 25, 2010.

Woodward, Bob. *Veil: The Secret Wars of the CIA*. New York: Simon and Schuster, 2005.

Wright, Lawrence. *The Looming Tower: Al-Qaeda and the Road to 9/11*. New York: Vintage, 2007.

Yergin, Daniel. *The Prize: The Epic Quest for Oil, Money and Power*. New York: Free Press, 2009.

Yom, Sean L., and Mohammad H. Al-Momani. "The International Dimensions of Authoritarian Regime Stability: Jordan in the Post-Cold War Era." *Arab Studies Quarterly* 30, no. 1 (Winter 2008): 39–60.

Zayat, Montasser. *The Road to al-Qaeda: The Story of Bin Laden's Right-Hand Man*. New York: Pluto, 2004.

Zogby, John, and James Zogby. *Impressions of America 2004: How Arabs View America, How Arabs Learn about America*. Washington, DC: Zogby International, 2004.

_____. *Arab Opinions on President Obama's First One Hundred Days: A Six-Nation Survey*. Washington, DC: Zogby International, 2009.

Index